Contents

List of Illustrations

Acknowledgements

A. F. Kersting (pp. 4, 6, 25, 45)
Fitzwilliam Museum, Cambridge (p. 82)
Trustees of the British Museum (pp. 93, 113)
Crown Copyright The Theatre Museum (pp. 99, 119, 217, 229, 232, 238, 281, 282)
Courtauld Institute of Art (pp. 114, 158)
Trustees of the Tate Gallery (p. 177)
National Theatre of Great Britain (pp. 178, 283)
National Monuments Record (p. 241)
Greater London Council Print Collection (cover, p. 225)

Introduction

This, as the title states, is a history of the theatre in Europe. A glance through the index will show that there are virtually no entries referring to the theatre in Poland, Netherlands, Belgium, Switzerland, Bulgaria, Romania, Denmark, or Iceland. This is not because there has not been any theatrical activity in these countries: on the contrary, each can claim to have enjoyed a distinguished theatrical history and to have established, in recent years, an important subsidized theatre (of which more will be said towards the end of this book). Selection is, of course, essential, to keep a book within manageable proportions; but in the case of a history of the theatre the selection is made in terms of the writers, actors, composers, designers, and directors who in one way or another have made a mark on the theatre of their own country and who in so doing have contributed to the European theatre as a whole. The influence on the rest of Europe of some theatrical periods, such as, for example, classical Greece, Elizabethan London, the French theatre under Louis XIV, and the German Romantic theatre has been so powerful that it is virtually impossible to write a history of theatre in any single country without constant reference to achievements elsewhere.

This book can therefore be likened to a piece of tapestry begun about five hundred years before Christ but never likely to be finished. Old colours are repeated, new colours are introduced, and many colours are never used at all and could only be used if the tapestry were very much wider in breadth.

This book has also been subject to considerable condensation since it deals not so much with the drama as with the theatre, of which drama, acting, décor, music, and dance are an essential part. It also deals, when appropriate, with audiences, who are perhaps the most essential element of all. For although it is possible, though highly unsatisfactory, for a dramatist to write a play without any thought of ultimate performance, it is simply not within the bounds of the way these things happen that an actor should act without an audience.

Perhaps the most serious abbreviation has been accorded to what is known as the lyric theatre, opera and stage dancing. These important theatrical forms have been mentioned when they have arisen in some significant manner or made some distinct contribution to the art of the theatre. This has been done simply in the interests of economy.

Many subjects have been mentioned, without being discussed in detail, when they have seemed to fit into the overall pattern. In this sense the book is full of signposts, inviting readers to pursue such subjects as interest them in greater detail. Some suggestions for further reading or investigation are appended to the end of certain sections.

The book is for the most part descriptive and not critical. This is partly a matter of space, but it is also because criticism is a very complicated process, almost as much so as the experience it is describing. A theatrical performance is a highly contrived affair; whatever efforts those concerned may make to give it a sense of reality, they can do no more than manipulate the ingredients of the performance, the words, the gestures, the space they are using, the relationship with the audience. Some people think that the theatre is the most artificial element of all and stage their performance in the open air or in a village hall; but this is no more than to change the nature, not the substance, of the performance. The very fact that the traditional concept of the theatre as a reflection of real life, 'holding a mirror up to nature' as Shakespeare says, is now seriously challenged, points to the complex nature of contemporary criticism.

There is no significant distinction between the words 'playwright' and 'dramatist'. I have preferred the former since the root 'wright' gives a suggestion of craftsmanship as in such words as shipwright and wheelwright.

I must confess to the greatest distaste for the common practice of using the Roman version of Greek names but have reluctantly submitted to the practice for fear of making well-known names unrecognizable. (Would Aeschylus be immediately identifiable as Aischulos?) But I have sometimes put a mild Hellenic gloss on Roman literary imperialism by substituting 'os' for 'us' and 'k' for 'c'.

As for pronunciation, the traditional custom is that if the last syllable but one of a Greek word is long, it will have the stress (Achílles, Agamémnon), but if the last syllable but one is short, the stress will be on the preceding syllable (Aéschylus, Thukídides).

Since the book is a compression of a lifetime of theatre-going, reading and discussion, I cannot hope to enumerate all those to whom I am indebted. In cultural matters we choose our friends and select our ancestors. To them all, living and dead, I am immensely grateful. I must, however, be precise in may gratitude to Dr Stephen Halliwell for help with the sections on the Greek and Roman theatre and to the readers and editors of Heinemann Educational Books for their wisdom, perspicacity and help.

1 The Athenian City-state

The theatre, *theatron*, the seeing-place, together with drama, were the creation of the Athenians in the fifth century BC. Drama is known to have existed many centuries earlier in such ancient civilizations as China, India, and Egypt but it was almost wholly ritual drama, which is to say that its enactment or performance had a life-giving purpose like the celebration of mass in a Christian church.

By the fifth century BC the city of Athens had reached political maturity. It had grown from a primitive community to the leading city in the Hellenic world in the space of about 500 years. 'We are the inhabitants of a city endowed with every sort of wealth and greatness', the great politician Perikles is reported to have said. Perikles was the last in a succession of politicians such as Solon, Kleisthenes, and Peisistratos who, over the previous two centuries, had been responsible for creating a democratic city-state which the Greeks called a *polis*, the word from which 'politician' is appropriately derived. Athens under Perikles was a city of about 200,000 inhabitants of which some half were slaves and many were foreigners; but there were no great tensions among the various social classes and there was a good deal of what is now called 'participation in government'.

Greece in the fifth century BC was not a country with a strong sense of nationality. Its proper name, then as now, was not Greece but Hellas, Greece being an anglicization of Graecia, the name the Romans gave Greece when in 146 they conquered the country and made it a Roman province. Hellas at this time was a confederation of city-states covering mainland Greece, the Greek islands, and the coast of Asia Minor (now Turkey), which had been colonized by the Greeks and was known as Ionia. The outstanding cultural characteristic of the confederation was the Greek language which, with local variations, was spoken throughout the area of the Aegean sea. By the fifth century Athens had won for herself a commanding political position; but Perikles's vision of a Hellenic Empire led by Athens came to grief through Athenian arrogance and the jealousy of rival city-states such as Korinth, Thebes, and particularly Sparta.

It was in this new and flourishing society that dramatic performances emerged as a major form of cultural expression.

There is a vast number of readable books on classical Greece such as, for example, H. D. F. Kitto's The Greeks*; but none give one so sure a 'feel' or so vivid a picture of the period as the works of the Greeks themselves. The* Histories *of Herodotus and Thoukukides are enthralling and available in excellent English translations.*

1. The Acropolis, from the west, seen from the hill of Philopappos.

2 | The Theatre of Dionysos

The centre of ancient Athens and the site of the earliest settlement was the Akropolis (*Akro-polis*), an immense rock on which, in the fifth century, the Athenians built a number of temples and administrative buildings of which the most outstandingly beautiful is the Parthenon, even in its present ruined condition still one of the wonders of the world. In the shadow of the south-east corner of this great rock they built the Theatre of Dionysos. Like every subsequent theatre it had three elements. The main (acting) area, and the earliest part of the theatre to be built, was a large circular dancing floor known as the *orchestra* which was mostly, if not wholly, used by the chorus. The second element, the audience, in earliest times sat on the slope that rose from the edge of the orchestra to the great rock wall of the Akropolis but as performances became more organized, improvised seating was replaced by a number of wooden tiers. Thirdly, there is the acting area. There may have been a long low wooden platform, perhaps cutting off a segment of the orchestra, and although this may have been used by the actors there is no evidence of a stage as we know it today. At a certain date, as backing or definition of the acting area, there was a building known as the *skene* which provided an architectural setting for the play, while its interior is thought to have been used as a dressing-room for the actors.

The present stone ruins are the remains of a new theatre that was completed by an administrator called Lykurgos who had control of the city's finances between 338 and 326 BC. There still exists the great tiled orchestra, sixty-six feet in diameter, the remnants of the stone auditorium with its front row consisting of sixty-seven throne seats, incised with the names of Athenian notabilities, and the throne for the priest of Dionysos in the middle. Of the *skene* nothing but the ruins remain. Sitting in the middle of those great stone terraces one can gaze, as Athenian audiences must have done, beyond the *orchestra*, beyond the actors, beyond the *skene*, to Mount Hymettos and the distant Aegean, so dearly loved by the Greeks. It is hard to believe that there can be a more exquisitely situated theatre anywhere in the world, except perhaps in Greece itself, at Delphi.

2. Theatre of Dionysos, Athens
Present remains of the reconstruction of the theatre by Lykurgos around 330 BC. The walls of the Akropolis are behind the auditorium to the left of the picture.

The standard work on the Theatre of Dionysos is A. W. Pickard-Cambridge's The Theatre of Dionysos in Athens. *But the book requires a knowledge of Greek to be of much use to the lay reader. Although the author has picked over and measured every surviving stone and crevice there are many details of this fine theatre that are the subject of considerable scholarly disputation.*

It is perhaps unnecessary to urge the importance of visiting Athens; but there are other fine theatres, especially at Epidauros, where performances of Greek plays are sometimes given by Greek companies.

3 | Athenian Dramatic Festivals

It is one of the curious but important features of drama that it has constantly emerged out of ritual. This of course tells us as much about ritual as it does about drama. Ritual, which is common to all ancient religions, derives from the belief that the imitation of an action can have a bearing on the action itself. The imitation of rain, or sound of rain, was thought likely to make it rain, for example. Primitive hunting societies believed that certain imitative and mimetic actions, often expressed in the form of dance, would lead to success in the hunt. Agricultural communities believed that the wooing of the Spring Queen by the Corn King was necessary to ensure the success of the spring sowing. In such a ritual as this an element of dramatic impersonation was involved. Further rituals were developed around the death of the tribal leader to ensure a continuity in leadership and that the strength and wisdom of the dead king should be passed on to his successor. Thus the celebrated cry – The king is dead! Long live the king!

It was the agricultural ritual that was most significant for drama, and indeed for society at large, since society depended even more than now on the harvest, and the cycle of sowing and reaping is related to the cycle of the seasons. The great festivals of early societies therefore took place at crucial times in the agricultural calendar, in the spring when the grain was sown, in late summer when the harvest was gathered, and in mid-winter when nature had to be reborn.

So it was in Athenian society. There were a number of festivals throughout autumn, winter, and spring, related to sowing the seed and the making of wine; but by far the most significant was the City or

Great Dionysia which was celebrated at the end of March. It was a public holiday with many kinds of civic functions from the conferring of honours on distinguished citizens to the rewarding of orphan children whose fathers had been killed in battle. Visitors came to Athens from all parts of the Hellenic world and the wealth of the city was put on show. Most remarkable of all is that its central feature was performances of dramatic and lyric poetry in the Theatre of Dionysos.

The explanation of how this came about lies in the word *Dionysia*. Greek religion of the time was in no respect like the Muslim or Christian religions which carefully prescribe the nature of the faith. It was also remarkably primitive in that many people still thought in anthropomorphic terms. This simply means that they tended to see abstract ideas in the form (*morphe*) of mankind (*anthropos*). In personifying the gods they looked on Zeus as the father and identified the other immortals with various human activities. But there was no pervading body of religious belief; there was no priesthood constituting an influential caste or class although there were a great number of priests and prophets who occupied the oracles and the temples.

Thus there existed a considerable variety of religious practices and local cults. One of the most influential of these cults was that of the god Dionysos. The cult first emerged in Thrace and had become widespread long before the fifth century. Of all Greek myths, those which tell the story of Dionysos are among the most savage. One of them recounts how, as a child, the god, the offspring of Zeus and Semele, was torn to pieces by the Titans at the instigation of Zeus's jealous wife. The Titans then threw the limbs into a caldron, boiled and ate them. A more palatable story tells of the marriage of Dionysos with a champion female athlete, the couple becoming identified with various fertility rites such as the wooing of the Corn King and the Spring Queen. (It was such competitive initiation ceremonies that gave rise to the Olympic Games, first established around 776 BC.)

But it was as god of the grape, of wine, of intoxication that Dionysos was chiefly celebrated and it is a curious fact that this rather disreputable immortal should have become the patron of the most important of all Athenian civic festivals. That this occurred was the achievement of the tyrant Peisistratos, an unconstitutional demagogue who ruled Athens for various periods during the sixth century. Although he did not advance the cause of democracy as a political principle, he made it a feature of his policy in championing the middle class, which was growing in size and power, and curbing the authority of the aristocracy. He confiscated land and gave it to the peasants, improved the coinage, developed export trade, and established a programme of public works that helped to make Athens a major city. He backed up these practical reforms with a vigorous cultural programme by founding or at least reorganizing one of the city's major festivals, the City Dionysia, and instituting competitive public recitals by Ionian minstrels of the Homeric poems which he had had edited for the first time.

The Greek tyrants were men, usually of aristocratic birth who, mostly in the seventh and sixth centuries, seized control of the polis *and established their own policy. They were responsible for great economic changes, often for the better, and were not usually 'baddies' as subsequently depicted.*

4 | The City Dionysia

The festival lasted for five or six days. It was a triumphant affair when slaves were freed, debtors exonerated, visitors welcomed, and the world went on holiday. The first day was devoted to the celebration of the god. His image was carried in triumphal procession from the temple in which it was habitually housed in the village of Eleutherai, an original centre of the cult, to the theatre where choruses were sung and a bull was sacrificed. At the end of the festival the image was ceremoniously returned.

The second day of the festival consisted of a competition in the singing and performance of dithyrambs by each of the ten tribes into which the citizens of Athens had been organized by one of the creators of Athenian democracy, Kleisthenes. There was a panel of judges elected by the Athenian Assembly and the winning tribe was awarded a bull as a prize.

The reason for the constant intrusion of the bull into the rituals of Dionysos is complex. A bull was held to be one of the common incarnations of the god. Worshippers who devoured the flesh of the bull believed that they were eating the flesh and drinking the blood of the god and so partaking of his strength and divine power. This concept of incarnation lies at the heart of many religions including Christianity; but it also provides one of the assumptions on which drama is based, that some dead or imaginary person can be incarnated or reincarnated, whether a dead king or a fertility spirit, in the person of the actor. This rather mysterious belief begins to explain why actors have frequently been treated by society as suspect and unreliable individuals. Someone who spends his life reincarnating other individuals cannot be as ordinary people are. But the crucial element is the attitude of the audience (or congregation or participants in the ritual). While some Christian worshippers believe in the doctrine of transubstantiation, that the bread and the wine actually turn into the body and the blood of Christ, to others it is a symbolic act, and none the less efficacious for that. Most theatre audiences agree implicitly to take part in a game of 'let's pretend'; but there are moments when the emotion runs so deep and the reality of the acting is so impressive that one is tempted to believe that the actors have actually lived their roles.

As for the relationship between the bull and Dionysos, this seems to have been the coincidence of two ideas. Since there is not a more noble animal than the bull, especially among domestic beasts, it is understandable that people who were accustomed to view the world in anthropomorphic terms should have seen the bull as the incarnation of fertility, the very quality they had associated with the god Dionysos. In fact the matter goes farther than that, for ancient societies have frequently tended to attach some special qualities to the horned beast. That is probably the explanation of how the goat comes into the story, for bulls are relatively rare and valuable creatures, whereas in Greece goats are prevalent, and being a great deal cheaper, provided an acceptable substitute.

On the third, fourth, and fifth days of the festival there was a competition in dramatic performances. A member of the Athenian Council, known as the *archon* was given the responsibility of choosing the best three groups of plays submitted by Athenian citizens. He then chose a *choregos*, a wealthy citizen who was responsible for bearing the cost of the production, a privilege that was known as a *leiturgia*, or public service, from which our word liturgy is derived, as well as a *didaskalos* for training the chorus and engaging a flute-player to accompany the singing. The prize was a goat in default of a bull. The word *tragoedia* (tragedy) seems to have meant 'goat song' and to have had nothing to do with subsequent meanings of the word.

There were five judges and the victorious poet, whose name was proclaimed by a herald, was crowned in the theatre by the *archon* with a wreath of ivy.

The group of plays, which each competing dramatist had to submit, consisted of three tragedies, not necessarily related in theme or story, and a satyr play. These four plays were known as tetralogies. What the Greeks seem to have understood by a tragedy will be discussed in the chapter on Aristotle. As to satyr plays not even Aristotle provides an adequate definition and since of this genre only a single play by Euripides and a few fragments survive, one cannot say more than that they seem to have been concerned with the debunking of the hero, and that the chorus consisted of satyrs, creatures that were half-human, half-animal, and of an ancestry of which we know nothing. The satyr play had nothing to do with Greek comedy, although it was presumably amusing, nor with what has subsequently become known as satire.

5 | The Creation of Dramatic Form

How did all this come about?

If this is the most vexatious subject of all it is because it is the most relevant to the subject of this book. Our only near-contemporary authority is Aristotle and he was writing nearly a hundred years after the events he is describing. Aristotle proposes a clear link between tragedy and the dithyramb. The dithyramb was a kind of choral dance that was first associated with the worship of Dionysos. The first person known to have composed dithyrambs was the Korinthian poet Arion who was also associated with another religious dance that was performed by satyrs, men crowned with flowers and ivy. Dithyrambs were danced by a chorus of usually fifty men and boys. Although few texts of dithyrambs exist, it is known that they dealt with aspects of the life and death of the god Dionysos. The man who saw the dramatic possibilities of the dithyramb was an actor-poet called Thespis who came to Athens at the time the City Dionysia was being reorganized and extended. He seems to have entered into some kind of artistic collaboration with the performers of the dithyrambs by delivering a prologue and breaking up the choral dance with some set speeches. This perhaps helped to give coherence and unity to performances which had originally been wild and unrestrained, as one would expect of ceremonies associated with wine. Aristotle says that Thespis 'entered into conversation with the leader of the chorus' which is the kind of form we find in the tragedies of Aeschylus. Thespis won first prize in the first tragic contest which took place in the year 534 BC.

As the dithyrambic chorus turned into a tragic chorus it became increasingly dramatic without ever wholly losing its choral nature. It broke into two parts and sang antiphonally while the leader became almost another actor. With the creation of a second actor tragedy assumed its independent form.

There was, however, another strand which in some way or other must have become related to the experiments that Thespis was conducting with the dithyramb. In 560 BC Peisistratos made himself tyrant of Athens. He was one of those men, of whom there were to be many more in the course of European history, who used art and culture for political ends, although there is no reason to believe that such people do not at the same time appreciate art for its own sake. One of the great achievements of Peisistratos was to arrange for the Homeric poems, the *Iliad* and the *Odyssey*, to be edited and presumably written down. This was necessary since, in the absence of printed texts, people could not read the poems for themselves but were accustomed to them being recited by *rhapsodes*, each of whom would have his own version. Peisistratos employed his scholars to establish a standardized version, and then arranged for there to be a competition among *rhapsodes* as a part of the great Athenian summer festival, the Panathenaea. Since this competition was established around 550, only a few years before Thespis comes into the picture, it is reasonable to assume that there was some kind of connection between the two developments. Moreover we know from what Plato and Aristotle wrote that the *rhapsodes* recited Homer in a highly theatrical manner. It was indeed from their number that the earliest actors may have been recruited.

Aeschylus doubtless played a part in these developments, but although he was the first dramatist to have written any plays which have survived, he was not the first tragic dramatist. There was Phrynikos whose name is coupled with Thespis as a creator of tragedy; Choerilos who won thirteen victories and competed against Aeschylus in the latter's younger days; and Pratinas who is thought to have introduced the satyr play.

These were the men who created the art of the theatre and of drama. It was a period of prodigious inventiveness in almost every aspect of Athenian life. The historian Thoukikides puts a vivid estimation of the Athenian character into the mouth of a Korinthian envoy – 'An Athenian is always an innovator, quick to form a resolution and quick at carrying it out . . . He is daring, resourceful, tireless.' So it was with the poets. Judging by the rapidity with which their achievement was given pride of place in Athenian public life it seems to have represented an act of will by the whole community. There has probably never been another period when drama was so close to the community that supported it.

In the early years of the century a group of Cambridge scholars, Gilbert Murray, Jane Harrison, Frances Cornford, and others, stimulated by Sir James Frazer's great work of anthropology, The Golden Bough, *produced some books on what they considered to be the origins of Greek tragedy. Scholarship is now more sober-sided and more recent books such as Sir A. W. Pickard-Cambridge's* Dithyramb, Tragedy, Comedy *and Gerard Else's* The Origin and Early Form of Greek Tragedy *emphasize the profound uncertainties about almost every aspect of Greek theatre and its drama. Nevertheless reasonable reliance can be placed on such books as H. C. Baldry's* The Greek Tragic Theatre *and J. Michael Walton's* Greek Theatre Practice.

6 | Aeschylus

Aeschylus lived from 525 until 456 BC. He came of an aristocratic family and was probably brought up as some kind of a priest. He made his début as a dramatist at the City Dionysia in the year 500 but he did not win first prize until fifteen years later. (It is a calamity that we have nothing by any of his competitors.) He is thought to have composed between eighty and ninety plays of which seven have survived. This amounts to about twenty tetralogies.

Persai (*The Persians*) is the only example of a play by one of the three great tragic dramatists on a contemporary theme. *Hiketides* (*Suppliants*) is a fine example of a play in which the chorus is protagonist. *Epta epi Thebas* (*Seven against Thebes*) is a splendid and deeply tragic play taken from the ancient history of Thebes and dealing largely with the unhappy life and descendants of Oedipus. *Prometheus Desmotes* (*Prometheus Bound*), the authorship of which is now in serious question, is a play of tremendous poetic and imaginative power dealing with the relationship of god to man in mythical terms that constitute a fascinating parallel to the myth that is described in the first chapter of Genesis. Though in some respects an even more powerful work than the *Oresteia* it is less well known since its philosophical attitudes are no longer of immediate relevance and it is virtually unstageable in any way that would do justice to its towering imaginative concepts.

The *Oresteia* (the story of Orestes), staged in 458 BC, is the only surviving example of a trilogy. The three plays are *Agamemnon*, which deals with the return of the king from the Trojan war and his murder by

Clytemnestra; *Choephoroi* (usually translated into English as *The Libation-bearers*) dealing with the return of Orestes, his meeting with his sister Elektra, and the murder of their mother and her lover Aegisthus; and *Eumenides* which is usually left at that, though a recent scholar has translated it as *The Gracious Goddesses*. This play deals with the trial of Orestes and the final establishment of Athenian justice.

Though Aeschylus was undoubtedly an innovator of genius it is impossible to tell the extent of his contribution to the development of tragedy for we know nothing about the work of his contemporaries. It is clear, however, that he was a supremely gifted poet, an art in which the Greeks had been pre-eminent since the time of Homer. Homer, and others whose names have been lost, was an epic poet. There was a vigorous tradition of lyric poetry, one of the most notable features of which was the variety of metres the poets used. Aeschylus and his colleagues were known not as dramatists but as dramatic poets. One of their finest achievements was to have adapted the richness of the Greek language and the metrical vitality of its poetry to dramatic purposes. The Greek language has the advantage in this respect of vowel sounds which are measured, rather like in French, as opposed to being stressed, as in English and German. This measured quality of the language is marked by lengthening rather than emphasizing the vowels and this is best done musically; and since there was virtually no distinction between words and music the Greek dramatists wrote their great metrical texts and the way they should be sung as a single operation in which the choreography was also an essential part. They called a metrical unit a foot (*pous*) because this is what it represented, a step. Metre comes from the word *metros* meaning measure.

Another aspect of tragedy which Aeschylus and his colleagues developed was its subject-matter, and this was taken very largely from myth. This is a subject about which so much confusion exists that a little unravelling is essential.

Critical works on Aeschylus abound. Of unusual interest is George Thomson's study of the relationship between his plays and contemporary Greek society, Aeschylus and Athens.

7 | Greek Myth

Myth must be distinguished from fairy-tale and legend although each may include elements of the other. Fairy-tales are for the most part a product of the fancy though there may be legendary or mythical elements that have fired the imagination of the story-teller. Legends are traditional stories that may have had a mythological origin but which do not go beyond the events the legend is recounting. Myth is more profound and far-reaching. It derives from ages when men were unable to make a distinction between cause and effect; before the art of writing history had demonstrated that men could see the difference between fact and fiction; before man had acquired the faculty for scientific analysis. Although there are no clear distinctions between myth and legend, the one frequently overlapping the other, myth is usually the explanation of a great variety of communal beliefs and experiences. The difficulty lies in interpreting them. The story of the Garden of Eden is clearly the attempt of early Hebrew scribes to lay down certain profound moral principles. Whether such a place as the Garden of Eden ever existed is beside the point: the truth of the creation myth, as expounded in the first chapter of Genesis, has been so widely accepted that it has survived until the present day. The Greek creation myth, which has not survived because it was more local and carried less of a universal truth, begins with the sky god Uranos who was the husband of the earth goddess. Their children were Titans and included the unattractive character of Kronos who castrated his own father. Another of their children was Zeus who made war on Kronos and the Titans and defeated them with his thunderbolts. Zeus, however, was one of the twelve gods associated with Mount Olympus. His recognition by the Greeks represents an advance in religious thought. All this may be interpreted as the way in which the Greeks recorded an invasion of fine-looking men and women from the north (the Olympian gods and goddesses) who overran an earlier and more primitive society.

The story continues in a most interesting manner. One of the more promiscuous of Zeus's many children was Tantalos who was sentenced to everlasting punishment (to be tantalized) for serving up the flesh of one of his sons in a banquet he was giving to the gods to determine whether they could detect human flesh from that of animals. (The emergence of a meat-eating society.) The son in question, Pelops, was restored to life but not surprisingly turned out to be a bad lot. For carrying out a particularly vicious murder, in order to secure the woman he wished to marry, he was put under a curse which took particular effect upon his two sons, Atreus and Thyestes. Atreus, King of Mykene (the myth is now moving into historical times) banished his brother for having seduced his wife but eventually recalled him and offered him a banquet which included a pie made of flesh of his own children. Thyestes fled in horror and in due course married a woman who bore him a son, Aegisthus, whom she exposed (left in the open to die) but who was discovered and brought up by a shepherd, and adopted by Atreus who was not aware of his real identity. As a young man he seduced the wife of the King of Mykene who was absent on military service fighting the Trojans. This King was Agamemnon and his brother was Menelaus who had become King of Sparta in succession to Tyndareus. This unfortunate man had a wife named Leda who was seduced by Zeus in the form of a swan and gave birth to Helen and Clytemnestra. Helen became the wife of Menelaus and Clytemnestra of Agamemnon. At this point Priam, King of Troy, sent an attractive young fellow called Paris on an ambassadorial mission to Sparta. It was a bad mistake and Menelaus made it worse by taking himself off to Crete on business leaving the attractive Paris with his wife Helen, who was reputed to have been the most beautiful woman in the world. By the time he had returned from Crete, Paris and Helen were safely in Troy. Menelaus, outraged, persuaded his brother, Agamemnon, to lead an expedition against Troy to regain Helen. At the outset of the expedition, the fleet was becalmed due to jealous rivalry among the Olympian goddesses. Calchas, the high-priest of the expedition, persuaded Agamemnon that the only hope of raising a wind was by the sacrifice of his daughter, Iphigenia. When Queen Clytemnestra back home heard of the sacrifice she swore to take vengeance on her husband and accepted Aegisthus as her lover. It took the Greek army nine years to conquer Troy, a period of time which itself has mythological significance. It is with the return of King Agamemnon to the Palace of Mykene that Aeschylus's great trilogy begins.

How great an element of historical truth lies behind this farrago of murder, revenge, cannibalism, treachery, seduction, and sheer bloody-mindedness? The probability, of course, is that the nearer we come to historical times, the stronger the factual and historical element is likely to be; and so it has proved. In the 1870s and 1880s a wealthy German archaeologist, Heinrich Schliemann, acting on an almost incredible flash of intuition, backed by some sound scholarship, organized archaeological 'digs', first on the site where he reckoned that Troy must have been situated, and then at Mykene and Tiryns. In each of these places he not only unearthed treasures of great beauty and skill in workmanship but found them to be precisely consistent with descriptions in Homer's epic, the *Iliad*. So Troy was real. The Trojan war took place. Agamemnon had been King of Mykene. Myth was shown to have had a basis in historical truth.

When the young Aeschylus took up play-writing around the year 500 BC there was an immense body of myth on which he could draw for stories. The Homeric and other epics, long since lost, had only recently been edited and so were readily available. There was a confusion of quasi-religious beliefs, practices, and superstitions which left the field clear for all kinds of speculation, and there was a vigorous tradition of lyric poetry.

Tragedy, therefore, constituted a further projection of and enquiry into the Greek view of life. One can detect these two elements in the plays of the tragic dramatists. On the one hand they embody traditional attitudes as enshrined in the myths; but at the same time they subject these myths to commentary and criticism. This critical element is explicit in the plays of Euripides, who was what we might now call an agnostic, and implicit in the plays of Aeschylus who does not directly criticize the ways of the gods but wrestles with the kinds of attitudes they seem to represent. What evidently interested him in *The Suppliants* was the existence of laws that imposed forced marriages on unwilling women. In *The Persians* he contrasts Persian arrogance with Athenian democratic ideals. 'A free people are not easily defeated', says one of the characters. *Prometheus Bound* contrasts, in the form of a violent and intensely dramatic debate, the old illiberal, aggressive, and irrational practices of Zeus, who had caused Prometheus to be chained to a rock in the Caucasus for having stolen fire from the gods and for giving it to man, with the innovatory hero who has helped man to acquire many of his most civilized skills and crafts.

But it is in the *Oresteia* that he reveals his hand most clearly. In the first two plays he shows how the blood feud which stretches back into the primitive origins of Greek society shows no signs of abating until new forms of justice are established. In one of the opening choruses in which the Mykenean elders rehearse the whole story of the curse, he dismisses the violent tyranny of the old god Uranos and then he seems to celebrate the unifying power of Zeus whom he sees no longer as the high-born seducer of the earlier myths but as a kind of Hebraic deity.

> Zeus is the name to cry in your triumph song
> and win the prize for wisdom.

In the third play Orestes is brought to trial by the avenging furies, the *Erinyes*, for the appalling crime of mother-murder. The goddess Athene listens to their case and then refers it to the Areopagus, the supreme Athenian court of justice which was accustomed to meet on the rock in the shadow of which, in the Theatre of Dionysos, the performance was taking place. Orestes is acquitted by the casting vote of Athene, the patron goddess of Athens. The Furies are incensed at having been outvoted by a younger goddess; but as they begin to understand the wisdom of the decision, they are transformed into the Eumenides, the good-natured ones. In this extraordinary play Aeschylus challenges the ancient myth and puts the gods themselves on trial. It is Athenian justice which must break the savage myth and Athenian justice which will bring peace and prosperity to mankind.

Another view of the myth, however, is quoted by the historian Herodotos who was in his teens when the *Oresteia* was first staged:

> It was the Greeks who were in the military sense the aggressors [he writes, referring to the Trojan war]. Abducting young women, in their opinion, is not, indeed, a lawful act; but it is stupid after the event to make a fuss about it. The only sensible thing is to take no notice; for it is obvious that no young woman allows herself to be abducted if she does not wish to be.

Greek myth is a subject of considerable academic controversy, understandably so, since myth by its very nature is imprecise and susceptible to individual interpretation. What myths are not are fairy-stories. A straightforward exposition of what the Greeks themselves wrote about their myths is to be found in H. J. Rose's A Handbook of Greek Mythology. *For extremes in the interpretation of myth one can turn to Robert Graves, Carl Jung, and many others. A sensible study of the whole subject is G. S. Kirk's* The Nature of Greek Myths. *But the whole nature of myth is now being reconsidered by anthropologists and even linguists on the grounds that myth is an early expression of thought processes and language.*

The importance of reading the works of the Greeks themselves has already been emphasized. Nothing shows the primitive savagery of the early myths more clearly than Hesiod's Theogeny *which traces the (mythical) history of the world from primeval chaos to the ascendancy of Zeus.*

For a background to other aspects of this section two works are indispensable, besides being finely written: Five Stages of Greek Religion *and* The Rise of the Greek Epic, *both by that fine scholar and poet, Gilbert Murray.*

8 | Sophokles

Sophokles (496–406) was thirty years younger than Aeschylus but old enough to have seen many of the old master's plays and to have competed against him. He wrote 123 plays which amount to thirty tetralogies, but these did not include any connected trilogies. That he won twenty-four victories testifies to his mastery as a dramatist and his popularity with audiences. This professional success is consistent with his public life. In spite of this prodigious output of drama he played a vigorous part in the life of Athens, accepted public office of various kinds, and enjoyed the friendship of Perikles who acted occasionally as his *choregos*. All references to Sophokles suggest that he was an exceptionally attractive and well-graced man, a loved and respected citizen of the *polis*.

This combination of personal distinction and professional brilliance is supported by the impression of the man we have from his seven surviving plays. In contrast with the tragedies of Aeschylus and Euripides they are the work of a conservative. He was not a thunderer like Aeschylus, wrestling with the imponderables of human existence, nor a complex and seemingly embittered personality like Euripides. He took the myths that were the subject of his plays at their face value, drawing from them every possible implication for what they have to say of the human condition, but neither challenging their assumptions nor attempting to reorder the values they express.

It so happens that all three dramatists handled the Elektra story. Sophokles's version is reasonably straightforward. He spends no time bewailing the horror of the primitive myth or warning his audiences against the outmoded tyranny of Uranos as Aeschylus does; nor does he turn Elektra into a vengeful and neurotic harridan as Euripides does. He dramatizes the events of the myth in full acceptance of the horror of the story, writing in superb poetry and showing a masterly sense of dramatic construction.

Most of his surviving plays come from the latter part of his life when Athens was conducting an ultimately disastrous war with Sparta. These lamentable events, which produced the most violent resentment in Euripides, do not seem to have affected him deeply as an artist but to have underlined that curious pessimism that runs throughout the work of these three dramatists and that can be summed up in the phrase, 'no man is happy until he is dead'. Three of his less popular plays seem to make that very point. In *Ajax* (?), *Trachiniae* (*The Women of Trachis*, *c*.430) and *Philoktetes* (409) he does not accuse the gods of being responsible for human suffering, but he does suggest that the best of us are victims of circumstances within which there is no opportunity for the operation of free will.

Three of his finest plays deal with aspects of the story of Oedipus, King of Thebes. *Antigone* (441), which takes up the story at the point that Aeschylus left it in *Seven against Thebes*, has become accepted as the classic statement of the rights of the individual against the state, though Sophokles was probably far more concerned with the religious aspects of the situation. *Oidipous turannos* (*Oedipus the Tyrant*, *c*.430) is the play that was singled out by Aristotle as the finest example of Greek tragedy. It tells the horrifying story of how Oedipus discovers that he has killed his father and married his mother. Twentieth-century psychiatry has taken the story as an archetypal statement of a basic human experience, an extreme case of a quality that is to be found in many other myths and which accounts for the surviving popularity of Greek tragedy.

In none of these plays, not even in those he wrote when Athens was facing total military defeat, does Sophokles allow himself a critical or querulous note. *Oidipous epi Kolonoi* (*Oedipus at Kolonos*) which he probably wrote in his ninetieth year and which was posthumously produced in 401, may be interpreted as having political references in scenes when the old King denounces Theban treachery, just as citizens of Athens may have done when the play was first produced.

Sophokles made important contributions to the development of theatrical technique. He is credited with having introduced painted scenery, however this was done, with increasing the size of the chorus from twelve to fifteen, and with introducing a third actor, so greatly extending the number of characters a dramatist could use.

It was with reference to Sophokles that the poet Matthew Arnold wrote his famous line, 'He saw life steadily and saw it whole.'

9 | Euripides

Although Euripides (484–406/7) was only twelve years younger than Sophokles he writes in so distinctive a style as to appear to be of another generation. This was probably the result of a unique artistic temperament which produced a wholly different and far more personal response to the brutalities and disasters of the Peloponnesian war. But whereas Sophokles played a prominent part in the political life of Athens, Euripides was a lonely figure, an extreme individualist of whose self-imposed isolation and morose nature there were many, though not very well-authenticated, stories. Although he was far less popular during his lifetime than Sophokles, winning only five victories from ninety-two plays, or twenty-three tetralogies, his work aroused considerable interest. There is a good deal of evidence, in addition to the fact that nineteen of his plays have survived, to suggest that subsequent generations found him the most approachable of the three dramatists. This is understandable. His attitude to human nature is more realistic. He does not inveigh against the gods but rather treats them with a certain contempt, presenting them on the stage with the human fallibilities of ordinary mortals. The lovely play *Alkestis* begins with Apollo explaining that as an act of petty vengeance his father Zeus has reduced him to the status of a mortal and this has involved him in playing a deceitful trick to save the life of Admetus. The superb play *Hippolytos* opens with an admission by the goddess Aphrodite that as a result of Hippolytos having no use for female company and spending most of his time hunting as a votary of the goddess Artemis, she has organized a plot that involves his stepmother Phaedra falling deeply in love with him. But having disposed of divine intervention in setting up the situation, Euripides seems to suggest that the rest is a matter of mortal cause and effect, and allows his interest in human psychology to come into play.

Similarly with his protagonists: they are not of heroic stature, projections of some great moral principal, but human in their submission to suffering even when he depicts such anguish, as he does in *Troades* (*Women of Troy*) in the most profoundly emotional terms. His heroes and heroines behave as free and responsible people; when they act improperly they take the consequences and do not blame the gods.

Euripides's handling of the Elektra story provides another useful opportunity to contrast the methods of the three dramatists. The Elektra of Euripides has been banished from the palace and is living alone and in poverty with an elderly husband. Her reunion with her brother is depicted in most moving and human terms. Orestes expresses the utmost distaste for the necessity of murdering his mother but having done so accepts the inevitable consequences.

Euripides returns to the subject in *Orestes*, which he wrote much later in his life (408). The play tells of the meeting of Orestes with Helen, whom not very surprisingly he hates for having been the cause of the nine years' conflict. They are also accompanied by Tyndareus, the father of both Helen and the now murdered Clytemnestra, who in a tempestuous fury demands of the citizens of Mykene the death of Orestes and Elektra. But Orestes, with his friend Pylades, proposes an alternative plot – to murder Helen. And so it goes on. The play is bitter and black, Orestes, Pylades, and Elektra behaving like a trio of gangsters, and Elektra making the point that if the gods have been involved in the whole sickening business, this is nothing to their credit. But it is clear throughout the play that Euripides is concerned with man's inhumanity to man, for which the gods must take their share of the blame, and not with the dispensation of Athenian justice.

Euripides found in the Trojan war a means of projecting his disgust at the war between Athens and Sparta which came to a disastrous conclusion for Athens at the time of his death. In one of his last plays, *Iphigenia in Aulis*, posthumously produced in 405, he expresses disgust that the whole Greek people should have banded together for no better reason than to recapture the wife of Menelaus, and that the very prosecution of the expedition at its outset should have depended on the sacrifice of the King's daughter. 'Prophets and their whole power-thirsty breed are damnable', says Agamemnon in reference to Calchas who had advised that a favourable wind could only be raised by the sacrifice of Iphigenia.

Sometimes the profound emotion with which he writes of war produces a masterpiece such as *Women of Troy* which is set in the burning ruins of Troy on the eve of the departure of the Greeks, with the surviving Trojans slaves to the Greek generals. Sometimes his indignation is so powerful, as in *Hekabe* (*Hecuba*, 424) or *Andromache* (426), as almost to destroy the credibility of the play.

Even though he shows a considerable variation in the tone of his plays, he is always probing the authenticity of the myth. In *Helen*, for example, he makes use of the astonishing suggestion that Helen, the universal whore, on whose account the Trojan war was fought, was only 'a living image compounded of the ether' while the real Helen was borne through the upper air and set down in Egypt whence she is rescued by her husband, Menelaus. 'So Priam and his people perished for nothing', says the Egyptian King, 'the Trojan war was fought for a non-existent image as a result of a personal feud among the goddesses over the beauty of a single woman'.

He probes the theme still further in *Iphigenia in Tauris* in which he shows how the daughter of Agamemnon was rescued from exile in a foreign land by Orestes and Pylades (whence she has been wafted through the upper air). Here he suggests that the endless chain of murder and revenge, action and reaction, which could perpetuate the myth until the end of time, must be brought to an end, not by political action, as Aeschylus suggests, but by a change in the heart of man.

One of his greatest achievements is the only surviving play that deals with the god Dionysos. *The Bacchae* has received considerable attention over the years for its powerful and disturbing statement of man's apparently uncontrollable irrationality, an unenviable aspect of human nature which accounts for atrocities and barbarities even in these supposedly civilized times. In this play Pentheus, King of Thebes, tries to suppress the orgiastic rituals of the followers of the young god among whom is his own mother, Agave. He spies on their rituals, is discovered, and torn to pieces. Agave, recovering from her frenzy, finds that she has killed her son.

No playwrights or poets have thrown up the problems of translation in quite so acute a form as the Athenian dramatists. This arises from the metrical variety of the language and the structure of many of the words for which there is no English equivalent. The reader of Greek is at a considerable advantage. The problems facing the translator are well-nigh insuperable. Yet even in translations that do not remotely measure up to these requirements, the power and majesty of the plays is apparent.

There are, of course, innumerable critical commentaries both on the plays themselves and their authors. Oliver Taplin's Greek Tragedy in Action *is of great practical help.*

10 | Greek Tragedy in Performance

A little imagination can get us some way towards envisaging the performance of a Greek tragedy in the Theatre of Dionysos. In the bright spring air an audience of many thousands occupies the curved and sloping auditorium beneath the great rock of the Akropolis. On the circular dancing floor, the *orchestra*, there is the chorus of twelve and then fifteen figures, sometimes speaking, sometimes declaiming, and singing and dancing the choral odes. Behind them are the actors, never more than three, on whatever kind of a stage there may have been.

It is the chorus that probably constitutes the biggest difference between a theatrical performance then and now; for in the plays of Aeschylus the chorus is an essential part of the action. Euripides uses the chorus, though in a less dramatically integrated manner, to give additional depth to the action by suggesting a wealth of poetic and imaginative associations. It is clearly no accident that Euripides writes some of his most exquisite poetry for the chorus of his plays. And in *Women of Troy* the chorus plays as important a role as Hecuba herself.

The three actors wore masks. By changing them they could play a variety of roles. Even so the number of characters a dramatist could introduce was strictly limited; but critics have pointed out the irony that could be derived from the 'doubling' of roles. Thus in *The Libation-bearers* of Aeschylus the chief actor (*protagonist*), undoubtedly played the leading role, that of Orestes; the third actor (*tritagonist*) played the servant, the nurse, Aegisthos, and Pylades, but the second actor (*deuter-agonist*) played both Clytemnestra, the mother, and her daughter Elektra.

Little is known about the masks that were worn in the fifth century. They were probably made of linen and fitted the actor's face closely. The great tragic masks with their high headpieces, together with the thick-soled boots (*kothornoi*) that are usually associated with the performance of Greek tragedy, were the creation of the fourth century or even later. But from the earliest times the actors are said to have worn splendid costumes.

The wearing of masks is one of the many indications of the ritual origins of Greek tragedy. It was a deliberately dehumanizing act. For the mask was a part of the process of incarnation that took place when

3. Theatre of Epidauros, Greece
The best preserved of all Greek theatres, still occasionally used for performances. This immense auditorium, built in the fourth century BC has superb acoustics and held 16,000 spectators.

the priest incarnated, or assumed, or acted the role of a god. A part of the secularization of a religious ritual, when the dramatic element began to replace the religious, was the replacement of priests by actors.

Of styles of acting little is known. Athenian audiences are known to have attached great importance to the actor's voice, both to tone and clarity of diction. The remarkable acoustics which we know the theatre of Epidauros to have possessed must have helped in this respect. As to movement, there is every indication that plays of the classic period had nothing statuesque about them but demanded considerable mobility and ease of movement from the actors. The dramatists directed and acted in their own plays and were known to be excellent dancers. The dramatists chose their actors, Aeschylus often working with Kleandros and Mynniskos, Sophokles with Tlepolemos.

With scenery we are on difficult ground. Aristotle says that Sophokles introduced painted scenery (*skenographia*) but one is not very convinced by the suggestion, for which there is a good deal of evidence, that painted screens were set up in front of the *skene*. There is much talk about the use of *periaktoi*, painted triangular prisms at each side of the stage, a crane (*mechane*) for raising and lowering the immortals from the top of the *skene*, and a *ekkyklema* or wheeled rostrum for rolling out the murdered bodies; but there is not much evidence of their use in classical times, and it is safer to concentrate on the vivid, colourful al fresco nature of the performance with its choreographic chorus and vigorous acting.

11 | Aristotle and Greek Tragedy

The only Greek to have produced a theory of tragedy was Aristotle. The work in question is called *Peri poetikes* (*About Poetry*) usually referred to as *The Poetics*. As Aristotle was not born until 384 he is unlikely to have written this particular book until at least seventy years after the death of Euripides. He seems to have written it as a rejoinder to the disparaging remarks made about tragedy by his master, Plato, in a book of seminal importance, *The Republic*. Plato was an extremely complicated personality, both poet and philosopher, as well as a kind of amanuensis or reporter of the sayings of the great dialectician, Sokrates. Plato-Sokrates advocated what might be described as a communistic structure of society. This rather restricted political outlook may have been the result of the two philosophers having lived through the final years of the Peloponnesian war. But since they must have been familiar with productions of some of the greatest plays of Sophokles and Euripides it is perhaps surprising that when they come to deal with the position of poetry and music in their ideal commonwealth, they banish the artists into exile.

By the time of Aristotle tragedies of distinction were no longer being written and by Aristotle's own admission in another of his works 'actors held greater power than playwrights'. But revivals were frequent and there is no reason why he should not have been familiar with the works of the three great masters in performance. Curiously he does not deal with the whole group of plays but singles out *Oedipus the Tyrant* (or *King Oedipus* as it is sometimes called) for special consideration. His book is of the utmost importance for two reasons: firstly because he provides a substantial definition of drama which is as valid today as ever it was, though none the less open to challenge; and secondly because it provides the theory on which most play-writing has been based from about the year 500 almost to the present day.

Aristotle agrees with Plato that drama, like music, is an imitation of life. It would all be much easier if we knew exactly what Aristotle meant by *mimesis*. That he describes music as being the most mimetic of the arts means that he does not mean what we mean by imitation. So we are tempted to assume that he meant something like the transformation or recreation of real life into poetic terms. (Not artistic terms, for the Greeks had a word for craft but not for art. Moreover the theme of the book is not drama but poetry and the differences between the three kinds of poetry – epic, lyric, and dramatic.) To Plato's accusation that dramatists have laid stress on the sensational aspects of life, when their social responsibility requires them to project a more idealized view, he replies (in chapter six) that the purpose of tragedy is not social but psychological. He does not use that particular word but it is what he implies. For tragedy, he says, is the reproduction of something done in action not narration (which is the field of epic poetry); that it is complete within its own terms and of a certain significance; and that by arousing pity and fear – and this is the rub and the psychological part – it affects a certain cleansing (*katharsis*) of the emotions. Ink galore has been spent in discussing exactly what he meant by *katharsis*; but the suggestion that we feel better as a result of having seen other people in trouble does begin to explain the problem that was posed in the introduction – why do we include tragedy in our concept of entertainment? Nevertheless it seems to be the case that the pleasure we take from the presentation in dramatic form of sensational or horrifying events at every level from the highest poetic reaches of Shakespeare and Racine to the most crude and rumbustious forms of Victorian melodrama supports the contention that drama is at its most prophylactic (healing? cleansing?) when it is projecting the fears and terrors, as well as the joys and rejoicings, of ordinary people. This is not to say that poetic tragedy and crude melodrama are on the same artistic or social level, for any art which expresses crude emotion is a debasement of human sensibility, just as the finest art is its ennoblement and extension; but it does begin to explain why we take such delight in other people's misfortunes.

Tragedy, says Aristotle, is the imitation of an action; its most important element is therefore its plot for which he uses the word *muthos* (myth); next in importance are *ethos* (character) and thought, for these are the motivations of action; then *lexis* (diction), *opsis* (spectacle), and *melopoiia* (song).

Now although Aristotle presents this as a definition of tragedy, it constitutes an admirable definition of drama in general. What then must be emphasized is that at least until the time of Aristotle the Greeks were not conscious of having created a new artistic form called drama, but only of a new form of poetry called tragedy. The fact that drama had a tragic quality in the modern meaning of the word was the accidental result of the nature of the myths on which drama was based, although it rapidly began to acquire that meaning. For as we have seen, the myths were basically concerned with the facts of life as they appeared to a primitive people – birth, resurrection, and death, and how these everlasting imponderables worked out in terms of the most important people in their society, their kings, rulers, leaders, tyrants, and heroes.

Nevertheless Aristotle does discuss the tragic element of tragedy, though he could hardly have done less once he had decided to take that most tragic of all tragedies, *Oedipus*, as his example: the human weaknesses that lead to personal disaster resulting from some kind of inadequacy in the hero (*hamartia*), and how this may be the result of overweening pride (*hubris*) and lead to a reversal of fortune, the disaster that suddenly attends a man who up until then had been happy and prosperous (*peripeteia*), and the tragic ending (*pathos*).

It is impossible to overrate the importance of Aristotle for an understanding of later developments in European drama. Let it be emphasized that About Poetry *is never dull, at any rate in those early chapters that deal specifically with drama. It is short and pithy. There are many translations and countless commentaries.*

Plato is another matter. He is for the enquiring mind. But he is the first to voice a scepticism about drama which has been constantly repeated. His accusation that the arts in general and drama in particular reproduce the superficial appearance of things rather than their basic nature or form is a challenge that has constantly to be answered afresh. Aristotle's reply was what we have called 'psychological'. Our answer today would be based on social considerations. Why? and with what validity?

12 | The Origins of Comedy

Aristotle, in chapter five of his book on poetry, says that the successive stages through which tragedy passed are well known, whereas comedy has had no history because at first it was not taken seriously. There is undoubtedly a great deal of truth in this remark. Comedy is notoriously difficult to categorize, analyse, or even to record, since laughter defies definition and the capacity to make people laugh, though exploited by the professional comedian, is something that many people are capable of doing under almost any circumstances.

There are other reasons why comedy tends not to be taken seriously. For one thing it is 'anti-establishment', it is critical of authority, it makes jokes at the expense of over-seriousness. There is nothing more satisfying than to see the overweening general slip on a banana skin or the pedantic professor fall over his own words. Comedy is indeed to do with slipping and falling, losing face, dignity, and respect. It tends to shock. And it is constantly rude.

There is really no evidence that comedy had a similar origin to tragedy in some kind of quasi-religious ritual, but that it was in its origins closely associated with the whole concept of fertility is clear. Early comedy seems always to have been associated with phallic songs and dances. The phallus, the distinctive male organ, was adopted by many primitive people as a symbol of fertility. Worshippers in their ceremonies attached a false and greatly enlarged phallus to the appropriate part of their person, and this was particularly common practice in the worship of Dionysos. Some scholars, using ancient masks, terracotta statuettes, and vase paintings as evidence, have suggested that from away back in the sixth century, the more serious fertility rituals were accompanied, though at another time and place no doubt, by knock-about farces in which mythological and legendary themes were 'sent up' with Herakles as a favourite buffoon.

So comedy took longer than tragedy to be established as a serious dramatic form; the competitive element for writers of comedy was not established until 486 and at the festival of the Lenaia, a less important occasion than the City Dionysia in about 440.

13 | Aristophanes

Of the earliest writers of comedy, Chionides and Magnes, only their names are known. They were followed by Kratinos, of whose output twenty-seven titles have survived but whose early brilliance was dimmed by enthusiasm for alcohol; and there was Eupolis, a near-contemporary of Aristophanes, who won seven first prizes.

Aristophanes (*c.*448–*c.*380) is the only writer of comedies from whom any plays have survived – eleven titles. Thus between 427, when the first of his plays was performed, and 385 when he died, he wrote forty plays at the rate of about one a year.

The comedies of Aristophanes are quite unlike those of any other dramatist. This may explain why, although he has always been highly regarded, his comedies have had very little effect on subsequent European drama, while that of the three tragic dramatists has been prodigious. The most obvious reason for this lies in the sharp topical satire of his plays, a reason, no doubt, why throughout history a large number of comedies which depended for their success on topical references have been meaningless in other times and places. But the greatness and uniqueness of Aristophanes lies in his practice of placing quite ordinary characters or contemporary figures, whom he usually identifies by name, in situations of extreme fantasy. Like Euripides he lived most of his life at a time when Athens was engaged in a disastrous war and much of his satire is directed at those whom he thought were, if not responsible for the defeat of Athens, at least contributing to a general decadence. Thus in *Acharnes* (*The Acharnians*) which was staged in 425 when he was in his early twenties, he makes fun of the Athenian magistrates for their conduct of the war and ridicules one of the city's leading politicians who put him 'on the mat' for his impertinence. In *Hippeis* (*The Knights*, 424) he suggests that Kleon, who had succeeded Perikles as a leading politician, was making such a mess of things that he might be better replaced by a sausage-seller. The knights were the Athenian aristocracy of whom Kleon was a distinguished member. In *Sphekes* (*The Wasps*) he satirizes the enthusiasm of the Athenians for litigation and their unwieldy jury system.

Eirene (*Peace*, 421) is one of his most delightful fantasies. The war-weary Trygaeus flies to Heaven on the back of a dung-bettle to remonstrate with Zeus about the continuation of the war but finds that the gods have emigrated and left their celestial abode to the Demon of War who is pounding up the Greek states in a gigantic pestle and mortar, while the goddess Peace has been shut up in a cave. On his return to earth he organizes representatives of the Greek states to help pull her out, only to meet with fierce opposition from the manufacturers of helmets, spears, and breast-plates, the armament manufacturers, who see themselves going out of business.

Some people consider his masterpiece to be *Ornithes* (*The Birds*, 414). This comedy is about two men who, disgusted with life in Athens, fly to the land of the birds, Nephelococcygia (Cloud-cuckoo-land) where they build an ideal city only to be harassed by all the tradesmen of Athenians who want to cash in on a good thing.

Batrachoi (*The Frogs*, 405) was written when the death of Euripides had left Athens without a major playwright. Dionysos, disguised as Herakles, goes to Hades to retrieve a distinguished dramatist but finds Aeschylus and Euripides arguing about their respective skills. This was the second play he had written involving Euripides which suggests what a controversial figure the great dramatist had been. In 411 or 410 he had written *Thesmophoriazusai* (*Women Celebrating the Festival of Thesmophoria*) which recounts how Euripides, hearing that the women of Athens, angered by his treatment of their sex, were planning to put him to death, persuades a relative to dress up as a woman, gatecrash the assembly, and plead his cause.

Perhaps the most accessible of all his plays, and the one that is most frequently revived, is *Lysistrata* (411) in which a council of women, led by Lysistrata, disgusted with the continuance of the war, band together to declare a sex-strike, banishing their husbands from their beds until peace is made. This move quickly brings the opposing Athenians and Spartans together in the cause of peace.

These extraordinary plays are written with tremendous vitality, in exquisite verse, and with even greater metrical variations than are to be found in tragedy. They centre round the chorus who in most cases supply the title of the play. The plays have an extremely formal structure with two parts separated by what was called a *parabasis* in which the chorus dropped any attempt at illusion and addressed the audience on a wide range of topical issues.

Although, as has been said, Aristophanes had little influence on succeeding generations of playwrights and was never copied, it was comedy which for many centuries was the dominating form of drama. Absence of genuine democracy and the freedom of expression that goes with it ensured that the theatre would almost never again have that liberty of comment that was enjoyed by Aristophanes. But why no other dramatist essayed the poetic fantasy of which he was so great a master is a question to which there is no answer.

In the absence of source material far less has been written about Athenian comedy than tragedy. Frances Cornford's The Origin of Attic Comedy *is invaluable.*

Aristophanes poses almost insuperable problems for the translator. While a detailed appreciation of his jokes and jibes requires a close knowledge of Greek, the general fun and fantasy of his plays are not difficult to appreciate.

14 | Athens in the Fourth Century

Athenian ambitions to be the political leader of a confederation of Greek states were finally destroyed by the Spartans at the battle of Aegospotami in 405. It is understandable perhaps that in the shadow of this deeply humiliating experience the Athenians should have looked for a scapegoat beyond the incompetence of their generals. Plato, who was twenty-two at the time, was critical of the sensationalism of tragedy. Aristophanes, who was critical of the conduct of the war, suggests in *Clouds* that the casuistical arguments of philosophers such as Sokrates, who could turn plain truths upside down, must take a share of the blame. Sokrates himself fell foul of the authorities for having questioned the validity of certain aspects of democratic government, and in a celebrated and infamous episode, described by Plato in the *Apology*, he was imprisoned and condemned to death by drinking hemlock.

Yet the new century was not a period of social and political deprivation for the Athenians. Two groups of people prevailed, the merchants and the philosophers. Having failed to become the political leader of the Greek states, Athens became the intellectual leader. Isokrates, one of the great teachers of the period, wrote in 381 that 'Athens has so outdistanced the rest of the world in power of thought and speech that her disciples have become the teachers of all other men'; and it is certainly true that the works of Plato and Aristotle and their school have had a greater effect on the development of European culture than those of any other thinker with the exception of the Jewish prophets and the early Christian bishops.

During the fourth century the Athenians paused and took stock of their position. They considered the past and the future, the nature of man and his relationship to the gods and to the *polis*, the city-state. And they developed in a practical manner their proclivity for trade. The Greek mainland is far too rocky to sustain an agricultural community and the country has little mineral wealth. The Greeks saw that their future lay in what Homer described as 'the wine-dark sea'.

It was a poor time for Aristophanes's armament manufacturers whose offices were taken over by brokers, agents, and bankers. But an expanding mercantile economy created a need for workers and an additional labour force was at hand in the slaves. While no one would wish to justify the use of slave-labour – though Aristotle does just that in his book on politics – the position of slaves in fourth-century Athens was in no way despicable. Social disruption and the loss of many able-bodied men caused by the war provided the slaves with opportunities to win their freedom. They exploited the security that had been provided by a good master, took further opportunity to educate themselves, and went on to fill the clerical grades in the vastly expanding Roman civil service.

The Athens of 320 BC was an entirely different place to what it had been a hundred years earlier. Gone was all pretension to political leadership, gone the democratic constitution, gone what was in some respects a heroic age. Athens had become a busy commercial centre, its streets full of merchants, their wives, their sons and daughters, and the curious social instability that grows up around ports where men from other countries drop in for a night or two.

It is a theme of this book that while the theatre is not an immediate reflection of the society of which it is an important aspect, it functions within certain limits laid down by that society. One would not expect to find the plays of Sophokles written at any other time or place than Athens in the fifth century BC. At the same time, the drama, like any other art, is not necessarily a precise expression or reflection of that society, since social reality is transformed by the creative imagination of the artist into a new fictional reality. Nevertheless this transformation can only take place within certain limits established by what can be called the spirit of the age, whether that spirit is established by philosophical ideas, historical traditions, economic pressures, or anything else.

It is only by considering the kind of changes that took place in Athenian society between the death of Aristophanes and the emergence of what is known as the 'new comedy' that one can hope to understand the transformation that took place in the writing of comedy in the space of much less than a hundred years.

15 | Menander and the New Comedy

Menandros (342–292), as he was called in Greek, was the leading exponent of what has been termed 'new comedy'. Indeed, he is the only dramatist of the period of whom anything is known and that is little enough. He was born of a good family, he was unpopular with the critics, and died at the age of fifty while bathing. He is thought to have written about a hundred plays but there may be duplication through confusion of titles. Of this great output only five plays survive in anything approaching recognizable form. The main source of our knowledge about Menander comes from the plays of the Roman dramatists, Plautus and Terence, who translated and adapted them into Latin.

His imaginative scope is extremely limited. An Alexandrian Greek, writing in the third century, had this to say about the comedy of Menander: 'Confrontations of husband and wife, father and son, master and slave, unexpected reversals of circumstance, raping virgins, suppositious children, recognition by means of rings and necklaces, these are the main constituents of recent comedy.'

Yet another Alexandrian critic, writing in the third century BC, says 'O Menander and life, which of you imitated the other?' This rhetorical question may have been occasioned by Menander's skill in depicting ordinary human beings. This impression of reality may also have been created by his verse which is fluid and flexible and far closer to what was probably vernacular speech than the great poetry of the fifth century.

Nevertheless what deterioration had taken place! This was not only the result of profound social changes in Athenian society but of changes in the structure of the theatre itself. The dramatist was no longer the dominating element. And we shall see throughout the history of theatre that whenever the creative energy of the dramatist flags, the actors take over; and although they bring a unique quality to theatrical art they impose a limitation on the creativity of the dramatists who tend, for example, not to create characters but repetitive types that suit the capabilities of the players. In seventeen of Menander's plays of which more than a hundred lines survive, there are, for example, four young men called Moschion, meaning 'little bull calf', and three country lads called Gorgias. He also wrote a number of standardized parts for soldiers who are usually called Polemon, from the Greek word *polemos* meaning war, or Stratophanes from *stratos* meaning army.

This tendency to fall back on what might be called social archetypes tends to happen in any theatre where masks are used. For although a mask carries its own theatrical quality it militates against the creation of original characters with their own fresh faces. Another limitation on the originality of playwright's invention tends to derive from Aristotle's emphasis on the importance of plot. If a playwright begins to write with a preconceived plot in his mind the characters will be subservient to that plot. But plot must be responsive to character. The development of an original story must depend on the subtle interplay between the characters concerned and the actions to which the characteristics of these characters give rise. The total submission of character to plot tends to create lifelessness; the total submission of plot to character leads to formlessness. The masterpiece requires a powerful organic relationship between the two. It was many hundreds of years before this happened.

It is interesting to note the persistency with which the chorus maintained its position in comedy. In the plays of Menander and the new comedies, the chorus has no role in the action of the play, but took the form of a band of revellers known as a *komos* who came on stage at various breaks in the action of the play and sang songs on a variety of subjects, usually irrelevant to the action. These interventions were known as *embolima*, a word that can almost be translated as interlude, a form of drama of which there will be a good deal to say in due course. It is probable that it was from these interventions of the chorus, breaking up the action of the play, that there developed the practice of dividing a play into acts. Menander was the first to do so, but why, or why five acts, no one knows.

This is not a period in the history of the theatre that has been the subject of much critical commentary. F. H. Sandbach's The Comic Theatre of Greece and Rome *is recommended.*

16 The Hellenistic Theatre and the Artists of Dionysos

It is a strange fever that suddenly drives a hitherto peaceful nation to take up arms and go abroad to conquer, subdue, or annex other people and other lands. The Assyrians, the Babylonians, the Egyptians and the Persians had at various times all caught the disease which Marxists attribute to powerful economic pressures and rivalries. The Greek people themselves were descended from invaders who had overrun the country from the north and then in turn had indulged in a limited form of aggression when they had besieged Troy and reduced it to a smoking ruin. But this was a struggle that may be seen to have been waged, less picturesquely but more pragmatically, for control of the Bosphorus through which a large part of the prosperous Asiatic trade had to pass. It was not in a spirit of adventure but of gain that Jason and his gang went in quest of the golden fleece. Wool was as precious a commodity to ancient Greece as it was to medieval Britain.

There are many reasons, however, for which men will explore foreign lands and settle down elsewhere than in their own country. The need for space and freedom are two of them. The Greeks were enthusiastic settlers. In the eighth century, the great age of the migrations, Greek colonists sailed east and settled along the coast of Asia Minor, then Ionia, now Turkey, and west as far as Italy and Sicily.

When the Athenians in their turn became aggressive they received their come-uppance from Sparta in 404; but peace did not last for long in the eastern Mediterranean. Trouble came next from the Macedonians, a somewhat military people of Greek stock who lived to the north of the Greek mainland. When Philip II of Macedon was assassinated in 336 he had become virtual master of Greece. He was succeeded by Alexander the Great (356–323) who, by the age of thirty-three, had overrun and subdued the whole of Egypt, the Middle East, Persia, and a large part of India. He was both an able administrator and a brilliant general, and since as a child at his father's court he had had no less a tutor than Aristotle himself he was not without cultural pretensions. It is not only trade that follows the flag but culture too, and Alexander left in the wake of his armies innumerable memorials to

Greek civilization. He founded, for example, the city of Alexandria which rapidly became one of the intellectual centres of the Hellenistic world.

So it happened that the culture of the Greek city-states was spread over the whole eastern Mediterranean and established what was known as the Hellenistic Age. Each country absorbed certain elements of Greek culture according to local conditions. Many built theatres on Greek models since they had no theatrical art of their own. By the first century BC there were some thirty theatres on the Greek mainland, fifty in Ionia, twenty in the region that is now Syria and Israel, sixty in central Italy, and a large number on the Mediterranean coast, countries that are now Tunisia and Algeria, as well as in Sicily, northern Italy, France, and the Rhineland.

Following the great age there was a decline in both the number and the quality of new plays, and the actors took over. Their importance can be dated from 449 when prizes for tragic actors were introduced at the City Dionysia and from 440 for actors in comedy at the Lenaia. With few new plays being written and an increasing number of revivals, the interest of the audience was switched from play to players whose contrasted interpretation of the great roles became a subject of considerable interest.

Such was their growing prestige that companies of actors not only toured extensively in Attica but increasingly throughout the Greek world. The more distinguished were granted diplomatic status and carried out negotiations between one city and another. Alexander was particularly enthusiastic about actors and musicians and organized contests and festivals on a lavish scale in the course of his aggressive perambulations.

By the third century dramatic festivals had become widespread throughout the Hellenistic world and were no longer confined to the spring festival of the god Dionysos. The result of this enormous and widespread demand for actors and musicians was that performing artists were obliged to organize themselves. The first of these guilds was known as the Artists of Dionysos. It was formed in about 280 and based in Athens. It was followed by others. Membership included not only actors of tragedy, comedy, and satyr, but singers, instrumentalists, rhapsodes, and bards, and those who trained the choruses.

The performer's art is notoriously evanescent. Our only source of knowledge of the activities of actors in the Hellenistic world is a variety of inscriptions on public monuments. These have been painstakingly recorded by Sir A. W. Pickard-Cambridge in Athenian Dramatic Festivals. *But many Hellenistic theatres, reasonably well-preserved, have survived and are described, with photographs, in Margaret Bieber's* The History of the Greek and Roman Theatre.

17 | Early Roman Comedy

The drive of the Macedonians was eastwards. This decision may well have represented a tacit acceptance of the power dominating the western world, that of Rome. Legend ascribes the founding of Rome to two brothers, Romulus and Remus, who were exposed by their parents, suckled by a wolf, and lived to become the leaders of a band of militant shepherds who decided to found a city on the River Tiber some miles from its mouth. The date when these curious events took place is accepted as 753 BC but it has as much validity as the suggestion that the events described in the first chapter of Genesis took place in 4004 BC. In due course there was a succession of kings who, with a consistently aggressive policy, established and then extended the territory of Rome. This period came to an end in 510 when a republic was established. But the territorial ambitions of the Romans were voracious and went on to cover the whole of the Mediterranean world, North Africa, the Middle East, and most of Western Europe. It was a new concept in imperialism. Roman interest in Greece was apparent in 452 when the Senate sent commissioners to Athens to study the country's reported wise and liberal constitution; but it was not until 146, the year in which the Romans finally destroyed the power of Carthage, that they invaded Greece and made it a Roman province.

Now it was a curious feature of this immensely able people that although they ultimately conquered and administered an enormous territory, in their cultural and artistic life they showed almost no originality. This they seem implicitly to have recognized for they did not destroy the Greek, Hellenistic or any other culture that seemed to them worthy of preservation, but showed considerable skill in adapting, copying, and assimilating existing cultural and artistic models. For this reason the history of the Roman theatre and its drama is neither easy nor satisfactory to recount. Indeed, if it had not been for the immense authority attached to the comedies of two playwrights many centuries later, and the effect of this on the whole development of European drama, it is likely that Plautus and Terence would have been lightly passed over in most theatrical histories.

The history of Roman comedy begins with short, probably coarse farces not unlike perhaps those that seem to have been prevalent in

Greece in earlier times. The first organized theatrical performances date from 364 and were known as *ludi scaenici*, a phrase which can be translated as 'theatrical games'. The place was Etruria, the country to the north of Rome inhabited by the descendants of a strange tribe with their own culture and their own untranslatable language, the Etruscans. The occasion was some kind of religious festival which in Roman society was always celebrated with games (*ludi*) usually in the form of athletic contests. The plays, which had as their subject-matter a variety of mythological and legendary stories, were full of singing and dancing. This is important to remember for when one comes to read the plays of Plautus in English prose translation one gets no sense of their abounding metrical vitality.

Of the early playwrights only names are known and in some cases the titles of their plays. Among the earlier was Livius Andronicus (*c*.284–204) who through his ability as a translator introduced the Romans to a considerable amount of Greek literature. He then went on to write plays himself on largely mythological themes and ended his life as president of an academy of poets. The historian Livy says that he was a fine actor and singer. Another was Gnaeus Naevius (*c*.270–*c*.201) who was more successful in writing comedy than tragedy but got into trouble with the authorities for jeering at Roman politicians.

All the earlier Roman comedies were translations, adaptations, or imitations of Greek plays and were known as *fabulae palliatae* (literally 'Greek cloak stories') while the rather later plays that were on Roman themes were called *fabulae togatae* (Roman cloak stories).

18 | Plautus

Plautus was by far the most successful exponent of the *fabulae palliatae*. He was born in Sarsina in Umbria around the year 254 BC. He went to Rome as a young man and seems to have had some early association with the theatre. It is suggested that he became an actor and played the stock role of Maccus, whence his full name of Titus Maccus Plautus. In due course he left the stage and went into some kind of business but was unsuccessful. He then became interested in

Greece and Greek drama and from the age of about forty began a new and successful career as an adaptor of Greek comedies for the Roman stage. He is credited with 130 plays of which twenty-one have survived. He died in 184 BC at the age of about seventy.

His plays are quite entertaining to read in an English prose translation for they are full of fun and vigour. But it is difficult to come to terms with their real flavour without a knowledge of Latin, since his outstanding quality is his verse, elegantly phrased and metrically varied and written to be spoken with some kind of simple instrumental accompaniment. It has been said that if the muses could speak they would do so in the language of Plautus. This mixture of linguistic elegance, metrical variety, musical accompaniment, and broadly comic characters and situations is very difficult to conceive and even more to reproduce.

One of his best-known plays is *Amphitryo*, a mythological burlesque of a kind that was very popular with the Greeks in the age following Aristophanes and one of which very few examples have survived. It is a neatly written comedy about the god Jupiter, who seems to have been as promiscuous as his Greek counterpart, Zeus, assuming the appearance of the general Amphitryon in order to make love to his wife while the general is away on active service.

The *Menaechmi* is the original of Shakespeare's *A Comedy of Errors* and the American musical, *The Boys from Syracuse*. Once one has accepted the basic premise of one identical twin searching the Mediterranean for his brother and both in the process becoming involved in a series of farcical misunderstandings, one can begin to enjoy these skilful variations on an overworked theatrical theme.

Aulularia (*The Pot of Gold*) is the prototype of Molière's *L'Avare* (*The Miser*). In the *Miles Gloriosus* (*The Splendid Soldier* or *The Swaggering Captain*) Plautus creates the prototype of another figure that has appeared constantly in European drama. The play is a mixture of sexual intrigue and a plot to deflate the swaggering self-esteem of the splendidly named soldier, Pyrgopolinices.

In some of Plautus's plays such as *Mostellaria* (*The Ghost*) the plot turns on the demonic and cynical inventions of a slave, who in this case is determined to prevent his master, on returning from a trip abroad, to enter his own house where his son has been spending the family fortune on riotous living. *Rudens (The Rope)* is about a girl who was stolen from her home in childhood and is now in the clutches of a pimp who intends to sell her to a brothel in Sicily. As was the case with Menander, from whom many of Plautus's plays are derived, the imaginative scope is limited: father and son compete for the favours of a courtesan (*Mercator, The Merchant*), the slave turns out to be the master's long-lost son (*Captivi*, *The Captives*), the attempts of a young man to raise enough money to prevent his mistress being sold to a Macedonian officer (*Pseudolos*). The standard assumption is that wives are unattractive, mistresses beautiful, slaves deceptive, and that the important values of life are money, clothes, jewels, and personal possessions.

19 | Terence

The only other comic dramatist whose plays have survived is Publius Terentius Afer, the last word referring to his dark skin and North-African origin. He was born around 190 BC and brought to Rome as a slave. On achieving his freedom he took the name of his master, Terentius Lucanus. He is thought to have died in 159 at the early age of thirty-one. Nothing more is known of his life although there is a tradition that he was accepted into a socially and intellectually distinguished circle. This may account for him having written in a more restrained manner that Plautus with less public success in consequence. Of his six surviving plays – and he is not thought to have written many more – four are translations or adaptations of Menander, and two are written in Menander's style.

Terence keeps fairly close to his Greek originals. He replaces the metrical variety of Plautus with a more limited but even more elegant form of verse. He avoids monologues and shows considerable respect for the coherence and unity of his plots. His plays are more discursive than Menander's, more disciplined than Plautus's, lacking farcical invention, but showing greater interest in the interplay of character. He was moving towards a more realistic form of comedy. His plays were not a great success with the public and in his prologues he criticizes the unappreciative stupidity of his audiences.

His plots are not significantly different from those already described. *Andria* (*The Girl from Andros*) is about a young man who is in love with a golden-hearted courtesan while his father wants him to marry the daughter of his best friend. *Hecyra* (*The Mother-in-law*) reverts to the unpleasant theme of the rape that took place in the dark. *Heauton Timorumenos* (*The Self-tormenter*) is a farrago of confused identities and complex father-son relationships. It includes the celebrated line:

Homo sum: humani nil a me alienum puto
(I am a man: nothing human is alien to me)

Eunuchus (*The Eunuch*) provides some of the material for the famous sixteenth-century English comedy, *Ralph Roister Doister*. *Adelphi* (*The Brothers*) moves in the direction of a serious discussion on education but concludes with the cynical suggestion that however you bring them up boys will be boys, that is, indulge their erotic urges. *Phormio* introduces the unpleasant figure of the professional parasite, the man who lives on his wits, engineering and undoing marriages according to the highest bidder.

After Terence very few new plays seem to have been written at all. One wonders whether the theatre-going public, such as it was, may not have been thoroughly bored with constant adaptations from the Greek and that their disenchantment with Terence may not have been part of a broader rejection of drama that must have lacked real relevance to Roman society of the time. Menander's variations on sexual intrigue and a very limited view of society may have amused fourth-century Athens, but there is no reason why the same fare should have meant much to second-century Romans. Their society was a very different one, and while the kind of entertainment it provided commands little respect, it was vigorous and is not to be wholly rejected because it was based on different values from our own.

The plays of Plautus and Terence have often been translated with the inevitable limitations. No opportunity should be missed to see a performance in the original Latin. Historically they are more important than their quality warrants.

20 | Roman Drama

In ancient Rome, as in Greece, theatrical performances took place only on religious festivals. Originally these festivals were celebrated with *ludi* or games which usually included chariot races and displays of military power. A festival, after all, is an opportunity for a community to celebrate and reaffirm what it believes in. The Romans paid plenty of lip-service to religion and built many temples, but when it came to the point it was the strong arm they believed in, not the spirit of god. As the Romans added to their victories so they increased the number of celebratory games. By the first century BC these were held on about fifty-five days of the year while by the middle of the first century AD there were over 150 public holidays on which games of one kind or another were held.

It is surprising that since *ludi scaenici* were added to the number of official festivals as early as 240 BC this did not give an impetus to the creation of an authentically Roman drama, but in this respect the influence of the Greeks appears to have been too strong. Nevertheless as the games became increasingly secularized and commemorative festivals became public holidays, so the activities that constituted the games became increasingly directed towards entertaining the people rather than reaffirming Roman military power or propitiating a god.

This trend was shaped by the habit of the official Roman mind to 'think big'. In some respects officialdom always thinks big, for a public occasion is just that, a public occasion, and has very little in common with more personal forms of culture. The relationship between the impressive official public occasion and more intimate manifestations is a complex one and teaches us a good deal about the structure of the society in question. In imperial Rome the spectacular survived and the drama went to the wall.

There is no obvious explanation for the absence of a strong dramatic tradition. The point has already been made that when the vitality of the dramatist flags, the actor takes over. And this is what seems to have happened in imperial Rome. The actors became 'top dog'. In the first half of the first century BC there were two actors in Rome to achieve considerable distinction, Roscius and Aesopus, though in whose plays they made their names we have no idea. Their success is the more remarkable since until the time of Plautus, actors had had the social status of slaves (*infames*) under the control of a manager (*dominus gregis*).

In 55 BC Pompey celebrated the second year of his consulship by building the first permanent stone theatre in Rome. When we read that it held 40,000 spectators we know that the art of the theatre was dead. In 13 BC the Theatre of Balbulus was built with a capacity of between 7,000 and 8,000, and years later the Theatre of Marcellus, of which a few columns can still be seen, with a capacity of 14,000. The great statesman Cicero, writing to a friend about a performance in Pompey's theatre, asks what pleasure there can be in the sight of 600 mules in a performance of Accius's tragedy, *Clytemnestra*.

The only kind of performances possible in such vast spaces were spectaculars, and as we know the skill of the Romans at military pageantry, gladiatorial combats, and throwing Christians to the lions, there is no reason to doubt their virtuosity as showmen. The actors and actresses – for these masters of brutality were not squeamish about exploiting nudity – became dancers, or mimes as they were called, and the Roman people were given their fill of pap and circuses. Livy refers to the 'mad extravagance' of the theatre of his time. Small wonder the early Christians had little use for drama.

21 | Roman Theatres

These great theatres in Rome, of which only a small portion of an impressive colonnade survives, were not typical of Roman theatre architecture. In the countries bordering on the Mediterranean there may be seen the remains of many a small Roman theatre in a sufficient state of preservation for one to glean a fairly clear idea of their appearance at the height of Roman civilization.

The first of all theatres, where any kind of drama other than the ritualistic was performed, consisted of a platform, or stage, resting on trestles, with a curtain behind and the audience in front. This is the kind of stage on which Sicilian-Greek and Roman farces may well have been played as far back as 600 BC. We have seen how this arrangement was given architectural form in the Theatre of Dionysos. Hellenistic and Roman theatres were not significantly different. The orchestra was semicircular and backed by a raised stage, the front of which was called the *proscenium*. The stage had an elaborate architectural backing, equivalent to the curtain in the booth theatre, and this was known as the *frons scaena*, and usually included three entrances. Unlike Greek theatres which were usually built against the side of a hill, Roman theatres, which were built on any level ground, had an ornate entrance façade. The Greek theatre, built to house a performance in which the religious and democratic elements were strongly emphasized, provided good seats for all. The Roman theatre, intended for public spectacles and entertainment of a far more secular nature, and often run on a commercial basis, reserved the front rows for public officials.

The raised stage, a development of the utmost importance, seems to

4. **Roman theatre at Jerash (Gerasa), Jordan**
Typical of Roman theatres built throughout the Mediterranean area and the Middle East. The stage backing shows the doorways that were advocated by Vitruvius and copied by Renaissance architects in theatres such as the Teatro Olimpico, Vicenza.

have been introduced around the year 200 BC, or even earlier, when plays no longer included a chorus. But better sight-lines undoubtedly played a part in new theatrical design.

Again we are frustrated at not having evidence with which to reconstruct performances. The picture we have given of a Roman theatre with its stone auditorium, stone stage, and stone *frons scaena* (stage backing), seen in the light of the remains of a large number of Roman theatres, suggests that they were impressive examples of Roman architecture, solidly built, well-proportioned and expertly decorated. But all this stone does not seem to create a suitable environment for bawdy comedies. One would have thought that the plays of Plautus would have been better suited to the rougher conditions of the booth theatres where in fact they were usually performed. Temporary theatres were set up in market-places and public squares and removed when the performances came to an end. But this does not help us to know whether scenery was used. Most Roman comedies require the entrance to two houses, one on each side of the stage; and although there are plenty of examples of audiences being satisfied with performances without scenery, locale is of some importance in the plays of Plautus and Terence. And if comedies were usually given on temporary stages we are left wondering whether plays, as opposed to spectacles, were ever given in the permanent theatres.

The most curious feature of the Roman adaptation of the Greek theatre is the introduction of a high raised stage. It is conjectured that the reason for this, in addition to (questionably) improving the sight-lines, may have been to add to the heroic proportions of the actors when they were playing tragedy; for it is known that in the Roman theatre they were given even higher head-dresses and thicker soled boots than they had worn in the later Greek theatre. But this theory has two disadvantages. The high stage was far less suitable for comedy, though the answer here may be that comedy was more often played on temporary stages rather than in the great stone permanent theatres. The second problem is that the high stage destroyed any direct or organic contact between actors and chorus. For the chorus continued to be used in such original Roman tragedies as were written as well as in the frequent revivals of Greek and Hellenistic tragedy.

The Romans were pragmatists. They acted with clear intentions. One feels that in the matter of theatre design there is some element which was important to the Romans but of which we are completely unaware.

In problems of staging we get no help from the ruins of Roman theatres, while the surviving evidence tends to come from what one can only call rather untheatrical sources. It is convenient however, to discuss the work of the Roman architect Vitruvius later in this book (section 41).

22 | Seneca

There is plenty of evidence of the enthusiasm of every class of Roman from the Emperors onwards for theatrical entertainment but little of an interest in traditional comedy or tragedy. Original plays were very occasionally written and old ones were revived but this was more often the work of eccentric amateurs than of the professionals. The only man who is known to have written tragedies probably did so for public reading rather than stage performance and he certainly did not depend on literature for his income.

This man was Lucius Annaeus Seneca. He was born in Spain between 4 BC and 1 AD of a wealthy Italian family. He led a varied and distinguished life in the course of which he attained high political position, was exiled for adultery, and became tutor and adviser to the Emperor Nero. He retired from public life in 62 AD but three years later was compelled to take his own life for alleged participation in an unsuccessful conspiracy against the Emperor.

He wrote a number of works on philosophical subjects and nine tragedies which are thought to have been inspired by Greek originals. They are so different in spirit from his philosophical works that scholars question whether they are really by the same man. The Seneca of the plays, however, though a fine dramatic poet, was no poetic dramatist. His plays are full of long, passionate speeches, rich in imagery, but with little sense of dramatic construction. He has no concept of the value of implication, suggestion, or irony, but presents dramatic situations head on. He is the master of the confrontation. Thus in his version of *Hippolytus* he commits the crudity which Euripides so carefully avoids of making Phaedra declare her love for her son-in-law to his face. His *Oedipus* is no gradual, carefully-constructed self-realization of the tyrant's guilt but a series of statements and set pieces. He provides a long and horrifying description of the bloody ritual in which Teiresias indulges in order to bring Laius back from the dead, and another which spares no detail of the horrifying manner in which Oedipus gouged out his own eyes.

There is every reason to concur with the suggestion that these plays were written not for performance in a theatre but for public recitation, a practice that was common among educated Romans and much enjoyed by the Emperors Augustus and Claudius. Today there is no great pleasure or profit to be derived from these lurid plays and they might hardly have merited a mention, let alone a chapter, in a history of the theatre if it had not been for their immense influence on the development of play-writing in Renaissance Europe. Whoever wrote these tedious tragedies seemed to have had need to express the most neurotic private fantasies.

23 | Roman Dramatic Criticism

In emphasizing the debility and general decadence of Roman drama one is in danger of belittling in too general a way the extraordinary achievements of the Roman people. They were superb architects even if their finest achievements lack something of the subtlety of the Greeks. They created a language from which a large part of many contemporary European languages is derived. They conquered and governed an enormous territory with skill and liberality for many centuries. They threaded this empire with superb roads and fostered the development of European trade by establishing methods of computation, a code of weights and measures, and a judicial system which has provided the basis for many subsequent codes. The Roman intellectual was more interested in the practicalities of life than its uncertainties. He preferred pragmatism to speculation. Even Virgil's great poem, the *Aeneid*, is more concerned with establishing the origins and growth of the Roman Empire than celebrating the fall of Troy or the wanderings of Odysseus. While the Greeks speculated and philosophized for the pleasure of so doing, the Romans tended to do so only when there was a practical end in view. They wanted clear answers, neat arrangements; they had no time for muddle. Thus they tended to produce critics rather than artists, analysis rather than works of art.

That there was not a great deal of dramatic criticism was the result of there not being very much drama to criticize. The first person to discuss poetry in general and dramatic poetry in particular was the poet Quintus Horatius Flaccus (65–8 BC), commonly known as Horace. His *Epistola ad Pisones (A Letter to the Piso Family)* is usually known as *The*

Art of Poetry, and although a far less interesting and penetrating piece of work than Aristotle's, it has over the centuries been almost as highly regarded.

His first precept is that the power of the eye is so great that only acceptable action must be shown on the stage, anything unpleasant being confined to narration. He says that a fourth actor can be introduced only in a small role, an interesting comment on the survival of the Greek practice of having no more than three actors in a performance. In his discussion on the chorus – another evidence of survival – he makes reference to the need for a play to be in five acts. The origin of this curious and arbitrary precept is not known but with hindsight one can say that five has always been a number with strange connotations and that five acts provide a convenient structure for a play. He has an interesting passage on metres, of importance only for those who can read Latin, and concludes his comments on drama with a warning to poets that they must combine, or choose between, instruction and entertainment, but that even if their object is the latter, they must preserve a certain truthfulness to real life, although it is a combination of the two that will win the fullest approval of audiences.

It is this last point which has proved to be of the greatest importance for the future of drama. Horace has put his finger on the ambivalent position of drama in society. No doubt the decadent cavortings that were taking place in the Roman theatres of his time enabled him to see that entertainment as the sole justification of drama leaves the door open for artistic irresponsibility.

Another important Roman critic was Quintilian (M. Fabius Quintilianus) who wrote an interesting treatise on rhetoric, oratory, and declamation. These related skills are of great importance in any society that does not rely on printed books as a main form of communication. Quintilian's analysis of the techniques required in public debate was of particular interest to scholars of later ages for whom rhetoric and oratory were essential elements in a liberal education.

The last of the Roman critics was Aelius Donatus who lived in the fourth century AD. In his short essay *De Commedia et Tragoedia* (*About Tragedy and Comedy*) he gives particular emphasis to the categorizations of comedy – the *palliata*, the *togata*, and the *atellana*, as well as other prescriptions such as the colour of costume each type of character should wear, and the conditions under which singing should be incorporated into drama.

The significant point is this, that while Greek dramatic criticism was concerned with analysis, the Romans were preoccupied with rules. This may be seen as a misguided attempt to analyse the ingredients of success. For what Western Europe has inherited from the civilizations of Greece and Rome, perhaps before anything else, is a sense of order, or proportion, or propriety. This is really the sense in which we use the word 'classical'.

The curious and in some ways rather depressing fact is that the collapse of drama, begun in Republican, completed in Imperial Rome, did not prevent subsequent generations from imbuing the vestigial remains of the Roman theatre with an authority out of all proportion to its actual achievement. That will be the subject of a much later section of this book. It was many centuries before Europe recreated the art of the theatre.

Dramatic theory can make tedious reading, but it is often most useful in helping us to understand why people did what they did in the way they did.

Books on the Roman theatre in general are disappointing but W. H. Beare's The Roman Stage *and F. H. Sandbach's* The Comic Theatre of Greece and Rome *are informative.*

24 The Emergence of the Early Christian Church

Anyone who has read the New Testament will be aware of the prodigious achievement of the apostle Paul in interpreting the teachings of Jesus and making them known throughout the eastern Mediterranean. If the early Christians had settled down to worship quietly in their own way along with a large number of other minority sects, the Romans would hardly have noticed them, for they were not an intolerant people. But there was a dynamic in Christianity; it challenged, indeed, it denied the supreme authority of the Roman Emperor. The Romans began to persecute the Christians not so much because they disliked their religion as because they saw them as politically diversive and destructive.

Although Christianity is founded on the teachings of Jesus and the passionate apologetics of St. Paul, it owes its growth to the physical courage, the administrative skill, and the doctrinal wisdom of the early leaders of the movement. For a religion, especially a religion that envisages conquering the world, requires a doctrine, an administration, a form of worship, a cohesive body of belief and behaviour that will enable a man to identify himself as a member of that religion. All this was achieved by the early leaders of the Church and their first bishops. They created a form of service (or liturgy) and they edited the Bible from a huge mass of Jewish, Greek, and contemporary writings, sorting out the authentic from the apocryphal and the relevant from the merely sensational. All this they achieved in the face of constant persecution and opposition from the Roman state.

As we know, Christianity gradually won the day: a religion that had seemed at first likely to destroy the Empire, proved to be a unifying agent. By 313 AD Christianity had made such progress that the Emperor Constantine himself was converted and demanded religious toleration throughout the Empire.

To conquer Europe for Christianity, however, demanded as great an effort as the Romans had had to make to conquer it militarily. This was the work of the bishops who were drawn from the ranks of well-educated, upper-class Romans and dispatched to every corner of the Empire where there was evidence of the new religion taking root. They carried with them all the administrative and secular skills of Roman civilization to each remote diocese where they combined the functions of mayor, town clerk, city treasurer, military governor, and spiritual father.

The policy of the Church in setting about Christianizing the soul of the European peasant is well set out in a letter of 601 which Pope Gregory the Great, one of the administrative giants of the early Church, directed to Augustine who had been given the task of converting the British.

> We have given careful thought to the affairs of the English and have come to the conclusion that the temples of the idols in that country should on no account be destroyed. He [Augustine] is to destroy the idols, but the temples themselves are to be cleansed within them . . . and dedicated to the service of the true God. In this way we hope that the people, seeing that its temples have not been destroyed, will abandon its idolatry and resort to those places as before . . . They are no longer to sacrifice beasts to the devil but they may kill them for food and for the praise of God . . . For it is certainly impossible to eradicate all errors from obstinate minds at one stroke.

Another skilful device was the Christianization of the calendar. Pagan ritual, like that of the Greeks, was seen as a life-giving process of recreation and regeneration. It was a means, based on unsophisticated but extremely human processes of thought, to secure the fertility of the crops, the health of the livestock, and the survival of man himself. The circle of the seasons and the clemency of the weather are matters of the utmost importance to any agricultural community. Men organized their lives and work according to the seasons. The Church therefore set about Christianizing the seasonal festivals in the same manner as Gregory had recommended the Christianization of the temples. The birth of Jesus was therefore identified with the winter solstice, the longest night and the shortest day, which suggested the birth of the new year. Lent was established early in February when food stocks were low and fasting was virtually obligatory. Easter was related to the spring equinox, when day and night are of equal length and farmers set about the spring sowing. The death of Jesus, which was closely related in time to his resurrection, reflected the burgeoning of the countryside. Festivals were established throughout the summer to take advantage of the good weather, and in the autumn, when the harvest had been gathered in, produce and animals were bought and sold, saints' days were established to coincide with autumnal fairs.

So it was that while the Church spread its civilizing influence over the face of Europe and the people increasingly accepted its wisdom and authority, there remained that obstinacy in the soul of man that treasured beliefs and practices which the priests found it more expedient to ignore than to attempt to eradicate.

The history of the Roman Empire has been the subject of many studies from Edward Gibbons's The Decline and Fall of the Roman Empire *onwards. The history of the Christian Church has become a popular subject in recent years and is of the utmost importance in providing a background to the following sections.*

25 | The Heroic Age

In 453, when Rome itself was occupied by a barbarian army, the writing was clearly on the wall. It must have been a daunting prospect for both the Roman and the Christian administrators. They were faced with a Europe that was under the control of kings and tribal leaders who held great military power. Society was advancing beyond a primitive agricultural and tribal culture and organizing itself in bigger units. There were no clearly-defined territorial boundaries. A king who wanted to wage war seemed to have little difficulty in recruiting the support of other kings. It was such an alliance that successfully invaded Italy not once but on a number of occasions.

It was from this strange, poorly chronicled period of invasion and counter-invasion that some of the Teutonic and Anglo-Saxon epics derive. Although the great German epic of the *Niebelungenlied* (*The Song of the Niebelungs*) was given literary form much later, it was in the courts of dark-age Europe that this heroic material was first put into song. Another was the celebrated *Beowulf*, a poem written in English though of Danish origin. The importance of such epics for the history of the theatre lies in the minstrel, scop, or bard – for he went under different descriptions – who was both composer and performer, as the Greek minstrels had been. At a time when nothing was printed and little written down, composition and literary survival were the responsibility of men who had a facility with the spoken word. Thus the minstrel was both a thesaurus of traditional material and a composer of new. There was no prize in those days for originality. The corpus of the epic grew through a series of accretions as the minstrels sought to entertain their masters during the long winter evenings. No less a leader than Attila enjoyed listening at his leisure to a couple of minstrels who sang his praises, recalled his victories, and celebrated the ancient history of the tribe; and if one of them had come across an effective piece of material which he had learnt from another minstrel, so much the better.

But the European tribes were not savages. They had their own culture and many of them were ready enough to absorb the obvious achievements of Roman civilization. The tendency was towards the creation of bigger political units. The whole long laborious movement came astonishingly to a head when on Christmas Day, 800, the Frankish Emperor Charlemagne (Carolus Magnus or Charles the Great) was crowned by the Pope as the first Holy Roman Emperor. It was an astonishing moment which seemed to some to be the realization of that ultimate vision when the political authority of the Roman Empire would be totally identified with the spiritual authority of the Christian Church. But the alliance quickly broke up. There were too many underlying tensions for success. And although the concept of the Holy Roman Empire emerged from time to time during the next seven hundred years of European history it never came so near fulfillment.

Charlemagne was a prodigious character, committed equally to secular and religious progress; he established schools of study, encouraged trade, took a great interest in literature, pressed for a definition of church dogma, insisted on discipline from church functionaries, took steps for the improvement of church music. He carried the work of the Popes into the heart of secular Europe and set Europe on the lines it was to develop over the next five hundred years.

26 | The Monastic Movement

Since the bishops tended to have their hands full with administrative and spiritual affairs, one of the most effective arms of the Church in pursuing its Christianizing mission was the monastic movement. The words 'monk', 'monastic', 'monastery', all derive from the Greek word *monarchos* meaning solitary and that is the key to the origins of the movement. The first Christian monks of whom anything is known were ascetics who went to live alone in the deserts of the Middle East in order to achieve a state of holiness through living a life of poverty, chastity, and devotion to the worship of God. Many of the early monks, however, were notable for their eccentric rather than their devotional behaviour and the movement did not achieve either respectability or official recognition until it moved into Western Europe and came under the attention of Pope Gregory the Great. The concept of a community of monks living according to strict administrative and spiritual rules was the work of the Italian, St. Benedict (*c.*480–*c.*550). These rules laid down in detail the manner in which the monks were to spend their day, how and when they were to eat, when to attend service, how often to remain in silent meditation, when to indulge in manual labour – for a monastic community was usually self-supporting – and when to study and read.

This was the period when Europe was subject to constant invasions from the east and Italy was overrun successively by Franks, Lombards, Visigoths, Ostrogoths, and Vandals. The establishment of Benedictine monastries throughout Europe between the sixth and tenth centuries was a stabilizing and civilizing influence during this stormy and restless period. For the Benedictine Order laid great emphasis both on education and the relationship of the monks to the local community. Thus the monks were able to provide leadership in farming methods, in establishing a calendar, in keeping accounts, in various kinds of husbandry; while their work in education, fostered by the vision of the Emperor Charlemagne, established the monastic movement as virtually the only form of education to exist throughout the Middle Ages. The importance of the various monastic orders in the development of European society between about 600 and 1500 cannot be overestimated.

27 The Development of Church Ritual and Ecclesiastical Design

Two of the greatest problems facing the early leaders of the Church was the nature of Christian worship, the Church service, and where it should take place, the church itself. The creation of the service, or liturgy, as it was called, was a gradual process, and the subject, as can well be imagined, of constant discussion. A certain arrangement of hymns, prayers, readings from the scriptures, and sermons raise no great doctrinal problems but the centre of Christian worship, the celebration of Mass, in which the worshipper partakes of the body and blood of Christ, proved to be a highly sensitive matter.

The celebration of mass involves a concept that must be clearly understood in view of subsequent developments. The mass was established for the purpose of bringing the worshipper as near as possible to experiencing the reality of Christ's Crucifixion and realizing the human redemption that was made possible by his death. Communion was therefore conceived as the symbolic re-enactment of events that took place in Palestine many centuries before, and it was intended to have the same force as if the communicants had been present at the death of Christ. Thus it was clearly emphasized in the service books of the time that the celebration of mass was a ritualized representation of the death of Jesus on the cross. The priest celebrating mass 'in the theatre of the church' – the words are those of a scholar writing around the year 1000 – 'represents by his gestures the struggle of Christ and the victory of his redemption, as by his silence he represents Christ as a lamb being led to the sacrifice, and by the extension of his arms the extension of Christ on the cross, and by his chant the cry of Christ in agony'.

It is not intended to be disparaging of the mass to say that the celebration had a powerful and deliberately intended theatricality, though the word would not have been used at the time. The setting was architecturally impressive, the 'performers' in the person of the priests, were clothed in finery reminiscent of the attire of a Roman Emperor, and the celebrant was involved in the symbolic re-enactment of a deeply significant and mystical event.

The text of the ritual was in Latin and it was sung. The Romans, however, had attached no great importance to music, and early Christian worship had been conducted as quietly as possible to avoid discovery and subsequent prosecution. When the Emperor Constantine made Christianity an official religion there was no musical tradition on which to draw and the leaders of the Christian Church turned therefore to the traditions of Greek and Jewish music, with important results that will be described in the next chapter.

They then had to create the architectural setting for this impressive ritual. Two areas are involved – that in which the central sacrifice or enactment of the ritual takes place, and a large area for the worshippers (or audience). The bishops based their design on the Roman basilica or meeting-place which lent itself for adaptation to Christian worship. The basilica was a long rectangular building with a curved recess at one end known as the apse, a large central area flanked by two rows of columns, on each side of which were two aisles, and a main entrance at the other end. When in due course the bishops began to build their own churches, instead of adapting basilicae, they let their passion for visual allegory come into play. The meaning of the term will be clear in the present context although it will be fully discussed in a later section. The basic symbol of Christianity has always been the Cross. The bishops therefore gave the basilica cruciform shape by adding two transepts. The area in front of the altar, where in a service the symbolic participation in the sacrifice takes place, was cut off from the nave by an area known as the chancel which was specifically reserved for the priests. At the back of the altar was an arrangement of small chapels, where priests could conduct more intimate services and which represented the crown of thorns around the head of Christ. But the most remarkable aspect of the whole concept was the passion for height. For three hundred years architects and masons experimented with techniques to raise the height of the nave and the thrusting elegance of the spires. The great tapering windows were filled with coloured (or stained) glass, one of the most extraordinary achievements of these remarkable people, while the echoing acoustics of these great spacious buildings gave that additional texture to the modal singing in which all services were conducted. All in all a medieval cathedral, abbey, or church is a marvellous – indeed it is a marvel – amalgamation of visionary idealism, technical skill, artistic form, and symbolic significance. In the great age of ecclesiastical architecture, between about 800 and 1350, some 5,000 churches, cathedrals, and abbeys were built in Europe, an astonishing achievement, economically, technically, artistically. Around the year 1065 a bishop wrote, 'I arose in the morning and behold the earth was covered with a white robe of churches'.

28 | Dramatic Tropes

By the ninth century Europe was beginning to take something of its present form and a certain economic stability was becoming established. Towns were being built and trade was increasing. It was on these emergent trade routes that the Benedictines established their monasteries. Among the most vigorous was the monastery at St. Gall, situated at the northern end of one of the passes through the Alps. In 850 or thereabouts two Irishmen visited the monastery, a bishop named Marcus and his nephew Marcellus. The nephew stayed. He proved himself to be a fine scholar and a good musician and the Abbot put him in charge of the monastic school.

Among his students were three remarkable men – Notker Balbulus, a gentle fellow who had a stammer, Tutilo who was something of a musician, and Ratpert who was a scholar. The three of them became interested in experimenting with the writing of tropes. The idea seems to have come from Balbulus (*c.*840–912) who was stimulated by a service-book brought to St. Gall by a monk from the Norman monastery of Jumièges which had been sacked by the Normans in 841.

A trope was a short original passage which could be added to one of the more formal elements of the service and was one of the few opportunities offered a musician or a poet for original work. Many of the regular psalms, hymns, and anthems ended with an 'Allelujah', a word deriving from the Hebrew and meaning 'Praise Jehovah'. Some enterprising musician hit upon the idea of extending the final syllable of allelujah, the ah, as a kind of coda. These additional musical passages were called tropes. The next step was for words to be written to these vocalized passages of music and then for the whole trope to be detached from the preceding anthem and to become an independent hymn. The practice became widespread and many tropes were written and passed from one monastery to another. The impetus for the whole idea came from Charlemagne's interest in the form of the liturgy and the development of church music.

The celebration of mass, however, was far from being the only occasion when a historical event was re-enacted in symbolic form. On Good Fridays, for example, worshippers and clergy would kiss a crucifix which was then ritualistically deposited in the church crypt or underneath or behind the altar, in the most solemn manner, to be brought forth amid acclamations, singing, and the ringing of the church bells on Easter morning. In this way the clergy reinforced the story of the burial and resurrection of Jesus. It was almost certainly the three monks of St. Gall who 'dramatized' the story even more effectively by composing a trope on the subject. In essence it consisted of a priest, or in one case two boys, wearing albs, we are told, standing in some elevated position in the area of the chancel and singing,

> Quem quaeritis in sepulchro, O Cristocolae?
> (Whom do you seek in the sepulchre, O Christians?)

to which three priests who were moving towards the altar (or sepulchre or crypt), according to the ritual that has already been mentioned, replied,

> Jesus Nazarenum crucifixum, O caelicolae
> (Jesus of Nazareth who has been crucified, O heavenly ones.)

to which the priest representing the angel replied,

> Non est hic. Surrexit sicut predixerat. Ite, nuntiate quia surrexit de sepulchro.
> (He is not here. He is risen as foretold. Go, announce that he is risen from the sepulchre).

It is not certain that this remarkable trope was really composed at St. Gall, but this was certainly one of the first monasteries where there is evidence of its having been performed, and it is in the library of the monastery of St. Gall that one can still see the earliest manuscript. Its success was outstanding. Four hundred monasteries from Winchester to Vienna copied, extended, or made their own versions of the trope.

This is less surprising than might at first appear. In certain respects the Romans left Europe more unified than it has ever been, bequeathing their roads, their laws, their civil service, their weights and measures, and above all their language. With many local variations Europe enjoyed a common Latin/Roman-Christian culture. For all the shortcomings in transport and communication, ideas and practices spread with remarkable speed, especially throughout the continental network of monasteries.

The fullest description of the trope in its more extended form comes from what is known as the *Regularis Concordia* (*c*.970). This was a document drawn up by three bishops at the instigation of King Edgar to regularize practices in Benedictine monasteries in England. The rubric states quite specifically that 'these things are done in imitation of the angel sitting in the monument and the women with spices coming to anoint the body of Jesus'.

Another indication of its success comes from the occasion of its performance. Originally this was in the course of an early morning service in the closed community of a monastery; but in due course a version of the trope was given full public exposure as a part of morning mass on Easter Day.

29 The Extension of the Liturgical Drama

It is prudent to use the word 'extension' rather than 'development' in considering the subsequent history of the dramatic trope. A very large number were composed and manuscripts have survived from monasteries in many parts of Europe, but there was no consistent development of the form and such extensions of the original trope as took place were piecemeal and inconsistent.

From Salisbury, for example, comes a version that begins with a series of laments by the three Marys (Mary the mother of Jesus, Mary Magdalene, and the Mary to whom Mark makes reference) followed by the *Quem quaeritis* sequence in its original form. Then comes a visit to the sepulchre by the disciples Peter and John and after that a short passage of liturgical poetry in praise of the Paschal lamb, a common medieval practice of identifying Jesus with the Jewish sacrificial victim. There is then a dialogue between the Marys and the disciples, and another song from the choir. The monastery at Prague introduced an ointment-seller from whom the women purchase perfumes to sweeten the shroud of

Jesus and later versions extend the sequence to include the Ascension. The monastic authors and composers studied the gospels closely for episodes which would provide material for a hymn, a scene, or some other extension of the situation, and this process involved the gradual introduction of other 'lay' characters, in addition to the ointment-seller, such as Pontius Pilate and King Herod.

Just as Easter had been marked by the laying of a crucifix within a sepulchre, so Christmas was marked, as it so often is today, with a crib or a representation of a manger. A sharp-witted monk, reading Luke 11 verses 8–20, saw that it would be an easy transition from 'Whom do you seek, O Christians?' to 'Whom do you seek, O shepherds?' or 'Whom do you seek, O wise men?' So there developed a collection of tropes around the Nativity which is a colourful story involving less doctrinal mystery than the Passion. The first surviving versions came from the monasteries of Limoges and Rouen and were followed by elaborate extensions, some of which include the massacre of the innocents and the flight into Egypt.

Having dealt with the miraculous birth and even more miraculous death of Jesus, the monks then turned their attention to establishing his historical authenticity. They based their play, which took the form of a procession of the prophets, on a passage in one of St. Augustine's sermons. Various versions include a bearded Moses, David dressed as a king, a pregnant Elizabeth, an Angel with a sword and, most striking of all, Balaam on his (speaking) ass.

The liturgical drama includes few plays of Old Testament subjects apart from the prophets. The most notable exception is Daniel who is the subject of a play from the monastery of Beauvais in northern France. From the New Testament the most popular subject, apart from a large number of plays grouped round the Nativity and the Crucifixion, is the story of the wise and foolish virgins. But there are also plays on the raising of Lazarus and the conversion of St. Paul. It is rather curious to find that in spite of the enthusiasm of the Catholic Church for the creation of saints, Saint Nicholas is the only one to have been often included in the liturgical drama. Perhaps his relative obscurity made him a convenient figure to which to attach miraculous and sometimes fictitious events. Lack of historical evidence gives freedom to the imagination.

And there we have the nub of the situation. For while on the one hand the 'dramatists' were clearly limited in their choice of subject, they were becoming increasingly enterprising in the way they handled their material. With the secular element becoming stronger than the religious it is not surprising to find that plays were becoming detached from the service or canonical office and being performed independently and in their own right. This secular element was increased when passages in certain plays were sung – we do not know whether they were ever spoken – in the vernacular.

As the monastery of St. Gall had played a large part in initiating liturgical drama, so other monasteries became a centre of further development. One of these was the monastery of Fleury, sometimes known as St. Benoit-sur-Loire. Fleury is near Orleans which in the twelfth century was considered to be the artistic centre of France. Fleury may well have been the home of Hilarius, a wandering scholar, English by birth and French by adoption, a former pupil of the great teacher, Peter Abelard, and a poet who is known to have written a *Raising of Lazarus*, a play about St. Nicholas, and a play about Daniel. But in those days when no great virtue was attached to originality, plays were passed from one establishment to another, altered, modified, adapted, and developed and then passed on so that authorship is impossible to determine. Anonymity was the order of the day.

Outside their context these plays are of no great interest either as drama or as literature, even for those who can read Latin. But they are nevertheless an extraordinary phenomenon, especially when one considers such details of their staging as have survived. In an *Officium Stellae (The Play of the Star)*, staged on 6 January, three priests dressed as kings walked towards the altar, where presumably the crib was set up, bearing gifts and following a star which was drawn along a cord. In a version of the *Sponsus*, the foolish virgins play ball instead of trimming their lamps. The Rouen version of the Prophets requires some kind of furnace for the incineration of the prophet. Most of the plays on Daniel include a good deal of pageantry together, in one instance, with a cage for the lions. In the Fleury play of the *Conversion of St. Paul* the rubric states that Paul and his disciples, in escaping from Antioch, are lowered to earth 'as if down a wall'.

We have no idea how all these effects were managed. But churches and cathedrals in those days were bare of chairs and pews and this left the great open space of nave, transept, and aisles free for the little stages, known as *sedes* or seats, which were built for each scene and which are known to have been decorated to various degrees of elaboration. But while this church drama was developing the cathedrals and abbeys were themselves being built. And the great innovators of all this were the Benedictines.

There was inevitable opposition from the ecclesiastical hawks, who roundly denounced the plays for their increasing secularization. The thirteenth-century theologian, Robert Grosseteste, Bishop of Lincoln, where dramatic tropes were frequently performed, was particularly severe in his denunciations, and even a century before him a German theologian had argued vehemently that the clergy were doing the work of Antichrist in turning churches into theatres (which leaves one wondering how in those days he knew what a theatre was).

But a kind of profanity was not only the outcome of these liturgical games. The Church had been unable, and in its wisdom perhaps unwilling to suppress a variety of irreligious celebrations that took place during the twelve days of Christmas and which included such cavortings as the crowning of the Boy Bishop, the Feast of Fools, and other survivals of the Roman mid-winter Saturnalia. Life was hard and the lesser clergy could not be expected to live on too tight a rein. But it all amounted to a good deal of tut-tutting on the part of the more sober-sided authorities.

While it is essential to consider the liturgical plays within the context of the Church at large, so it is essential to see the Church within the broader context of European society. By the thirteenth and fourteenth centuries, when denunciations were plentiful, the face of Europe was very different from what it had been in the tenth century at the time of the modest experiments of the monks of St. Gall. The development of political power had been immense. The concept of a Holy Roman Empire in which state and Church should enter into everlasting compact, had long since proved unworkable, though the ideal was still remembered. A coronation service, then as now, was religious and took place in a cathedral. The kings considered that this ceremony invested them with divine powers. They therefore increasingly used the Church as the spiritual arm of their own supreme political authority. Some of the more aggressive and politically motivated Popes protested vigorously, while the Church as a whole was quick to realize that it must employ every device to maintain, if not increase its authority. In these circumstances one can see the conflict created in the mind of the ecclesiastical authorities by the liturgical drama: on the other hand it provided a vivid reinforcement of some of the basic beliefs, myths, and legends of Christianity, while on the other it tended to be a diversion, an emasculation of true faith. But more was to come.

There are no anthologies of liturgical plays, but examples are sometimes included in anthologies covering the whole medieval drama. Every known liturgical text, however, has been collected and studied in Karl Young's two volume The Drama of the Medieval Church.

The most comprehensive study of the period, with every known fact recorded, is Sir E. K. Chambers's The Medieval Stage, *a monument of scholarship. A shorter study of the whole period is Glynne Wickham's* The Medieval Theatre, *particularly useful for the breadth of background provided. Another treatment of the subject, enlightening on practicalities, though rather dense in style, is William Tydeman's* The Theatre in the Middle Ages.

30 | European Folk Drama

It is now necessary to revert to an earlier theme. During the early Middle Ages a liturgical drama was developed in the churches of Western Europe while a secular drama was developing outside the churches: that will be the subject of the next chapter. In addition to all this there was a persistent tradition of folk festivals, rituals, and ceremonies. Although they were pagan and agricultural in their origin the Church authorities tolerated their survival, partly because they could do nothing else, but also because such games and dances were increasingly enjoyed for their own sake rather than for their ritualistic significance. After all, Pope Gregory had admitted as much.

An interesting example of this was the Morris dance, the origins of which go back into the remote past, but in which certain ritualistic elements are still faintly to be observed, even in the innocuous form in which they have been preserved. Of greater dramatic significance are the plays of St. George and the sword dance, both of which feature a death and resurrection, in the one case of a hero, in the other of a booby. Even Sir Edmund Chambers, a great scholar by no means given to unsupported speculation, has suggested that there was an original and ancient resurrection play from which all subsequent variants have evolved.

The election of the May Queen and the practice of dancing round the maypole on the village green are recent memories but they clearly are of the same origin as the primitive dance of the Corn King and the Spring Queen; but plenty of people have enjoyed the dance without the least idea of its anthropological significance, just as we can enjoy Father Christmas in a red cloak and a Christmas tree lit with candles without feeling guilty at doing so in defiance of the Church's teaching. It is therefore in no way surprising that the medieval peasant had no difficulty in conforming to the requirements of the Church while still enjoying his May Queen, his Plough Monday, his Pace Eggs, his Morrises, and Mummings.

The society of the early Middle Ages differed from that of the so-called 'dark ages' in the number of towns that now existed and the vigorous nature of urban life. Nothing was more natural than that these urban communities should develop their own activities, in particular those that gave expression to some aspect of communal life as Greek tragedy had been, in a way, an expression of Athenian life.

The two dynamics operating in the early Middle Ages were the state and the Church. The state, the public authority, the town council, whatever form it took, created the conditions in which drama, along with many other social, cultural, and artistic activities could take place, and the Church provided the spiritual dynamic, the belief, what it was that was to be incarnated or expressed. This is the setting for the medieval secular drama.

From a not very extensive bibliography, Christina Hole's A Dictionary of British Folk Customs *deals with its subject in a varied and comprehensive manner. Literature on the folk play, in its efforts to be authentic, tends to be insipid. There is little available apart from Sir E. K. Chambers's* The English Folk Play *and Alan Brady's* The English Mummers and their Plays. *Mumming will be dealt with more fully in a subsequent chapter.*

31 Medieval Secular Drama in France

Le Mystère d'Adam (The Mystery Play of Adam), the first play of its kind to have survived from anywhere in Europe, was written in France between the years 1150 and 1200. The subject, taken from the first chapter of Genesis, the fact that it was written to be performed outside a church but in front of one of its main doorways, the detailed stage directions written in Latin, and the need for a choir familiar with singing liturgical plainsong, all emphasize the play's close relationship with the Church. The dialogue is written in delightful verse and the detailed stage directions are both playful and reverential:

> Then shall a serpent cunningly contrived climb up the trunk of the forbidden tree; Eve shall put her ear to it as if listening to its advice.

From the same period comes *La Seinte Resureccion* (*The Holy Resurrection*), a play which tells the story of the Crucifixion, probably written in the south of England in Norman–French by an author who was surprisingly skilful at exploiting the dramatic possibilities of the subject.

Since there is nothing heretical in these two plays, and since in spirit they do not exceed the limitations of the liturgical drama, it is reasonable to believe that the author was a cleric. But at this point continuity breaks down and the professionals step in in the person of the *jongleurs*. These were the latest in the long line of mimes, minstrels, scops, and bards that provide a kind of continuity in popular entertainment from Roman times right through until the later Middle Ages. Although these poet-entertainers and their like were to be found throughout France as well as in other European countries, it was in the town of Arras, then in Burgundy, now in Belgium, that they made their mark. Arras was in those days a flourishing town whose prosperity was founded on the wool trade. It was an international centre for woven fabrics. Its wealthy business community showed considerable interest in literature and the arts and supported a Guild of *Jongleurs*.

Various members of the Guild took up drama. The first we can identify by name was Jean Bodel (d. 1209/10). He seems to have been an attractive and respected man and a poet of some ability. He died miserably of leprosy but not before he had written a remarkable play, *Le Jeu de St. Nicholas* (*The Play of St. Nicholas c.*1200). Although there are a number of liturgical plays on this now very important saint, Bodel's is of a very different calibre and shows clearly the distinction between a liturgical text and one written free of religious constraint. The play has a kind of double plot, one depicting tavern life in Arras with low-life scenes of gambling, drinking, and quarrelling, and a second plot set in the Middle East with vigorous scenes between Christians and Saracens testing the potency of an icon of St. Nicholas. It is a curious mixture of high and low life, tragedy and comedy, typical of the way in which the medieval secular drama was to develop.

Only isolated plays have survived but they are enough to suggest that the tradition continued. From 1228 or thereabouts comes an entertaining dramatization of the parable of the prodigal son. The play is called *Le Courtois d'Arras* (*The Courtier of Arras*) and it shows how the courtier of the title was duped by a couple of prostitutes before returning to his welcoming father. From around the year 1266 comes a savage little play, *Le Garçon et l'aveugle* (*The Boy and the Blind Man*) about a sharp-witted boy who in the most cynical manner outsmarts an old blind beggar.

A writer comparable in many ways to Jean Bodel was Adam le Bossu or Adam de la Halle or Adam d'Arras as he was variously called. Like Bodel he recorded many details of his life in his writings, his attractive young wife, his studies in Paris, and his departure for Sicily in the employment of a French nobleman and where he died between 1285 and 1289. His two surviving plays are extraordinarily original pieces. *Le Jeu de la feuillée* (*The Play of the Greensward*, 1276/7) has little plot but combines a wealth of topical references, many of an autobiographical kind, a monk who is challenged to prove the efficacy of what he claims to be his marvellous cures, with a curious invasion of fairies who involve themselves with the other actors and some of the distinguished citizens of Arras.

His second play, *Le Jeu de Robin et Marion* (*The Play of Robin and Marion*) is a simple pastoral about a pretty shepherdess, her lover, Robin, and the unwanted attentions of a passing knight. The play is full of songs and dances and the games of Robin, Marion, and their friends.

It is tempting to speculate whether there was any connection between the play of Robin and Marion and the English Robin Hood plays. That the English Robin's girl should have been called Marian seems to be more than coincidental. Unfortunately there are only fragments of Robin Hood plays surviving and these are of a later date; but some scholars believe that the two Robins had a common ancestor in some ancient mythological hero from whom perhaps St. George was descended. This in no way precludes the possibility of identifying the English Robin with a real outlaw, Robert Fitzooth, Earl of Huntingdon, who died in 1325; while the supposition that Marian might be identified with the May Queen who in the thirteenth century was in turn identified with the growing cult of the Virgin Mary is supported by the subtitle of one of the fragmentary plays, *Robin Hood and the Friar* which reads, *Here beginnethe the playe of Robyn Hood, very proper to be played in Maye Games.*

Also from the thirteenth century comes the Parisian poet Ruteboeuf who wrote a play called *Le Miracle de Théophile* (*The Miracle of Theophile c.*1261). It is a curious version of the Faust story. Theophile, having been dismissed from his job as clerk to a bishop, makes in despair a pact with the devil who promises to restore his fortunes. The bishop thinks better of his action and offers to re-employ Theophile. The clerk arrogantly refuses the offer and lives according to the values of the devil for seven years when he makes full confession of his sins to Our Lady who restores him to a state of Christian grace.

Of the plays mentioned in this section, French editions are usually available, English translations occasionally.

Critically the period is well described by Grace Frank in The Medieval French Drama *and Richard Axton's* European Drama of the Early Middle Ages, *and for readers of French, Gustave Cohen's* Le Théâtre en France au moyen age.

32 | The Thirteenth Century

Historians look on the thirteenth century as the highest point of medieval achievement. Although the political situation remained unstable, the various countries were coming to terms with issues on which the structure of more recent society came to be based. There was an extraordinary German (Hohenstaufen) Emperor, Frederick II, who raised in acute form the relationship between a political Empire and a universal Church. In Britain the century began with that unique charter of the rights of man, the Magna Carta (1215) on which seven hundred years of parliamentary democracy has been based.

Medieval society had a hierarchical structure. The classes were sharply differentiated but collaborated within more or less accepted relationships. The more flexible and productive capitalist system was taking over from feudalism but had not yet begun to exert corroding social tensions. Pictures of medieval towns show a city wall encircling a tight compress of buildings each with its church, its market-place, and its castle, standing for its spiritual life, its economic life, and its protection. This is not to give a romantic picture of a period which in many respects was still both crude and cruel but to emphasize the unity on which some remarkable cultural achievements were based.

Medieval social life was noisy, colourful, vigorous; full of rituals and formulae; nothing was done simply. These prodigious cathedrals, in the building of which many people from the local community played a part, and which embodied a wealth of allegorical concepts, were not the creation of a prosaic society. The Church was immensely influential and did its utmost to dominate every aspect of life; and since illiteracy was widespread it used to the full the powerful language of visual images. And what images it imposed upon the people: the history of the world in visual terms (or more accurately the history of Christendom); visions of the creation of the world and visions of the Last Judgement; visions of the prophets, of Hell, and of the angelic hosts. And it exploited, although the bishops themselves would not have put it in these terms, the inability of the medieval mind to detect the difference between reality and fantasy. Hell was real. The Devil was real. Witches were real. Between his Crucifixion and Resurrection Jesus descended into Hell – the episode is referred to in the Apostle's Creed – and freed the suffering souls. This Harrowing of Hell, as it was called, was a reality, like the visions of the Last Judgement which were the stock-in-trade of every artist who was let loose in a church with a bare wall and a box of paints, from anonymous Tuscan apprentices to the great Michelangelo himself.

This widespread use of the visual image was a part of the common medieval practice of thinking and expressing in allegorical terms. Allegory has already been mentioned. It is a kind of anthropomorphism which was common in the ancient world. To use allegory is to give a physical body to an abstract idea. The best way of understanding how allegory was used is to look at one of the most important examples of medieval literature, which is wholly allegorical in form, *Le Roman de la Rose* (*The Story of the Rose*, part one 1230, part two 1275). A man enters a walled garden which is protected by Idleness. Here he finds the God of Love around whom are dancing Mirth, Beauty, Riches, Gladness, Generosity, Candour, and Courtesy. He gazes into a pond in which he sees reflected a rose tree guarded by a hedge of thorns. He raises his hand to pick a rose and is shot through the heart by the God of Love. And so it goes on, not in such a soppy manner as the opening might suggest, but to give a broad, glowing, though in the second part often satirical picture of contemporary life.

Every society is involved to a greater or lesser extent in a continuous process of transforming traditional social customs into a new social order. The somewhat rigid structure of medieval society often made this very difficult, and created tensions that were expressed in unexpected ways. An example of this was the institution of chivalry. This was a brilliant move on the part of the Church to legitimize the predatory and aggressive instincts of the military and to divert their disposition for butchery into creative forms. The knights accepted the blessings of the Church because they recognized the value of strengthening the structure of society and of the moral force which was given to their role. The complex code of behaviour that developed around the concept of chivalry affected many aspects of medieval society, even to the manner of conducting military campaigns. The well-known tournament was not only a useful training for war but an invaluable outlet for pent-up aggression. It was a highly ritualized war-game. For not only did the knight wear on his lance, with which he intended to unhorse his opponent, the favour of his lady, thereby establishing the insidious relationship between aggression and sex, but when he entered the lists from a simulated castle, built like a stage set, a minstrel would provide a long poetic explanation of his fictional identity, placing him in an imaginative and allegorical setting. There was an occasion in a French tournament in 1449 when the knights, dressed as shepherds, rode forth from pavilions disguised as thatched cottages which of course it was their intention to defend.

The readiness to assume a role was a partial result of the emphasis on the visual at the expense of the cognitive, on the eye at the expense of the mind. It weakened in turn the distinction between reality and fantasy and sharpened the old instinct to achieve an objective by a process of identification. This helps to explain the enthusiasm for acting which was common throughout Europe. The most remarkable example is the subject of the next section.

The literature of chivalry is immense but fortunately for English readers, it is largely summed up in the masterly prose fiction of Sir Thomas Malory. Though written three hundred years after Geoffrey of Monmouth's fascinating History of the Kings of Britain *it shows the medieval mind still lurching inconsistently between history, legend, and romance.*

The dramatic element of the tournament has been fully treated by Glynne Wickham in the first volume of Early English Stages. *Of innumerable books on various aspects of medieval life, the one most directly relevant to the section is J. Huizinga's classic* The Waning of the Middle Ages; *see also Joan Evans,* Life in Medieval France, *G. G. Coulton,* Medieval Panorama *and the* Penguin Book of the Middle Ages.

33 The Corpus Christi Mystery Plays

In the year 1264 the Church authorities found it expedient to establish another major festival. There are various versions as to its origin such as one involving an Italian priest who, having questioned the doctrine of transubstantiation, saw blood flow from consecrated host. Such stories were taken as reason to reiterate, in ritual form, the basic mystery of Christianity, the partaking of wafer and wine at communion (Corpus Christi means the body of Christ). A celebratory festival was proposed by Pope Urban IV and the office was composed by St. Thomas Aquinas, a leading Catholic intellectual, who had been educated by the Benedictines at the monastery of Monte Cassino but had subsequently joined the Dominicans.

This gives one a clue as to the basic reason for the festival. The Dominicans were a teaching order and teaching was achieved in those days largely by preaching. The aim of the Dominicans was to project faith into action. They were less interested in contemplation in a closed community than in preaching the word of God to people in the street. This became an essential activity in a society that was largely illiterate and when all Church services were conducted in Latin. Evidence suggests that there were many skilful preachers who mastered the techniques of an actor to hold their audiences.

The Feast of Corpus Christi was therefore conceived as a further means of projecting one of the basic doctrines of the Church into the lives of the people. The festival was to take place on the Thursday after Trinity Sunday, which is the first Sunday after Pentecost, the Greek name for a Jewish festival which coincided with the revelation of the Holy Spirit to the Apostles (Acts 2:1) and is usually known as Whitsun (white Sunday, when the newly baptized wore white garments). The festival was to consist of a procession through each town followed by a celebration of mass in the church.

Processions were a regular and popular feature of medieval life. They were one of the ways in which both state and Church authorities kept in touch with the people. Resident and visiting dignitaries all had their processions with a splendour related to their importance. The dignitaries rode in coaches or on horseback followed by decorated carts and chariots, banners, and every kind of device to impress the crowds who were expected to line the streets.

The extraordinary feature of the Corpus Christi procession is that soon after it was established, in 1311, it involved the staging of plays. And this occurred in most countries where the festival was held. One can only conjecture that this took place through a coming together of many of the practices that have been mentioned in the last few chapters. At the beginning of the fourteenth century church-goers would have been familiar with liturgical plays. It is probable, although there is no evidence for this, that in many European cities the minstrels were responsible for some kind of simple plays. The year 1311 is not very long after the days of Adam of Arras. The Dominicans, with their histrionic methods of preaching, had introduced a modified form of street theatre. And there was a general disposition to think visually, allegorically.

Another factor has not yet been mentioned. The development of trade and vigorous urban life in the thirteenth and fourteenth centuries had led to the establishment of a large number of guilds and associations of men of different crafts, professions, and persuasions. The last term refers to the formation, more commonly in France than England, of religious fraternities which might be likened to what we now call the

Friends of a certain organization. In this case the organization in question was of course the Church. All these associations and brotherhoods developed their own range of activities and there is no reason to suppose that these did not include something of the dancing, the singing, and even the acting that was so common a feature of medieval life.

Any ceremony that takes place in the streets of a town involves the people of that town. It is therefore not surprising that the earliest records of royal and civic processions indicate the inclusion of the various trade and craft guilds, the power and authority of which were considerable by the fourteenth century. They would therefore have been given a distinguished representation in the Corpus Christi procession.

The inclusion of plays in the procession was not general. In Britain there are records of plays from Aberdeen, Bath, Beverley, Bristol, Canterbury, Dublin, Ipswich, Leicester, Worcester, Lincoln, and London, though no manuscripts have survived. We have four complete cycles and the remnants of one from Coventry.

They are referred to as cycles because this is what they were, sequences of plays. The process of creation was a more ambitious form of the process that had led to the extension of some of the liturgical plays when, for example, the Nativity of Jesus was extended in one direction by the Annunciation and in the other by the massacre of the innocents.

Unfortunately we do not have any examples of cycles in their simplest form, but if the liturgical drama is anything to go by, the writers and organizers probably began with the two basic sequences of the Nativity and the Passion, both of which eventually became the subject of a whole sequence of plays. They then moved backwards in time to include the plays about the prophets, Noah and the flood, Cain and Abel, the Garden of Eden, the fall of Lucifer and the creation of the world; they moved forwards in time to include the Ascension and the Last Judgement. Not all the cycles include all these episodes and some include others. But their uniqueness lies in the fact that they constitute a sequence of plays dramatizing the history of Christianity from the creation of the world to the Last Judgement.

Of the four surviving cycles the earliest is probably the one from Chester. It consists of twenty-five plays, nine dealing with Old Testament subjects, eight with events concerning the Nativity, one on Lazarus, one on John the Baptist, five on the Crucifixion, and seven on subjects subsequent to the death of Jesus. Municipal records make clear that the cycle grew by a series of accretions over the years, mostly in the latter part of the fourteenth century.

The Wakefield cycle, often referred to as the Towneley plays from the Lancashire family in whose library the manuscript was found, consists of thirty-two plays that follow the same grouping as the Chester cycle. It is distinctive, however, in including six plays by a rich humorist and gifted dramatist who is usually referred to as the Wakefield Master. Among the six are two plays on the shepherds, the second of which is perhaps the best-known play from the whole range of the cycles. *The Second Shepherds Play* is often anthologized and performed.

The York cycle consists of forty-eight plays and is notable for extensive treatment of the Passion sequence, the work of another poet with a grim and sardonic sense of humour. It also includes a doctrinal element in plays dealing with the Creed and the Lord's Prayer.

The cycle known as the *Ludus Coventriae*, sometimes referred to as the Hegge plays or the N. Town cycle, is unique in several respects. Since it is not associated with a craft guild, it was probably the work of a religious fraternity, or the monks of a monastery. In some respects it is more sophisticated than the other cycles, and uses more allegory. It was written to be staged not processionally, as was the case with the other cycles, but on a collection of stages, a practice that is put to particular effect in the Passion sequence where the action moves quickly from one stage to another. The stage directions are unusually full. For example:

> Here goeth the messenger forth and in the mean time Caiaphas sheweth himself in his scaffold, arrayed like to Annas, saving his tabbard shall be red furred with white; two doctors with him arrayed with cloaks after the old guise and furred caps on their heads . . .

In spite of its title the cycle has nothing to do with Coventry but is thought perhaps to have come from Lincoln.

Coventry had its own cycle of Corpus Christi plays but it was shorter than the others, and only two of the plays survive, though one of them is a charming and lyrical version of the Nativity.

The whole phenomenon of the cycles must have been the result of close collaboration between Church and civic authorities, though what part may or may not have been played by the minstrels and the wandering scholars, there is no way of finding out. The latter may well have made a significant contribution. For men intending to become priests there were a number of grades or 'orders'. Between the higher orders required for senior positions in the church and the lower grades for intending clerks, there was a large grey area. A monk might write with a strong feeling for secular values, while a layman, educated by the Church, might write with strong religious convictions.

Just as critics in the eighteenth century applied the word 'Gothic' to medieval cathedrals in a perjorative sense, finding them anything but admirable, so it was customary at the time to dismiss the Mysteries for the naivety of their subject-matter, the roughness of their alliterative verse, so crude in contrast to our cherished romantic poets, and the simplicity of their characterization. In recent times we have learnt to value these very qualities just as in painting we feel no longer that the marvellous directness of the two Lorenzettis and Simone Martini is outfaced by the great masters of the High Renaissance. No other writers, or groups of writers, not the Greeks, the Elizabethans, and certainly not the Romantics, ever conceived, let alone executed, work on the scale of the cycles. *Paradise Lost* alone is perhaps comparable. For beneath their apparent simplicity there lies a profound statement of the relationship of God to man and the real significance of the death of Christ on the Cross. One may not believe in or wish to identify with the attitude expressed in these plays; but it is difficult not to be impressed by the scale of their artistic achievement, the depth of their religious conviction, and their resonant alliterative verse. Mention has already been made of the humour of the Wakefield Master, the York Passion sequence, and the Coventry Nativity; and he is a dull fellow who does not respond to the wit of the Chester *Deluge*.

Originality was not highly prized. The plays were copied and adapted between one writer or town and another. The writers drew their material from a variety of sources: the Bible of course but also a number of contemporary works such as the *Northern Passion*, the translation of a popular French work with the significant title of *La Passion des jongleurs*, which was written in dialogue form and much used by preachers. Another useful piece of source material was *Cursor Mundi*, a popular and lengthy poem bringing together all the legends, traditions, and hagiography (material concerning the saints) related to Bible history and told in the manner of a chivalric romance. *The Golden Legend* was a compendium of the lives of the saints written by Jacope de Voragine (*c*.1230–98), a Dominican who became bishop of Genoa. The debate of the four daughters of God pleading for the soul of man, which opens the Hegge plays, was taken from the *Meditations* of St. Bonaventura (*c*.1217–74), an Italian theologian; but the source of most allegory was *Psychomathia*, the work of a fourth-century Spaniard named Prudentius, the first to describe a contest between the allegorical figures of Good and Evil for the soul of man.

Though a student may be discouraged from reading the liturgical plays, nothing should deter him from tackling the great cycles. Texts are available in the original as well as modernized language; but the more one is able to cope with the original Middle English, the nearer one comes to savouring the bite of the language with its mixture of Anglo-Saxon monosyllabic hardness and alliteration, and French linguistic elegance. And the metrical structure of the plays is remarkably varied.

Wide-ranging discussions on every aspect of the cycles can be found in a number of books: Glynne Wickham's Early English Stages, *William Tydeman's* The Theatre in the Middle Ages, *Stanley J. Kahrl's* Traditions of Medieval English Drama, *Hardin Craig's* English Religious Drama of the Middle Ages, *V. A. Kolve's* The Play Called Corpus Christi, *and Rosemary Woolf's* The English Mystery Plays.

34 | The Cycles in Performance

Although the manner of performance varied between one town and another and even more between the different countries, it is possible to build up a generalized if not too accurate a picture.

Rehearsals began soon after Easter by which time the participating companies had been assigned their play, presumably by some kind of central organizing committee. There was obviously an attempt to relate the subject-matter of the play to an appropriate craft but this was not always possible. The play was called the 'pageant', which was also the name of the mobile stage or 'pageant-cart' on which the performance was given. These carts are not at all easy to reconstruct since they had to be large enough to provide a playing space for a number of actors, and sometimes a change of scene, and small enough to be manhandled without too much difficulty through the narrow streets of a medieval city.

The players of the first pageant gave their first performance at the earliest light of dawn and then moved on to a series of 'stations' where they repeated their performance. These stations were significant places in the town such as the market-place, outside the town hall, and in front of the residence of the more distinguished citizens. At these stations, scaffolds were erected for the public. Actors were paid according to the length or importance of their roles. God at Coventry received 3*s*. 4*d*., a soul, whether damned or saved, 2*d*., but a worm of conscience 8*d*. (Needless to say, these amounts bear little relationship to subsequent value of money.) At Hull Noah was paid 1*s*. but his wife rather less. All performers were members of a guild, but the minstrels, who had a guild of their own, contributed the music. The actors dressed for their parts but usually in variations of contemporary costume. Perhaps that is why the authors of the Hegge cycle were specific about the clothes that were to be worn.

To get thirty or forty pageants following each other at different intervals of time in orderly fashion, each dragged or pushed by a group of men through the twisting streets of a compact medieval town, must have required considerable organization. A simple calculation based on the playing time of each pageant being in the region of thirty minutes, and allowing time for one to move and the next to take its place, makes clear that a performance of the whole cycle must have been spread over several days. But it must be emphasized that the whole subject of pageant design and overall organization are subjects of the greatest uncertainty, and some people are convinced that after the procession the plays were performed as stationary pageants.

The Mysteries had a life of around two hundred years. The period of greatest growth was the fifteenth century; their end came in the sixteenth. Even in countries where the Catholic Church remained the dominant form of worship they did not survive the pressures of the Reformation. But by this time they had had their day and were supplanted by other, more contemporary forms of drama. They were representative of a dying tradition, an outstanding part of that aspect of medieval religious practice which was ready for reform. A certain George Gilpin (*c.*1514–1602) translated a Dutch Calvinist satire on the Catholics and their plays which smells as if it carried a grain of truth.

> In summer, Christ hath not done aniething in his death and passion, but they do plaie and counterfeite the same after him, so trimlie and livelie that no plaier or juggler is able to do it better. I speake not of their perambulations, processions, and going about the towne carrying their crucifixes alongst the streets and there plaie and counterfeit the whole passion . . . as though it had been nothing else, but a simple and plaine Enterlude, to make boyes laugh at, and a little recreat heavie and sorrowful hearts: for these matters fall out onlie upon church holy dayes or solemnities, when the Catholikes are determined to be merrie, and drinke themselves so dranke that they tumble from their seat.

A little malicious, indeed. But the Reformation would not have taken place if there had been nothing to reform. Let us now look at parallel developments in Europe.

35 | Religious Drama in Europe

The dramatic trope was common throughout Europe just as the form of Christian worship, of which it was a part, was largely unchanged between one country and another. But any tendency towards political unification, a Holy Roman Empire, or a United States of Europe, has foundered on the rocks of nationalism; and as each country developed its national identity, free from ecclesiastical control, so its drama acquired an increasingly individual form.

The liturgical drama in Spain seems to have included some rather more spectacular elements than are found in other countries: a pentecostal dove was propelled by some kind of firework; braziers were used to brighten the sun and the moon; masks were worn by both the Apostles and the Jews; and there was considerable use of emblematic animal figures; a knight and a winged dragon; a cloud machine which opened to reveal an angel who handed a branch of palm to Mary; all this together with the prohibitions against dancing suggests that early Christian culture in Spain was less rigid than in the more emotionally constricted north.

In Italy the transformation of various religious songs into what in France and England were known as Mysteries was an achievement of the Florentines. The plays were known as *sacra rappresentazioni* (sacred performances) and were performed, not as elsewhere as part of the Corpus Christi celebrations, but on various popular festivals which were in fact Christianized survivals of old Roman *ludi*.

These performances were usually given on a row of fixed stages, as in France, rather than processionally as in England. Though very serious in intent they were blown up by the powerful visual imagination of the Italians into extravagant open-air spectacles comparable to the lavish pageants staged by Italian princes on every kind of civic occasion. The most complicated machinery was designed by the great Florentine architect, Filippo Brunelleschi (1377–1446) and described by Giorgio Vasari in his autobiography.

In France there are fairly consistent traces of the development of a secular drama by the minstrels throughout the twelfth and thirteenth centuries when there was widespread liturgical drama. But in the fourteenth no form of secular drama appears to have emerged in connection with the festival of Corpus Christi. French religious drama developed in a different manner, though scanty records do not provide us with details.

In 1402 the French King Charles V granted to the Confrèrie de la Passion the right to establish the first permanent public theatre in France; and it was here that the Confrèrie was responsible for staging a collection of forty plays known as the *Miracles de Notre Dame* (*Miracles of Our Lady*). These forty plays are preserved in two small manuscript volumes and date from 1380. They are a delightful collection of plays, immensely varied in subject-matter, and all demonstrating that even the greatest criminal may be forgiven if he offers up prayers of repentance to the Virgin – perhaps not a wholly acceptable belief to the modern mind but one that shows the importance of the cult of the Virgin Mary as a stabilizing influence in a country that was fighting to establish its national and territorial identity.

The Confrèrie, which had been given permission to establish itself in Paris, was composed of lesser clergy and the more devout members of the general public and tradesmen with the particular object of performing Mysteries and Passions. There was no element of that spacious civic involvement, that rich vernacular street theatre that makes the performance of the English Mysteries so unique. This accounts no doubt for the far greater solemnity of the developing religious drama in France. It was more of a religious and less of a civic celebration.

The first of the great French Passions, *La Passion du Palatinus*, a play deriving much of its material from the *Passion des jongleurs*, is written with some of the brutal wit that is found in the York plays. The first play to have the scope of the English Mysteries was the *Passion de Sémur* of 1448, written to be played over two days with a few lines at the end of the first part inviting the audience to return the next day. This was followed by the *Passion d'Arras*, almost certainly the work of one Eustache Mercadé, a somewhat heavy-footed theologian. The play is 25,000 lines in length and took four days to perform.

The masterpiece of the period is Arnoul Gréban's *Le Mystère de la Passion*. The author was a native of Le Mans but he probably wrote most of his Passion while he was choirmaster in the cathedral of Notre-Dame in Paris. The conformity of the job seems to have irked him and soon after 1456 he returned to Le Mans where he died in 1471. His Passion, which is 34,450 lines in length, was immensely popular in its own day and manuscripts were borrowed for performance by a number of other French cities. It was revived from time to time by the Confrèrie de la Passion and has been successfully staged in recent times.

The third Passion of the group was the work of Jean Michel, who extended Gréban's Passion to 45,000 lines and completed it around 1486. Jean Michel, as others had done, drew heavily on the work of his predecessors, which he did little to improve and much to spoil; but his Passion was extremely popular and among the first works to benefit from the invention of printing (by Johannes Gutenberg of Mainz *c.*1400–68).

During the latter part of the fifteenth century and earlier decades of the sixteenth there was considerable enthusiasm for the writing and staging of Passions or cycles of Mystery plays, many of which were pieced together with scenes from existing works. An *Actes des Apôtres* (*Acts of the Apostles*), attributed to Simon Gréban, the brother of Arnoul, was nearly 62,000 lines and when performed at Bourges in 1536 is said to have lasted forty days; and there was a *Vieux Testament* of similar length. The Bourges performance was played in a restored Roman amphitheatre with considerable pomp, preceded by sumptuous processions, attended by every dignitary in the region, and staged with tremendous technical elaboration. It was clearly what we should now call a spectacular.

In the staging of these plays, clergy of every level were involved and there was considerable support from the municipal authorities. Performances were given indoors, as in the 'theatre' provided by the Confrèrie de la Passion in Paris as well as in the open air. They were staged at any time of the year, clearly because their great length prevented them from being closely identified with a single Church festival; while the discovery of various account books, particularly from Mons in 1501, provides evidence of the enormous organization involved.

The extent of the effort and resources put into these performances may have something to do with the fact that in 1453 the Hundred Years War came to an end and France was at last in a position to begin establishing itself as a modern and independent nation. There are examples throughout history of countries having used drama as a means of helping to establish national identity.

This brings us to the end of a period. Mysteries, Passions, cycles of religious plays all came to an end in the sixteenth century. The reasons will now have to be considered.

Not only have the French Passions and Mysteries not been translated, but they are extremely difficult to acquire even in French. The best one can hope for, without investigating some learned library, is a collection of selected scenes which at least provide a taste of these remarkable plays. Of great historical importance is Le Livre de Conduite du Régisseur et le Compte des Dépenses pour le Mystère de la Passion, joué a Mons en 1501 *(prompt script and account book), edited by Gustave Cohen who in a number of books has written illuminatingly on the whole period.*

36 | The Morality Plays

Another achievement of medieval playwrights was the morality play. It was an outcome of the allegorical way of thinking. A man who had read Prudentius's dramatic description of a debate between the Seven Virtues and the Seven Vices for the soul of man and had seen some kind of a dramatic performance would have had little difficulty in putting the two together and dramatizing the debate. Would-be playwrights must also have realized that freed from the necessity of sticking to a canonical story the morality play gave them considerable scope for exercising both their fantasies and their passion for moralizing. The whole concept of such a form of drama now has a cold and intellectual flavour; but it must be remembered that in those days people were accustomed to 'think' in anthropomorphic terms and it was by no means unusual for them to see figures of the Virtues and the Vices featured among the iconography (the statues and carvings) and the stained glass windows that adorned their churches.

The first surviving English morality is *The Pride of Life*, a sharp little play, written around the year 1350. It features the King of Life who with the support of his warriors issues a defiance of Death couched in such arrogant terms that his Queen, in alarm, invokes the help of the local bishop to bring the King to a sense of Christian humility. One can imagine its relevance at a time when the nobility habitually rode roughshod over the peasants.

From about 1375 comes what is perhaps the finest of the English moralities, *The Castle of Perseverance*. It takes up the earlier theme of the contest for man's soul between allegorical characters representing the World, the Flesh, and the Devil on the one side and the Seven Virtues and the four Daughters of God on the other. The Goodies secure Mankind in the castle which is then attacked by the forces of evil led by Belial 'with gunpowder burning in pipes in his hands and ears', as the stage direction puts it, and defend themselves by showering the attackers with roses.

The play has become particularly well-known in theatrical history for the diagram included in the manuscript which indicates the manner in which it was to be performed. The castle stands in the middle of a circular ditch of water which in turn is surrounded by scaffolds or stages; but whether the audience, which is not referred to in the diagram, sat within or without the circle of scaffolds and ditch is quite unclear. But the circular arrangement of stages was evidently common at the time.

Since the moralities were written free from the biblical context of the Mysteries, they reveal in a most fascinating manner the preoccupations of their authors. There was clearly a great interest in political power represented by Emperors thundering out their demands for total loyalty; and there are daring excursions into the real world. In *Mary Magdalene* (*c.*1475), for example, Mary, on the death of her father, is persuaded by the Seven Deadly Sins to go on a pub-crawl in Jerusalem where she enjoys the hospitality of a jovial Taverner and the flattering attentions of a Gallant. The archetypal pattern of a contest between the forces of good and evil is clearly expressed in *Mankind* (*c.*1465–70), in which the latter are represented by New Guise, Nowadays, and Mischief, urged on by Titivillus 'arrayed like a devil'. Plays like *The Conversion of St. Paul* and *The Play of the Conversion of Ser Jonathas the Jewe by Myracle of the Blyssed Sacrament* are full of a wild mixture of historical, fictitious, and allegorical characters.

But one can see the secular element gradually taking over. In those days the Devil had the best, or at least the more original tunes and these no doubt are what the audiences of the time found most entertaining. *Hickscorner* (*c.*1510), who goes around with a couple of ruffians, rather significantly called Free Will and Imagination, boasting about the countries he has visited and the crimes he has committed, is a far more entertaining character than the rather colourless Pity, Contemplation, and Perseverance. In *Nice Wanton* (*c.*1550) a play about an irresponsible mother with one good child and two delinquents who refuse to go to school, the moral of the story is hammered home in the last few pages with allegorical figures playing a minor role.

A great many moralities were written in France during the fifteenth century, some of them approaching the prodigious proportions of the Mysteries, plays of 30,000 lines and eighty characters. But these mammoth productions had become so many dinosaurs with immense bodies and little brain. They were supplanted by a new form of drama which had little body and too much brain. That is a subject shortly to be discussed.

An admirable study of the circumstances in which the moralities were written is to be found in the fourth volume of Glynne Wickham's Early English Stages.

Some of the better known moralities, especially the superb Everyman, *probably the finest example of the genre, manage to keep in print, and although they do not always make easy reading, many of them contain splendid passages and cannot be ignored by anyone interested in the evolution of the European drama.*

37 | The Interludes

The morality spawned the interlude although the distinction is far from precise. The interlude is a more embracing term since almost any morality could be an interlude, but many of the more secular interludes could never be considered moralities.

The distinction largely arose out of conditions of performance. The moralities of the fourteenth and fifteenth century were associated, like the Mysteries, with specific Church festivals, feast days, and holidays, but being independent plays they could be more easily transferred from one occasion to another. And as the moral element decreased in significance, the association of a play with a specific occasion became less relevant. Similarly there was far more latitude in venue, as well as occasion, for the performance of a morality, as they were played, not only in town squares, market-places and on village greens but in the halls of the nobility which throughout the Middle Ages had been designed for social intercourse and ceremonial junketings.

The last point introduces another important development. The text of some of the moralities refers to a collection being taken. This marks the change from the amateur player who takes a collection to defray expenses and the professional who does so because this is what he lives on. Moralities such as *The Castle of Perseverance* and the great French productions with their immense cast lists could never have been played by professionals; but the small casts of the later moralities were not the result of a self-denying ordinance on the part of the author but of his willingness to write for small companies of professional actors, usually numbering between four and six. Many of the surviving texts give details as to how the parts should be distributed between them.

The rise of the professional player can be dated from this period, the early sixteenth century, the beginning of the Tudors. The religious drama was collapsing, a secular drama was emerging with all the social authority that throughout the Middle Ages had been accorded to religious drama. The plays and entertainments that became known as interludes were just that, interludes in a banquet or some other kind of festivity. In the course of the century the term was applied in different European countries to a great variety of performances and entertainments that were complete and self-sufficient in their own right, but that

5. **A booth theatre**
This detail from *A Village Festival*, by Pieter Brueghel the Younger (1564–1638), shows the kind of improvised stage that was commonly used, and the conditions under which open-air performances were given from earliest times until well into the eighteenth century.

was because no other term had been invented. At the beginning of the period, in England, the dramatic interlude is easy to identify.

It is also possible to identify some of the playwrights. One of the first surviving interludes is the utterly delightful *Fulgens and Lucrece* (*c.*1497), the work of Henry Medwall, a gifted dramatist of whom unfortunately nothing is known. A number of references in the text make clear that the two acts were written to serve as interludes between courses. Then there was the minstrel-poet, John Heywood, the author of three surviving farcical interludes. *The Play of the Weather* (*c.*1535) is an allegorical piece in which a number of characters argue in front of the throne of the Great Jupiter about which weather suits them best. *The Playe Called the Four P.P.* is about a contest between a Palmer, a Pardoner, a Pothecary, and a Pedlar to tell the biggest lie and implies some interesting criticisms of medieval institutions. But his best play is the far too little known and extremely amusing farce of *A Merry Playe betwene Johan Johan, the Husbande, Tyb, the Wife, and Sir Johan the Preest*. We now have a form of drama with no pretentions but to make people laugh.

At this point the interlude in England rapidly loses its identity and becomes involved with the extraordinary outburst of dramatic activity which took place from about 1580 onwards, and led to the creation of a dramatic form as we have it today.

The word 'interlude' (*entremets*) was not much used in France although there were plays of a similar kind. Initiative in this case came from the law students who refreshed themselves from the cares of serious study by forming themselves into societies which constituted a 'send up' of established society with a King, a University Chancellor, and so on. In due course their hilarities led to the writing of short farces, some of which involved burlesquing the moralities and even the Mysteries. Groups of these *Basochiens*, as they called themselves, were established in many French towns and lasted from about 1300 till 1590.

But the ribald humour of the French went even farther. There was widespread enthusiasm for forming Brotherhoods of Fools (*Confrèries de sots*), constituting something closely similar to the clerical frivolities of the Feast of Fools. These *sots* wrote and staged *sottises* of the most extravagant kind, satirizing, burlesquing, turning everything upside down. They even produced in Pierre Gringoire (*c.*1475–*c.*1538) a strange kind of bohemian poet and entrepreneur, constantly in trouble with the authorities though for a time the friend of Louis XII. Pierre Gringoire had something in common with that tragic, dissolute but exquisite poet, François Villon, who was forty years his senior.

Out of a large number of farces and farcical moralities, one masterpiece emerged, *The Farce of Maitre Pierre Pathelin* (*c.*1464). It is not known who wrote it, whether a *Basochien* or a *sot* or anyone else, but it was associated with and performed by one of the earliest professional companies which, as in England, were emerging in France at that time. There will be more to say about these companies in due course.

The outstanding historian of the French medieval theatre is Gustave Cohen. Pierre Gringoire features in Victor Hugo's heavily romanticized picture of the period, The Hunchback of Notre Dame. Pierre Pathelin *is available in English translation. François Villon is an outstanding and exquisite European poet.*

38 | The Renaissance

The movement that finally broke up many medieval institutions is known as the Renaissance. It is impossible to define the Renaissance in a few words because it was just that – a movement, a stream of new thought that began as a trickle and went on to break up into innumerable streams that flowed into every aspect of life. It was a shift of emphasis in the European consciousness. It led to new habits of thought and new ways of doing things and, as always when society goes through a period of violent change, it made life painful and difficult for many people.

The most convenient starting-point in a history of the theatre is the rebirth of classical studies. This may seem a somewhat trivial beginning for a movement that was to transform European society but that is how it was. Throughout the Middle Ages there had been men who were familiar with Latin and Greek but they were mostly Catholic theologians locked up within their monasteries. Latin, of course, was far better known than Greek for it was the language of the Church, the law, and a number of other professions. But a language can be as interesting though as irrelevant as a crossword puzzle. The study of Latin and Greek suddenly became alive when it was realized that these languages opened up new cultures, new civilizations. It is of course a profound criticism of medieval society that the culture of two ancient societies should have been seen as so advanced and progressive. Nevertheless in some respects this study of the past produced the incentive that was needed to open new areas of thought and activity although in others it was a misapprehension and something of a retrograde step. By the year 1500 the European theatre, for example, had lost its sense of direction. It was breaking out in all directions; but the imposition of classical values prevented natural development.

The first men to establish the classical Renaissance as a recognizable movement were Francesco Petrarca (1304–75), best known for his sonnets to his unattainable Laura, and Giovanni Boccaccio (*c.*1313–75) even better remembered for his somewhat unsalubrious collection of stories known as the *Decameron.* Both were passionate scholars and produced a considerable amount of classical studies in Latin. It was men like these who contrasted their own culture most unfavourably with what they considered to be the splendours of Greek and Roman civilization. The new movement was even more sharply articulated by the Florentine scholars who were encouraged by the Medicis. Pico della Mirandola (1463–94) summed up the new philosophy when he wrote that man was created to master the world. 'To thee alone', he makes the Creator say to Adam, 'I have given possibilities of growth dependant on your own free will.'

It is not difficult to see why this new attitude to life became known as humanism. Man was the measure of all things. It was most vigorously projected by the painters and sculptors of the period who turned men into gods and depicted gods as men.

Of all the figures of antiquity the one who was most revered was Plato. It is extremely difficult to explain how scholars came to develop a neo-Platonic philosophy because they tended to read not what Plato had written but what they would have written if they had written Plato. Plato was a kind of inspiration for their own new concepts, extremely confused though at first they were. The most important aspect of this neo-Platonic philosophy for the arts was that it stood for a sense of harmony, order, and proportion. Men began to realize how these qualities could be expressed in music, in architecture, in dancing. Even the great astronomer Galileo Galilei wrote in 1632 a work in which he establishes a relationship between the imaginative and discursive methods of the artist and the science of the mathematician.

The result of this passion for classical literature was a vigorous search for Greek and Roman texts. A manuscript that had gathered dust over the centuries now became the basis of an industry: it was edited, printed, translated, and commented upon. Moreover since criticism and the work being criticized go together, and genuine criticism is not a cavilling, a finding fault, but an analysis, an appreciation, and an elucidation, the humanists were as pleased to have to hand the critical works of Aristotle, Horace, Donatus, and Quintilian as the plays of the classical dramatists. The manuscript of Aristotle's book on poetry, for example, had been preserved in the Middle East, translated into Syriac, then into Arabic, into Latin in the thirteenth century, and then into Spanish. It was again translated into Latin in Italy in 1498, and then published in its original Greek in 1508. Further editions of the text were published throughout the sixteenth century along with the inevitable commentaries. Every manuscript had its own strange history.

It requires no great effort of the imagination to perceive the enormous difference between the highly confined, tightly organized, and formally constructed plays of the classical dramatists, with the great sprawling, shapeless masterpieces of the Middle Ages, which quite clearly, by the late fifteenth century, had become lamentably out of control. It is therefore hardly surprising that the French and Italian critics, in writing commentaries upon the classical critics, and under little compulsion to keep strictly to what their subjects precisely wrote, tended to use classical authority to support their own views. They became more classic than the classics. They assumed and were granted an authority that resulted in their sometimes ill-judged admonitions shaping the course of European drama for nearly five hundred years.

39 | Neo-classical Dramatic Criticism

Greek and Roman plays were printed, performed, translated, and imitated with increasing frequency from the 1490s onwards. Major works of criticism did not begin to emerge until the 1540s but it is more convenient to consider them first since they established the theories that guided the new dramaturgy.

The first treatise on the art of poetry appeared in 1536. It was written by one Bernardino Daniello. Among his successors was the delightfully named Giulio Cesare Scaligero (1484–1558) who was born in Padua but became a naturalized French citizen and so is usually known as Jules César Scaliger. Lodovico Castelvetro (1505–71) was an irascible and lonely man who spent much of his life wandering about Europe and published his translation of and commentary upon Aristotle in Vienna in 1570. The only Englishman to have made a significant contribution to the debate was Sir Philip Sidney whose celebrated work, *An Apologie for Poetrie* (written *c.*1580), is an example of classical conservatism. He rejected the mixture of tragedy and comedy that was becoming a feature of the emergent English drama and derided the constant changes of scene which were common in Tudor plays.

The main points to emerge from these various critical works, which, it must be admitted, do not always make easy reading, were these:

– Tragedy must concern itself with the death of kings and the ruin of great Empires; with great and terrible events, with grave and weighty happenings.

– But it must show how men of high rank fall into misery through human error or fallibility.

– It must depict only what can be properly shown on the stage. While this is a requirement that can be interpreted in a number of ways, it is really insisting on what the French came to call 'vraisemblance', a kind of truth to life. Hence, says one French critic pointedly, no murders and certainly no representation of the Crucifixion.

– Plays that deal with the middle and lower strata of society can only be comedies.

– Both tragedy and comedy must respect the unity of time, place, and action. There was considerable debate on how much time the unity of time permitted. It was generally agreed that the action of a play must be kept within the range of twelve hours to two days. Observation of the three unities proved to be one of the most obdurate demands of Renaissance critics, perhaps as a result of what was to them the rather horrifying example of the Mysteries which sometimes took days to perform. It is important to remember, however, that on this question Aristotle has very little to say: he mentions unity of action as desirable rather than necessary; he contrasts unity of time, which is to be found in many Greek tragedies, with the timelessness of epic poetry, but draws no conclusions; and of unity of place he says nothing at all.

– The critics gave much thought to the purpose of drama. Aware of the moral power of the medieval drama and of the unstable society in which they lived, they insisted on the didactic responsibility of drama; but aware of the reality of the situation, they also agreed that drama must entertain and delight. This combination of instruction and pleasure is as applicable to tragedy as to comedy.

Perhaps the most destructive of all these admonitions to a free and organic development of dramatic form was the insistence on the three unities and the sharp social distinction between tragedy and comedy. Nevertheless they would have been totally ignored by the dramatists, as they were by Shakespeare and his contemporaries, if they had not had a certain validity at the time. A great deal of sixteenth-century art and culture was firmly based on certain classical values. But much of this culture in turn was both a reflection and an arm of politics and it suited some of the Emperors and Kings and Heads of State to build up their own authority with specious references to Roman imperialism. Art, in this way, was conditioned to serve certain political and social purposes.

But it must always be remembered that art is an expressive form, and that just as an artist has to find the appropriate form through which to express his ideas or sounds or images, so an audience or a reader or a listener has to learn to interpret them. Some artists have tried to find an (artistic) language that will be understood by a popular audience, like the authors of the medieval cycles, while others have been satisfied to write for a more limited audience. Their work can then be properly understood only in terms of the culture of that society. Examples of this will be given throughout the remainder of this book.

40 Drama in Italy in the Sixteenth Century

For the next few chapters we shall concentrate on Italy, for in spite of an unhappy political history the country continued to be the centre of lively artistic experiment throughout the century. It was in Italy that humanistic views were applied to the theatre with the greatest energy. In this cultural ferment the Church played no significant role: its problem was survival. When this was finally assured it made a renewed contribution to culture of a very different kind from what it had made in the Middle Ages.

The Renaissance of European drama began at Ferrara. This was due to the enthusiasm of Duke Ercole I. When he wanted a celebration, he arranged for his staff to stage an intermezzo. Although this is the same word as the English interlude, in Italy it constituted an extravagant mixture of medieval pageantry, classical mythology, elaborate costumes, scenery, masks, and a considerable amount of music and dance. His attention having been drawn by the scholars on his staff to the comedies of Plautus, he arranged in 1486 for the staging of *The Menaechmi* (*The Twins*) in the courtyard of his palace, not as an independent production but as part of a succession of intermezzi; and although no records exist it seems probable that he followed this with other Roman comedies.

The inspiration for these courtly theatricals came largely from a young man, Ludovico Ariosto (1474–1533) who was the son of a court official. Like many other young intellectuals of the time he became an impassioned humanist; but he was also a very considerable poet and in due course composed one of the great Renaissance epics, *Orlando Furioso*, a work which is set in the same curious medieval-romantic-allegorical world as Edmund Spencer's *The Faerie Queen*.

He also became interested in drama and began to compose original plays, copied from Plautus and Terence, but set in contemporary Italy. The first of these was *La Cassandra* (the name of the heroine), which was staged in 1508. He followed it in due course with *I Suppositi* (roughly *Conjectures*), entertainingly translated into English later in the century by George Gascoigne under the title *Supposes*, and then *La Lena* (1528).

In Bernardo Dovizi's *La Calandria* (1513) we have a comedy combining two plays of Plautus, father and son as rivals in love (*Cassina*) and identical twins (*Menaechmi*). When the author became a Cardinal he entertained the papal court with his comedy. Other writers followed the fashion. There was the brilliant Pietro Aretino (1492–1556), a Venetian who wrote several plays while on a visit to Mantua where there was another stage-struck duke. *Il Marescalo* (*The Stable-master* or *Farrier*, 1526–7), though amusingly written, turns on a single, not particularly funny joke about a stable-master, a vowed celebate, who is threatened by his Duke with a wife, who turns out to be a page-boy in disguise.

A typical play of the time was *Gl' Ingannati* (*The Deceived*, 1538), a group composition by members of a literary academy. An old man loves a pretty girl who loves a young man. She disguises herself as a page and is sent to court the lady with whom the man is in love, and so on, the source of Shakespeare's *Twelfth Night*, in fact. But these Italian dramatists were not Shakespeares and seem to have been unable to escape the limited theatrical conventions which they imposed upon themselves and which they lacked the creative energy to break.

The most interesting writer of the whole period is Angelo Beolco who wrote under the name of Ruzzante (Gossip) (*c.*1520–*c.*1542), a character which he introduces into some of his plays. He was a young middle-class landowner with estates in the region of Padua. Among his compositions are three curious orations in praise of what must then have been a very beautiful town and the splendid men and women who inhabited it. In his longer plays he shows evidence of being familiar with Plautus, but even in these plays he introduces a fresh vernacular note, while in his shorter plays, of which *Ruzzante Returning from the Wars* is a fine example, he writes in a dense Paduan dialect inscrutable to many contemporary Italians who have to read his plays in modernized versions. There is no evidence that he died early but it is extremely disappointing that a writer of such outstanding talent, who might have pointed contemporary comedy in a realistic and relevant direction, should have vanished from the scene before he made any lasting impression on contemporary dramaturgy. His plays are eminently revivable.

The best-known play of the period, and one that is still successfully revived, is Niccolo Machiavelli's *Mandragola*, a play which the notorious Florentine diplomat wrote in 1518 when he was forty-nine and in exile and disgrace. Though a neatly constructed play it is difficult to work up much enthusiasm for a piece that turns upon the cynical and rather brutal seduction of a beautiful young lady by a wealthy lecher and the dishonouring of her husband.

The first successful neo-classical tragedy was the work of Giangiorgio Trissino (1478–1550). His subject, and the title of his play, was *Sophonisba* (1514), Queen of Carthage, the story of whose unhappy marriage he culled from Livy's *History of Rome*. He wrote eight other plays but none so successful.

Giambattista Giraldi (1504–73), another Ferrarese, wrote a number of Senecan tragedies, full of blood and sensation. He wrestled bravely but not very successfully with forms of verse, problems of construction, and what he took to be the rules of Aristotle, while ransacking Roman authors for possible subjects.

In addition to the opposing forms of tragedy and comedy, there was a kind, known as Pastoral, derived very largely from Virgil's rural poetry. The excuse was the opportunity offered to create a fantasy world of pure delight, usually known as Arcadia, to which courtiers could escape as relief from a world of increasing social and religious constraints. The first of all Renaissance plays had been a pastoral, Angelo Poliziano's *Orfeo*, produced in Mantua in 1480. Another fine example of the genre was *Il Sacrifizio* (*The Sacrifice*, 1550) by another Ferrarese, Agostino de Beccari. The scene in Arcadia and the characters are all shepherds and shepherdesses, though none of them had ever seen a sheep. Even better written was *Aminta* (1573), the work of the tortured poet of the court of Ferrara, Torquato Tasso; and in Gian Guarini's *Pastor Fido* (*The Faithful Fido*, 1588) we return to Arcadia on which Diane has set a curse through the infidelity of a nymph.

This strange form survived for another two hundred years. It produced no literary masterpieces. Spencer's *Arcadia* was repudiated by Spencer himself and Philip Sidney's *The Shepherd's Calendar* is not a great work. It is only in painting, especially in the great *fêtes-champêtres* of Watteau that the pastoral achieves a powerful reality.

Many of these plays are not very rewarding to read. If however, they can be studied in the light of the authors' intentions they become far more interesting. It was a formative period for the theatre. The playwrights of the time had no immediate predecessors on whose work they could build. Religious drama of the medieval kind was politically prohibited and artistically objectionable. They chose their ancestors from among the Greeks and Romans with not altogether satisfactory consequences. But they faced the problems squarely. There was, for example, the question of language. Since comedy was about ordinary people it was arguable that comedy should be written in the vernacular. But there was a strong tradition that plays should be written in verse. There was thus a search for a verse-form that would respond to the rhythms of ordinary speech. It was a problem which, as we shall see, troubled the composers.

The writers of tragedy had the problem of *katharsis*. It was extremely difficult to reconcile the idea of cleansing the mind of an audience with a story of pity and terror with the Christian insistence on the virtues of repentance. Crime must be punished. But the Greek heroes had not committed crimes: they were often the victims of malevolent forces over which they had no control. It was all very difficult.

There are plenty of translations of Mandragola *since critics have decided that it is historically important and theatrically impressive. Translations of various plays are sometimes available but tend to be of little more than historical interest. Ariosto's great poem,* Orlando Furioso, *has been translated into English.*

41 | Renaissance Theatre Architecture

Theatre and drama had to be rediscovered, in a sense recreated. Once the Italians, with all their wealth and ingenuity, saw the need, they set up endless experiments. At the court of Mantua in 1501 there were fumbling but costly attempts to stage the great *Triumphs* of Mantegna which in turn were a kind of reproduction of the great literary triumphs of Petrarch. One cannot now even imagine how they set about it.

Another ducal court where there was enthusiasm for drama was Urbino. One of those who had had a hand in the staging of Bibbiena's *La Calandria* in 1513 was Baldassare Castiglione (1478–1529) who was a friend of Bernardo Dovizi who went on to write another play on the same theme at Ferrara. Castiglione, who some years later wrote an important book on courtly life, *Il Cortegiano* (*The Courtier*), described the setting in a letter to a friend.

> The stage represented a very beautiful city, with streets, palaces, churches, and towers. The streets looked as though they were real. Everything was done in relief and made even more striking through the art of painting and well-conceived perspective.

The discovery of perspective was one of the great achievements of Italian Renaissance painting, and its application to scene design was of the greatest importance. Another crucial factor, governing the design of theatres rather than theatrical scenery, was the discovery in the monastery of St. Gall of the manuscript of a book, *De Architectura* (*About Architecture*) by the Roman architect Vitruvius. We do not know what kind of reputation Vitruvius enjoyed in his own lifetime but in the sixteenth century his book was enormously influential on architecture in general even more than on the theatre. This book emphasizes all those qualities which the Renaissance valued highly, symmetry, proportion, and the relationship between these basic artistic principles and the proportions of the human body. Vitruvius also discusses the theory of 'perfect numbers' and the purity of mathematics, establishing rules for the diameter and height of columns and subjecting them to the most precise and sophisticated rules of proportion. In chapter five he deals with the theatre, placing particular emphasis on the clarity and quality of human speech which he relates to the science of acoustics which in turn is the basis of the art of music. This was the kind of information Renaissance architects valued highly and they put it to immediate use.

By 1518 a number of temporary theatres were being built on Vitruvian principles, by the great Raphael himself in the Castle of Saint Angelo in Rome, by the architect Bramante in the construction of St. Peter's, and by Sebastian Serlio in Vicenza.

Sebastian Serlio (1475–1554), a pupil of Baldassare Peruzzi, one of the most distinguished of Renaissance architects, built a temporary theatre in Vicenza in the 1530s. He describes the principles on which he

6. The Liberation of Tyrrhenus
An engraving by Jacques Callot of Bernardo Buontalenti's design for an intermezzo staged in the Uffizi Palace in Florence in honour of the Grand Duke of Tuscany in 1617. This was probably the first permanent theatre in Europe with movable stage scenery.

worked in the second volume of his *Regole Generali di Architettura* (*The Principle Rules of Architecture*) where he gives detailed instructions for designing a stage and auditorium in the banqueting hall of a palace. His theatre, following precisely the rules of Vitruvius, is based on a circle, one half of which is designated for the stage, the other half for the auditorium.

Vicenza continued to be a centre of theatrical experiment through the establishment in the 1550s of the Accademia Olimpico for the study of antiquity in general and the production of classical and neo-classical plays in particular. A distinguished member of the Academy was the architect Andrea Palladio (1508–80) who was responsible for turning the city into a paradise of neo-classical architecture. The Academy commissioned Palladio to build a permanent theatre. He began its construction in 1580 but died the same year. The work was completed by his pupil Vincenzo Scamozzi (1552–1616). Palladio designed the Teatro Olimpico on the basis of a commentary on Vitruvius by Daniella Barbaro and although he applied some of his own modifications, the resulting theatre was impractical and unworkable. Unfortunately he was more influenced by Vitruvian theory than theatrical practice. The huge richly decorated *frons scaenae*, as the Romans would have called it, with a large central doorway and two smaller ones on either side, made no provision for the kind of settings required by contemporary dramatists or even by Plautus and Terence. The place was a dead end, a monument to unrealizable ideals.

The next permanent theatre to be built was the Teatro Farnese at Parma, completed in 1618–19. The feature of this theatre was a proscenium arch in front of the acting area. The logic of this much disputed element in theatrical design is clear. Renaissance dramatists gave their plays a setting. A setting requires painted scenery. Painted scenery requires a frame. The frame was provided by the *pro-* (in front of) *scaena* or *skene* arch. Whatever Vitruvius may or may not have implied the Italians were far too visually alert to accept a remorseless stone background to every play wherever it was set. Then having provided a proscenium arch or frame, the way was clear for the introduction of changeable scenery. The centre for this development was Venice where the theatres had to meet the demands of a new and insistent theatrical form known as opera.

The Teatro Olimpico at Vicenza is still a tourist attraction in all its rather drab splendour; but the Palladian city is a splendid sight. The superb Triumphs *of Mantegna are on public view at Hampton Court Palace.*

42 | The Creation of Opera

The Italian intermezzi (interludes) were the product of a period of the utmost confusion in theatrical form. There was a long tradition of lavish entertainment in the ducal courts but the form of these entertainments, resulting from the prodigious inventiveness of the people, was a wild farrago of drama, dance, song, and every kind of lavish pageantry. In these displays the elements of music and dance were not minor partners. Dances, usually performed by professionals, were known as *balli* or *balleti* and generally took as subject a theme from classical mythology. A love-affair between a god and a mortal seemed to hold particular attraction for the choreographers as it did for the painters. These ballets often formed a major element in the intermezzi which in the early sixteenth century had developed into a sequence of dances, madrigals, motets, and acted scenes with no clear distinction between one art form and another.

Things changed in the latter part of the century. For one thing Monteverdi arrived upon the scene. Claudio Monteverdi was born in Cremona in 1567 and as a young man joined the staff of Vincenzo Gonzaga, Duke of Mantua. The Duke was extremely interested in original works of art, and in addition to supporting a school of music he built a theatre, though we have no details of its design, and placed it under the direction of Leone di Somi (1527–92), an extraordinarily gifted Jew who wrote poetry in both Hebrew and Italian, staged elaborate court entertainments, and wrote four dialogues on acting and drama in the course of which he advocates the establishment of a public as opposed to a private theatre.

In 1583, Claudio Monteverdi, a young man of sixteen, accompanied the Duke on a visit to Florence for a Medici wedding. The Grand Duke Ferdinand de Medici had inherited the taste of his forebears for sumptuous spectacles which he staged for a variety of political motives. The entertainment, which was watched by the visiting Mantuans, was a prodigious intermezzo entitled *Il Combattimeno d'Apollino con Serpente* (*The Fight between Apollo and the Serpent*). It seems to have been an elaborate multi-media production full of allegorical significance and classical illusions. It was the work of four young Florentines – Giulini Caccini (1558–1615), a composer who had come to Florence from

Rome; Iacopo Peri (1516–1633), a Florentine by birth and also a composer; Ottavio Rinuccini, a poet; and their patron, a wealthy young nobleman, Giovanni Bardi, Count of Vernio.

At some date, probably subsequent to 1583, Count Bardi formed an Academy of his young friends, calling themselves the Camerata or Comrades and meeting in his house. Bardi's great interest was in music; he expounded his views in a short treatise, *Discorso sopra la Musicale Moderne* (*A Discourse on Modern Music*) where he wrote that 'in composing you will make it your principle aim to arrange the verses well and to declaim the words as intelligently as possible, not letting yourself be led astray by the counterpoint'.

Caccini was also interested in this subject of declamation and counterpoint and in 1601 published *La Nuova Musicale* (*The New Music*) in which he argued that language must predominate over the musical element. The source of their anxieties was that polyphonic music, which is choral music written with different parts for the various voices, had become so complex in the hands of a master such as Palestrina that the words had become wholly obscured.

They were also extremely interested in Aristotle and other classical critics and the commentaries that had been written on them. From all this reading they formed the impression that Greek tragedy had provided a perfect fusion of the arts of poetry, music, dance, and spectacle. We have seen that this is only partly true and that we really have not the least idea how the fusion was achieved. But the Camerata, like the critics, read into Aristotle what they wanted to find and turned their attention to what they believed to be the recreation of Greek tragedy by taking a story from the classics, writing a poetic text, and setting it to a single melodic line with simple instrumental accompaniment.

We do not know exact details of their experiments. But in 1597 Rinuccini the poet and Peri the composer completed a version of the story of *Dafne* which they staged with considerable elaboration in Count Bardi's private theatre. The work, now unhappily lost, does not appear to have been very successful; but the collaborators were not deterred and, joined by Caccini, wrote and staged a version of *Eurydice*. The musical style was a slightly uneasy balance between declamation and singing proper, but by giving each syllable a single note, they preserved the clarity of the text.

Monteverdi, meanwhile, a captive in Mantua, was kept informed of the experiments of his friends. The Duke, though an enthusiast for the arts, paid him poorly and refused to release him. Monteverdi therefore had to work on his own, which may have been an advantage. Probably learning by the mistakes of the Florentines he brought their experiments to ultimate success by writing and composing the beautiful and celebrated *Orfeo*, which was staged in 1607 at the marriage of the Duke's son. He described the work as 'dramma per musica', a musical drama, separating the recitative, in which he tries to follow the inflections of ordinary speech, from the declamatory passages. There were no songs or arias as they were later called.

What the Camerati in Florence and Monteverdi in Mantua had done was not to recreate Greek tragedy, which was based on a different set of assumptions, but to create a wholly new theatrical form which came to be known as opera. In 1612 Monteverdi was released from Mantua and went to Venice, then one of the wealthiest cities in Italy, where he was provided with opportunity to exploit this new theatrical form. He wrote a large number of music dramas of which only two have survived, *Il Ritorno d'Ulisse in Patria* (*The Return of Ulysses to his Fatherland*, 1641) and *L'Incoronazione di Poppaea* (*The Coronation of Poppaea*, 1642).

The subsequent history of opera lies outside the scope of this book, although its influence on theatrical development has been such that it will be necessary to refer to it from time to time. It is enough to say that the Venetians were quick to realize the possibilities of this new theatrical form which admirably satisfied their love of music and drama. Between 1636 and 1700, 300 operas by 66 composers were staged – in a city with a population of 150,000 – and eight theatres were built. During the same period opera houses were built in many German cities. These were often designed by members of the Italian Bibiena family who also provided many of the stage designs. But perhaps the greatest designer of them all was Giacomo Torelli (1608–78) who had worked at the Teatro Farnese at Parma and was of much assistance to Molière at the Théâtre du Petit-Bourbon. But it was the fantastic and spectacular settings and effects that were required by opera that gave considerable emphasis to technical developments back-stage. Torelli, in fact, was known as 'the great magician' for the splendour of his effects.

43 The Commedia dell' Arte

Italy, during the early years of the sixteenth century was in a state of political turmoil. The country had been invaded by the French in 1494 and the sordid game of power politics played by some of the Italian despots, notably the Sforzas of Milan, as well as by Pope Julius II, with the greater powers of France and Spain and the Emperor Charles V, came to an end in 1559 with what amounted to the division of the country into three separate kingdoms, the south dominated by Spain, the Papal States occupying the area around Rome, and the north under the domination of the Austrian Hapsburgs, a condition of unhealthy stability that lasted for two hundred years.

But the artistic achievement of the Renaissance was not obliterated in a moment. Leonardo da Vinci was at the height of his power between 1480 and 1520 and Michelangelo between 1490 and 1560. The more placid decades in the second half of the century, which saw the developments described in the last chapter, were the period of the great Venetian painters, Titian (d. 1576), Paulo Veronese (d. 1588) and Tintoretto (d. 1594).

The Commedia dell'Arte – the phrase is untranslatable and of unknown origin – was a creatiòn of the early professional companies of actors. We have seen in the case of Greek and Roman comedy that when the actors get the upper hand in the theatre they tend to create types. It began to happen in the emergent French theatre at the beginning of the sixteenth century and this may be an unusual example of the French having influenced the Italians. Indeed it has already been pointed out that during the time in question, the first thirty years or so of the sixteenth century, Italy was invaded by French troops. The French may have pointed the way, but it was the Italian comedians who went to the end of the road. This may well have been because they found theatrical conditions, and the domination of the literary neo-classic drama of the humanists, intolerable. We do not know. The fact is that groups of actors began to get together and to improvise their own plays; and since actors are often brilliant at making up their own dialogue and inventing comic 'business', but poor at thinking out stories, they began by taking the stories they were familiar with, those of Plautus and Terence, but transforming them into their own indivi-

7. Balli di Sfessania
Engravings by Jacques Callot of characters from a Commedia ballet of the early seventeenth century. The physical vitality of the characters is superbly apparent.

dual, improvised kind of comedy, at the same time finding a contemporary equivalent for the not very original 'types' that are to be found in these plays. So once again there was a popular theatre of lecherous old merchants, pedantic doctors, and intriguing servants. The lecherous merchant became the Venetian *magnifico* with long red tights, a loose black cape, and a long straggly beard that was blown about in the wind. He was always elderly, wealthy, retired, and obsessively mean about money. He was known as Pantalone.

The actors got their own back on the pedantic humanist by transforming him into Il Dottore, the learned doctor from the university town of Bologna; but he had a degree from every other university, he was a member of every existing academy, he was immensely learned in all the arts and sciences but confused his facts and sent everyone asleep with his interminable disquisitions.

The swaggering Captain was another well-known figure of the time, a boaster and a bully, with a large nose, a bristling moustache, and an immense sword that quivered like a peacock's tail at the mating season. The names of the Capitanos roll of the tongue with impressive splendour – Cocodrillo, Papirotondo, Rodomonte, and Escobombardo. When they fought there was not a piazza in Italy large enough to hold them.

Pulcinella was a kind of Neapolitan clown, slow and deliberate in movement and speech; Brighella came from Bergamo, a bizarre, cynical character with a hook nose and sensual lips. He prowled rather than walked. He could insinuate his lithe body into any nook or cranny – a man of infinite ingenuity but a little scary.

The most famous and distinctive character of all was Harlequin, Arlecchino, dressed in the well-known parti-coloured jacket and trousers and using his slapstick as a sword, a wand, a fan, and a red-hot poker. His play was a string of extravagant tricks, outrageous rogueries. He was ingenious, inept, insolent, craven, agile, and infinitely mercurial.

Actors of outstanding creative ability invented their own characters but most actors created individual variations of one of the stock types or 'masks' as they were called. For another curious feature of the Commedia was the use of half-masks, usually made of leather and fitting close to the face, and worn only by the comic characters.

The love element in the scenarios was played more or less 'straight' and in a formal manner. The young lovers of both sexes tended to improvise less and to use set speeches which they adapted to different situations.

Each company invented or selected its own scenarii. Between seven and eight hundred titles have been identified but there was undoubtedly a great deal of overlapping. The quality of performance rested less on the story than the improvisation. This the actors exploited in two ways.

The more experienced built up a considerable repertory of vocal tricks, quips, pieces of repartee, and choice remarks which they would vary between one performance and another according to the response of the audience. But their improvisational methods were expressed even more strongly in their physical creation of character and the enormous amount of comic 'business' or *lazzi* which they became highly skilful at inventing.

It was an actor's theatre and as such it was immensely variable between one company and another. One of the earliest troupes included the celebrated actress Isabella Andreini, who was a distinguished Latin scholar, and her husband Francesco, who could speak five languages and was a member of various learned academies. Closely related to them was the company known as *Gli Gelosi* who in 1576 were invited by Henri III to visit France and play both at the French court and in the Hotel de Bourgogne.

But for the most part these companies led a nomadic existence, playing what are now called 'one night stands' on improvised stages which they carried with them and set up wherever they could find an audience. They visited most countries in Europe and often made a considerable impact on the native drama. This occurred particularly in France: in Britain their influence had different and even more surprising results.

The Commedia dell' Arte does not lend itself to academic study and many of the books that have been written on the subject are informative but dull. The Italian comedy was often trivial, frequently obscene, but it is hard to believe that it was ever boring.

Many of the characters have been superbly recorded in the engravings of the French artist, Jacques Callot.

In recent years there has been an attempt in Italy to rediscover some of the techniques of the Commedia. Giorgio Strehler's production of Goldoni's A Servant of Two Masters *at the Piccolo Theatre, Milan, was a landmark in this respect. But it is an essentially Italian creation and attempts by actors of other nationalities to find something of the comic verve in voice and body have rarely been satisfactory.*

44 | The Reformation

The movement known as the Reformation marks the ultimate failure of the Catholic Church, henceforth to be called Roman, to achieve the ideals that were embodied in the concept of the Holy Roman Empire. For this failure the Church itself was largely to blame. In practical affairs the Popes and Bishops had too often tried to play the kings of Europe at their own game. In administrative matters they allowed the development of widespread corruption often in matters in which they themselves had set a lamentable example. In spiritual affairs they had been guilty of a doctrinaire pedantry from which not even the example of the great theologians such as St. Thomas Aquinas had been enough to free them.

It was in this last respect, in spiritual affairs, that their failure was the most fatal; for as has been described, a new wind was blowing through Europe bringing with it an intellectual excitement which even at her most unified the Church would have been hard pressed to resist. Yet it could have been done; for the great medieval theologians had been students of Plato and had shown how humanism, in the sense of an absolute respect for the sanctity of the human body and mind, could be contained within the teachings of the Church if it were not interpreted in too narrow a way. Similarly the great reformers did not want to destroy the Church but to reform it, to see an end to scandal and abuse, while men such as Martin Luther (1483–1546) looked for a more spiritual approach to religion based on close reading of the Bible.

It was a tragedy that at this moment of supreme crisis the Church lacked a leader of wisdom and authority. The Church Fathers replied to the dynamic of the protesters and reformers only with great stubborness. They they did what everyone does in a crisis – called a conference. After many years of postponement through niggardly points of procedure, an example of the very weaknesses that had to be overcome, a Church Council met in 1545 in the German city of Trent; but instead of concentrating on internal reform, as the Catholic Emperor Charles V vigorously advocated, it turned its attention to the least important of the great issues, the clarification of minutiae of dogma. The Council spun out its life over the pontificate of three Popes, missed all opportunities for working out an ecumenical compromise, a set of beliefs with which all sects could agree, and virtually declared war on the reformed Church.

Nevertheless the basic issue was a very deep one and closely affected the history of every kind of art and culture. The controversy really turned on whether an individual had the right to his own interpretation of the Bible, or whether the interpretation of centuries of thinking by learned theologians was sacrosanct and not to be questioned. In this sense the art and drama of the later Middle Ages were the beginning of the breakup, for they were increasingly the expression not of Christian art but of Christian artists. The great Mysteries and moralities had expressed a view of Christianity projected by the Church, accepted by the people as part of a great communal celebration. Since then there has been no communal art, only the work of individual artists.

The political and religious ferment that developed throughout Europe was immense. Henry VIII broke with Rome and destroyed the monasteries. In France, a little later in the century, and in central Europe in the next century, there were religious wars of a protracted and devastating nature. This was the legacy of the Reformation to which society had to adapt itself.

45 French Drama of the Sixteenth Century

In 1494 Charles VIII, King of France, invaded Italy. This initiated a series of campaigns that continued until the French were ultimately defeated in 1559 and Henri III thought it more prudent to concentrate on troubles at home than forays abroad.

Whatever the political results of the war may have been, the cultural outcome, as is often the case, was immense. Although the French had been by no means unaware of Italian achievements in art and culture, they returned home laden with evidence of the marvellous artistry of their neighbours. The booty included not only works of art galore but architects, musicians, and dancing masters. Even Leonardo da Vinci went to work at the court of Francis I in 1517 where he was given the flattering title of 'leading painter, architect, and engineer of the King'.

The French were not slow in demonstrating their enthusiasm for humanism. Teachers of Latin and Greek were in business. There was, for example, Jean Dorat, a peasant by birth and a pedant by profession, but a much sought-after teacher. People came from far and wide to hear him expound classical texts in the obscure establishment in Paris where he taught and to which he gave the impressive name of the Collège de Coqueret.

Another distinguished teacher was James Buchanan, a Scotsman, who for a time was professor of classics in Bordeaux and numbered the young Montaigne among his pupils. He translated a couple of plays by Euripides and wrote two classical tragedies in Latin. And then there was Marc-Antoine de Muret (1526–85) who taught at the Collège de Boncourt in Paris. From such Colleges as these came the theorists with their commentaries on Aristotle and a number of young playwrights.

Among Muret's scholars was a group of young poets. There was Jean-Antoine de Baïf who in 1547, when first they met, was fifteen, Pierre Ronsard who was twenty-three, and Joachim du Bellay who was twenty-five. They combined their enthusiasm for the classics with a great interest in their own language. Indeed it was the one that led to the other, for they were exasperated to find how much superior the works of such Italian poets as Petrarch and Dante were to French poems of roughly the same date, such as *Le Roman de la Rose*. Ronsard and du Bellay, having published in 1549 a translation of Horace's poem on poetry, brought out a celebrated work, *La Deffence et illustration de la language Française* (roughly, *An Explanation and Description of the French Language*) in which they argued that properly used, and with the introduction of some Greek and Latin words, there was no reason why a country with the most beautiful scenery in the world should not have the finest language. The logic may be shaky but the confidence is admirable.

The initial group was joined by others until, numbering seven, they described themselves as La Pléiade after a group of Alexandrian Greek poets. Their interests included drama. In 1549 Ronsard translated Aristophanes's *Plautus* and in 1552 Etienne Jodelle, one of the more recent recruits, wrote one of the more significant plays of the whole period, *Cléopâtre captive* (*Cleopatra in Captivity*). This play, together with a hastily written comedy called *Eugène*, was staged in Rheims before an audience which included the King, Henri III, and received a reward of 500 gold crowns. A second performance was given a year later for members of the group and their friends and concluded with a kind of pagan celebration, of no great significance to the participants but shocking to Catholic and Protestant members of the audience.

In precision of construction and respect for the unities *Cléopâtre captive* is faultless. In act one Cleopatra declares her intention of dying; in act two she discusses her reluctance to die; in act three she bargains over the inheritance of her treasure; in act four she prepares to die; and in act five there is an announcement of her death, the rules forbidding anything so inappropriate as her death on the stage.

Soon after, the Pléiade broke up and its members went their own way as poets; but the interest in humanist drama continued. The next significant writer was Jacques Grévin (1538–70), a tall blond man who studied the classics with Muret and became a convert to Calvinism. In 1560–1 he wrote a short commentary on Aristotle and a classical tragedy, *César*. In some respects the work is superior to Jodelle's. It is written in alexandrines, a form of verse which had been advocated by the Pléiade and which conformed to the rhythms of French vernacular speech. It has since become the standard form of French dramatic poetry as the iambic pentameter has for English. In act one of this play Caesar discusses with Marc Anthony the implications of government by toleration or by force; in act two the conspirators plan to assassinate Caesar; in act three Calpurnia expresses her fears and tries to dissuade her husband from going to the Senate; in act four a messenger describes the assassination; in act five Brutus tries to justify the murder to the citizens and Anthony to mollify the fury of the army: a less unified play than Jodelle's but opening up dramatic form to new possibilities. One can see the rapidity of development by contrasting this play with Shakespeare's *Julius Caesar* written only fifty years later.

Grévin's comedies are a rather interesting example of an attempt to reconcile the classical ideal with the need to express contemporary life. *La Trésorière* (*The Tax-collectors Wife*) is about the efforts of two suitors to raise the money with which to purchase the affections of the heroine. *Les Ebahis* (*The Astonished Ones*) is about an old merchant who, believing his wife to be dead, makes plans to marry his closest friend's eldest daughter, who is herself in love with a young lawyer. The various servants do their ingenious best to frustrate the former proposal and further the latter, while an Italian rogue named Pantalone appears with a woman who turns out to be the missing wife of the old lecher.

Performances of these plays were usually given by amateurs and college students. Professional companies scraped a hazardous existence, unable to cope with the intellectual demands of the humanist drama, and lacking the authority and the expertise of the Italian comedians. Gli Gelosi paid the first of their visits to France in 1571 and established themselves as *Comédiens ordinaires du Roi*. The effect on the development of French comedy is questionable, for while on the one hand they set an example in standards of performance, they placed a restraint on any natural development through the very limited subject-matter of their performances.

With tragedy things took a very different and extremely interesting course. All religious drama had been banned by the French Parlement in 1548. Since the Mysteries, which were now somewhat despised, were closely associated with the Roman version of Christianity, the new dramatists were almost wholly Protestants; and since in the new religion there was a considerable emphasis on the study of the Bible, it was here that the dramatists found their subjects. Théodore de Bèze (1519–1605), for example, a humanist as well as a theologian, wrote *Abraham sacrifiant* (1550) as a piece of Protestant propaganda. Louis Desmasures (1515–74), a cheerful and easy-going fellow, wrote a fascinating trilogy on David, *David combattant*, *David tromphant*, and *David fugitif* (*David the Fighter*, *David in Triumph* and *David in Flight*) in which he tried to relate something of the religious passion of the Mysteries with the disciplines of classical tragedy. Jean de la Taille published an important work, *The Art of Tragedy* in 1562 and a fine tragedy, *Saul le furieux* (*Saul in Fury*, 1572).

The most significant dramatist of the century is sometimes considered to be Robert Garnier (1545–90). Between 1573 and 1583, when he was a kind of magistrate at Le Mans, he wrote seven tragedies and a tragi-comedy which, while showing an obsession with cruelty, doubtless a reflection of the horrors of the Wars of Religion, are the work of a man who was strenuously trying to create a valid dramatic form. His masterpiece, *Les Juives* (1583) is about the captivity of the Jews under Nebuchadnezzar. Another man of the greatest interest both as a personality and a writer was Antoine de Montchrétien (1575–1621), poet, dramatist, adventurer, duellist, bandit, industrialist, and contemplative. On his death at the age of forty-six his body was burnt and the ashes thrown to the winds. He was the author of a fine play on no less a subject than Mary, Queen of Scots, *La Reine d'Ecosse* (1601).

The difference in the development of drama in France and Italy in the sixteenth century is explained by the wholly different state of religion in the two countries. The Central States of Italy were under the direct control of the Vatican, and the two powers of Spain and Austria that dominated the south and the north respectively were also strongly Catholic. The humanist drama in Italy, therefore, remained humanist and like the country itself was wholly unaffected by the reformed religion. In France, however, Protestantism combined with humanism to provide a powerful incentive to new forms of writing; and although the religious settlement was ultimately a Catholic one, the Protestant experiments of the sixteenth century provided a basis for one of the most impressive periods in the whole history of the theatre.

Few of the plays mentioned in this section have been translated into English but most are available in French. The period is well covered critically and historically by Brian Jeffrey's French Renaissance Comedy *(1552–1630) and Geoffrey Brereton's* French Tragic Drama in the Sixteenth and Seventeenth Centuries.

46 | Classical Ballet

Like the Camerata in Italy, so the young poets who formed La Pléiade read Aristotle and envisaged the possibility of a kind of theatrical art that unified story, character, song, poetry, dance, and spectacle. The Greeks, they conjectured, must have subjected music to a strict control of rhythm and pitch to support and give particular effectiveness to spoken poetry. This was a subject of particular interest to Jean-Antoine de Baïf (1532–89) who in 1570 formed the Académie de Musique et de Poésie for the studying of such subjects, though it was not long before it collapsed under pressure of the religious wars.

Pierre Ronsard (1524–85), also a poet and a very great one, read Aristotle and Plato, and developed a concept of music and dance as having a kind of cosmic significance representing all that was most harmonious and orderly in the universe. Ronsard was by no means unique in entertaining such views. In broad terms they formed the basis of a humanistic philosophy that was known as neo-Platonism, for philosophers had developed their own interpretation of Plato as writers had done of Aristotle, and used such theories as a basis for their own. But to the philosophers as much as the artists concerned, music and dance were significant forms of art since the one expressed an orderly structure of time and the other of space. This concept of dance as representing the basic pattern of the universe is beautifully expressed by the English poet, Sir John Davies, in his poem 'Orchestra' which he wrote in 1596 when he was twenty-seven. The sun, the moon, the stars all have their own measures . . . the universe itself is one great dance, and at the centre of the universe was Queen Elizabeth and her court. This was not a piece of gratuitous flattery but a way of making the point, of great importance to monarchs of the time, that the order of the universe is reflected in the body politic, the political structure of the country.

Ronsard found a ready listener to his views in Catherine de Medici, the Queen Mother. This formidable lady was born in Florence in 1519 of a French mother and an Italian father, Duke Lorenzo de Medici II. At the age of fourteen she was married to Henri II, King of France, but she did not achieve real power until 1560 when at the age of forty-one she became Regent during the minority of her second son, Charles IX. By then she was the mother of nine children, three of whom were to become kings of France. She conducted diplomacy with the flair and unscrupulousness of an Italian despot, playing off the Catholics and the Protestants (Huguenots) against each other and pursuing a policy of peace only when protracted bloodshed had led to stalemate.

Being a passionate humanist, however, she exploited the artists in conducting her diplomacy. Her son Charles IX went so far as to promulgate a statute declaring that a country's music reflected the quality of its society, for when music is crude and disorderly, social manners are depraved. Well-ordered music is the corollary of a well-governed state.

This was the translation of Ronsard's neo-platonic theories into political terms. Their further transformation was the work, among others, of Balthasar Beaujoyeux, an Italian whom Catherine had imported from Italy, under the name of Balthazarini Belgiojoso, for his fame as a violinist, and then made him her court valet. Beaujoyeux expressed his own humanist passions not in music but in dance, believing, as was the fashion of the times, that the universe itself is one great dance comprising many lesser dances.

Beaujoyeux was an outstanding choreographer and stage-director whose talents she exploited to the full in a series of spectacular entertainments which she properly called *Magnificences*. These she staged on every occasion that called for an impressive diplomatic gesture. Thus at a great festival at Chenonceaux in 1564, organized in the interests of religious toleration, she created an earthly paradise; the water-festival at Bayonne in 1565 was intended to secure the union of France and Spain 'for the good of Christendom'; there was a notable *Magnificence* at Fontainbleau in 1564 in the course of the King's royal tour of the country; and in 1571 to celebrate the triumphant entry of Charles IX into Paris, Catherine staged *Le Paradis d'amour* (*The Paradise of Love*) in which the King and his brothers defended the gates into the Elysian Fields against a troop of knights who, it need hardly be said, were defeated and consigned to the underworld.

In 1573 Beaujoyeux came into his own with an ambitious *Ballet of the Provinces of France*; but his greatest achievement was his celebrated *Ballet comique de la Reine* (*Comedy Ballet of the Queen*) of 1581. The performance, which lasted for six hours and finished at three in the morning, cost one million gold crowns. The details of this important ballet fall properly within the history of dance; but the results for the theatre are important. The story, which was full of political and allegorical significance, even to the inclusion of an updated version of the contest between the Vices and the Virtues, was based on the Greek enchantress Circe (Kirke) who represented Civil War, but who was finally worsted by the King of France. The choreography, of which Beaujoyeux has left a detailed description, came to a climax with a sequence of forty geometrical figures all carried out with intricate precision. This was neo-Platonism indeed.

Behind Beaujoyeux was Ronsard with his poetry, Dorat with his scholarship, and at least the spirit of Baïf's Academy of Music and Poetry. But Beaujoyeux was clearly a powerful artistic personality. And the French loved dancing. On the death of Catherine de Medici, *ballet de cour* as it came to be called, was sustained by her daughter, Catherine de Valois. For the great Henri IV and his Queen, Marie de Medici, dancing was a passion, and so it was with his son, Louis XIII, and his grandson, Louis XIV. As a young man and a young King, Louis XIV not only took part regularly in court ballets but in 1661 founded the Académie Royale de Danse, composed of thirteen dancing masters who were required to re-establish the art in all its perfection. But as the king grew older and the cares of state weighed on him more heavily the development of ballet was left to the Paris opera which Louis had also founded in 1661 and which had remained for some years under the control of the composer, Jean-Baptiste Lully. But this is material for a later section.

The whole subject of sixteenth-century diplomatic pageantry has been dealt with by Roy Strong in his beautifully illustrated Splendour at Court. *The intellectual background to Renaissance thought is clearly summed up in E. M. W. Tillyard's* The Elizabethan World Picture. *Other books cover the great age of patronage; such as Hugh Trevor-Roper*, Princes and Artists *and A. G. Dickens (editor)* The Courts of Europe.

There are many admirable and well-illustrated books on the history of classical ballet. It should not be forgotten that, like opera, it has remained one of the basic theatre arts.

47 | The Court Masque

Throughout the Middle Ages and well into the times of Henry VIII there was a tradition of seasonal games which took different forms among different groups of people. The records, as well as our knowledge of human nature, are enough to tell us that these activities persisted but not enough to tell us the details. The seasonal nature of these games was very marked since Britain was still a wholly agricultural country and even life in the towns was not so remote from rural life as it is today.

Games and rituals were played and observed among the aristocracy as well as the peasantry though they were often different in character. There was, for example, a curious custom known as a 'mumming', the essence of which was that around the Christmas season a group of men on horseback would visit the house of some notability, distribute gifts, play dice, dance with the inmates of the house they were visiting, and then go away. Sometimes the visitors dressed in green and sometimes they were masked. The reasons for this are obscure but of ancient origin. There are occasional records of mummings from the fourteenth century but nothing very precise until the time of Henry VIII who as a young man was an enthusiastic mummer. The masks and the greenery suggest an anthropological origin to the mumming but as they lost their meaning so they ceased to be a feature of the custom. The element that survived was that a group of visitors paid a ritualistic visit and danced with their hosts.

Henry VIII was a Renaissance prince of high calibre. He was not willing to be outfaced by Pope, Emperor, or King. He was something of a poet, a dancer, a musician, and he loved pageants and interludes. To administer such frivolities he established a special office known as the Revels Office which was run by an official who played an increasingly significant role in the history of the English theatre.

Under Henry VIII the mumming was transformed into a more organized form of entertainment known as a Masque; it was not dissimilar from, though perhaps on a slightly smaller scale than, one of Catherine de Medici's *Magnificences* or an Italian intermezzo. It was the customary mixture of medieval dramatic allegory, with a lot of music and dancing, in a strongly classical setting. There were performers and there were spectators who at the end of the performance always danced with each other.

Henry VIII's passion for this kind of diversion waned as he became increasingly involved in a costly and complex game of dynastic politics. Edward VI was a weakling and died at the age of sixteen. Mary Tudor was similarly poor in health and though far less of a tyrant than often supposed, she was beset with far too many problems to have any interest in cultural diplomacy in the manner of her father, Henry VIII, or her cousin, the Emperor Charles V.

With Elizabeth the scene changes. This brilliantly cultured woman won the deepest respect of many of her subjects. Her sense of monarchical responsibility is legendary. But she was not an ostentatious queen. She encouraged her artists to the full but she did not rule by means of extravagant artistic displays. There were seldom Masques at her court. One of the few of which there are records, planned to be performed at a projected meeting between the Queen and Mary, Queen of Scots, never took place. But the tradition survived and was vigorously resurrected by Anne of Denmark, the wife of James I.

Anne was a frivolous lady and interested in entertainment, dress, and jewels. A contemporary described her court as being 'a continued maskeranda where the Queen and her ladies like so many nymphs appeared to the ravishment of the beholders and made the night more glorious than the day'.

It was as a nymph, though a black one, that she appeared in the first of the great Court Masques she was responsible for having staged. It was called *The Masque of Blackness* and revealed the Queen with eleven of her ladies as Daughters of the River Nile, seated in a great concave shell seemingly constructed of mother-of-pearl 'curiously made to move on those waters and rise with the billows', says the author, Ben Jonson.

In 1605 Ben Jonson, one of the leading dramatists and poets of the day, had come to the attention of the King as the author of one of the set pieces that had been staged to greet him on his slow progress from Scotland to London in 1603, and of two of the seven 'stations' at which the King had stopped on his coronation procession. His close collaborator in this and many following projects was not a composer or a choreographer but an architect, Inigo Jones (1573–1652), who had visited Italy where he had become familiar with the intermezzi, and more recently done some work for Anne's brother, King Christian IV of Denmark.

Between 1605 and 1632 these two remarkable men collaborated in some twenty-five Masques. A good deal is made of the row that finally terminated the collaboration but the remarkable thing is that two such intense individualists should have worked together as long as they did. In all some hundred Masques were staged between 1605 and 1642, mostly in the Whitehall Banqueting House. Many were the work of other poets, but Inigo Jones remained the dominant designer and stage-director, and was responsible for fifty.

Jonson's Masques are a remarkable fusion of allegory, classical allusion, and sheer fantasy. Within a limited and repetitive structure, Jonson finds great imaginative freedom. Order gives place to chaos until order is restored again. The earthly paradise is seen somewhat in terms of the Italian pastoral, a visionary land for the depiction of which Jonson found a form of verse that dances off the page. His texts are especially delightful to read for their vivid descriptions of Jones's scenery, his own elaborate stage directions and the explanations of his many classical allusions.

Jones, though a superb draughtsman and designer, turned increasingly to Italy for his ideas. For every Masque he had to build a stage, framed with a proscenium arch, at the end of some great hall. He achieved the necessary transformations by means of three major devices. First, a revolving stage which enabled two scenes to be set at the same time, one on the part of the semicircle facing the audience, the other behind it so that, at the appropriate moment, it could be moved into view with a half turn of the revolve. Secondly, there was a series of shutters at the back of the stage which slid open to reveal a new scene; and thirdly there was a complex machinery for flying gods and goddesses through the air and revealing groups of immortals sitting comfortably among the clouds. It is hardly surprising that there were complaints from members of the audience about the noise of these great transformations. Nor is it unusual that Inigo Jones, who was much influenced by Italian methods, should have made great use of perspective scenery.

These Masques were not intended altogether as straightforward entertainments. There was as much behind them as there was behind Catherine de Medici's *Magnificences*. They were a positive statement of neo-Platonic ideas, using to the full the relationship between number and proportion, measure and light. Jonson saw his Masques as 'mirrors of man's life', Jones his designs as 'pictures of light and motion', the Court saw the performances as a revelation of the body politic with the King at the head of an ideal universe.

In 1609 King James declared to Parliament:

> The state of monarch is the supremest thing upon earth; for Kings are not only God's lieutenants, and sit upon God's throne, but even by God himself they are called Gods.

One may think that this is going a bit far; but James's son, Charles I was similarly convinced, and paid the penalty. Indeed, under Charles the Masque became increasingly an allegorical representation of self-

8. **The Dutch Pageant**
When in 1604 James VI of Scotland entered London as James I of England, his procession passed under seven arches or pageants, designed by Stephen Harrison. At each a short allegorical welcome composed by Ben Jonson or Thomas Dekker was given. This one was erected by Dutch merchants working in London. The central tableau represents the provinces of the Netherlands. The figure at the top is the King.

9. Design by Inigo Jones
For Zenobia, Queen of Palmira, in Ben Jonson's fine *The Masque of Queens*, 1609, the third of Jonson's Masques in which Queen Anne appeared as chief masquer.

rule and monarchical authority. Jonson, by this time, had retired, but Jones went soldiering on and with the skilful use of perspective scenery placed the King at the centre of the stage, the state, and, lest anyone should miss the point, the universe.

The slightly contemptuous attitude of the public to these expensive charades is summed up in almost the opening lines of a famous Jacobean play, *The Maid's Tragedy*, by Beaumont and Fletcher.

– What think'st thou of the masque? will it be well?
– As well as masques can be.
– As masques can be!
– Yes; they must commend their king, and speak in praise
Of the assembly, bless the bride and bridegroom
In person of some god; they're tied to rule
Of flattery.

Although the Masque was an expression of monarchical authority and came to end when that authority ceased to exist, it made a great contribution to the public theatres in its unusual combination of poetry, music, and dance and in many technical innovations which Inigo Jones had copied from the Italian intermezzi.

Anthologies of the better-known Masques are not difficult to find. A large collection of Inigo Jones's designs exists at Chatsworth House in Derbyshire; many of these are reproduced in histories of the theatre and the whole collection has been reproduced in a work of splendid scholarship, Inigo Jones: the Theatre of the Stuart Court *by Stephen Orgel and Roy Strong.*

48 The Emergence of the Professional Actor in England

During the Middle Ages it had been increasingly the custom for kings and noblemen to attach minstrels to their staff. As drama became secularized and society became more complex the minstrels were replaced by small companies of players. These were the first professional actors.

The increase in the number of these companies was made possible by the growing number of secularized interludes which they could perform and for which there was a demand. When a troupe, which at first numbered between four and six players, was not required to perform for its patron, it went on tour to local towns where the demise of the cycles had left potential audiences short of entertainment. Arriving in a new town they would give a performance in front of the mayor and members of the town council who would then give them permission (or not) to play public performances.

An actor's life has always been hard. Anyone whose livelihood depends on entertaining people places himself in a basically unstable situation; for there is nothing predictable about public taste. If the public does not care for an entertainment that is being offered, it stays away. The actor, after all, is the man who makes his living by assuming the roles of other people, feigning madness, making love, murdering the king. Has he a life of his own? Is there a stable personality behind all those masks? In the sixteenth century the medieval tradition that assigned to every man a place in society had not died out. How could the actor be placed in any recognized category? The authorities, many of whom were unable to smother their prejudices, demanded that as a limited guarantee of respectability an actor should acquire the 'protection' of a baron or 'a personage of very high degree', as the Act put it, and wear his livery. This was not altogether a disadvantage for generous patrons helped their players with clothes, money, and influential support in times of difficulty.

The actor who was unattached to a member of the established social order was therefore a social outcast and classed with rogues and vagabonds, an attitude of which the acting profession has divested itself completely only in the present century. Fortunately for the actors a powerful dynamic came from the dramatists. The land was suddenly filled with plays, and actors were required to act them. The profession then had a basis on which to organize itself.

The new dramatists tended to come from the ranks of the teaching profession, from the universities, the newly-founded grammar schools, and the Inns of Court where the legal profession was educated. The Catholic clergy had come to be slightly ashamed of the Mysteries and the Protestant clergy were downright critical. In fact there were a number of non-conformist sects, centring particularly around the teaching of Calvin, who were disposed to be hostile to all forms of drama and found reasons for their opposition in the abuses attendant on it.

The Puritan opposition to the stage came under four headings – a general dislike of all actors, a general disapproval of what they called 'the counterfeiting of wanton behaviour on the stage' together with impurity of speech and gesture, a profound disgust at men dressing up as women, and the waste of time and money involved in play-going and play-acting. This attitude was in general supported by the public authorities who considered that the gathering of crowds at a theatrical performance was a breeding ground for the plague and a meeting-place for undesirables.

There had been periodic attacks on drama throughout the Middle Ages. Such attacks gathered force during the reigns of Henry VIII and Edward VI especially when interludes were written with a religious content. Religion was far too delicate an issue to be subject for entertainment and that actors should be in the position of moralists was unthinkable. When London was provided with a couple of theatres and a growing body of plays to fill them, the attacks increased. At least two playwrights underwent conversion and wrote powerful pamphlets in condemnation of the theatre. There was Stephen Gosson whose *The School of Abuse* appeared in 1579 and Anthony Munday who wrote a further diatribe which was published in 1580. A violent attack on the stage was contained in Phillip Stubbes's *Anatomie of Abuses* (1583), while the clerical opposition was led by Archbishop Grindal of York who finally suppressed the last residual staging of the Mysteries.

The whole controversy was the more delicate since in England at the time the relationship between religion and politics was very close, the one reacting sensitively on the other. The aldermen and councillors of the Corporation of the City of London were mostly Anglicans and basically hostile to the theatre, while Queen Elizabeth and her court, especially her advisory body, the Privy Council, a group of about twenty of the most influential men in the country, were humanists and sympathetic to the stage – so long as it preserved a certain decency. Throughout the reign of Elizabeth there was an unresolved conflict between the Privy Council, representing the Queen and the nobility, and the Corporation, which stood for middle-class interests, who constantly invoked plague, political tension, or artistic scandal to persuade the Council to join them in total suppression of the stage. It was one of the skills of Elizabeth to know how to handle such contradictions. The Stuarts did not know and the result was civil war.

The changing composition and the endless comings and goings of the theatrical troupes under Elizabeth I is an extremely complicated story; but there is little doubt that the most significant company was the one attached to the Earl of Leicester. The leader was James Burbage (*c.*1530–97) who before becoming interested in the theatre had been a carpenter. In 1576 he built a theatre and called it the Theatre. More will be said about it in the next chapter. The Earl of Leicester's Men changed their patron from time to time, as was customary, and appear in 1594 as the Lord Chamberlain's Men, then under James I as the King's Men. From about 1592 they included William Shakespeare in their company, both as an actor and dramatist and were clearly, with only one serious rival, the leading theatrical company in the country until the closing of the theatres in 1642. All of which suggests that James Burbage, together with his sons Cuthbert, who was an administrator, and Richard, who was one of the great actors of the age, were a family of considerable theatrical flair and ability.

The comings and goings of the other companies are a subject for specialist study. The only company that proved a serious rival to the Lord Chamberlain's Men were the Lord Admiral's, who after a period of obscurity during the 1580s, appear strongly upon the scene from 1594. They owed their distinction firstly to their leading actor, Edward Alleyn (1566–1626) and secondly to the fact that in 1592 Alleyn married a certain Joan Woodward who was the stepdaughter of Philip Henslowe (d. 1616), a pawnbroker, property speculator, shrewd man of business, and first outstanding theatrical manager in English history.

It is impossible to say how many theatrical companies scratched a living in England at the end of the century. The minor ones spent most of their time touring the provinces. There were about six major companies who spent the winter months playing in London and the summer on tour. The existence of these companies was made possible by the richest crop of plays that any country has ever produced during a single period of some twenty or thirty years. But before considering the plays it will be helpful to consider the theatres in which they were first staged.

Useful books on the material covered in this section are David Bevington's From Mankind to Marlowe: Growth and Structure in the Popular Drama of Tudor England *and M. C. Bradbrook's* The Rise of the Common Player.

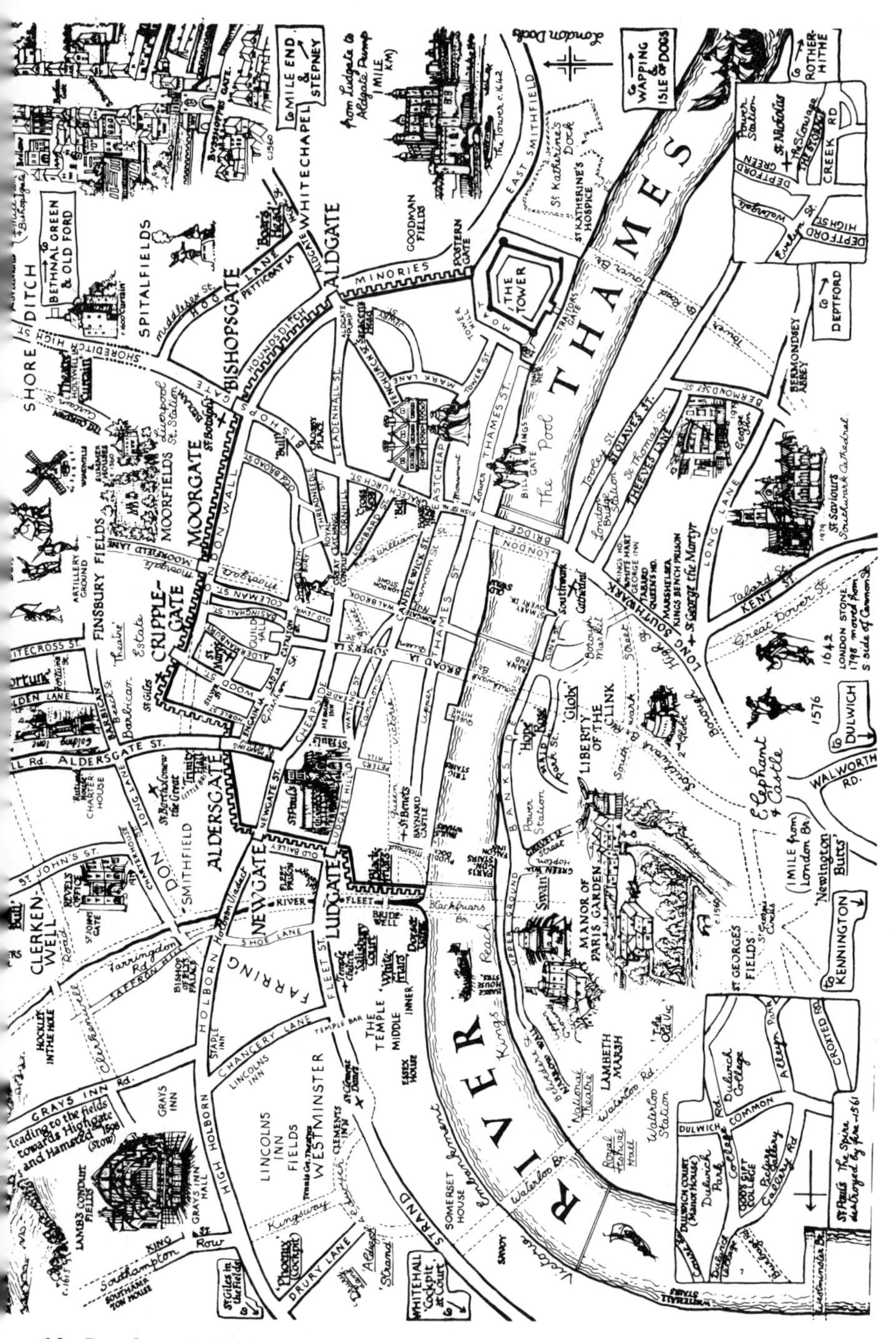

10. London playhouses
This formal plan by Grace Golden shows all the playhouses of the sixteenth and seventeenth century in relation to London of the twentieth century. The old city wall with its gates is clearly marked.

49 Elizabethan and Jacobean Theatre in London

The impetus to build a permanent home in the form of a theatre was largely a result of the Vagrancy Act of 1572 which was intended to rid the country of vagabonds among whom unattached companies of actors were included.

In the early 1570s there were various theatrical venues in London, mostly consisting of inn yards where open-air performances could be given under somewhat unsatisfactory conditions. There was the Bel Savage Inn on Ludgate Hill, the Bull Inn in Bishopsgate, the Bell in the same area, and several others. But being within the city walls, and so under the jurisdiction of the Corporation of the City of London, whose members were basically opposed to theatrical performances, they were under constant threat of closure and could enjoy little security or continuity of policy.

James Burbage therefore built his theatre outside the city walls, a mile or so to the north, in an area already associated with entertainment, known as Finsbury Fields. The Middlesex councillors, in whose country the theatre stood, were less hostile than those of London.

The Theatre cost James Burbage £700 to build. He borrowed the money from his wife's brother-in-law, James Braine, who was a grocer. We know little about the details of the Theatre except by inference. It was probably octagonal with a very large stage around which the audience stood in an area known as 'the pit'. This in turn was surrounded by three galleries in which patrons sat on payment of a higher entrance fee. The Theatre probably had a capacity of over 2,000.

That the venture was a success is suggested by the fact that a year or so later a certain Henry Laneman built a second theatre close by and called it the Curtain; but little is known about its design or use.

The third theatre to be built in London was the Rose. This marks the entry of Philip Henslowe into theatrical management. He had it built in 1588, choosing a site south of the river in an area known as Bankside, which was also outside the jurisdiction of the Corportion of London. Its most distinguished period was between 1594 and 1600 when it was the home of Edward Alleyn and the Lord Admiral's Men, and the scene of the first production of many important plays.

A fourth theatre, the Swan, was built by Francis Langley in 1595. It was also on Bankside about as near the Rose as the Curtain was to the Theatre.

So by the turn of the century there were four theatres in London, two to the north of the city and two to the south. They were a source of great concern to the City councillors, who did their best to persuade their opposite numbers in the counties of Middlesex to the north and Surrey to the south to join their prohibitions; but they got little positive response.

By this time important developments were taking place at the Theatre. In 1597 the original twenty-one-year lease ran out and complicated negotiations ensued between the Burbages and Giles Alleyn, the landlord. Alleyn was exasperatingly vague. The company moved to the nearby Curtain. Alleyn then produced a new lease. The terms were unacceptable and the Burbages refused to sign. Alleyn retorted that the Theatre thereby became his property and that he intended to pull it down and put the materials of which it was made 'to better use'.

Cuthbert reported the situation to his colleagues. There appears to have been a kind of Committee of Management consisting, in addition to the Burbages, of leading members of the company who included John Heminge, Augustine Phillips, Thomas Pope, William Kemp (the clown of the company), and William Shakespeare. They decided to forestall Alleyn by pulling down the theatre themselves and erecting it elsewhere. There were few alternatives to Bankside where there were already two theatres and a bear-baiting ring.

They carried out their plan in December 1598, carted the timbers across the Thames and rebuilt their theatre on the South Bank. They called it the Globe. Outside the main entrance they erected a sign of Hercules bearing the world on his shoulders and beneath it the legend, *Totus mundus agit histrionem*, which roughly means, 'All the world's a stage'.

Henslowe withdrew from direct competition and the next year commissioned Peter Street, a carpenter who had had the job of dismantling the Theatre and building the Globe, to build a replica back in Shoreditch, half a mile west of the Curtain. This theatre was called the Fortune.

Meanwhile the Lord Chamberlain's Men had acquired another theatre. It was known as the Blackfriars and consisted of the upper floor of a priory which had been 'suppressed' in 1538, and converted for theatrical use by one of the children's companies which were popular at the time. Burbage, however, did not use the theatre himself but leased it back to the children until 1608. The King's Men then occupied the theatre themselves with considerable effect on Shakespeare's style of writing. The masque-like quality of his last plays, *Cymbeline*, *A Winter's Tale*, and *The Tempest* is often attributed to indoor staging with a smaller and more select audience.

Theatre-going in late Elizabethan and early Jacobean London was a popular way of spending the afternoon, especially among the well-to-do. In 1600 the City had a population of about 160,000. There were five theatres giving performances every day of the week. The average daily attendance at the Rose, for example, is reckoned to have been about 1,250 or about 50 per cent of capacity. While there is considerable uncertainty among historians on the social composition of audiences, research suggests that the most influential theatre-goers, though not necessarily the most numerous, were those with money to spare and time on their hands.

So great was the demand for new plays that by the turn of the century collaboration was virtually essential. Writers were paid £1 an act or between £5 and £10 for a complete script, which then became the property of the company who witheld publication so that it could not be copied or played by a rival company, there being no copyright laws in those days. The 'hack' playwright Henry Chettle (1560–1607) claimed to have had a hand in forty-eight plays and Thomas Heywood (*c.*1570–1641), the author of that fine play *A Woman Killed with Kindness*, claimed to have had 'at least a finger' in 220.

Performances began at 2 p.m. and played without a break. When plays were printed they were sometimes, though erratically, divided into five acts. But in performance there were no intervals and there was little, if any, scenery. But the costumes, which the players were often given by their wealthy patrons, were said to have been very fine. Although there are many records of theatres having been closed during the summer on account of the plague, there are none of winter closures owing to bad weather. The ability of the plays and their players to attract audiences and to hold their attention in such conditions was extraordinary.

The Elizabethan theatre was London's theatre. In 1576 when the population was about 150,000 the population of the next largest cities, Bristol and Norwich, was 12,000. By the end of the reign London was a thriving centre of commerce, education, and entertainment. There were innumerable shops selling a vast array of goods. In the Strand alone there were fifty goldsmith's shops. There were few comparable cities anywhere.

Attendances have been worked out on the basis of receipts of which Henslowe kept careful records. These can be studied in his Diaries. *The composition of Elizabethan theatre audiences has been fully discussed in a number of books.*

The design of the Globe has been the subject of considerable controversy, fully discussed and illustrated in The Globe Restored *by C. Walter Hodges.*

A book covering many important aspects of the Elizabethan theatre is G. B. Harrison's Elizabethan Plays and Players.

50 English Drama in the Sixteenth Century

The fundamental reason why English drama developed on wholly different lines from French and Italian drama was that England enjoyed a form of political freedom that had been established by Magna Carta in 1215. Over many hundreds of years England was associated in the minds of many Europeans with a freedom that was not enjoyed elsewhere. There was no other country with so assured a sense of national identity or a political structure so firmly established.

This begins to explain why the classical revival made far less impact in England than it did elsewhere. It was not that English scholars were less interested in the literature of Greece and Rome than their French and Italian counterparts, but they studied it for its own sake, not for its political and cultural associations. Humanism did not become a cult as it did in Italy because in England there was no cultural gap which classical literature was seized upon to fill; and neither Henry VIII nor Elizabeth needed to reinforce their authority by assuming the role of a Roman Emperor.

Much of the art that England did produce was essentially English. This is particularly true of her drama. There was no violent change of style under the impact of humanism, although there was a process of incorporation. Nor did the English playwrights need to be warned off religious drama, though some rashly dabbled in the subject and were sharply rebuked. The executions of Catholics under Henry VIII and of Protestants under Mary Tudor were warning enough. Even so, a certain number of plays were written between about 1550 and 1570 that were Protestant in content and allegorical in manner. One of the better known is *Kynge Johan* by John Bale (1495–1563). This play, though a kind of chronicle in the manner that was to be developed by

Shakespeare, is full of such characters as Sedition, Civil Order, Private Wealth, and Dissimulation. But such plays were discouraged under Queen Elizabeth as dangerous to social stability and there even became established a limited form of censorship under the Office of Revels.

Most plays that we would now call comedies were still referred to as interludes. Two such plays were Nicholas Udall's *(Ralph) Roister Doister* (*c*.1553) which the author, who was for a time headmaster of Eton, claimed to have been written in the manner of a Roman comedy, and *Gammar Gurton's Needle* probably written by William Stevenson, who was a Cambridge don.

It is no accident that the last two authors were educationists. They represented the growing interest of teachers in classical drama. But whatever they may have owed privately to reading Plautus and Terence it is difficult to imagine anything more wholly English than these two plays. *Roister Doister* is a boisterous comedy about the courting of Dame Christian Custance by Mathewe Merrygreeke, and in *Gammar Gurton's Needle* the author manages to spread over five acts a story that turns on the search for a needle that is eventually found in the seat of one of the characters' trousers. In George Gasgoyne's *Supposes* (1566), which the author claims to have been a translation of Ariosto's *I Suppositi*, the dialogue is so racily English that there is hardly a trace of the Italian original.

Then there is the case of tragedy. Seneca was held to be as powerful a model for writers of tragedy as Plautus and Terence were for comedy. Yet one wonders how seriously English tragic dramatists took their model. Humanism, which inspired this reverence for Seneca, had insisted upon the responsibility of man for his own actions; yet Seneca, a dour and depressing philosopher, saw man as the victim of forces beyond his control. A considerable number of Senecan tragedies were written in the 1560s and 1570s. They conform to a Senecan model in their five-act structure, their overwhelming sensationalism, and their obsession with horrifying events. But the better examples of the kind have an authentic flavour that owes nothing to the Roman dramatist. The best-known English tragedy is probably *Gorboduc* or *Ferrex and Porrex* (staged in 1561). It was the work of two young laywers, Thomas Sackville and Thomas Norton; but it is a butchery of a play about a king who divides his kingdom between his sons, one of whom murders the other only to be murdered in turn by his mother who is then killed by a rebellious people. (It seems to have been intended as a warning against a divided kingdom.)

At about the same time the Vice-Chancellor of Cambridge University wrote *Cambises*, a play about a tyrannical Persian monarch, which includes three soldiers called Huf, Ruf, and Snuf, two clownish countrymen called Hob and Lob, and a crowd of allegorical characters such as Shame, Diligence, and Councell. There is nothing very Senecan about this.

All this is not to deny that the Tudor dramatists were deeply concerned with the nature of writing plays and their responsibilities as artists. Few of them would have denied that art has some kind of didactic function. Art should be used to reduce reality to moral order and to show that the good survives at the expense of the bad. The high moral tone of the Mysteries persisted. Thus Sir Philip Sidney proposes in his important essay, *An Apologie for Poetrie* (written in 1580 but not published until 1595) that the artist who can organize reality according to his own rules is more meritorious than the historian who must record the unpleasant aspects of real life without being able to do anything about them. The question then arises whether the poet-playwright reorganizes reality according to his inner vision or a moral order that is accepted by society. The problem exercised the acute intelligence of Sir Francis Bacon who in *The Advancement of Learning* (1605) laments that the stage has been inadequately used to establish 'a means of educating men's minds to virtue'. Does the playwright present reality as he sees it or as he thinks it ought to be? And what are the values on which he should base his judgement?

Another problem which exercised the playwrights of the time was that of the form of verse they should use, and this of course was related to the development of vernacular speech itself. The alliterative verse of the Middle Ages was out of fashion. The moralities employed a variety of verse-forms. *Cambises* was written in heavy jog-trot seven-foot rhymed couplets. *Supposes* was written in prose. But throughout the period there gradually emerged the iambic pentameter, the five-stressed line which responded to the rhythms of vernacular speech. It was used successfully in *Gorboduc* and developed by succeeding dramatists.

The moral element in the plays was finally destroyed by the existence of a large permanent theatre, followed shortly by a second, drawing on a popular audience that paid for admission. These theatres created a tremendous demand for new plays, for it was extremely unusual for a play to be revived, once it had run for a few performances. Writers were quick to respond to this growing market. And the kind of plays they wrote were shaped less by classical models on which they probably were lectured at university, and moral issues on which the philosophers constantly held forth, than by the demands of an audience of a thousand men and women who paid to be entertained on a cold winter's afternoon.

The first group of writers who tried to earn a living by their pen and who turned with varying degrees of success to the theatre were nearly all university educated. The eldest was John Lyly (*c.*1554–1606) who had been to both Oxford and Cambridge. But he did not write for the public theatres. In his mid-twenties he wrote a book called *Euphues*, which was a model of elegant, witty, and highly artificial prose and enormously influential in high-class society. He then became Vice-Master of the Children of St Paul's who, with the Children of the Chapel Royal, formed the major choir schools of London. For them he wrote a number of plays in his elegant euphuistic style and these were staged at court before the Queen. The best known are *Campaspe* (1584) and *Endimion* (1591). The theatrical quality of these plays is negligible but the prose dialogue is of unparalleled elegance.

Thomas Lodge (1557–1625) wrote poetry, romances, and plays. Thomas Nashe (1567–1602) wrote a number of pamphlets in a brilliantly vivid and racy style, collaborated in several plays and composed himself *Summer's Last Will and Testament* (1592). George Peele (1558–96) wrote some exquisite lyric poety and a number of plays including *David and Bethsabe* and *The Old Wives' Tale*. Robert Greene (1558–92) wrote prolifically during his short life. His play *A Looking-Glass for London and for England* (1588), which he wrote in collaboration with Thomas Lodge, still shows traces of the morality, but his *James IV* (*c*.1590) is one of the best plays of the period. Thomas Kyd (*c*.1557–94) led a short unhappy life but wrote one of the most important of these early Elizabethan plays, *The Spanish Tragedy*, a furious farrago of bloodshed and revenge.

These young men did not constitute a coherent group, school, or academy, though they are often referred to as the 'University Wits'; but they exercised a considerable influence on each other and frequently collaborated.

By far the most important of the group was Christopher Marlowe (1564–93), an astonishing young man who wrote six extraordinary plays and some exquisite poetry before being killed in a tavern brawl at the age of twenty-nine. Marlowe's achievement was to establish drama as a major form of art of considerable distinction and great popularity. The response of the public to his plays was immediate. *Tamburlaine* and *Dr Faustus* were two of the most outstandingly successful plays of the period and provided Edward Alleyn with his finest acting roles.

Christopher Marlowe received a classical education at King's School, Canterbury, and Corpus Christi College, Cambridge, and while in no sense a humanist in the continental sense he expressed in his plays the spirit of the Renaissance perhaps more than any other writer, even Shakespeare. His heroes are powerful, fearless, questing independent individuals. *Tamburlaine* is about a Scythian shepherd who becomes King of Persia and sets out to conquer the world. At the climax of part one he comes on stage in a chariot drawn by seven conquered kings with bits in their mouths; but in part two his lust for power ends in his ruin. *The Jew of Malta* shows a man who envisages using his immense wealth for some outstanding purpose, and *Dr Faustus* is the man who makes a compact with the devil in return for unlimited power. *Edward II*, though depicting a weak king, is a reflection of the intrigues that were typical of Renaissance politics, and *The Massacre at Paris* (the notorious Massacre of St. Bartholomew) shows those politics operating in a particularly brutal manner.

Marlowe was able to present these prodigious themes in verse of similar splendour. When Ben Jonson wrote of 'Marlowe's mighty line' he referred to the extraordinary manner in which Marlowe was able to give the iambic pentameter, the five-stressed line, a remarkable weight and length. He lacked the poetic flexibility that Shakespeare developed but he also lacked the flexibility of thought that made such linguistic flexibility necessary. Marlowe's heroes are of heroic proportions but limited psychology.

Most of the plays mentioned in this section are available, usually in collections of pre-Shakespearian drama. Much of the work of the pamphleteers is also available and provides a fascinating picture of the social background. Useful critical studies of the period include Wolfgang Clemen's English Tragedy before Shakespeare.

51 | William Shakespeare

In 1592 or thereabouts, at the height of all this activity, Shakespeare arrived in London. He had been born and educated in the Warwickshire town of Stratford-on-Avon, and was married, the evidence suggests, none too happily. By then he was twenty-six and there is much interest in how he passed his early twenties. Arriving in London he seems to have found employment with the Lord Chamberlain's Men and quickly began writing plays. From a comment by George Greene one gathers that he introduced a competitive element that was not altogether welcomed by his rivals. He also became an actor and in due course a shareholder in the company.

Within the space of about twenty years he wrote thirty-six plays and a great deal of poetry. (Although he died in 1616 he seems to have given up writing and retired to the country in 1611.) This is a considerable output and evidently confirms a comment made by Ben Jonson after Shakespeare's death 'that he ne'er blotted out a line'. In his own time he is credited with having had a hand in thirty other plays. This is by no means unlikely. Many plays were written in collaboration to meet the huge demand and as Shakespeare was by far the most successful dramatist of his day it is not surprising that managements tried to exploit his genius.

Shakespeare wrote for the large bare architectural stage that was common at the time. He wrote in the medieval, not the neo-classical manner. He shows absolutely no interest in Aristotelian rules but changes the scene as the action of the story and his own sense of form demand, a practice which exasperated classicists of his own and subsequent times. Nevertheless it must not be thought that his plays are clumsily put together: in matters of construction Shakespeare worked according to his own dramatic logic in a way that becomes evident as soon as one begins to 'move' any one of his plays.

He wrote in every genre that was current at the time, except of course the neo-classical tradition, and developed each to a high degree of perfection. He picked up the historical chronicle-play tradition from the start. Among his earliest plays (not in chronological order) were the three parts of *Henry VI*, an amazing achievement for a man in his twenties, *Richard II*, *Richard III*, *Henry IV* in two parts (among his supreme masterpieces), *Henry V*, and *Henry VIII*. One learns from these plays very little about English history but a very great deal about the nature of man as a political animal and the nature of political and historical thought at the time of the Tudors.

With *Love's Labour Lost*, *As You Like It*, and *Twelfth Night* he wrote three of the most tender, lyrical, and witty comedies in the language and in so doing freed comedy for all time from the dreary lechers of Plautus and Terence. *Much Ado about Nothing* has a rather bitter undertone in spite of the title.

Although Ben Jonson sneered at his 'little Latin and less Greek' Shakespeare was far from uninterested in the culture of Greece and Rome and, using a translation of Plutarch and similar publications for his sources, wrote four great plays on classical themes – *Troilus and Cressida*, *Julius Caesar*, *Coriolanus*, and *Antony and Cleopatra* (and perhaps one should include the bitter *Timon of Athens*). All this only fifty years after *Cléopâtre captive*.

In tragedy his output was similarly extraordinary. From the rather crude and melodramatic *Titus Andronicus*, which perhaps should have been included among his Roman plays, he went on to write, between 1601 and 1608, four of the greatest tragedies of all time, *Hamlet*, *Othello*, *Macbeth*, and *King Lear*, the only tragedies ever to have been written comparable with the Greeks. The philosophic density of these plays, their superb poetry, their vivid depiction of a great variety of human beings, have led some critics to claim that they are better read than staged. This is a matter of taste. Among their many outstanding qualities is their intense theatricality. Shakespeare was as much a playwright as a poet.

From the period of his tragedies comes a group of plays of intense bitterness – *Measure for Measure*, *Troilus and Cressida*, and *Timon of Athens*; but he weathered whatever experience it was that soured his view of life and ended his career with three rich, complex, difficult plays – *Cymbeline*, *The Winters Tale*, and *The Tempest*.

And even this catalogue omits some of his lesser but still interesting plays like *Two Gentlemen of Verona* and *Alls Well that Ends Well*.

Shakespeare's immense stature can be considered under a number of headings. First, there is the variety of his subject-matter. Although he selected his themes from a great variety of sources, as was the custom of the time, he created in each of his plays a new reality, a world of his own devising. In all his thirty-six plays he never repeats the same imaginative idea or returns to the same setting although there are a number of philosophical themes that run through his major works.

He projected this immense range of imaginative experience through a vast array of characters. He was as much at ease in depicting the rogueries of Falstaff, the weaknesses of Richard II, the villainy of Richard III, the exquisite eroticism of Rosalind, the complexities of Hamlet, the passion of Cleopatra, the bitter transports of Lear, the jealousy of Leontes, the furies of Hotspur, the felicities of Viola, the venom and humanity of Shylock.

His tool was a consummate mastery of language. He could switch in a moment and with complete conviction from the murder scene in *Macbeth* to a drunken porter, from the sophisticated wit of Beatrice to the absurdities of Dogberry and Verges, from the jealous rage of Othello to the ironic villany of Iago.

Some years after Shakespeare's death there took place an event unique in the publishing history of the time. Two of his fellow actors, James Heming and Henry Condell, made a collection of his plays and had them published in a large folio edition. It was a hazardous undertaking. In their introduction they refer to Shakespeare as 'a happy imitater of Nature' and 'a most gentle expresser of it'. Indeed, the constant tenor of the introductory essays and poems is that Shakespeare was of a gentle and amiable temperament. Ben Jonson, in the poem that refers to him as 'sweet swan of Avon', 'To the Memory of My Beloved, the Author, Mr. William Shakespeare', and twits him for his lack of classical scholarship, concludes with the moving lines:

My Shakespeare rise; I will not lodge thee by
Chaucer or Spencer, or bid Beaumont lye
A little further, to make thee a roome:
Thou art a monument without a tombe,
And art alive still, while thy Booke doth live,
And we have wits to read and praise to give.

He is, and we have.

Nothing perhaps points so clearly to the unparalleled and inexhaustible richness of Shakespeare than the books and commentaries that continue to pour forth in many different languages. The output amounts to many thousands of books a year. Shakespearian scholarship is an industry in itself. But no critical work, of course, can replace a careful reading of the plays themselves or an imaginative and thoughtful production.

Shakespearian criticism has now become a study in its own right. Those interested in the subject will turn to Samuel Johnson, Charles Lamb, A. C. Bradley, J. Dover Wilson, Wilson Knight, and the many admirable critics who have dealt with one aspect or another of this prodigious dramatist.

Perhaps the most authentic and reliable biography is by S. Schoenbaum.

52 | Jacobean Comedy

Queen Elizabeth died in 1603 leaving the monarchy uniquely strong and respected. A mere forty-six years later the King of England was executed. Nothing shows more clearly the changes that had taken place in British society during this short period.

The most obvious change was that the wisdom of Elizabeth had been replaced by the bigotry of the Stuarts. Any kind of autocratic rule by a monarch who was less than a genius at manipulating the government was no longer possible. Less obvious but in some ways even more important were the economic changes that had taken place in a country which had been socially more stable than its political history suggests.

The influx of Spanish-American gold and the development of productive techniques had led to a considerable increase in the number of people with a great variety of financial, industrial, and territorial interests. This was the class from which Cromwell recruited his Ironsides, Anglican, commercially-minded, against autocracy but not necessarily against the monarchy. It was the absolute failure of James I and his son Charles I to respond to the demand of this class for political representation that led to the disaster of 1649.

The new social status of the theatre made things both more interesting and more difficult for the playwright; for instead of writing to suit the tastes of the king, the patron, and a small circle of courtiers, whose inclinations could be fairly accurately gauged, he had now to entertain a vast and heterogeneous public with unpredictable tastes and reactions. Since James I and his Queen were far more interested in their Masques than in the theatre, the Jacobean dramatists were free to exploit a mixture of private and public fantasy.

It is the nature of things that an artist, however original his conceptions, should work very broadly within certain conventions and attitudes laid down by his immediate predecessors and the nature of contemporary society. It is difficult to think of a single artist who has created work right outside the atmosphere of his own age. Indeed, since most artists are dependent on the approbation of a patron or the public for their living, they are only too willing to cut their coat according to the fashions of the times. It is therefore not surprising that against the background of an increasingly mercenary society, Jacobean playwrights should have dealt increasingly with social and economic problems. Shakespeare is virtually the only major dramatist of the time whose comedies are entirely free from this prevailing obsession with money. One finds this tendency in the plays of the eldest of the Jacobean dramatists, George Chapman (*c.*1559–*c.*1634). He was a man of great intellectual power, a distinguished scholar who is still respected for his fine translation of Homer. His earliest comedies, written round the turn of the century, are on classical models, but *Monsieur D'Olive* (*c.*1606), though a rather stupid story, gives a vivid picture of a social upstart, and *Eastward Hoe* (*c.*1605) of life among London apprentices and their masters.

Eastward Hoe is additionally interesting for three reasons: it is a good example of a play that was written as a result of collaboration between three distinguished writers, the other two being Ben Jonson and John Marston; it contained some slighting reference to the Scots which offended the King, and led to the three dramatists, all in their forties, being imprisoned; and it was first performed by one of the Companies of Children at the Blackfriars Theatre.

The unhappy consequences of *Eastward Hoe* emphasize another hazard faced by Jacobean playwrights. A play on a similar theme was the better-known *The Shoemaker's Holiday* of Thomas Dekker (*c.*1570–1632). Dekker was a Londoner and the author of a number of pamphlets which give a vivid picture of life in the capital. Yet a gifted writer who might have been expected to exploit this kind of social realism, wrote only one other play in this style, and that only remotely so, *The Roaring Girl*. The reason was probably the operation of the censorship laws. In 1559 Queen Elizabeth, who had inherited an extremely delicate political situation, sent out an order nationwide to all mayors and justices of the peace that they were to give particular attention to the performance of interludes and to permit none to be played wherein matters of religion or the government of the country were depicted. In 1581, under pressure from the Corporation of the City of London, she strengthened this control by giving additional powers of censorship to Edmund Tilney, Master of the Revels. But there were so many interested parties and the regulations were so imprecise that playwrights and players did not feel themselves to be unduly threatened. It was in writing comedy, which is largely concerned with jesting at the more pompous or absurd aspects of society, and is therefore more vulnerable than tragedy, that playwrights had to be particularly circumspect.

A writer who turned frequently to social comedy and satire was Thomas Middleton (*c.*1570–1627), another Londoner and a friend of Dekker. Many of his plays are full of social comment. *Michaelmas Terme* (1607) is on the popular subject of a wealthy landowner who feigns death to test the love of his wife and son. *A Trick to Catch an Old One* (1608) is about the strategies of a young waster to extract money from a wealthy uncle. *The Roaring Girl* (1611), already mentioned in connection with Dekker, is about low-life society in London. All these and many other plays turn on the existence of a leisured class and the need for money to sustain its privileged position.

Another playwright who was clearly interested in the existence of an acquisitive society and of marriages that are arranged on the basis of the dowry that goes along with the bride who thereby becomes a piece of property, was Philip Massinger (1583–1640). *The City Madam* (1632) makes a sharp comment on how social status is increasingly measured in terms of food, clothes, and property, and *A New Way to Pay Old Debts* (1633), a play which includes the great acting role of Sir Giles Overreach, is about a landowner who has acquired great wealth by blackguarding his neighbours.

But it is in the plays of Ben Jonson, who after Shakespeare is the most important writer of the age, that we find the greatest preoccupation with social themes, and, as with Chapman, this is the more surprising since he was a leading classical scholar. Ben Jonson (1572–1637) was of working-class origins; but he was educated by the great scholar, William Camden, who gave him a passion for the classics. On leaving school he seems to have found difficulty in securing employment and worked for a time as a bricklayer and as a soldier in the Netherlands. He then became a dramatic hack for Henslowe and wrote his first original play, *Every Man in His Humour*, in 1598. It was staged at the Curtain by the Lord Chamberlain's Men with Shakespeare in the cast. The next year he wrote *Every Man out of His Humour*. These two plays, though not directly concerned with an acquisitive society, in which his interest was to come later, give a vivid picture of London life, teeming with vigorous characters and lively dialogue. (By humour Jonson was referring to that aspect of human naure which we might call temperament.)

In his Preface to the latter play he makes his intentions clear:

> I'll strip the ragged follies of the time
> Naked as at their birth . . . (the satirist)
>
> I fear no mood stamp'd in a private brow,
> When I am pleased t'unmask a public vice (the moralist)

while elsewhere he writes disparagingly of plays about York and Lancaster with their 'creaking thrones', their simulated thunder, and all the paraphernalia of theatrical effects, clearly poking fun at Shakespeare.

It was soon after this that he began to write Court Masques and at the same time to deliver himself of four of the most satirical, amusing, and inventive comedies in the language. *Volpone* (1606) is the very archetype of the acquisitive monster who feigns illness in order to cheat rich presents from similarly rapacious creatures who hope to benefit from his will. *Epicoene* or the *The Silent Women* is a gigantic farce about a wealthy old eccentric on whom a crowd of tricksters foist a pretending wife to rob him of his wealth. In *The Alchemist* (1610) a trio of tricksters, left to look after their master's house, set out to cozen, cheat, and deceive a succession of sharply satirized characters of extreme gullibility by claiming the ability to work various miracles through alchemy. *Bartholomew Fair* (1614) is far less taut in construction but gives a great, bawdy, sweaty, steaming picture of a popular London fairground.

It is curious that with all his gifts as a poet, a dramatist, and a scholar his two attempts at classical tragedy should have been so poor. One can immediately see the weakness of *Sejanus* and *Catiline* by comparing them with any of Shakespeare's Roman plays. He is, moreover, the only dramatist who began writing plays in the last years of Queen

Elizabeth and was still writing them during the perilous years of Charles I. His latter plays are not without interest, but they have none of the ferocious vitality of his early comedies.

The period comes to an abrupt end in 1642 when, with the outbreak of the Civil War, the theatres were closed. But while politics were becoming more brutal, plays were becoming softer, less preoccupied with social problems, more of a diversion. The most notable dramatist of the time was James Shirley (1596–1666), a man who combined the two professions of dramatist and schoolmaster. He wrote some forty plays. Of his comedies, which with their romantic patina are quite amusing, the best known is *The Lady of Pleasure* (1634), a charmingly elegant play about the social pretensions of a young wife and the devices employed by her husband to cure her extravagance.

No play shows the change of atmosphere more clearly than *The Jovial Crew* by Richard Brome (*c.*1590–1652), who was secretary for a time to Ben Jonson. This play, written in 1641, gives an almost defiantly idealized picture of a vagrant life, as a group of young middle-class people seek the 'natural life' by joining a band of beggars. There was nothing very enjoyably natural in country or town in the ensuing years.

53 | Jacobean Tragedy

We are dealing with the most formidable body of plays in the English language. In the forty years between the accession of James I in 1603 and the closing of the theatres in 1642 a dozen or so dramatists produced a number of plays which are notable for their lurid stories, their savage, vigorous verse, and their mastery of dramatic form. They are all written in the medieval narrative tradition, and owe nothing to Aristotle or the humanists. They provide a large number of superb acting roles.

They are a testimony to the incessant demand by managements and public for new plays; but they present us with some interesting problems. Some critics have dismissed Jacobean drama as sensational melodramas written to satisfy the depraved appetites of a degenerate public. While this is far too superficial a judgement, the reason for it must be faced. Jacobean tragedy presents us with a gallery of ambitious, lusting, predatory, and unscrupulous men and women. What attracted the dramatists to such themes? If it was a response to public demand, what created this demand?

While it is impossible to answer these questions with any kind of accuracy, one can make a few observations. The first thing to be noted is that Jacobean drama was a new phenomenon. It will already have been noted that most of the leading Jacobean dramatists, men whose plays were staged in the first fifteen years of the seventeenth century, were all born in the 1570s when there was virtually no significant professional drama. As they grew up they created an expressive dramatic form. Their tastes and public taste were synonymous. But what created this taste?

The times were exceedingly brutal. Within a very short distance of the theatres on the South Bank there stood the bear-baiting ring where it was common sport for bears and bulls to be set upon by dogs and mastiffs; or for a blind bear to be whipped into a state of frenzy by half-a-dozen ruffians. A popular entertainment was a public execution at Tyburn (which was roughly on the site of the present Marble Arch). When the victim had been hanged, his body was cut down, his bowels were cut out and burnt, his heart was removed by the hangman who showed it to the people, his head was cut off, and his body quartered. In 1610 two Catholic priests were taken 'to the place of execution' followed by a crowd of 3,000 'among them many great ladies and gentlemen'. After the quartering, the Catholics in the crowd tried to gather the blood of the martyrs and even pieces of the bodies for relics. Many more stories of a similar kind are recorded.

France had been the scene of prodigious depravities during the Wars of Religion. In Italy depravity was a way of life. The Italians had been as prodigal in their crimes as in their works of art. Poison, murder, massacres of whole families were the counterpart of rape, incest, and every kind of sexual enormity in which the despots were more frequently involved than ordinary citizens, since in their pursuit of power and wealth they had more to gain and lose by the removal of their rivals.

Thus the playwrights created an image of the world in terms of the prevailing brutality. It was a vision of the real world transformed into a poetic world. At the same time it is possible to make a distinction between plays that are clearly 'hack' jobs, written with professional competence but simply to make money, and those that are genuinely creative and written from an inner compulsion with a sense of poetic reality.

Many writers chose France, Italy, and vaguely remote countries like Bohemia as a scene for their plays because it was safer. The court of

James I has been described as a scene of unkempt luxury and dirty splendours in which the King sloped around in an atmosphere of negligent grandeur. No one would accuse James and his descendants of the depravities that were common in the courts of Italy, but in a deteriorating political situation the sharper vices of Italy seemed to provide a safe and enlarged projection of anxieties that haunted Englishmen. When on one occasion a dramatist took an overtly political theme, as Thomas Middleton did in *A Game of Chess* (1624), on the subject of Anglo-Spanish politics, even though he wrapped it up in obscure allegorical trappings, proceedings were taken against author and actors and the play was banned.

The suggestion that the Jacobean writers of tragedy saw their society as bordering on chaos, whether or not they were justified in this view, is born out in the prodigious savagery of George Chapman's tragedies. In *The Tragedy of Charles Duke of Byron* (1608) there occurs the following passage:

> When the thick air hid heaven, and all the stars,
> Were drown'd in humour, tough and hard to pierce,
> When the red sun held not his fixed place;
> Kept not his certain course, his rise and set . . .
> When th'incomposed incursions of floods
> Wasted and eat the earth; and all things shewed
> Wild and disordered: nought was worse than now;
> We must reform and have a new creation
> Of State and government; and on our Chaos
> Will I sit brooding upon another world.

One could hardly have a more explicit statement than that.

Something has already been said about the aloof and independent Thomas Middleton whose finest tragedies are *The Changeling* (1623) and *Women Beware Women* (*c.*1620) though his other plays are far from negligible. An important writer of both tragedy and comedy in the early part of the period was John Marston (*c.*1575–1634) whose plays are complex and embittered. But the greatest tragedies, after those of Shakespeare, are generally considered to have been those of John Webster (*c.*1580–1625). *The White Devil* (*c.*1612) and *The Duchess of Malfi* (*c.*1614) are still revived. He is often credited with having been largely responsible for *The Revenger's Tragedy* (*c.*1607), a great play usually attributed to Cyril Tourneur.

Some critics see the collaboration between Francis Beaumont and John Fletcher as introducing a more romantic note into the violence of Jacobean tragedy. This is certainly true of *Philaster* (1611) but *The Maid's Tragedy*, written in the same year, is of sterner stuff. The romantic element marks a stage in the developing independence of the theatre. Although the medieval and Elizabethan drama was far from being naturalistic, it was concerned with the realities of its times. But it became increasingly the view, both of authorities who had it in their power to control the theatre, and the public who supported it, and who in doing so exercised even greater control though of a different kind, that the drama should concern itself less with religion and politics and more with subjects of a generally entertaining nature. This represents both a gain and a loss.

Beaumont was twenty-two and Fletcher twenty-seven when in 1606 the two men became working partners. John Fletcher (1579–1625), son of a bishop and a would-be courtier, was the more productive of the two, writing fifteen plays in collaboration with Beaumont, sixteen of his own, and a number in collaboration with other writers. Francis Beaumont (1584–1616), who was trained for the Bar, was of a more critical disposition.

By the time of Charles I the two most significant writers of tragedy were John Ford (1586–1639) and Philip Massinger (1583–1640). The shift of emphasis continues. Their plays project a picture less of a tormented world than of tormented individuals inhabiting that world. Ford's masterpiece *'Tis Pity She's a Whore* (*c.*1663) is far too finely written to be dismissed as sensational, although its subject, a passionate affair between brother and sister, is horrifying.

Massinger was the author of some forty plays of which half are lost; but those which survive, of which the fine tragedy, *The Duke of Milan* (1620), and *The Great Duke of Florence* (1627) are among the most successful, continue the movement towards a kind of romanticism.

On the whole however, the Jacobean and Carolingian dramatists maintained the distinction between tragedy and comedy but defined them differently. The distinction was no longer one of class but of subject-matter, tragedy dealing with problems of politics and power, comedy with social and sexual matters often related to money and property.

But the really extraordinary feature of the whole period is the speed with which a popular drama developed. In 1580 plays were being written by academics, intellectuals, schoolmasters, and enterprising amateurs: twenty years later there were five theatres in London, a number of professional companies, at least a dozen dramatists earning their living from the theatre, and a couple of outstanding genius. The only comparable phenomenon was Athens at the time of Sophokles.

The plays that were written between 1590 and 1630 were as remarkable for their subject-matter as they were for their quantity. The dramatists could look for little help from their ancestors. Plautus,

Terence, and Seneca were of little help to authors who were writing for a popular audience and who in any case were interested in projecting on to the stage some kind of an image of contemporary society. The Mysteries were unsuitable in form and of a content that was forbidden; the moralities, like all these forms, left lingering wisps of material but not a substantial tradition. So the dramatists turned to every possible source, English and European history, particularly the invaluable chronicles of Raphael Holinshed, contemporary translations of Plutarch's lives of the Greeks and Romans, and the increasingly popular Italian romances and short stories.

It must be emphasized: a certain popular vigour of expression was imposed on them by the necessity of entertaining an audience for whom Plautus was little more than a name. That the dramatists were able to achieve such vigour was partly due to their mastery of language. One has only to read a few lines of Chaucer, who died about two hundred years previously, and almost any of Shakespeare's plays to see the development that had taken place. 1609 was the year of publication of the finest of all translations of the Bible, a work which along with the plays of Shakespeare is the greatest piece of literature in the language. Shakespeare used a vocabulary of well over 20,000 words, Milton some 8,000, the Authorized version about 6,500, but the contemporary Englishmen uses a couple of thousand if he is well educated. The depth and breadth of Shakespeare's imagery and thought is due to his ability to make use of this prodigious vocabulary.

The plays of Shakespeare's contemporaries, less intensely poetic, were nearly all written for this same popular audience. The sheer vigour of expression which is as evident in a pamphlet by John Nash as it is in *King Lear*, the constant playing with and intricate manipulation of words, which obscure the sense for contemporary audiences, make absolutely clear that the Elizabethan public delighted as much in language as in a powerful story. In no respect is the difference between the present age and the Elizabethan more marked than in our own increasing distrust in the capacity of language to communicate the human condition contrasted with the Elizabethan confidence in the capacity of man to express every aspect of human experience in words.

There are many critical works on this important period but perhaps the most accessible is Volume 3 of the Revels History of Drama in English.

54 | The Children's Companies

Nothing shows more clearly the curious attitude of society towards women than the fact that no women ever appeared on any stage until the middle of the seventeenth century with the exception of a period in the late Roman theatre when they appeared as dancers. In the Elizabethan and Jacobean theatre women's parts were played by boys. This practice partly accounts for the prevalence of plays in which the women for some reason or other assume men's clothes.

The professional companies often recruited their boys from the children's companies. The practice of acting plays at school was a direct result of the establishment of grammar schools and the classical education they offered. Eton College, for example, was founded in 1441 and maintained a company of boy actors until the 1570s. There was a company at Westminster school where in 1521 an anonymous author was paid 16d. 'for wryting of a play for the children'; but after a period of great popularity they succumbed like most other boys' companies to the growing popularity of the professional theatres.

Companies, however, from the choir schools attached to St. Paul's Cathedral and the Chapel Royal not only survived the challenge of the 1570s but became serious rivals of the adult professional companies. Between 1558 and 1576 they gave more performances at Court than the professionals – forty-six against thirty-two – and although they then lost favour for a time they came back strongly in 1599 when the Master of the Children of the Chapel, Nathaniel Giles, leased from the Burbages the Blackfriars Theatre and staged regular weekend performances.

The success of the children's companies, like that of any theatrical company, depended on the skill of their teacher-director and his interest in creating some kind of permanent organization. Men such as William Hunnis, Richard Edwardes, Nathaniel Giles, and Henry Evans, who at various times were Masters of one or other of the companies, were not motivated simply by the ambition to show off the skill of their boys in public: education was based on the study of the classics; Plautus and Terence not only wrote excellent Latin but had the advantage of being amusing. The step from reading plays to acting them was prompted by the importance attached by Renaissance educationists to the art of rhetoric. This involved not only the ability to speak well and clearly in public, with appropriate gesture, intonation, and inflection, but to assemble one's thoughts, order them logically, and express them clearly. Until the 1580s most of the plays staged by the children's companies were by Plautus and Terence or new plays written in imitation. The practice of doing new plays in English became common only when such plays were available. The first to exploit this new demand, as we have seen, was John Lyly whose delicate and artificial plays evidently suited the style of these gifted children. Productions of his plays by the Children of St. Paul's became particularly popular at Court.

In 1599 the Children of the Chapel took over the Blackfriars Theatre. Over the next two or three years there was a kind of dramaturgical war, fought chiefly between Ben Jonson, John Marston, and Thomas Dekker in which the playwrights satirized each other and their plays in what can only be called dramatic caricatures. The most typical plays, in what has been called the War of the Theatres, are Jonson's *Cynthia's Revels* (1601) and *Poetaster* (1602), Marston's *Histriomastix* (1599) and Dekker's *Satiromastix* (1601). They are not very interesting plays except in demonstrating the extraordinary vindictiveness of the writers, the interest of the public in a very limited debate, and the ability of young boys to cope with extraordinarily complex and unrewarding texts. All three writers showed themselves capable of far more interesting work.

For the next few years it becomes increasingly difficult to identify any particular style of play that was staged by the children at the Blackfriars. They were responsible for *Eastward Hoe* in 1605 and Jonson's *Epicoene* in 1609 and they played Chapman's savage *Bussy* plays. During these years the organization of the company changed, they broke away from the Chapel Royal, but under the patronage of the Queen became known as the Children of the Queen's Revels. They maintained some kind of existence throughout the Jacobean period but were no longer of much significance in the history of the theatre.

55 | Spanish Drama of the Golden Age

The Spanish people have not on the whole been distinguished for their contribution to European drama. All the more remarkable, therefore, is the outburst of dramatic writing that lasted between 1550 and 1650 and which has been called 'the golden age'.

To understand the nature of this outburst one must take a look at the historical background. The Arabs invaded Spain in 711 and conquered the whole peninsula in seven years: it took the Spaniards 700 years to regain control. The thirteenth century was the period of most energetic reconquest but the impetus slackened around the year 1270 and there was no all-out drive to rid the country of the Arabs until the remainder of the country had been unified and a sense of national identity established. This came about with the union of the two principal states, Aragon and Castile. Aragon, occupying the north-east of the country, was based on the port of Barcelona and had developed a vigorous Mediterranean trade and a cosmopolitan outlook. Castile, lying to the north-west, was largely pastoral and more directly concerned with the war against Islam. Thus when federation was achieved in 1469, as a result of the marriage of Ferdinand of Aragon and Isabella of Castile, Castile was the senior partner so far as internal affairs were concerned. Granada was finally conquered in 1492, a few months before Columbus was authorized to set sail on his adventure.

The Arab-Muslim conquest, however, had not been wholly without its advantages for the Spaniards. The Arabs were a brilliant people and at the time of the conquest their military ardour had been matched with considerable achievements in mechanical, agricultural, and architectural techniques, in mathematics, scholarship, and the arts. The Spaniards were generously paid for the inconvenience of conquest.

In cultural terms the two people established a reasonable co-existence: it was the Church that could not accept a Muslim-Jewish population occupying a large part of the country. The notorious Spanish Inquisition was established in 1478 less to purify orthodox Christians of heresy than to rid the country of Jews and Arabs.

As a result of difficult racial and economic conditions – for the land of Spain is not rich in natural resources – the kings of Aragon and Castile had governed the country in an authoritarian manner, and had been supported by a powerful nobility. Many aspects of Spanish society, such as an extreme inequality between the sexes, the debased position of women, and a rigid code of moral behaviour, they had absorbed from the Arabs. All these elements are evident in the Spanish drama of the Renaissance.

Isabella was a clever and powerful woman. She managed to impose Castilian culture, and in particular its language, on the whole of Spain; at the same time, with a skilful exercise of authority and strong support from the Church she was able to encourage scholarship, classical studies, and all the fresh and vigorous culture of humanism without providing opportunity for the establishment of the reformed religion. Furthermore, within a few years of the death of Isabella (1504) and

Ferdinand (1516), their children, through a process of intermarriage, brought Spain into the mainstream of European politics. Thus the unification of the country, Isabella's leadership, and the influx of American gold gave the country a power and authority that enabled it to play its part in cultural developments along with those in other European countries.

Spain therefore enjoyed a cultural continuity that was unique in Europe; her medieval institutions absorbed Renaissance ideas without being transformed by them. This was particularly true of drama. Not only did the Corpus Christi plays survive into the sixteenth century but became a major dramatic form known as *Autos Sacramentales* (sacred plays) exploited by many of the leading dramatists.

The domination of cultural life by the Church did not prevent the emergence of a lively secular drama at about the same time as in England, France, and Spain. Both the two earliest Spanish dramatists, Juan del Encina (1469–*c*.1529) and Bartolomeo de Torres Naharro (*c*.1485–*c*.1424) came from Salamanca, a lively university town, and both visited Italy. The former wrote some simple secular pieces in addition to a number of *autos*, while Naharro not only wrote amusing comedies but introduced the Spanish public to the dramatic theories of the humanists; they made no deep impression, however.

The most prolific of the first wave of professional dramatists was the Portuguese, Gil Vicente (*c*.1465–*c*.1536). Of his many plays forty-four survive, sixteen in Portuguese, eleven in Spanish, and seventeen in a kind of bilingual dialect. The range of his work seems to have been considerable but difficulty in acquiring texts of his plays and the almost complete absence of translations makes it difficult to compare Spanish dramatic achievement with that of other countries, though clearly it did not lag far behind.

The creation of a Spanish professional theatre is associated with Lope de Rueda (*c*.1510–1565) who was a playwright, an actor, and the manager of a touring company. Cervantes, the famous author of *Don Quixote*, has left a short description of primitive touring conditions. The stage consisted of a few planks lying across some benches and a single sack held the company's costumes and properties. Agustin de Rojas Villandrando (*c*.1572–*c*.1625) has left another entertaining account of a theatrical touring company doing 'one night stands' in his picaresque novel *El Viaje Entretenido* (*Entertaining Journey*).

Development was similar to that in Britain. By the end of the sixteenth century there were permanent theatres in Seville, Valencia, and Madrid. These had evolved from performances given in inn yards with the stage at one end and the audience standing around or watching the performance from overlooking windows. In the 1580s this arrangement was incorporated into the design of permanent theatres which, with their open thrust stage and surrounding galleries, were not dissimilar from their Elizabethan counterparts. In Madrid, the first of these theatres, the Teatro de la Cruz (the Theatre of the Cross) was run by a religious fraternity to help pay for its hospital just as happened in Paris.

Performances nevertheless were thoroughly popular. There was music to begin with, a recited prologue to say what the play was about, then the play, with short farces called *entremes* – the familiar interludes or intermezzi – between the acts, and more music and a dance to finish. The whole performance was accompanied by loud comments, catcalls, and applause from the audience.

The greatest writer of the age and one of the giants of European literature was Miguel de Cervantes Saavedra (1547–1616). Although he wrote a number of plays and delightfully fresh and realistic *entremes* (interludes), none had anything like the stature or the success of his great novel *Don Quixote*.

The first of the giants of Spanish drama was Lope de Vega Carpio (1562–1635), almost an exact contemporary of Shakespeare. He himself claimed to have written 1,500 plays but this is probably an exaggeration. Nevertheless 458 of his plays survive and that is phenomenal enough. In addition to this colossal output he found time to lead a vigorous and promiscuous private life; he sailed with the Armada, writing 11,000 lines of epic poetry while on board, but returned in safety, married a number of times, produced numerous children, and at one time contemplated taking holy orders.

Lope had two great qualities as a playwright: he was a fertile inventor of plots and a fine poet. He employs far more verse-forms than any French or English dramatist and frequently puts dialogue into sonnet form as Shakespeare does once in *Romeo and Juliet.* He is not the most profound of dramatists but he is one of the most felicitous. He provided the growing Spanish drama with a flow of immensely actable and entertaining plays and left a treasury of themes and stories which subsequent playwrights were not slow to exploit.

Of the immediate descendants of Lope de Vega, the two most distinguished were Gabriel Tellez, better known by his pseudonym, Tirso de Molina (1583–1648) and Juan Ruiz de Alarcon y Mendoza (1580–1639). Molina claimed to have written four hundred plays of which eighty-six survive. They are of three kinds – religious plays (*autos*), a few historical plays, and a large number of plays of intrigue which include the first play on the story of Don Juan, *El Burlador de Sevilla* (*The Seducer of Seville*).

Alarcon was a hunchbacked Mexican who came to Spain at the age of twenty, attained high office in the Council for the Indies, wrote twenty-five plays and was widely mocked for his deformity.

The other giant of the period was Pedro Calderon de la Barca

(1600–81). He was educated by the Jesuits and studied for the priesthood although as a youth he was something of a 'tearaway'. At the age of twenty-five he was given a position in the service of a Duke and became an official court playwright. With occasional lapses he enjoyed royal favour throughout his life. As early as 1637 he was awarded a high order of knighthood by Philip IV as the greatest living Spanish dramatist. In 1651, after a period of military service and some domestic upheavals, he was ordained a priest. He continued to write plays, though most were *autos*. When criticized for so doing he defended himself energetically.

His plays fall into the familiar three groups, religious plays and *autos sacramentales*, secular plays on largely contemporary subjects, and what are broadly called 'cloak-and-dagger' plays. Like Lope he employed a variety of metres but unlike Lope he was a deeply thoughtful writer and something of a mystic.

One of the paradoxes of Spanish drama of the sixteenth and seventeenth centuries is that in a country and at a time when there were rigid codes of behaviour and a highly ritualized court life, drama was as free to develop naturally as in Elizabethan England. This was partly due to the innate vitality of the Spanish people who were extremely fond of dancing, though the activity was much condemned by the Church, and also to their freedom from humanistic or other constricting theories. That the dramatists were aware of prevalent ideas about drama is clear from frequent references. Cervantes includes a passage about drama in the forty-eighth chapter of *Don Quixote*. Here he criticises contemporary dramatists for failing to follow the precepts which he incorrectly attributes to Cicero, that drama should be a mirror of human life and a model of good manners, whereas in fact, he says, it is morally licentious and artistically formless. He wrote that in about 1605.

In 1609 Lope de Vega produced his *Arte Nuevo de Hacer Comedias en Este Tempo* (*The New Art of Writing Comedies in This Age*) in which he writes fairly knowledgeably about Aristotle, Menander, Plautus, and Terence, but disclaims all interest in the rules. The mixture of tragedy and comedy, he says, is delightful, follows reality, and gives pleasure. After listing various artistic proprieties he claims: 'I banish Plautus and Terence from my study . . . and write in accordance . . . with the applause of the crowd.'

He did just that. His racy four-stress rhymed couplets move the action with great speed. His vivid stories give a colourful picture of the world in which he lived. He is on the side of the true-hearted peasant against the oppressive overlord – see the fascinating *Fuente Ovejuna* – and frequently represents the King as an idealized, resplendant and highly regarded Head of State, encapsulating the very spirit of justice.

Calderon is no different in spirit but pursues his themes in far greater depth. It is not ridiculous to see something of the spaciousness of Shakespeare in a play like *The Mayor of Zalamea* and his poetic visions in *La Vida es Suena* (*Life is a Dream*, 1635).

The Spanish dramatists established a 'genre' of considerable influence, the so-called 'cloak-and-dagger drama' (*comedia de capa y espada*). (The phrase is derived from the dress of the noblemen who feature in such plays with their enveloping cloaks and their habit of settling disputes with sword and dagger.)

The story of these plays is usually based on the passion of a nobleman for a woman of outstanding beauty. Women were far more free than they had been in the days of the Arab occupation and the sight of girls no longer hidden behind veils sent a wave of passion through the chauvinistic aristocracy. But the determination of high-born men to possess the girl of their desires was frustrated by the rigid social code by which young ladies were controlled, however low of birth. In this sense the Spanish drama is much more limited in range than the Elizabethan and reflects the more constricted social atmosphere in which the dramatists themselves lived. But within those constraints the Spanish dramatists of the golden age produced some plays of great imaginative power.

Historians find it difficult to explain why after about 1680 Spain went into rapid decline both culturally and politically. But that is what happened. Having dominated the continent for two centuries she suddenly ceased to play any significant role in the life of Europe.

Critical and historical books on the Spanish drama are not nearly as plentiful as the interest of the subject demands. N. D. Shergold's A History of the Spanish Stage *and Hugo Rennert's* The Spanish Stage in the Time of Lope de Vega *give the necessary facts.*

The texts of the better-known plays are available in Spanish but there is a lamentable absence of translations. The astonishment with which a production of The Mayor of Zalamea *at the National Theatre in 1981 was received emphasizes ignorance of the Spanish drama even among critics.*

A useful book on the historical background is J. H. Elliott's Imperial Spain 1469–1716.

56 French Drama of the Seventeenth Century: Corneille

The religious wars of the sixteenth century were fiercely fought throughout the French provinces. Uncontrolled by three weak kings and the regency of a middle-aged foreigner, warring factions brought desolation to the hard-won unity of France. The Protestant, Henry of Navarre, with a timely conversion to Catholicism, became Henri IV and brought stability to the country. Reconstruction was then the order of the day. His successor Louis XIII was no less energetic and took advantage of the organizing genius of his chief minister, Richelieu.

This was a crucial period in the development of France as a modern state. Catholicism as a state religion seems to require a more centralized political authority than the non-conforming varieties of Christianity, and this centralization, strongly developed by Louis XIV, is still evident in contemporary France.

The civil wars were disastrous for the French economy but there was still considerable wealth in the hands of the aristocracy who closed ranks round the king. But the strengthening of the central authority led to the impoverishment of the provinces and it was nearly two hundred years before the tensions thus created exploded in the Revolution of 1789.

The religious wars, though delaying economic development, did not destroy the country's cultural life which was much encouraged by the Valois kings. The educated classes received the impact of humanist ideas with considerable enthusiasm and among the distinguished scholars, poets, painters, and artists who are associated with the French Renaissance were two writers of supreme ability, François Rabelais (*c.*1494–1553) of Gargantuan fame, and the essayist, Michel de Montaigne (1533–92). These two writers are examples of humanism at its finest. Both took the fascinating nature of man as their subject. Rabelais looked outward and wrote with a bawdy imaginative spaciousness; Montaigne looked inward and contemplated the curious aspects of human nature. They were examples of humanism, not neo-classicism.

Political consolidation was thus supported by a strengthening of the country's cultural life. In this the intellectuals played a vigorous part.

The humanist movement produced in France, as in Italy, academies and centres for all kinds of study. Henri III had created an academy for the discussion of philosophical questions. There had been Baïf's short-lived academy for the study of music and poetry. In the seventeenth century academies were established for music, fine art, science, literature, and dance. The celebrated Académie Française was set up by Richelieu himself to bring together a distinguished group of writers who had been meeting informally for a number of years and to whom he gave the task, still uncompleted, of compiling a dictionary of the French language.

Along with the official academies were the *salons* where the women played their part. The most influential was that of Catherine de Vivonne, Marquise de Rambouillet (1588–1665). Between about 1618 and 1650 this amiable and serious-minded lady opened her house to many of the most distinguished writers of the day for discussion of a very wide range of subjects. Although such groups descended into preciosity and pedantry and were satirized by Molière in *Les Précieuses Ridicules* the *salons* are an example of how the French envisaged the reconstruction of society as involving every aspect of behaviour, manners, and language. While the Académie Française had the responsibility of establishing the purity and correct use of the French language, the *salons* were particularly concerned with questions of behaviour. These attitudes are expressed in a number of words and phrases of great significance to this narrow but influential Parisian society but which are really untranslatable – *comme il faut*, *galanterie*, *bon sens*, *bon esprit*, *sensibilité*, and *vraisemblance*.

By far the most prolific dramatist in the early years of the seventeenth century – and it must be remembered that he was a near contemporary of Shakespeare and Ben Jonson – was Alexandre Hardy (*c.*1570–1632). Although he used a large number of stories from the classics he treated them in so sensational a manner that the humanists were outraged. His contemporaries did no better.

Not only were there no good plays but there were few good theatres. The Confrèrie de la Passion still held a monopoly of professional acting in Paris and had acquired a theatre on the site of the old Hotel de Bourgogne, a building to the north of the city. The theatre was a long narrow room with a stage at one end and rising tiers of benches and boxes on each side.

For scenery a strange practice had grown up. However sensible the concept of unity of place may have been in theory, it did not work out in practice. The unities imposed impossible restrictions on the playwrights. Changes of scene were necessary and the permanent background of the Teatro Olimpico made this impossible. The solution arrived at was to put as many small pieces of scenery on the stage as the action required. In a French play with a story similar to *A Winter's Tale*, there was a seascape, a temple, a Sicilian palace, and a prison, all on stage together, an arrangement known as simultaneous or multiple setting. Its clumsiness reinforced the argument of the classicists in favour of unity of place, that is, confining the action of the play to a single scene, a requirement which forced playwrights into extremes of improbability and destroyed the *vraisemblance* (truth to life) it was intended to create.

Between about 1590 and the assassination of Henri IV in 1610, the leading company was led in turn by a fine actor named Valleran le Conte and then Robert Guérin, a coarse, jovial comedian whose stage-name was Gros-Guillaume. He established himself at the Hôtel de Bourgogne; his players were known as the Royal Company and received many privileges. He was succeeded by Bellerose who in 1647 persuaded Floridor, the best actor at the Théâtre du Marais and a close friend of Corneille, to join his company. The Hôtel de Bourgogne remained the home of the royal troupe, Les Grands Comédiens, until it combined with Molière's company in 1681.

The centre of interest shifts temporarily to Rouen, the capital of Normandy, one of the liveliest of the French provinces. Rouen had a vigorous printing and publishing industry, it was frequently visited by touring companies, and there was a large Jesuit college. It was here that Pierre Corneille (1606–84) received his education. As a young man he was influenced both by the plays in which he acted at college – for the Jesuits were enthusiastic about drama – and the plays of the visiting companies.

One of these companies was run by a certain Guillaume Desgilberts who acted under the name of Montdory and to them he gave a comedy he had written called *Mélite*. In 1629 Montdory's company arrived in Paris, attracted attention, achieved success, and in 1634 was given use of a tennis court which they converted into the Théâtre du Marais. This was in the eastern part of Paris near the fortress of the Bastille. Here they staged the early plays of Corneille with sufficient success to attract the attention of Richelieu himself.

Armand du Plessis, Duc de Richelieu, was not only principal minister of the King, Louis XIII, a man of great political ability but also an enthusiast for the arts. He founded the Académie Française in 1634 and composed a tragedy which is said to have been of no great merit. Nevertheless he arranged for it to be staged in a temporary theatre he had built for the purpose in the Palais-Royal. This theatre, in the middle of a royal palace surrounded by public gardens, was to play an important part in the history of the Paris theatre over the next few decades.

Richelieu considered that the French drama should be purified as well as the French language. He therefore chose five authors, of whom Corneille was one, to write plays under his direction. This proved to be a dubious blessing for Corneille. The first two plays he wrote under this impressive patronage were *Medée*, a fairly straightforward account of the classical story of Medea, and a very curious comedy called *L'Illusion comique*. Neither appears to have received much attention. His next play, *Le Cid*, based on a Spanish play by Guilhen de Castro, produced in 1637, created a sensation. It is by any standards a fine play, written in powerful and resonant alexandrines and developing a theme that Corneille was to use in many of his later plays, the conflict between duty and passion. Paradoxically enough it was because of its success with the public and a rather boastful poem that Corneille was rash enough to publish, that it was attacked by Richelieu and his critical myrmidons, and officially censured, as it were, in papers produced by members of the French Academy, for its style, its grammar, and its failure to respect the Aristotelian unities. Corneille in fact had done his best by cramming the action into twenty-four hours, a compression which led one contemporary critic to remark that for the hero the day had been well spent and the one thing of which he could not be accused was laziness. It is interesting to consider how Corneille might have constructed his play if he had been writing with the freedom that Shakespeare enjoyed.

Pierre Corneille, however, was no polemicist. He did not enjoy controversy. He was a fussy, timid, and insecure man who subjected his manuscripts to constant revision. He was a bit of a provincial and never came to terms with the great Parisian public. Nevertheless he weathered the storm created by *Le Cid* and after a short rest in Rouen went on to write the plays on which his fame securely rests. They are neither timid nor fussy but immensely strong and firmly constructed. His interest is in authority and all that that implies. Where does a man's loyalty lie, to his family, his religion, his country? His attitude to erotic passion is that it must be controlled by reason. His heroes and heroines are men and women of tremendous stature whose private emotions assume national significance.

Horace (1640) is powerfully theatrical, full of what the French call *coups de théâtre*, striking developments in the action. *Cinna* (1641) is still grander, placing the issues of personal passion and political responsibility in sharp relationship. *Polyeucte* (1641) takes a religious theme from a play by Calderon and in the most skilful manner presents three sets of interrelated loyalties. *Rodogune* (1644) balances the political ambitions of a Syrian Queen against the erotic ambitions of a seductive Syrian captive. Passion and duty are tightly interlocked.

In 1651 he wrote *Nicomède*, a tremendous pageant of Roman politics set in the Middle East two centuries before Christ. In the introduction he says that it is his twenty-first play and that he is finding it increasingly difficult to discover appropriate stories. A sense of strain clearly enters his work. He wrote little between 1652 and 1659 and the plays he wrote in the last twenty years of his life have little to commend them. He was outshone by two younger dramatists, one of whom befriended him while the other was a rival.

57 | Molière

The man who befriended Corneille was Jean-Baptiste Poquelin who took the professional name of Molière (1622–73). Like Corneille he was educated at a Jesuit college where he received a thorough grounding in classical literature and perhaps an initiation into acting. The theatre was clearly 'in his blood' for in 1643, when he was only twenty-one, he formed his own company which he termed L'Illustre Théâtre. Failing to establish himself in Paris, he spent fourteen years, from 1645 until 1658, touring the provinces with his Illustrious Theatre Company, for whom he acted, managed, and wrote plays.

The results of this long slog 'on the road' is evident in his later work in a number of ways. He became familiar with the work of the Italian improvised companies who were also constantly on tour, and whose vigorous acting style clearly made a deep impression on the young dramatist. The character of Sganarelle appears in six of his comedies and in others he wore a mask. It was familiarity with popular audiences and the ability to hold their interest under difficult conditions that explains the theatricality of his plays, the quality that makes them eminently stageable. Years of touring no doubt fostered in him a certain contempt for the fopperies of high society and the courage to satirize the foibles even of those on whose favours he depended for a living.

Fortunes changed when in 1658 he managed to win the patronage of the King's brother who helped him to secure temporary accommodation in Paris. At one of his first performances the King himself was present.

With great daring he staged Corneille's *Nicomède*. The King was not greatly impressed. Molière asked for permission to play his own short *Le Docteur amoureux*. The King was delighted and arranged for him to have better accommodation in another temporary theatre in the Hôtel du Petit-Bourbon. This theatre was used for a variety of functions and had been the scene of the famous *Ballet comique de la Reine* nearly a century earlier. It was long and narrow and must have been highly inconvenient for dramatic purposes; but two years later, when the Petit-Bourbon was to be pulled down to allow for an enlargement of the Louvre, he was able to move to the Palais-Royal which, however, he had to share with the Italians.

The evidence suggests that Molière and his company introduced a fresh, more realistic and less declamatory style of acting into the French Theatre. In this lies their daring in having staged *Nicomède* and the probable explanation of their failure. For they invited direct comparison with the company at the Hôtel de Bourgogne which under the fine actor Floridor specialized in classical tragedy and had staged the major plays of Corneille. In *L'Impromptu de Versailles* he jeers at the tragic style of the rival company: their aim, he says, was to 'ronfler les vers et faire le brouhaha' (untranslatable).

He not only challenged the acting styles of rival companies but styles of behaviour in society itself. He attacked *salon* society in *Les Précieuses ridicules* (usually translated by some such title as *The Ridiculous Ladies*, 1659), sexual hypocrisy in *L'Ecole des femmes* (*The School for Wives*, 1662), religious hypocrisy in *Tartuffe* (1664), the humanists in *Le Misanthrope* (*The Misanthropist*, 1666), the new rich in *Le Bourgeois gentilhomme* (1670), and *Georges Dandin* (1668) and the medical profession in *Le Médecin malgré lui* (*The Doctor in Spite of Himself*, 1666) and *Le Malade imaginaire* (*The Imaginary Invalid*, 1673). It is not surprising that he was fiercely attacked in return. There were those who said he was a reincarnation of the devil. One's heart warms towards the anonymous voice which called out at the end of the first performance of *L'Ecole des femmes*, 'Courage, Molière, voilà une bonne comédie!'

He also wrote a number of lighter and less satirical plays, some of which he took from Latin originals. *Amphitryon* and *L'Avare* (*The Miser*, 1668) came from Plautus, *L'Ecole des maris* and *Les Fourberies de Scapin* from Terence; but he translated these classics into his own contemporary world with complete success.

Among those who recognized his genius was fortunately the King himself, Louis XIV, then a cheerful young man sixteen years younger than Molière whom he defended with remarkable consistency. He constantly invited Molière to bring his company to his various palaces, Versailles, Saint Germain, Fontainbleau, Chambord on the Loire as well as the Louvre and the Tuileries in Paris. He also arranged for Molière to collaborate with the court musician, Lully, in the composition and staging of a succession of court entertainments on the lines of the old *ballets de cour*. Molière wrote fourteen *comédie-ballets*, as they came to be called, two of which were *Le Bourgeois gentilhomme* (1670) and *Le Malade imaginaire* (1673), in which he was playing the part of the hypochondriac when he died.

Molière is one of the world's great comic dramatists. His plays are still more widely performed than those of any other dramatist except Shakespeare. He is virtually unique in his all-round abilities. He was manager of his company as well as its artistic director. He wrote a succession of masterpieces which he directed himself as well as playing the leading role. Some of his contemporaries wondered how the author of *Tartuffe* could stoop to play a role like that of Scapin, which requires him to be tied up in a sack and beaten. Molière replied that his presence on the stage was necessary for the sake of the performance and the livelihood of sixty people.

He died at the age of fifty-one of tuberculosis, but worn down by the jealousies, rivalries, and slanders to which he was constantly subject, and sheer hard work.

The most frequently performed plays of Molière at the Comédie-Française since 1680 have been, in this order, Tartuffe, L'Avare, Le Medecin malgré lui, Le Misanthrope, Le Malade imaginaire, Les Femmes savantes, L'Ecole des maris, L'Ecole des femmes, Les Fourberies de Scapin, Les Précieuses ridicules, *and* Le Bourgeois gentilhomme.

58 | Racine

Both Corneille and Racine saw the success of the third great dramatist of the century. Jean Racine (1639–99) was born near Paris. His parents died while he was still young and he was brought up by relatives who sent him to school at the Jansenist monastery of Port-Royal where he received a thorough education in the classics. The Jansenists were a kind of Puritan sect within the Catholic Church, believing in predestination, guilt, sin, and the general incapacity of man. This, together with their educational practices, did much to shape the curious artistic personality of Racine. While subjecting their students to a rigorous training in the classics, the Jansenists believed that no student should be expected to write or speak Latin or Greek until he could use his own language with grace, fluency, and clarity. It was a form of education in rhetoric.

Racine was a credit to his teachers. He grew up to be personable, handsome, a brilliant conversationalist, and immensely attractive to and attracted by women. With a succession of sinecures acquired through the influence of his relatives he gained a position at court and enjoyed the friendship of the King throughout his life.

He defied the efforts of his relatives to force him into a career in the Church and frequented the society of actors and writers. He began to write plays and gave his first, *La Thébaïde* (*The Theban Story*, 1664) which deals with the story of Oedipus, to Molière; similarly his second *Alexandre le Grand* (1665). But no doubt he realized that the actors at the Hôtel de Bourgogne were better suited to tragedy and gave his next play, which dealt with Alexander the Great, to the rival company. And along with the play went Molière's leading lady, Marquise du Parc. The rift between the two companies was complete. This may have been why Molière cultivated the friendship of Corneille.

Between the years 1667 and 1676 Racine wrote eleven masterpieces, beginning with *Andromaque* and ending with *Phèdre*. His private life was a source of constant salacious gossip and he was bitterly attacked by his former teachers of Port-Royal for becoming involved in the theatre, and for the sensuality of his plays. But controversy and criticism, far from weakening his resolve, sharpened his pen, and it was not until the most bitter of all controversies following the production of *Phèdre* that his creative energy appeared to be exhausted. He teetered with becoming a Carthusian monk, changed his mind, married plump and plain, fathered seven children and became official historian to the King. Many years later he wrote, at the instigation of the King's wife, Madame de Maintenon, two great plays on religious themes, *Esther* (1689) and *Athalie* (1691) for production at a seminar of young ladies of which Madame was a governor. The latter play was subsequently described by Voltaire as 'le chef d'œuvre de l'esprit human' (a masterpiece of the human spirit).

Racine's plays are the only masterpieces of dramatic art that obey the rules. This is not only because he was a devoted classicist but also because he found a formula that suited such precision. In most of his plays, A loves B who loves C who loves both or neither. The serpent dies devouring his own tail. Thus in *Andromaque* Oreste is in love with

Hermione, Hermione with Pyrrhus, Pyrrhus with Andromaque, who is the widow of the dead Hector and cares for no one but her child. Yet love is not really the word to describe the total devouring obsession of these introverted characters with each other. Reason plays no part. It is a profound statement of the Tristan myth, summed up by Phèdre, dying for love of her son-in-law Hippolyte, when in a famous couplet she says that it is Venus devouring her prey, but much stronger in the French:

> Ce n'est plus une ardeur dans mes veines cachée:
> C'est Venus tout entière à sa proie attachée.

No wonder nice-minded contemporaries were shocked.

Perhaps the most remarkably disciplined of all his plays is *Bérénice* (1670) in which he demonstrates the extreme simplicity which he claims in the Preface to the printed version to be his object. The story of the play is simply the rejection of Bérénice, an Eastern princess, by the Emperor Titus, after a platonic affair that had lasted five years. The action has been described as the Queen's illusion (of becoming Empress) in act one; her doubts in act two; her disillusion in act three; her despair in act four; and her departure for Rome in act five. It is profitable to compare this play with *Cléopâtre captive* written 120 years earlier. The form has not advanced at all, but Racine has found a way of exploiting a far deeper range of emotion.

Similarly in *Phèdre*. Theseus loves his wife Phèdre, Phèdre loves her stepson Hippolyte, Hippolyte loves Aricie. There are no love scenes, there is nothing but a brutal eroticism expressed in the most elegant language that has ever been employed on the stage. All the Jansenist insistence on predestination, guilt, and obsessive sin is encapsulated in this tremendous play. It is perhaps understandable that Racine had burnt himself out.

Racine was as fortunate as Corneille in his players. In 1647, when Corneille was past his best, the great actor Floridor moved from the Théâtre du Marais to the Hôtel de Bourgogne and so having played Corneille's greatest heroes, went on to play those of Racine. The beautiful and talented Madamoiselle du Parc has already been mentioned, and when in 1668 she died at the age of thirty-five she was succeeded by the even more accomplished Madamoiselle Champméslé.

There is no doubt that the French neo-classical dramatists functioned under more rigorous critical constraints than those of any other period. But it was a time when people cared. Many of the demands of the critics were not absurd. Even the grave and humourless Jean Chapdelain (1595–1674) insisted that a play must please its audiences through moral propriety and the artistic treatment of its story. This is fair comment. He and others invoked a term that was of considerable significance at the time, the need for *vraisemblance*, a reasonable appearance of reality. Another of the *salon* set, François Hedelin, Abbé d'Aubignac, demanded that the stage should present things not as they are but as they ought to be. This is requiring a playwright to project the dominant values of his society which is to put in question his own imaginative revision of reality. But in the circumstances one can see how artists were expected to transform the chaos of reality into some kind of order, whether that represented the views of the artist, or the views of the artist of society.

Corneille in the last years of his life examined these questions in short essays he attached to his published plays. He asks how the rules of Aristotle are to be interpreted, what is the permissible scope of the Unities, and so on. Racine was more imperious. In his short Prefaces he advises his critics to bother less with the rules and pay more attention to their enjoyment of the play.

But the key figure in all this was Louis XIV himself. He has left an image applicable to his years as the Sun King, le Roi Soleil, when he was leading actor in a great court drama set in the palace of Versailles (completed in 1682). But as a young man he had been of a cheerful disposition, extremely fond of acting and even more of dancing, and a great lover of literature. He was a clear and stylish writer himself. One of his first acts, on assuming personal rule in 1661, was to draw up a list of writers deserving a state pension.

It is a critical pastime to compare the plays of Corneille and Racine; but they cannot be compared; they are wholly different. Corneille was interested in the great moral issues that lie at the heart of a civilized nation. His themes are of Roman grandeur. Racine was in a way an immoralist. He was interested in the private torments of the human heart. He does not stipulate a provoking beauty in women that creates a possessive passion in men. His men and women, plain or handsome, fat or thin, are in love with each other, and their love is a destructive passion from which there is no escape.

And between the two stands Molière. When Louis XIV once asked Jean de la Bruyère, one of the most perceptive critics of the time, who was the greatest master of the age, he received the reply, 'Sire, c'est Molière'.

A great deal has been written about this, one of the great periods in the history of the theatre. Much of it concerns the theatrical conditions of the times, a prerequisite to a full understanding of the plays. Professor T. E. Lawrenson's The French Stage in the XVIIth

Century *deals with the period of simultaneous décor; but there is much invaluable information in Geoffrey Brereton's* French Tragic Drama in the Sixteenth and Seventeenth Century, *John Lough's* Paris Theatre Audiences in the Seventeenth and Eighteenth Centuries *and Georges Mongrédien's* Daily Life in the French Theatre at the Time of Molière.

The language of Corneille and Racine defies translation, and their themes are somewhat remote from interests of our own day. Molière does much better although there is an unfortunate tendency to 'tart him up'. Many of Molière's plays are not so closely related to his historical context as those of his great contemporaries.

59 | A Note on Theatre Audiences

Even the closest scholarly scrutiny finds it difficult to establish the exact social composition of audiences. Yet this is a subject of the greatest importance for a full understanding of the theatre of any period. It is the basic responsibility of an author, through his actors, to make a relationship with his audience; but while a novelist must hold the attention of his readers through the interest of the story, the playwright, however interesting his play, ultimately depends on the relationship his actors make with their audience; and this depends to a large extent on their physical relationship. In the Elizabethan theatre, the largest part of the audience stood round the stage (on three sides). Those who could afford a higher entrance fee sat in the galleries, more comfortably, but in less close contact with the players. The social composition of those standing in the pit, and so in closest contact with the actors, is therefore of great importance for the playwright. In the French theatre of the seventeenth century the pit was known as the *parterre*, for which the entrance fee was lower than for the surrounding boxes (*amphithéâtre*) or the two higher rows (*loges*). The playwright was therefore in a quandary since the people with whom he must keep closest in contact were those of the middle and lower classes who stood in the *parterre*, while the most socially influential people were those who could afford a higher price and sat in the *amphithéâtre* and *loges*. Even a dramatist of the distinction of Voltaire was so acutely aware of the importance of the *parterre* that he organized a *claque* (people paid to applaud) at the first performance of a new play.

The change in the nature of English and French drama in the mid-eighteenth century is usually attributed to the rise of the middle class. This term is difficult to define since the middle class is not a clearly identifiable section of the population. What it really means is that the political and economic power of the industrial and professional classes became stronger as that of the aristocracy declined; and since they represented the productive resources of society, culture increasingly reflected their interests: the appreciation of the business man became more important than that of the King and his courtiers. The biggest change in the social structure of the theatre took place when in the course of the nineteenth century the most expensive seats were those closest to the stage and the cheapest seats were in remote galleries. The implication of this is that in the seventeenth century those in the *parterre*, the cheaper seats, had a considerable influence on what was going on on stage through their proximity to the actors, but that distinction broke down as the various interests of the different classes began to converge.

The most significant single change in actor-audience relationships was the banning of audiences from sitting on the stage. This custom had grown up in England in Elizabethan times. Thomas Dekker wrote an amusing essay on how a gallant should disport himself in the theatre. And the same custom was common in Paris. When in 1689 a new theatre was built for the Comédie-Française, five rows of benches were provided on each side of the stage so that it was often difficult for the audience in the *parterre* to tell players from spectators. These privileged people often abused their position and were referred to by Voltaire as *petits-maîtres*. He was therefore delighted when in 1759 they were banished from the stage. Garrick did the same four years later.

While we are on the subject of audiences there is one further point to be made. We now expect an audience to sit quietly and attentively except when they laugh. It was quite different in the eighteenth century when for all their rough behaviour audiences were so keenly aware of the finer points of an actor's art that they would applaud a finely delivered speech or a well-executed piece of 'business'. When in 1782 a new theatre, built for the Comédie-Française, provided seats for those who had previously stood in the *parterre*, or pit, a critic complained that this resulted in lethargy. Close contact between stage and pit was broken. 'The almost incredible enthusiasm of the old days gave place to calm silence and silent disapproval'.

11. Salmacida Spolia (final scene)
Staged on 21 January 1640, this was the last of the Caroline Masques. Behind a false proscenium arch there were four sets of shutters on which the four buildings were painted in perspective with a back shutter for the bridge and background. The cloud machine was suspended upstage of the shutters. The scene represents a vision of architectural and cosmic harmony.

60 | London Theatres of the Restoration

By an Act of 1642, the First Ordinance against Stage Plays and Interludes – it is interesting that the term was still in use – such theatres as existed in London were not only officially closed but destroyed – the Globe, the Blackfriars, Salisbury Court in Fleet Street, the Phoenix in Drury Lane, the Fortune and the Hope were all pulled down during the following years. There is evidence that a certain amount of theatrical activity continued more or less secretly outside London throughout the period of the Civil War and the Protectorate but in the history of the mainstream theatre there is a gap of eighteen years.

With the Restoration of Charles II two theatres were established in London. They were the responsibility of two remarkable men. First off the mark was Sir Thomas Killigrew (1612–83), a humorous, outspoken man and a great favourite of the King. He had written a number of plays before the closing of the theatres and had spent much of the ensuing eighteen years travelling around Europe.

Within a few months of the return of Charles II to London Killigrew secured from him a licence to open a new theatre under royal patronage. This was a converted tennis court in Vere Street, a little to the north of the present Aldwych. He called it the Theatre Royal and his company the King's Men. It was not, however, a satisfactory building and in 1663 he moved to a new theatre in nearby Drury Lane, using the Vere Street premises as a training school for young actors. Colley Cibber, whose autobiography gives a vivid picture of the period, says that 'ten members of the company were on the royal household establishment, having each ten yards of scarlet cloth with a proper quantity of lace, allow'd them as liveries'. The old system of patronage was far from dead.

The other licence was granted to Sir William Davenant (1606–68). He had been Poet Laureate under Charles I and had written some twenty undistinguished plays. On the defeat of the King he joined the royalist faction in France and was sent by the Prince of Wales, the future Charles II, on an expedition to Virginia; he was captured by the Parliamentarian navy, brought back to London and was lucky to escape with his life. He finally settled in London where in 1656, with considerable diplomatic skill, he staged theatrical performances in his private house in Aldersgate. The second of these was a production of what is virtually the first English opera. More will be said about this in a later chapter; but it was a symptomatic gesture for during his eight years as a theatrical manager he showed particular interest in opera and spectacles with music.

In October 1660, six months after the return of the King, he was granted a licence to open a theatre. This was also a converted tennis court in Portugal Street off Lincoln's Inn Fields, and very close to Vere Street; but it was inconvenient for his purposes. Killigrew's company was the more successful with straight plays and Davenant therefore set about indulging his interest in musical spectacles, commissioning Sir Christopher Wren to design and build him a new theatre in Dorset Gardens, near the Thames and the present Waterloo Bridge. Unfortunately he died in 1671 before the theatre was completed and his interest passed to his widow and his son. The new theatre, by far the most magnificent London had yet seen, was opened in 1674; but it had poor acoustics which affected attendances. The company got into financial difficulties and in 1682 the two companies combined. Dorset Gardens Theatre was never used regularly again. Between 1682 and 1695 the Theatre Royal, Drury Lane, was the only theatre in use; and then Thomas Betterton, in dispute with Christopher Rich, reopened the theatre in Lincoln's Inn Fields.

Continued restrictions on the number of playhouses in London were not due to puritanical opposition to the theatre as much as to fear of plague and fire. In 1665 and 1666 there were fearsome examples of both. Thus only two licences were issued, one that was held from that day onwards by Drury Lane, as it always came to be called, and a second that was transferred from one theatre to another until Covent Garden was built in 1732. In due course a limited licence was given to the Haymarket Theatre.

We know little about the principles on which an architect such as Sir Christopher Wren, who built the Dorset Gardens Theatre, based his designs; but for stage arrangement and scenery Davenant turned to John Webb (1611–72) who had been Inigo Jones's principal assistant in the creation of Court Masques. This was the tradition, therefore, that was revived in public theatres of the Restoration.

There was a permanent proscenium arch with an opening about twenty-five feet wide behind which there was a small acting area about fifteen feet deep. Behind this there were three or four painted and immovable wing-flats and at the back of the stage a number of shutters that ran on grooves and were painted to provide the various scenes of the play. In front of the proscenium arch there was a gently raked apron-stage – the origin of this term is obscure – about seventeen feet deep, on to which there was access through a door on each side surmounted by a box. The pit sloped upwards with straight rows of benches. Around the auditorium, which was curved, were two rows of boxes. Thus if the stage arrangement owed something to the Masque, the auditorium was very similar to that of the Hôtel de Bourgogne in Paris with which both Killigrew and Davenant would have been familiar.

When in 1682 the two companies combined, the management fell into the hands of one Christopher Rich (d.1714) who proved to be a commercial manager of the most notorious kind. Since making money was his whole objective, he increased the value of the house by reducing the size of the apron-stage to make room for additional rows of seats. He removed the proscenium doors and replaced them with boxes, thus obliging the actors to enter the fore-stage from above the proscenium. Since this was an awkward movement actors tended to play above the proscenium which increased their distance from the audience with unhappy results on their audibility. 'The voice', wrote Colley Cibber, 'was then no more in the centre of the house' and everything on stage was more distanced.

It would be extremely interesting to know how Killigrew and Davenant recruited their actors. Davenant apparently took over a company which had been formed at the Cockpit Theatre, also in Drury Lane. The Cockpit was a roofed theatre which had been built in 1616 by Christopher Beeston and had usually been used by boy's companies. Davenant had been connected with it in a number of ways. Killigrew's leading actors included Michael Mohun, who had fought with distinction in the royalist army, and Charles Hart, both men in their forties with some pre-war acting experience. Several had been boy players with the Beeston company. And then there was Thomas Betterton (*c.*1635–1710), reputed to have been among the greatest of English actors. During the Protectorate he had lived in Paris and through his familiarity with the French theatre Charles II sent him back on several occasions to pick up ideas. In 1695, when the dishonesty of Christopher Rich became unendurable, he formed his own company and opened the theatre in Lincoln's Inn Fields with Congreve's *Love for Love*. But it is as an actor that he is remembered. Cibber gives a detailed description of some of his performances. 'Could HOW Betterton spoke', he writes, 'be as easily known as WHAT he spoke, then might you see the muse of Shakespeare in her triumph'.

Also of note is the first appearance of professional actresses on the London stage. In the licenses granted to the two theatres in 1660 it is stated that not only must all plays be cleaned of offensive passages but that all women's roles must be played by women on the grounds that this is a more moral practice than for women's roles to be played by boys. The first actress to appear on the stage was probably Margaret Hughes, though we do not know for certain. Nor do we know how Killigrew found or trained her. Others followed. Of many of them Cibber speaks highly. The celebrated Nell Gwynn played her first role at the age of fifteen and became the mistress of Charles at nineteen. Elizabeth Barry, Betterton's most accomplished leading lady, was born only in 1658 and made her first stage appearance in 1673. She is said to have been taught to act by that notorious wag, the Earl of Rochester, when she became his mistress.

When the theatres reopened in 1660 people turned for precedents and practice to the pre-war theatre. But the London of Charles II was a very different place to the London of his father, Charles I, and became increasingly so in the course of the reign. The theatre was quick to develop its own practices and by the turn of the century, when George I and the Hanoverian succession had established a period of political peace and economic stability for the country, the theatre took the shape that it has today.

By far the most helpful study of the design and structure of Restoration and subsequent theatres in Richard Leacroft's beautifully illustrated The Development of the British Playhouse.

61 | Restoration Comedy

In 1660 few if any new plays had been written for eighteen years, for people do not on the whole write plays when there are no theatres to stage them. Fortunately there was a considerable reserve of plays in all those that had been written earlier in the century. Killigrew and Davenant therefore appeared to divide the spoils between them, neither staging those plays which were in the share of the other.

But a living theatre depends on new plays and it took time for the would-be dramatists to respond to a wholly new theatrical situation. A new drama had to be created and it was understandably the work of new young dramatists. The first to write a play of any real interest was Sir George Etherege (1634–91) who was one of a group of somewhat wild young men who had received much of their education in France, become friends of the King, and gave the court its reputation for witty conversation and audacious behaviour. The play was *The Comical Revenge* or *Love in a Tub*, staged by Davenant at his theatre in Lincoln's Inn Fields in 1664. It is a light-hearted piece of an understandably uncertain form, with the more serious passages written in rhymed couplets. But Etherege was not prolific. His second play, *She Would if She Could*, came four years later (1668), and his best play, *The Man of Mode* or *Sir Fopling Flutter* in 1676. Others in the first wave of new playwrights were John Crowne (*c*.1640–1703), Thomas Shadwell (*c*.1642–92), a writer who concentrated on adaptations, of which more later, and texts for musical productions, Nathaniel Lee (*c*.1653–92), and the strange figure of Mrs Aphra Behn (1640–89) who was the first professional woman writer, a prolific and hard-working author, and a thoroughly unconventional character.

The only comic dramatist of real distinction was William Wycherley (1640–1716). He was the son of a staunchly royalist father who had had him educated in France during the Protectorate. In Paris he had become familiar both with the French drama and the English court in exile. While the influence of Molière is evident in his four comedies, he provides a fascinating contrast with the French dramatist. For while Molière, even at his most satirical, writes with the elegance that was obligatory for a dramatist whose plays were staged at the court of Louis XIV, Wycherley writes with the brutality and the outspokenness of a far more permissive society. *Love in a Wood*, staged at Drury Lane in 1671, is rather dull and diffuse; but *The Gentleman Dancing Master* is a charmingly written satire on bourgeois behaviour as two young men compete for the hand of the beauteous Hippolita. In *The Country Wife* (1675) and *The Plain Dealer* (1676) he wrote two of the great comedies of the English language, plays that are to be set alongside Ben Jonson's masterpieces. The former play is at once so amoral and so amusing that one tends to ignore the acute and cruel analysis of sexual relationships that it contains, while in the latter play Wycherley creates a hero, based broadly on Molière's Alceste in *Le Misanthrope*, whose rejection of society is so savage and whose relationship with his mistress is so revealing that the play hardly constitutes a comedy at all. There are elements of tragedy in the remainder of his life. This brilliantly talented writer lived another forty years without writing another play. One wonders whether this had anything to do with the fact that he became involved with the celebrated beauty, Barbara Villiers, Countess of Castlemaine, who had already given the King no less than five illegitimate children, and that in 1682 he was imprisoned for debt and languished in Newgate gaol for almost seven years.

Another great dramatist was William Congreve (1670–1729) who in 1692 arrived in London from Trinity College, Dublin, where he had been schoolmaster of the great Jonathan Swift. He was young and witty and had a manuscript of a comedy in his pocket. The story goes that he met John Dryden, then the Grand Old Man of English letters, who did a little work on the play and then gave it to Thomas Betterton, then manager of Drury Lane, with whom and which he had connections. *The Old Bachelor* was produced in 1693, followed in successive years by *The Double-Dealer* and *Love for Love*. The latter, together with *The Way of the World*, staged at Lincoln's Inn in 1700, are two more of the great comedies that give the period its distinction and its authentic flavour. It must be said, however, that both plays are confused in plot and ramshackle in construction and owe their mastery to the dialogue which reverberates and dances as no other dramatic prose.

Congreve's particular qualities can be seen by comparing his plays with those of Sir John Vanbrugh (1664–1726). This witty and irrepressible man is as well known as an architect as a playwright. In the former capacity his masterpieces are Blenheim Palace, which he built for the Duke of Marlborough in 1704, and Castle Howard in Yorkshire. He also went into collaboration with Congreve in building a theatre in the Haymarket, but of this more will be said anon. His comedies, which for all their wit have a certain coarseness of texture, include *The Relapse* (1696), *The Provoked Wife* (1697), and *The Confederacy* (1705). He wrote with great facility and Cibber says that of all the dramatists of the time the actors found Vanbrugh's plays the easiest to learn.

The most distinguished writer of the age was John Dryden (1631–1700), although it is difficult to place him as a playwright. He received a classical education at Westminster and turned at once to poetry; but with the opening of the theatres in 1660 he became interested in drama. He wrote his first comedy, *The Wild Gallant*, in 1663 and between 1667 and 1680 wrote mostly plays. His comedies are on the whole far less successful than his heroic tragedies which will be considered in the next section. Indeed, some of them are so graceless that it is difficult to believe that he was not cynically exploiting the licentiousness for which in due course the stage was vigorously attacked. Such vulgarity is surprising from a man who was a notable scholar, a fine poet, and a penetrating critic. It is only in the poetic and fanciful *Marriage à la Mode* that one feels he was at all at ease in comedy.

62 | Heroic Tragedy

The origins of this curious form are not altogether clear; but as Dryden was the leading exponent of the form it is reasonable to base one's definition on what he had to say. Dryden was a great classicist. He was also a poet. His models were therefore the great classical epics. But he was also familiar with the canons of the humanists for whom the great epic poets were not only Homer and Virgil but Ariosto, Tasso, and 'our English Spencer'. Tragedy, for Dryden, was an attempt to find a stage version of the epic poem, heroic because it should be concerned with knights, arms, love, gallantry, women, and heroic actions. To this he adds a very curious rider: the emotions to be aroused by a tragic play are wonder and admiration, while at the same time it is more important to entertain an audience than to instruct it. This suggests that he was familiar enough with the theatre to realize that if one did not entertain an audience, there would be no audience to instruct. So the two parts of *The Conquest of Granada* (1669–70) consist of a wild concoction of military and amatory exploits, battle, murder, and sudden death; *Aurengzebe* (1676) is only a little more controlled, but the rivalry of an elderly father and his two sons for the love of a captive princess produces plenty of absurdities.

Yet he was clearly aware of what he was about, for in the epilogue to *The Conquest of Granada* he boasts about the wit and refinement of the age, which he ascribes to the example of the King who had the opportunity of travelling and 'being conversant in the most polished courts of Europe'. Elsewhere he talks about his aim to achieve 'an absolute dominion over the minds of the spectators'.

He knew all about the French dramatists but he did not copy the methods of Corneille or Racine since he had the very worthy aim of writing plays that were authentically English. The only real success he had in the genre was *All for Love*, a play in which he rewrites Shakespeare's *Antony and Cleopatra* to conform with the three unities. Here he reveals his contempt for the great sprawling Jacobean tragedy by reducing Shakespeare's prodigious canvas to a closet drama in which the focus is entirely on the introspective relationship of the two lovers. In his Preface he refers to the rules but argues that English dramatic genius is less refined than the French even though his play is closer to Racine than to Shakespeare.

A strange man whose adaptation of *The Tempest* introduces the most inept vulgarities into Shakespeare's marvellous play; who wrote a version of *Paradise Lost* in rhymed couplets, calling it *The Age of Innocence*, and yet whose essays on drama and dramatic criticism are among the most perceptive in the language.

A feature of Dryden's heroic tragedies is their use of rhymed couplets. Other tragedies were written at the time in blank verse and without the heroic element. The problem was one from which English poetic drama never escaped. The domination of Shakespeare and the Jacobean dramatists was fatal. Every dramatist writing poetic tragedy, right up into the present century, has used the same verse-form, and the more it has been used the more pedestrian it has become. A play like *Venice Preserved* (1681) by Thomas Otway held the stage for many years because it had some fine acting roles, but one's sympathies are with those who satirized the genre like Buckingham in *The Rehearsal* (1671), a play that gave Sheridan the idea for *The Critic* more than a hundred years later, and a number of sallies by Henry Fielding before he turned away from the theatre in disgust and devoted his tremendous talent to writing novels.

63 | Restoration Society and its Drama

Restoration comedy is one of the most individual types of British drama. It is often referred to as the 'comedy of manners' which helps to clarify its particular nature: it is very much concerned with people's behaviour and requires for its successful performance a sense of style in speech, deportment, and carriage. Most people are aware that Restoration comedy is witty rather than humorous and frequently very indecent. In order to understand how it acquired these particular qualities one must look at the society which gave rise to it.

In many respects it was an unhappy society which was preoccupied with assuaging the tragedies caused by the Civil War. It was also an unstable society which had to set about rebuilding much that had been destroyed in people's lives. This is not to say that the Protectorate had been responsible for disasters which the new regime had to put right but simply that the effect of violent transition from monarchy to republic and back to monarchy again required a vigilant attempt to restore those permanent elements on which any stable society must be based.

A certain degree of stability was established between the King and his parliament in the Bill of Rights; the religious settlement was established in the Act of Uniformity; the legal rights of the individual were established in the Act of Habeas Corpus (ensuring that no man can be imprisoned without trial). The interest of the King in many practical activities led to the formation of the Royal Society, the intention of which was to substantiate the word of God through science and the order of creation through scientific enquiry, and thus to free mankind from error and superstition.

It was what the dramatist, Henry Arthur Jones, writing two hundred years later called 'the flowering time of English prose'. But it was also the flowering time of English poetry when John Milton produced the greatest epic in the English language, *Paradise Lost*, a poem which, incidentally, he had originally conceived as a play. One wonders whether he ever conceived that fine dramatic poem *Samson Agonistes*, the product of his old age, ever being played on a stage.

The curious fact is that against this rather sombre background the theatre seemed to thrive on and to exploit an amoral and almost antisocial profligacy. For this the character of Charles II and his court were largely responsible. Charles was sardonic, witty in an ironical way, and cynical about the way things happened after eighteen difficult years in exile. He combined deep seriousness with passionate sensuality. His closest male associates were men he had known during his exile or who had joined him on his return. They were a wild bunch and included John Wilmot, Earl of Rochester, poet, drunkard, sensualist, and enthusiastic theatre-goer; Thomas Killigrew, who was known as 'the King's jester'; the playwrights Etherege and Wycherley; Sir Charles Sedley, another spare-time dramatist, and George Villiers, Duke of Buckingham, a most distinguished and important politician. These men had every excuse, after the miseries they had endured, to enjoy their own company and their own laughter; but it was a misfortune for the theatre that although from time to time a serious note emerges in their work, they reduced the theatre to an ignominious position in society. The great diarist Samuel Pepys sums it up when he refers to 'a sad, negligent, vicious court'.

It is as always difficult to gauge the nature or extent of the public. It seems to have been extremely mixed although it did not include the poorer paid to anything like the same extent that the theatres of James I had done. The King himself was a frequent theatre-goer, but he was more interested in pretty actresses than dramatic art. Behaviour in the theatre seems to have been very poor; there are many references to audiences being small but noisy; there was a lot of shifting about, drunkenness was common, and people carried on their own conversations throughout the performance. Many women, for reasons of modesty, hid their faces behind masks. Yet Samuel Pepys, a serious-minded, hard-working civil servant in the Navy Office, visited the theatre seventy-three times between 1 January and 31 August 1668, often with his wife, their friends, and his maid, Deb Willett. His wife and Deb sometimes went alone which they are unlikely to have done if behaviour was as rough as has sometimes been suggested.

Nevertheless it is clear that by the end of the century and with the accession of the sober-sided William and Mary there was general concern about moral laxity throughout society. For its share in the prevailing licentiousness the stage was attacked by Jeremy Collier in *A Short View of the Immorality and Profaneness of the English Stage*. The author was an ordained priest who came to live in London in 1685 but excluded himself from the ecclesiastical office by refusing to take the oath of allegiance to the King and Queen. He based his attack on the theatres on what he described as 'the intolerable liberties of stage-poets', the smuttiness and indelicacy of their language, their abuse of the clergy, the profligacy of many stage characters, the success of their debaucheries, and much besides. He singles out for particular attack Dryden, Congreve, Wycherley, Vanbrugh, and D'Urfey, the last an author of many indecent comedies now lost and a particular friend of the king. There followed a pamphlet war which lasted until 1726. Wycherley, who was let off most lightly, did not participate, having long since lost interest in the stage; nor did Dryden, who was nearing his seventieth year; and the ripostes of Congreve were disappointing although at the time he enjoyed considerable public support.

It is difficult to say whether Jeremy Collier's diatribe had any direct influence on the dramatists; but it seems to have acted as a kind of danger signal to such a potentially licentious dramatist as George Farquhar showed himself to be in his early plays. But under Queen Anne and the Hanoverian kings we move into a new political and cultural climate in which drama for a time lost grace and favour.

The best plays of the Restoration dramatists should be readily available. The Diaries *of Samuel Pepys, which cover the period 1660–9, have many references to the theatre and provide an invaluable source of information on as well as giving a vivid picture of what theatre-going was like at the time. The other great diarist, John Evelyn, was not a regular theatre-goer, but his diaries are valuable for their social and political comment. Antonia Fraser in* Charles II *gives a fine portrait of a King who in addition to a wife had twelve illegitmate children by seven mistresses. There are many books on the complex subject of Restoration comedy and heroic tragedy as well as on the more important authors.*

64 | English Opera

Sir William Davenant was author of the last Carolingian Masque to be performed. Its name was *Salmacida Spolia* and the date was 1640. This was a form of theatre that clearly interested Davenant, for in 1639 Charles I had given him a patent to build a theatre in London. It was to have been an all-purpose theatre for the performance of opera and ballet as well as drama; but the closing of the theatres put an end to what might have been a fascinating project. However, the Puritans, who formed the core of Cromwell's party, were not as opposed to music as they were to drama, and in the 1650s, after a skirmish with the military and naval authorities, Davenant obtained permission to stage some musical entertainments at his home in East London. *The Siege of Rhodes*, which was first performed in 1656, was a musical play. The music was by four composers. It was written in recitative, a kind of declamatory style of singing fairly close to the rhythms and inflections of speech. The composers described this style as being 'in the manner of the ancients'. Davenant, one suspects, was a kind of Count Bardi, infected with humanistic ideas, but really more interested in theatrical performance than the recreation of Greek tragedy. Nevertheless it is known as the first English opera.

It will be remembered that it was at this same time, the mid-seventeenth century, that opera was making rapid progress in Venice and indeed throughout Italy. The Italians were not slow to export their new creation. We do not know when the first Italian opera singers visited London, but men like Davenant had probably seen Italian opera for the first time in Paris. When in due course an Italian opera arrived in London, the English did not like it. They called the Italian singers 'canary birds'. They considered the stories to be stupid, which they usually were, and found the words inaudible. Traditional drama of Shakespeare and his Jacobean contemporaries with their exciting stories and tremendous language was far more to their taste. They were not averse to music, and welcomed it in the form of interludes in a way that did not interfere with the drama.

There is evidence that a man such as Betterton was far more impressed with French *comédie-ballet* of the kind that Lully and Molière produced and that this is what he was sent to study and report on the second time he went to Paris. On his return he arranged for the playwright, Thomas Shadwell, to collaborate with the composer, Matthew Locke, in the composition of something on similar lines; but the result was too much like a Masque to be satisfactory.

In 1676 Betterton commissioned the eighteen-year-old genius, Henry Purcell (1659–95), to compose the incidental music for Dryden's heroic tragedy *Aurengzebe*; then for an adaptation of Shakespeare's *Timon of Athens*. Throughout the remainder of his lamentably short life Purcell wrote a considerable amount of theatre-music. Among his masterpieces are Dryden's *King Arthur* and musical versions of *The Tempest* and *A Midsummer Night's Dream* which he converted into that supreme masterpiece, *The Fairy Queen*. Only once did he write an opera in the Italian manner and that was the short but exquisite *Dido and Aeneas*. It was commissioned by one Josias Priest, a former dancing-master in Betterton's company, for performance at a girl's school in Chelsea of which he was then headmaster.

Italian opera was finally imposed upon the English by the authority and genius of George Frederick Handel (1685–1759). This great composer first visited England (from his native Germany), in 1710. He was twenty-five and had already composed a number of operas. *Rinaldo* was staged at Vanbrugh's theatre in the Haymarket and was an immediate success. Handel settled in London and dominated English music until his death.

There has never been a lack of admiration in England for Handel's many masterpieces of choral and orchestral music. But admiration has stopped short of idolatry. They have not been imitated or absorbed. There developed no tradition of operatic composition. Whether this was through the domination of the dramatic tradition, which was certainly not as powerful in any other country, it is impossible to say. The whole tradition of English music, which had been one of the glories of Elizabethan England, faltered during the eighteenth century, but the possible reasons are outside the scope of this book.

65 | The Eighteenth Century

The eighteenth century opened in most countries in a spirit of considerable confidence. In France it is referred to as *le grand siècle* (the great century); in Germany as the *Aufklärung*, the enlightenment, and in Britain as the Augustan age, when society would enjoy the assumed splendours of the Roman Emperor Augustus. Neo-classicism took a long while to cross the Channel, and when it did the English anglicized it, as was their way, and made no great fuss about what the Greeks and Romans had said and done. But it was one of the three articles of faith on which English culture in the eighteenth century was based.

Of the others there was firstly the word of God as revealed in the Bible. As the century proceeded, however, biblical scholarship revealed that the text of the Bible, behind the inspired translation of King James's scholars, was riddled with textual uncertainties. When the Christian turned away from the Bible to the world in which he lived he realized that Christendom was divided into two great armies composed of deeply religious people who missed no opportunity to butcher each other, while the Protestants themselves, lacking the unity provided by the authority of the Pope, were proliferating into a number of sectarian divisions. The century ended with less confidence in the Bible and what it stood for than it had begun.

At the same time there was tremendous confidence in the potential of scientific achievement. Restoration scientists such as Sir Isaac Newton saw a synthesis between the ways of God, the words of the Bible, and the scientific analysis of the natural world; for it was God himself who had given man the ability to analyse his own universe. Science, however, developed at a pace and in a manner – with its agricultural and industrial revolutions – that destroyed the stability of traditional society and created an unbridgeable gap between industrial productivity and humanitarian values. As the population rapidly increased the rich became richer and the poor poorer.

As for Augustanism, it was as far as the British went in subscribing to the ideals of classical culture. Study of the classics was the basis of British education. The exquisite proportions of eighteenth-century architecture were derived from a study of Greek and Roman, not medieval models. There was a widely-held belief in the authority of the individual, although dramatists such as Corneille and Racine, in revealing that every hero had an Achilles heel, had gone a long way to cut the hero down to size.

But there was a reverse to the clean lines and fine proportions of Augustan art. A style known as 'baroque', a word of obscure derivation, had been cultivated in Italy since the beginning of the seventeenth century. It was florid and theatrical in a slightly vulgar way, since it was an attempt to create a more vivid sense of reality and an emotional response in the spectator. But response to what? While baroque art was not the creation of Roman Catholic artists and architects the Church made considerable use of the baroque style in its fight to re-establish its authority, the movement that is known as the Counter-Reformation. In the best examples of baroque art there is a fine balance between a classical sense of proportion and elaborate exterior ornamentation. One can see this very clearly in the great choral works of Bach and Handel; but the excesses of baroque art are usually to be found in the work of architects and sculptors.

Some of the practical problems that artists were facing are summed up in an early statement issuing from the Royal Society which included the most learned men at the time of the Restoration. It attacked all forms of 'poetic' language, rejected all the 'amplifications, digressions, and swellings of style' and proposed a return to 'the primitive purity, and shortness, when men deliver'd so many things, almost in an equal number of words' and 'a close natural naked way of speaking . . . bringing all things as near the Mathematical plainness, as they can; and preferring the language of Artizans, Countrymen, and Merchants, fore that of Wits, or Scholars'.

While one can look on this as a philistine attack by scientists on artists, it is nevertheless a very significant statement of a problem that exercised many people, and that was how to establish a real relationship between science and art. This is too complicated a subject to deal with at length, but the contradictions were very clearly expressed by the Augustan poet, Alexander Pope (1688–1744) in his *Essay on Man*:

> All Nature is but Art, unknown to thee;
> All Chance, Direction, which thou canst not see;
> All Discord, Harmony, not understood;
> All partial Evil, universal Good:
> And, spite of Pride, in erring Reason's spite,
> One truth is clear, 'whatever is, is Right'.
> Know then thyself, presume not God to scan;
> The proper study of Mankind is Man.

This was a philosophy widely accepted by the philosophers as well as the artists. But the more they studied man the clearer they became that man is not merely a thinking creature but a feeling one, and that man's emotions are lamentably irrational and uncontrollable. It was this aspect of man, the unpredictable side of human nature, that became the main interest of eighteenth-century dramatists with some curious consequences.

It was during the eighteenth century that European culture became uniquely divided. Let us take Britain as an example. There was rapid growth of the country's cities, in particular Norwich, Bristol, Manchester, Leeds, Sheffield, Birmingham, and Liverpool. The country enjoyed a political stability unique in Europe. It was governed by an elected government supporting and supported by a free market economy. The Protestant succession had been firmly established, the Act of Union with Scotland had been passed, French expansionism had been blunted. The middle class set about expressing its independence with the acquisition of property and possessions. They bought land, built country houses, and had their estates exquisitely landscaped. It was the age of the great gardeners and horticulturalists – William Kent, Lancelot (Capability) Brown, and Humfrey Repton.

But another curious movement developed in the course of the century. The prosperous business man with his landscaped estate began to build a ruin in his grounds and planted ivy to grow over it. 'Is it not picturesque?' is the sort of question he might have asked a friend he wanted to impress. He relegated the novels of Richardson and Fielding to an inaccessible shelf of his library and began to read the 'Gothic' nonsense of Horace Walpole. (*The Castle Otranto* was published in 1764, only fifteen years after *Tom Jones*.) Walpole himself, fourth son of the Prime Minister, Robert Walpole, of whom more anon, had built himself a Gothic castle in Twickenham which he called Strawberry Hill. And the money for all this came from two sources – the immense improvement in agricultural techniques which resulted in a spectacular improvement in agricultural productivity, and the accompanying industrial revolution which produced immense wealth for Britain at the expense of covering large parts of the country with Blake's 'dark Satanic mills'. The century ended with total confidence in the economic stability of Britain, somewhat undermined by strange forebodings and misgivings in the soul of man which it became the work of the Romantic artists to express.

The Gothic Revival *by Kenneth Clark provides a useful description of this strange but important phenomenon. Books on the history of landscape gardening and horticulture are useful in showing one of the most productive aspects of eighteenth-century culture. Nothing shows more clearly the disintegrating sensibilities of the English middle class than a comparison of* Tom Jones *with* The Castle of Otranto *and Mary Shelley's ridiculous* Frankenstein. *Alexander Pope lived only a few yards along the road from Strawberry Hill which has been finely restored and may be visited by the public.*

66 English Drama in the Early Eighteenth Century

Colley Cibber gives no impression of being aware of social or political change; but he records in great detail the constantly changing managements of the London theatres. For the fact was that buildings were falling increasingly into the hands of business men who leased them to the managers, who were usually playwrights or actors, who actually staged the plays.

The emergence of the man who owns the theatre rather than stages plays is a development of considerable significance. His existence turns the theatre into an industry, a source of profit-making, and this in turn affects the policy of the producing management whose first concern is not to pay the actors but the rent. His chief concern is not artistic quality but commercial success. In the theatre of Shakespeare the two concepts were more or less synonymous. But increasingly the producing managers were obliged to make public taste their first consideration in choosing repertory. This dependence on public approbation was summed up by Dr Samuel Johnson in a Prologue he wrote for the opening of Drury Lane Theatre in 1747.

> The drama's laws the drama's patrons give,
> And we that live to please must please to live.

A change in the style of play-writing was a reflection of a change in the cultural climate of the whole country. The Restoration rakes, who for good or ill had been enthusiastic supporters of the theatre, and influential in what was written and staged, had gone, and managers faced the need to find new audiences. That it was a gradual and not an immediate change can be seen in the plays of George Farquhar (1678–1707). Here was another brilliant young Irishman who came to London and enjoyed great success with his second comedy, *The Constant Couple* (1699) which is licentious, indecent, and very funny. His next play, *The Twin Rivals* (1702), is not funny and was not successful. Then, having married, and finding it necessary to secure a regular income, he took a job as a recruiting officer in the north of England, an experience that provided him with material for his two best plays. *The Recruiting Officer* (1706) and *The Beaux' Stratagem* (1707) are plays written for the new emerging society. They are set outside London, the sexual intrigue decreases, there is more concern with a logical plot and developing characterization. They are gentle, amusing, stageable plays, showing a broader social outlook and a more tolerant view of humanity than is to be found in Restoration comedy.

This increasing gentility is also evident in the plays of Richard Steele (1672–1729) who was also of Irish birth though educated in England. It was at school that he met and made friends with Joseph Addison (1672–1719). Richard Steele interested himself in the theatre both as a manager and dramatist. His plays do not constitute a major contribution to British drama but his work in collaboration with Joseph Addison on the *Spectator* and the *Tatler* established a new kind of journalism, with a delicacy of wit that would have been quite unacceptable thirty years previously. Their occasional references to the theatre are vivid and often quietly malicious.

But a gentler form of Restoration comedy and was not enough to give the theatre the support it needed from a new society. The uncertainty of playwrights can be seen in the feeble plays of the supremely gifted Henry Fielding (1707–54). Before finding his true vocation as a novelist he wrote a number of dramatic satires and burlesques, sniping at the government with such success that the humourless Prime Minister, Robert Walpole, imposed a permanent censorship on the theatre. One of the most successful plays in the first half of the century was John Gay's *The Beggar's Opera* (1728), a delightful joke at the expense of Handel's operas combined with some sharpish social satire. This unpretentious little ballad opera was played throughout England in its own day and has been frequently revived during the present century.

The limitations of the patent did not help matters. Only two theatres were allowed in London though it did not matter which two. One was Drury Lane. The patent for a second theatre was bought and sold like a commodity, while the actors themselves moved from one theatre to another and back again according to the salaries they could command and the roles they were offered.

Since no outstanding playwright emerged to give a sense of direction to the faltering English drama the managers had to look for other ways of drawing a public. Italian opera singers had invaded London with limited success, though Handel's version of Italian opera was now well established at Vanbrugh's theatre in the Haymarket. Another Italian invasion was made by actors from the improvised companies. They seem to have come as individuals rather than in troupes and to have offered to managers and public what were called Harlequin dances; these evidently consisted of a curious mixture of mime, acrobatics, and talented fooling, or slapstick as it came to be called from the 'prop' they always carried with them. English playwrights were not slow to seize the opportunities that were offered. In 1697, for example, a certain William Mountfort wrote *The Life and Death of Doctor Faustus, made into a Farce with the Humours of Harlequin and Scaramouche*. So much for the great Elizabethan myth that had been the glory of the Renaissance theatre.

The piece was staged by John Rich, son of the notorious Christopher. He combined his father's interest in management with considerable skill as a Harlequin dancer (and a passion for cats with which his office used to be filled). With the real flair of a showman he ransacked myth, fable, and legend for suitably fantastic plots into which he could insert his Harlequin dancer, and so give some kind of unity and coherence to the episodic repertoire of the part. Such was his success with the public that Sir Richard Steele, who at the time (around 1712) was manager of Drury Lane, suffered from the competition. He turned for help to John Weaver (1673–1760), a man who was both dancer and scholar. Weaver was horrified by the general English attitude towards dance teaching as was exemplified, for example, in Wycherley's *The Gentleman Dancing Master*; he was familiar with the French *ballet de cour* through having translated into English various French theses on dance, and he was fascinated by the Harlequin dancers who visited London from the French fairs. He responded to Steele's invitation by creating a composition that seems to have been a mixture of mime and dramatic dancing. He called it *The Loves of Mars and Venus*, described it as a pantomime and staged it at Drury Lane in 1717. From that moment the pantomime become one of the most authentic and individual forms of British theatrical entertainment.

Cibber takes a rather dismissive attitude towards the whole story, ascribing it to competition between the theatres. Each was obliged 'to exhibit some new-fangled foppery, to draw the multitude after them. Of these expedients, singing and dancing had formerly been the most effectual; but at the time I am speaking of, our English music has been so discountenanced, since the taste of Italian operas prevailed, that there was no purpose to pretend to it. Dancing was now the only weight in the opposite scale.' To improve dancing, and to make it something

12. **The Beggar's Opera, 1728**
A painting by William Hogarth of the original production. The players are the five central figures, with Macheath in the middle. The people behind the tables are members of the audience. The stylishness of the playing and the distraction that must have been caused by the audience on the stage will be apparent.

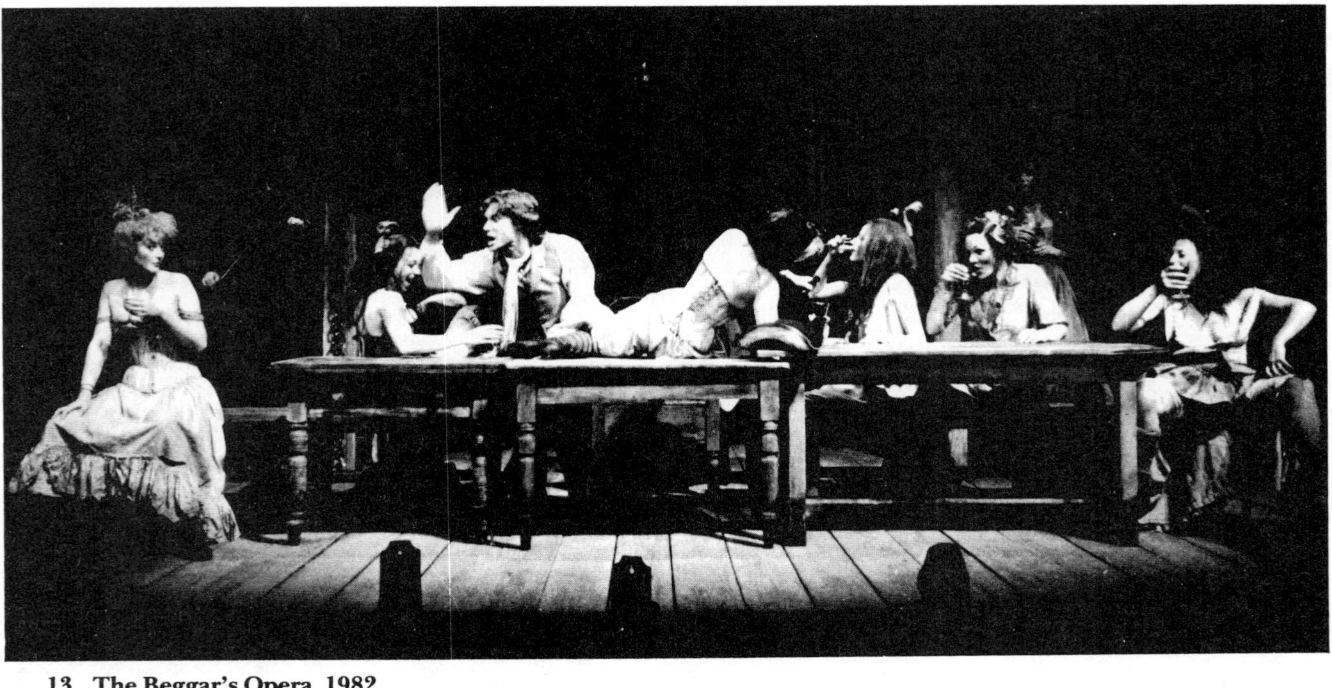

13. The Beggar's Opera, 1982
Produced in 1982 by the National Theatre. The scene shows Macheath 'with his doxies around'. A comparison of the two pictures will show how in the 1982 production period style has been discarded in favour of social realism.

more than motion without meaning, the fable of Mars and Venus was form'd into a connected presentation of dancers in character' which was so intelligently achieved that 'even thinking spectators allow'd it both a pleasing and a rational entertainment'. From this beginning, he goes on to say, there sprang 'that succession of monstrous medlies that have so long infested the stage . . . poetical drama, these gin-pots of the stage, that intoxicates its auditors and dishonours their understanding, with a levity for which I want a name'.

John Rich, however, was on to a good thing. Such was his success that in 1732 he gave up the theatre in Lincoln's Inn Fields and built a new theatre in Covent Garden to which he transferred the patent. He opened it with a revival of Congreve's *The Way of the World* but although he had had a great success with *The Beggar's Opera* – a production which contemporaries said made 'Rich gay and Gay rich' – it was his harlequinades, as they were first called, and his pantomimes, as they came to be called, that were the money-spinners. The success of this new form of entertainment with its spectacular transformation scenes was so great that David Garrick himself had to limit Shakespearian revivals in favour of pantomime. He apologized for so doing in 1750 in a Prologue in which he underlines again the dependence of the actor on public taste.

> Sacred to Shakespeare was this plot designed, [Drury Lane]
> To pierce the heart and humanize the mind,
> But if an empty house, the actor's curse,
> Shows us our Lears and Hamlets lose their force,
> Unwilling we must change the noble scene,
> And in our turn present your Harlequin . . .
> If want comes on, importance must retreat;
> Our first great ruling passion is – to eat.

67 English Tragedy in the Eighteenth Century

Heroic tragedy had been a seven-day wonder. Tragedy, as it survived in the eighteenth century, was something of a cross between the Jacobean and neo-classical, and hardly warrants serious attention. Of

Nathaniel Lee, one of the most enthusiastic authors of tragedy among Restoration poets, Cibber has this to say: 'In what raptures have I seen an audience at the furious fustian and turgid rants [of Betterton] in Nat Lee's *Alexander the Great.*' Thomas Otway has already been mentioned. Nicholas Rowe (1674–1718) was Poet Laureate for the last three years of his life, edited Shakespeare's plays, and wrote some abominable tragedies of which the two most successful were *The Fair Penitent* (1703) and *The Tragedy of Jane Shore* (1714). The former is a hysterically melodramatic Jacobean-style play about the rivalry of two young noblemen for the lovely Calista and her deceitful attitude towards them both. It is full of such couplets as

> Is it the Voice of Thunder, or my Father?
> Madness! Confusion! let the storm come on . . .

The other play is rather more controlled but only emphasizes the continual debilitation of tragedy. Playwrights clearly had no sense of direction. They took their ideas from the Greeks rather than the Romans, from Racine rather then Corneille, and, most unfortunately, from Voltaire (of whom more will be said later). They did this not because they were interested in the unities or the rules but because Racine's sexual themes were of some interest to them.

Tragedy, in fact, had no longer either social or theatrical validity. In its neo-classical form it was a product of the Renaissance because the values of classical tragedy accorded with the outlook of its highly influential audiences. But English society in 1750 was very different from French society in 1650, and the theatre-going public even more so. What is surprising is that would-be dramatists continued to write classical tragedy even as long as they did. They achieved some success when, as in the case of Nat Lee, they wrote good acting parts. But that a change was taking place can be seen in Ambrose Philip's translation of Racine's *Phèdre*. He gave it the subtitle, *The Distressed Mother*. The tormented classical heroine was becoming a tearful bourgeois matron.

But even the players clung to the sharp distinction between tragedy and comedy. Owing to the royal and aristocratic associations of the former, tragic actors considered themselves to be a higher species than comedians and hated to see the comedians as well-dressed as themselves, even off the stage.

The most significant play of the period is *George Barnwell or The London Merchant*, a title which is sometimes reversed as *The History of the London Merchant or George Barnwell*. Very little is known about its author, George Lillo (1693–1739), except that he was a man of amiable disposition and devoted to the theatre. The play is about a young business man who is brought to ruin by a villainous beauty who persuades him to rob his employer and murder his uncle, in both cases for their money. The dialogue carries the crudeness of poetic tragedy to even further extremes.

> Expiring saint! Oh, murdered, martyred uncle! lift up your dying eyes, and view your nephew in your murderer! – Oh, do not look so tenderly upon me! Let indignation lighten from your eyes, and blast me ere you die! . . .

It will be noticed that this debased prose falls easily into even more debased pentameters.

But the play had an enormous influence throughout Europe, presumably because it did represent an escape from prevailing dramatic forms. But it is a strange commentary on the Age of Enlightenment that this kind of nonsense should have been so popular.

68 | Sentimental Comedy

Restoration comedy and its aftermath had run their course by the 1720s. The extraordinary fact is that not a single other dramatist of note appeared until the arrival of Oliver Goldsmith and Richard Sheridan later in the century. As so often happens when dramaturgy, the writing of plays, is in decline, the prestige of the theatre was maintained by the players. In this case particularly the status of the London theatre was immeasurably improved by the work of David Garrick who was manager of Drury Lane between 1747 and 1776.

Garrick was a many-sided man with a ready pen, although as a dramatist he was no genius. One of his less admirable activities was to continue the Restoration practice of rewriting Shakespeare to suit, as he considered, the tastes of his time. But a play like *The Clandestine Marriage* (1776), which he wrote in collaboration with George Colman, is a most interesting work and a forerunner of what came to be called 'the well-made play'. With its preoccupation with money, social status, property, and possessions, it is a social tract in itself. Nothing else he wrote is as interesting.

Oliver Goldsmith (1728–74) has won for himself a small but significant niche in theatrical history by virtue of a single play. He was an improvident Irishman who had tried his hand at innumerable occupations in Britain, Europe, and America, before finding success as a novelist with *The Vicar of Wakefield* (1766). The next year he wrote his first play, *The Good-natured Man*, but it had no success. Although he admits in his Preface that he wrote the play in imitation of those in a former age, with emphasis on character and humour, the play is deficient in both and hampered by an improbable story.

In 1772 he wrote an *Essay on the Theatre or Sentimental Comedy* in which he regrets that tragedy and comedy are encroaching on each other's territory and that 'a new species has been introduced under the name of sentimental comedy in which the virtues of private life are exhibited rather than vices exposed . . . and the distresses rather than the faults of mankind make our interest in the piece'. This new genre, he says, has been very successful but had driven genuine comedy out of the theatre.

He exemplified this rather reactionary attitude in his next play, *She Stoops to Conquer* (1773), the early scenes of which are delightful enough to compensate for the rather feeble and contrived events with which he keeps the story going. It is generally considered to be one of the great, even if slightly overrated comedies of the English stage.

The outstanding dramatist of the age was yet another Irishman, Richard Brinsley Sheridan (1751–1816). He was the son of an actor who held eccentric views. On completion of his education at Harrow he began almost at once to write plays but not before he had married, in somewhat romantic circumstances, a young singer called Elizabeth Linley, described by Leigh Hunt as 'a charmer for beauty and song'. In January 1775, when he was only twenty-four, his first comedy, *The Rivals*, was produced at Covent Garden; *St. Patrick's Day or The Scheming Lieutenant* in May of the same year and *The Duenna* in November. This last was rated far more highly than it is today and was a great success. Over the next two years, having a good deal of the gambler in his nature, he bought Drury Lane from David Garrick with the help of his father-in-law, various friends, and a large mortgage. In 1777 he wrote *A Trip to Scarborough*, a purified version of Vanbrugh's *The Relapse*, but the public did not care for it. He was saved from disaster by the success of his own masterpiece, *The School for Scandal*, produced in May of the same year. Although the story had been in his mind for some time, he wrote it at great speed, prodded to overcome his innate laziness by David Garrick who was breathing down his neck. The play went into rehearsal before the text was complete and it was not until a few days before it was due to open that he was able to write at the bottom of the manuscript – 'Finished at last – Thank God – R.B.S.', to which the prompter added 'Amen'. Unbelievably, the play was looked at askance by the Lord Chamberlain and was granted a licence only on Sheridan's personal intervention. The applause at the final curtain of the first performance was so great that a passer-by took to his heels for fear the theatre was going to collapse. One of the morning papers summed up the occasion like this.

> Yesterday morning Mrs Sheridan was delivered of a son. The mother and child are likely to do well. In the evening of the same day Mr Sheridan's muse was delivered of a bantling that is likely to live for ever.

In the autumn of the same year his exquisite satire, *The Critic*, was staged, another timeless work. Sheridan wrote only one more play and that was *Pizzarro* (1799), a free adaptation from a German original. One wonders how he came to put his name to a work which his own Mr Puff, the critic of *The Critic*, would have laughed out of the theatre for its idiotically artificial heroics and drivelling sentimentality.

It was perhaps because he had overstretched himself. In 1780 he entered Parliament where he proved himself to be a brilliant orator. He continued to run Drury Lane, which he had rebuilt in 1791 and again in 1809 after it had been destroyed by fire. He was neither an efficient nor a successful manager. He took large sums of money at the box-office, partly through having the greatest actress of the age, Sarah Siddons, in his company; but he was financially improvident almost to the point of dishonesty, and frequently left his players unpaid for long periods. During more than twenty years of management he did virtually nothing to help the theatre either by encouraging new dramatists, improving methods of production, or even properly exploiting the talents of his often brilliant company.

In 1812 he lost his seat in Parliament and the next year was imprisoned for debt. He passed the last years of his life in obscurity and extreme ill health but was well cared for during his last illness and was buried triumphantly in Westminster Abbey.

It is hardly necessary to add that the plays referred to in this chapter are eminently readable and stageable. But a careful reading of the masterpieces of Goldsmith and Sheridan will show how soft the social satire had become in contrast with the bite of Congreve and Vanbrugh. Sheridan has been the subject of many biographies.

69 French Comedy in the Early Eighteenth Century

The death of Molière in 1671 and the virtual retirement of Racine from the theatre closes a chapter in the history of the French theatre. The new chapter opens with two important events, the creation of the Comédie-Française and the Comédie Italienne. The former was the result of a decision by Louis XIV that the two companies working in Paris should combine. This amalgamation was brought about by Molière's widow in 1681.

It will be remembered that the Italians had established themselves in Paris in 1658 when they shared the Palais Royal with Molière's company. With the formation of the Comédie-Française, for whom a new theatre was built on the site of the present Odéon, they were given full use of the Hôtel de Bourgogne. Their work must have been interesting; for although they were given permission by the King to play occasionally in French, they continued at the same time to play their own traditional improvisations which did not require much speaking in either language.

They were thus in the curious position of requiring short scenes written in French which they could link together with improvisations. The first writer of the time to oblige was Jean-François Regnard (1655–1710), a witty young man who in the course of travelling around Europe was captured by pirates and made to work as a slave until ransomed by his wealthy parents. On his return to Paris he became interested in literature and the theatre, and so to amuse himself rather than to make money, he began writing at first short scenes and then full-length plays for the Italians. Unfortunately in 1697 the company was accused of having slighted Madame de Maintenon, the wife of the now sombre and autocratic Louis XIV, who banished them from Paris. Regnard then began writing for the Comédie-Française and produced two of his best known works, *Le Joueur* (*The Gambler*, 1696) and *Le Légataire universel* (*The Residuary Legatee*, 1708). Both plays are written in verse. The first is about an inveterate gambler who pays for his obsession with the loss of his lady and the second is a rather cynical play, of the kind that was popular with the Jacobeans, about the far-fetched devices employed by a group of relatives to secure the inheritance of an old and dying man.

Other writers of the period show an increasing interest in contemporary manners and behaviour. In the case of Florent Carton Dancourt (1661–1725) this can be seen in the titles of his farces – *Le Bourgeois à la mode* (*The Fashionable Bourgeois*, 1692), *Le Chevalier à la mode* (*The Fashionable Knight*, 1687), and *Le Bourgeois de qualité* (1724) – the titles are really untranslatable. Alain Réné Lesage (1668–1747) writes more bitterly about money as a motive force in social life. His use of prose gives more reality to his satire. His famous play, *Turcaret* (1709), was bitterly attacked by the financiers it satirized.

This is the period when the life of the old King was slowly drawing to its close. He died in 1715 and his son who succeeded him as Louis XV did little to change the face of French life. The aristocracy, increasingly impoverished through having spent time dancing attendance on the King in Versailles when they should have been administering their provincial estates, were losing authority, while the bourgeoisie, whose increasing importance was a subject of such interest to the dramatists, lacked political representation. These were some of the tensions that led to the revolution of 1789.

With the succession of Louis XV the Italians were allowed to return to Paris. They arrived in 1716 and settled in the Hôtel de Bourgogne under the direction of a most distinguished actor, Luigi Riccoboni (1675–1753), son of a famous Pantalone and the author of an important book on the Italian comedy. Parisian taste in the meanwhile had changed. The now old-fashioned pantomime, no longer acceptable, was replaced by a variety of musical entertainments, including ballet-pantomimes and the increasingly popular vaudevilles. Of greater importance was their invitation to young French dramatists to supply them with plays. It was thus that they discovered a dramatist of genius in Marivaux. By the 1780s they had achieved official subsidized status but the price they paid was loss of identity. Italian actors were replaced by French; and when in 1752 an Italian comic opera company arrived in Paris the two companies amalgamated to form the Opéra Comique.

By the time of the return of the Italians to Paris, dramatists were at liberty to write for either company, the Comédie Italienne or the Comédie Française. One of those who wrote for both was Pierre Carlet de Chamberlain de Marivaux (1688–1763). Never did a playwright exploit so narrow a range of subject-matter with such rich invention. His subject-matter is falling in love rather than being in love: he is in no way a Racine; he is not interested in Venus or love-potions, but simply in the complex psychological process that takes place when a man and woman meet each other and find a growing and unexpected emotion in their relationship. In view of the fact that he deals with the process of falling in love in considerable detail, and that his plays are almost wholly without physical action of any kind, depending entirely upon a succession of emotional shifts, it is surprising that he preferred writing for the Italians rather than for the French. The reason may well have been the contradictory one that it was simply because the Italians were graced with a natural physical vitality that they were able to supply an additional element of physical expressiveness that was absent from the script. To many of his characters he gives the name of Italian actors and actresses, and even preserves them from one play to the next. Arlequin, Silvia, Lelio, Columbine appear in one play after another so that the audience (or the reader) could concentrate on the subtly changing relationships of characters they knew rather than on coming to terms with new ones.

He found his style with *La Surprise de l'amour* (1722), by no means his first play but one of his best. And nothing happens but that the Countess and Lelio abjure all interest in love only to discover after three acts that they are in love with each other. In *La Double inconstance* (*The Double Inconstancy*, 1723), one of his masterpieces, two pairs of lovers slowly change partners. In *La Seconde surprise de l'amour* (1727) a Marquise, inconsolable at the death of her husband, finds her friendship with the Chevalier transformed into love. In *Le Jeu de l'amour et du hasard* (*The Game of Love and Chance*, 1730), often considered to be his finest play, a young woman and her servant, her intended fiancée and his servant, change roles in order better to observe the character of their opposite. A change of role leads to a change of emotional relationships.

The plays of Marivaux are like a highly organized dance in which the most deft and subtle variations are evolved out of the most limited material. They are devoid of theatrical effects, they need neither furniture nor properties. They take place in an abstract world that cannot reflect more than a tiny facet of his society; yet they make compelling reading and are often very moving.

Nevertheless it is interesting to find that even in the cloistered world of Marivaux a bitter note creeps in, especially to his later plays. His heroines become a little more bourgeois, a little less aristocratic, and an increasing concern with money gives a slightly sordid edge to the game of love.

Most of the plays mentioned in this section are classics of French literature. Many of them are still revived at the Comédie-Française. But they do not translate well, Marivaux least of all. The Game of Love and Chance *is by far the best known in English. In recent years there has been a striking increase in the popularity of Marivaux especially among younger and more 'progressive' directors.*

Since 1680 Molière has been by far the most frequently performed dramatist by the Comédie-Française, followed, in this order, by Racine, Corneille, Musset, who has gained favour in recent years, Dancourt, Regnard, Marivaux, and Voltaire, who is now rarely played at all.

70 | Sentimental Comedy in France

As the century progressed, French audiences, like those in England, became tired of sexual intrigues among the aristocracy, dishonest noblemen, fatuous uncles, duplicitous lovers, rascally servants, and depraved soubrettes. Marivaux had introduced a new note into French comedy, and even if his slightly ironic and sometimes bitter style is not exactly sentimental, it is full of sentiment.

Two other dramatists had a hand in changing the theatrical climate. These were Philippe Nericault Destouches (1680–1754), whose best-known play is *Le Glorieux* (1732) and Pierre-Claude Nivelle de la Chaussée (1692–1754). Both were moralists and typical of their age in considering that vice is an illness rather than a crime; that man is to be pitied rather than censured; that the aim of drama must be to reform rather than to rebuke, attitudes which suggest that the age was a good deal more tolerant than in fact it was.

But *comédie larmoyante* (tearful comedy), as sentimental comedy was called in France, produced no more distinguished playwrights than it had in England until two writers of note appeared. Denis Diderot was one of those prodigious figures who cover a vast range of human activities and have something original to say about everything. He was not, however, much of a dramatist. His first play, *Le Fils naturel* (*The Natural Son*, 1757) was what we might call a Gothic melodrama, full of violent passion and striking theatrical situations for which the French have an untranslatable term, *coup de théâtre*. What is of interest is not the play but the theatrical analysis, written like much of his work in dialogue form, accompanying the published version under the title of *Entretiens* [*Conversations*] *sur le Fils naturel*. In this he takes a contrary and far more positive view of the theatre than Oliver Goldsmith, arguing that tragedy and comedy are no longer valid as separate genres since what was wanted was a form that depicted the lives of ordinary people with whom an audience could feel a certain sympathy. He goes on to discuss a large range of theatrical topics: the unities; the old French concept of *vraisemblance*; the value of large stages enabling scenery to be easily changed; and large auditoria so that a collective emotion can be engendered in the audience.

In the following year, 1758, he wrote his second play, *Père de famille* (*Father of the Family*) and published it along with a *Discours de la poésie dramatique* in which he discusses the art of the dramatist in more general terms than he had in the *Entretiens*. In these works he makes a powerful plea for realism in subject-matter, a natural style of acting (instead of the fashionable declamation), and simplicity in scenery and costumes.

The other considerable figure of the period was Pierre-Augustin Caron de Beaumarchais (1732–99), another man to spread his energy over an enormous area of human activity. He was at various times musician, financier, man of business, diplomat, merchant, shipowner, army-contractor, secret agent, publisher. He was something of an adventurer, highly argumentative by nature and not always scrupulous in his dealings. He was not a professional liberal, against the government and the establishment, but he did not suffer fools, prejudice, or pomposity gladly. He used his pen not so much to earn a living as to provide a diversion from his intensely busy practical life. His first two plays, *Eugénie* and *Les Deux amis* (*The Two Friends*) were heavy-going dramas of a kind he defends in his *Essai sur le genre dramatique* arguing that this type of play has taught us how to enjoy the touching spectacle of domestic unhappiness while providing a more direct and appealing interest than is to be found in heroic tragedy and more profundity than in light comedy.

He then changes key and writes two of the most elegant comedies in the whole of dramatic literature, *Le Barbier de Seville* (*The Barber of Seville*, 1772) and its sequel, *Le Marriage de Figaro* (1775), both now better known through the operatic versions of Rossini and Mozart respectively, than as original plays, although *The Marriage of Figaro* was extremely successful in its own day and is still sometimes revived by the Comédie-Française. In his introduction to *The Barber* he seems to repudiate his early work and claims to have written an amusing play in the style of older comedies. Indeed, *The Barber* takes up the theme of Molière's *L'Ecole des femmes* with its amorous old man, pretty ward, and noble lover. As Sheridan ran into trouble with the censor over *The School for Scandal*, Beaumarchais ran into constant opposition from the liberal sentiments expressed by his traditional comic servant, the barber Figaro. It did not need the French Revolution to create a high degree of political sensitivity. We are moving into the period of romanticism with its political idealism and artistic liberality.

71 | Voltaire

French tragedy of the eighteenth century is a pretty dull affair. It is dull in the hands of the chief exponent of the genre, Prosper Jolyot de Crébillon (1674–1742), and it is dull in the hands of the least dull of men, the sprightly, sharp-witted and highly sagacious François Marie Arouet (1694–1778) who wrote under the name of Voltaire. Yet it is astonishing to meet a writer of such unquestionable eminence who did not write a single work that is essential reading. Among his letters, his articles, his poems there are golden nuggets. *Candide* is a small masterpiece but it does not say much except, in the wittiest of terms, that what is, is by no means necessarily right. In his own day he enjoyed a European reputation and when his constant polemics against church and state had made France too hot to hold him, he retired to Ferney in Switzerland from where he conducted a correspondence with many of the leading figures of his time which, when ultimately published, will fill sixty volumes. Here he had his own small theatre and the actors and actresses who visited him speak of his skill as a teacher and director.

His witty tongue and satirical pen got him into trouble from the start. As a young man he spent eleven months in the Bastille, where he wrote a tragedy on Oedipus and part of an epic poem. He was in trouble again in 1726 and freed from imprisonment on condition that he went to England where he lived for three years. Here he became the close friend of Pope, Swift, Gay, and many others and developed a life-long love-hate relationship with Shakespeare.

In spite of great persistency he had no success in the theatre until the production of *Zaïre* in 1732. In spite of his natural wit, it was tragedy that interested him. His plays, rather like those of Dryden, combine a colourful story in a picturesque setting with a classical severity of structure; but his verse is pedestrian, his stories far-fetched, their theatrical interest negligible. To most of the printed versions he attaches a delightful Preface or Dedicatory Epistle. In these essays he expresses his horror of social injustice (*Alzire*, 1737); the importance of writing tragedies that do not depend on an erotic relationship between the protagonists (*Mérope*, 1743), and in the long Preface to *Sémiramide* (1748) which takes the form of a dissertation on ancient and modern tragedy he argues that the contemporary form most similar to classical tragedy is opera, and then continues with a delightful analysis of *Hamlet* which he describes as a vulgar and barbaric play which can only be the imaginative product of a drunken savage (*un sauvage ivre*); while in the Preface to *Tancrède* (1760) he writes of the social importance of the theatre and the pre-eminence of Greek tragedy.

One feels that in his *La Mort de César* (*The Death of Caesar*, 1731) he had learnt nothing from Corneille and Racine but reverted to the naivety of the sixteenth century. The play opens with Anthony asking Caesar why he is so depressed. Caesar replies with a speech of thirty-nine lines complaining that he is tired with conquering the world (as well he might be) and concludes with an unemotional Anthony demanding vengeance for the murder, with the citizens replying in stereotyped alexandrines.

Voltaire, writing a hundred years after Molière and Racine, is still insistent that the stage should reflect the 'bon sens', the good manners, the social values of real life. In his *Letters Concerning the English Nation*, he complains again about *Hamlet*.

In the first scene the Guard says 'not a mouse stirring'.

> Yes sir, a soldier might make such an answer when in barracks; but not upon a stage, before people of the highest distinction who express themselves nobly and before whom every one should express himself in a similar manner.

Voltaire's tragedies, though rarely played today, were constantly revived on the stage of the Comédie-Française. Their heroic themes accorded with the aristocratic outlook and the high social pretensions of the theatre's audiences. But only eleven years after his death, the country went up in flames and the Bastille, to which Voltaire had paid a couple of enforced visits, was seized by a revolutionary mob. Classical tragedy had finally had its day. Society was no longer interested in legendary heroes, unless, as increasingly rarely happened, they provided good acting parts. Hamlet, Lear, Othello, and Macbeth have lived because they have an independent existence in an imaginative reality unrelated to any particular class or social or political outlook. With an increasing preponderance of the middle classes in the audience, it was middle-class interests that were projected by the playwrights; these interests included the disaster that could befall the ordinary citizen, and that was none the less tragic and moving for being on a low rather than an elevated social level, for being concerned with the ordinary fellow and not with princes. The new direction that tragedy was likely to take had been pointed out by the success of Lillo's *George Barnwell* and that is why the play, with all its absurdities, was so successful throughout Europe.

72 | The Comédie-Française

The success of the Italians with Marivaux left the company of the Comédie-Française to deal with the more conventional plays of the time and to revive the classics of the previous century. Under Louis XIV they had been 'la seule troupe des Comédiens du Roi', the King's special company, and took over the privileged monopoly previously held by the Confrérie de la Passion. They numbered fifteen actors and twelve actresses and their rights and privileges together with the extent of their annual subsidy were carefully defined. The King was in absolute control, interfered frequently, even in matters of casting, and delegated only to his brother.

Nevertheless the company went through a difficult period. One theatre after another was for one reason or another unsatisfactory, and even with subsidy finances were difficult. Under the new King matters improved. The company included players of considerable ability both in tragedy and comedy. Some of them achieved considerable social standing among the *grands seigneurs* from whom they learnt physical deportment, taste in dress, and standards of speech, matters of great concern to members of high society who formed the greater part of their audiences. It is therefore not surprising that the French revolutionaries saw the Comédie-Française as a hotbed of the *canaille aristocratique* (aristocratic mob). Under the Terror of 1791 their theatre, which was on the site of the present Odéon, was closed and their survival was due to the republican sympathies of the great actor Talma, and the interest of Napoleon Bonaparte himself. The theatre reopened in 1799 in what is virtually its present building. Napoleon insisted on a classical repertoire to the exclusion of new work, befriended Talma, took the company's leading lady, Madamoiselle George, as his mistress, and redrafted its constitution on route for Moscow (1812).

In the eighteenth century the Comédie-Française was of considerable importance. French culture was dominant throughout Europe and French comedy was a part of this culture. This domination collapsed when the political authority of which it was an expression disintegrated.

With the Romantic movement, which has yet to be discussed, British culture became far more influential. But the British, for all their success in building an Empire, have never been cultural imperialists. Indeed it was nearly two hundred years before the British built a subsidized national theatre. The tradition of French culture has been aristocratic, centralized, and authoritarian. The British, in their more haphazard but democratic way, have left responsibility for culture to those who both create and benefit from it.

More will be said about national theatres, subsidizing the theatre, and similar subjects in a later section. One is happy to be able to say that at the time of writing, the early 1980s, the Comédie-Française is in good health. A stay in Paris should include a visit to the senior permanent theatre in the world.

73 Italian Drama of the Eighteenth Century

The aftermath of the Renaissance was not a happy time for Italy. The country was politically divided and spiritually exhausted. The opera singers sang and the Harlequins danced. Giovanni Tiepolo painted immense canvasses illustrating the epic poems of Greece and Rome, and his son, Giovanni, left some delightful caricatures of the curious types who were to be found in the streets of the towns. But of the neo-classical theatre, nothing more is heard. Italy had no equivalent to the Jacobean drama in England, the drama of the golden age in Spain, or the neo-classical French drama of Corneille, Molière, and Racine. By the eighteenth century even the Commedia dell' Arte was showing signs of exhaustion.

It was not until the latter part of the eighteenth century that a dramatist of any distinction emerged and that was Vittorio Amedeo Alfieri (1749–1803). The spirit to which he gave expression was Italian nationalism which was to become a most powerful movement in the nineteenth century. He did this by trying to create an authentic Tuscan-Italian drama. There were many regional dialects in Italy then as now and Tuscany, which includes the great artistic centre of Florence and the commercial city of Milan, was accepted as the cultural capital of the country by sheer weight of achievement. But in spite of Alfieri's admirable intention of wishing to arouse feelings of nationalism and liberty, he was imprisoned within the classical tradition and wrote plays on such threadbare subjects as Orestes, Antigone, Agamemnon, and Brutus with strict regard for the rules. Far more was achieved by a writer like Carlo Goldoni who had very little interest in politics and who wrote a large number of plays that presented a vivid picture of Italian life. He was interested in theatrical not political reform. For the Commedia dell' Arte had run out of steam. Its themes had become increasingly repetitive and there was a widespread reliance on comic 'business' and well-worn routines many of a most indecent kind. This is what tends to happen in a theatre dominated by actors rather than writers. This is no disrespect to the acting profession. Actors and actresses have as deep a store of creative fantasy as every artist, but it does not emerge in conceptual terms. That is to say, an actor creates characters through the instrument of his own body: he does not re-create reality in terms of stories in which his own contribution is only a part. When he possesses this faculty he ceases to be an actor and becomes a writer.

Some, however, saw the possibility of regeneration. Such a one was Carlo Gozzi (1720–1806), an unhappy, down-at-heel aristocrat who was always turning to the past and searching for a lost society, to restore the purity of the Italian language, and to recreate classical literary forms. In his autobiography Gozzi describes how he tried to revitalize the Commedia dell' Arte by writing original scenarios for the Commedia troupe of Antonio Sacchi. Although his ten stories did nothing to arrest the decline of improvised comedy, their imaginative inventiveness and delightful fantasy have appealed greatly to a number of writers and composers. *Gli Amore della tre Melarance* (*The Love of the Three Oranges*) has been turned into a opera by the Russian composer Prokofiev, *Turandot* into an opera by Puccini, and *Il Re Cervo* into a popular children's play.

Carlo Goldoni (1707–93), towards whom Gozzi directed all his bitterness and frustration, was described by the English poet, Robert Browning, as 'good, gay and the sunniest of souls'. He was a Venetian by birth, trained in the law. This he practised for a time while he wrote scenarios for various companies. After seven years he was persuaded to throw over the law and to join a Commedia company as 'resident writer of scenarios'. But he soon came to realize the limitations of the form, resigned, and became an independent author of comedies. Only one of his earlier pieces has survived; but *Il Servitore di Due Padroni* (*The Servant of Two Masters*) is a brilliant example of the way in which he gave style and form to the traditional 'masques'. Goldoni was infinitely prolific. Gozzi was justified in describing him as inventive, observant, and superficial. He settled down to write for the manager of the Sant' Angelo theatre in Venice, writing in the year 1750 no less than sixteen comedies. In 1753 he moved to another theatre in Venice, the San Luca, but it proved to be too big for his neatly composed and delicately stylish comedies. He was attacked not only by Carlo Gozzi but by a rival playwright, the Abbe Pietro Chiari (1711–85), the author of Gothic extravagances of the kind that were becoming popular in England and France. Gozzi loathed them far more than the comedies of Goldoni for which he had a certain sneaking regard.

Goldoni, however, was no fighter and in 1761 he accepted an invitation to visit Paris where he settled down to write for the Italians. He did not find life easy in Paris although it was here that he wrote two of his best comedies. He was far too genial a man to cope with the excesses of the French Revolution and he died in poverty.

He wrote in all 150 comedies, ten little-known tragedies and eighty-three texts for various kinds of light opera that were popular at the time. His earlier plays have a carefully contrived plot. *The Servant of Two Masters* is a fine example. *Il Bugiardo* (*The Liar*) is based on the complications resulting from a young man's compulsive lying. *Il Due Gemelli Veneziani* (*The Two Venetian Twins*) has all the predictable complications associated with identical twins, who in this case were played by the same actor. But in his later plays he develops the facility to contrive a play out of the most trivial of incidents. *Il Ventaglio* (*The Fan*, 1765) is about the gossip and the misunderstandings that arise when a woman drops her fan in a café. *La Locandiera* (*The Hostess*, sometimes known by the name of its heroine, *Mirandolina*, 1753) and *La Vedova Scaltra* (*The Artful Widow*, 1748) are both about attractive ladies playing off their admirers against each other.

With the death of Goldoni Italy ceased to play a part in the mainstream of European drama for more than a hundred years. The innate passions of the Italian people were fully expressed, however, in two ways. The great movement of Italian nationalism, known as the *Risorgimento* (resurrection), began to take shape around 1815 and resulted in the unification of the country in 1870. During this period the spirit of Romanticism, which was closely associated with political freedom, was expressed by a remarkable group of opera composers. Gioacchino Rossini (1792–1868), Gaetano Donizetti (1797–1848), Vincenzo Bellini (1801–35), and Giuseppe Verdi (1813–1901) gave a unique emphasis to the lyric as against the dramatic theatre. One wonders what strange deep social forces were at work that the Italian genius in the visual arts should have deserted them, while in music, and a particular kind of music, there should have been so impressive a burst of creativity.

Gozzi's autobiography, Memoirie Inutile della Vita di Carlo Gozzi *(*Useless Memoires of the Life of Carlo Gozzi*) is available in English translation. There is at least one English version of* King Stag.

A number of Goldoni's plays have been translated and should be readily available. They are staged by no means infrequently.

The Italian theatre of the period has not been adequately dealt with in English. The opera composers have always been treated from a musical rather than a theatrical standpoint.

74 | Romanticism

The movement that spread over Europe in the second half of the eighteenth century was another major shift in human consciousness similar to that of the Renaissance three centuries previously. Nor can the Romantic movement, any more than its predecessor, be dated from a single event. People began to compose, to write, to paint, to build in a way markedly different from their predecessors, until there came a time when all this activity could be identified as a movement. But it was the French, who have always enjoyed a particular gift for metaphysical speculation, who first identified Romanticism with a particular political and artistic programme.

The Romantic movement has been foreshadowed in much that has already been described. The collapse of heroic tragedy, the tearful hysterics of George Barnwell, the ivy-covered ruins on Capability Brown's estates, Gothic novels, all these were portents of a great change, to repeat the phrase, in European consciousness. People looked at the world differently, and understandably so, for in some ways it was a new world, a world of factories and industrial productivity. The population increased rapidly and so did the size of the towns. But while the main streets had bigger and better shops, in the industrial districts there were even more horrifying slums.

All these great social changes were closely related to political change. The single most violent and far-reaching event of the late eighteenth century was the French Revolution of which the war-cry was Liberty, Equality, Fraternity. If the last two have remained somewhat unattainable ideals, the idea of political liberty was of great significance for people who felt that they had been for too long suffering from autocratic government. The new consciousness in the way that people looked at things was very closely related to the way they felt about things, and one of the things they felt most strongly about was political freedom.

The eighteenth century began with a widespread belief in the rationality of man and ended with an equally strong belief in his irrationality, his emotionalism. Men looked at the world not in terms of the orderliness expressed by Alexander Pope but of the great stormy skies that were painted by J. W. M. Turner. The new outlook was explicitly stated by William Wordsworth in his Preface to *Lyrical Ballads* (published in 1800) where he writes about the importance of the poet using 'the real language of man in a state of vivid sensation . . .' his concern to 'make the interests of common life interesting . . .' by the association of ideas 'in a state of excitement'. He defines poetry as 'the spontaneous overflow of powerful feelings', taking its origin from 'emotion recollected in tranquillity'.

The artist of the Romantic period was no longer concerned with legendary heroes but humble peasants. He did not assume an objective attitude to his art, based on a number of precise rules and principles, but gave expression to his own inmost feelings in the most personal and individual manner. The writings of the great Romantics such as Jean-Jacques Rousseau and Goethe are full of this new consciousness: an intense individualism, a close relationship with nature, religious mysticism, the exaltation of emotion, a preoccupation with the supernatural and a revolt against political authority. The Alps, the German forests, the great cathedrals of medieval Europe, all suddenly came into their own.

A word of warning. To suggest that Romantic art is concerned with feelings, colours, textures, the picturesque, the exciting, is not to imply that it is necessarily inferior to classical art, but simply that it is different. The distinction between good and bad art is outside the scope of this book, though the distinction between good and bad theatre has been constantly noted. Classical art, paying too much attention to rules, can be dry and pedantic, just as Romantic art, paying too little attention to rules, can be hysterical and superficial. In any case, such comparative terms as 'good' and 'bad', 'better' and 'worse' are well avoided, unless one can establish absolute standards for one's comparisons.

It is, nevertheless, an extremely puzzling phenomenon that, generally speaking, the Romantic theatre was a disaster with nothing to compare with what was achieved in music, literature, and the visual arts. The reasons for this are distressingly obscure.

Anyone wishing to understand this important movement is recommended to study Romanticism not only in literature, but in music and painting. From Mozart's early works, for example, to Beethoven's last, the Ninth Symphony, for example, is a period of about fifty years, but one does not have to be a highly-trained musician to hear the tremendous extension of emotional range that was achieved.

75 | The Emerging German Theatre

Historical maps show that the territory comprising central Europe has undergone constant political change from the dark ages until the end of the nineteenth century. Renaissance ideas, which exercised so powerful an influence in France and Italy, were slow to take root since the conditions in which these ideas could flourish did not exist. Development was considerably delayed by the policies of the Emperor Ferdinand II (1578–1637) who used military means to suppress growing Protestantism. The ensuing war, which is known as the Thirty Years War (1618–48), was brutal and bloody even by standards of the age and involved at one time or another every country in Europe. The Catholics were led by the Habsburg Emperors and the Protestants by the King of Sweden. The war resulted in the death of at least half the population of Germany. The eventual Peace of Westphalia changed the political map of Europe.

Germany in the late seventeenth and early eighteenth century consisted of a large number of independent duchies, principalities, and dukedoms of which the Kingdom of Prussia was the largest and most powerful. The extension of Prussian territory was an objective of the two kings whom the Hitlerian regime saw as the founders of the modern German state, Frederick William I (1688–1740) and his son, Frederick II, known as Frederick the Great (1712–86).

For the Kings of Prussia and the independent princes and dukes, the dominant culture in Europe was not that of Britain, which was far too domestic to satisfy the ambitions of growing political nationalism, but the French, although Louis XIV's territorial ambitions made France Prussia's political rival at the same time as being her cultural ideal. Aggressive dog admires aggressive dog. In Potsdam, a small town some short distance to the south of Berlin, Frederick II built the Palace of

Sans Souci. Its name was not the only French thing about it. It is a kind of replica of Versailles with symmetrically laid-out gardens and an inordinate number of neo-classical sculptures. The library is lined with books in French, and in particular the works of Voltaire who was a close friend of, and literary adviser to the King. But Sans Souci has something that is absent from Versailles – an enormous parade ground where Frederick William drilled his troops, which included a regiment of men of immense physical stature. Thus the two kings, aided by a powerful army and an efficient civil service, laid the foundations of the future German Empire; but they did little to create an authentic German culture. That was the work of the more enlightened dukes who, by turning their courts into miniature Versailles, each with its library and its theatre, to which they frequently invited French touring companies, created the conditions in which natural growth could take place.

There were three traditions in the German theatre. The first was that of amateur drama. Although his work has been rather poorly documented we know that Hans Sachs (1494–1576), the shoemaker of Nuremberg, wrote over two hundred short plays covering a wide range of historical, biblical, and classical subjects such as were treated by French dramatists of the sixteenth century. They were performed by groups of university students and professional organizations as happened in England and France.

The second tradition was that of the Jesuits. The Society of Jesus had been founded in 1534 by St. Ignatius Loyola to fight the so-called refôrmed religion and encourage the Counter-Reformation. A part of their programme was the establishment of colleges where the students could be thoroughly indoctrinated. The Jesuits brilliantly realized that it would be safer to absorb humanism than fight it. The Colleges were therefore encouraged to write and produce Latin plays on largely Old Testament subjects. Though strongly propagandist in content they were often spectacular in form, thus assailing the audience with the intensity of their content and the brilliance of their presentation.

Thirdly, there were the court theatres where, in default of an authentic German drama, the repertoire consisted largely of French dramatic and Italian operatic touring companies. Most generally detested was the work of the poor itinerant German troupes.

So by no means for the first time in this book we are considering the formation of a new drama. The first of the great visionaries was Johann Christoph Gottsched (1700–66), a literary critic who in a series of pamphlets and plays did something to prepare the way for reform. Though a Prussian by birth, and being a man of exceptional height, he had moved to Leipzig, a vigorous centre of German culture, to avoid conscription into Frederick William's regiment of giants. First he tried to establish a single German language based on Saxon forms of speech; then he turned to the theatre and entered into collaboration with Caroline Neuber (1697–1760), the leading actress of the day and the head of a company that was based in Leipzig. The collaboration lasted ten years. Gottsched tried to collect a body of German plays written in the French manner, the only one he knew. But the two styles were not compatible and Gottsched, who was both pedantic and arrogant, lacked the flexibility to work out a realistic compromise.

By the middle of the century some of the books and plays that had been influential in the British and French theatre were becoming known in Germany – Richardson's novels, Lillo's *London Merchant*, sentimental comedy, *comédie larmoyante*, *drame sérieux*, and Shakespeare. And the man who did more than anyone else to draw all this together was Gotthold Ephraim Lessing (1729–81).

As a young man Lessing had worked in a modest way for Caroline Neuber and among other literary activities had translated Dryden's *Essay on Dramatic Poetry* and a number of plays. In due course he became *dramaturg*, a function that might be described as literary editor, to a theatre in Hamburg. In this capacity he wrote a series of theatrical comments and criticisms which were published as the *Hamburg Dramaturgy*. Of the 104 numbers the most important are those in which he uses the theories of Aristotle to justify contemporary bourgeois tragedy of which he himself became a distinguished exponent. He loathed Voltaire's tragedies and found much to admire in Shakespeare.

He was also successful as a dramatist. Several of his plays are still regularly staged in German theatres. The better known are: *Miss Sara Sampson* (1755), .. bourgeois tragedy that was strongly influenced by Richardson with the Seven Years War as a strikingly realistic background; *Minna von Barnhelm* (1767); *Emilia Galotti* (1772), a powerful piece of social criticism; and *Nathan the Wise*, a plea for religious toleration written in the last years of his life. The most frequently performed of these plays is the subtle but rather sentimental *Minna von Barnhelm.*

But the German theatre was exceedingly unstable. Companies came and went, and changed their composition; they were all itinerant, dependent on touring, always on the move from court to court and town to town with occasional forays abroad to Zürich, Vienna, or even Moscow.

In default of a body of plays it was an actor's theatre and the significant figures were the actor-managers. Caroline Neuber has already been mentioned. Konrad Ekhof (1720–78) was an outstanding actor and manager who introduced a naturalistic manner of playing into the German theatre as a change from the declamatory style copied from the French. He founded an academy of acting in Schwerin (1757), and this became a centre of theoretical discussion on style, methods, and standards.

Konrad Ackermann (1710–71) was an actor-manager who in 1765 settled in Hamburg, a city which was overtaking Leipzig as a commercial and cultural centre. Here, in collaboration with Lessing, he tried to establish a permanent theatre with an emphasis on German plays and better conditions for the actors. Even more important was that the two men conceived the idea of a 'national' theatre, and although the project failed it was taken up elsewhere, notably by Count Dalberg in Mannheim. This project was greatly helped by the fine actor August William Iffland (1759–1814) who had been trained by Eckhof and became manager of the Mannheim theatre before moving on to Berlin. He wrote sixty-five plays himself and took the lead in many of Schiller's dramas. Another fine actor was Friedrich Ludwig Schröder who succeeded Konrad Ackermann as manager of the Hamburg theatre which he directed from 1771 until 1800. It was he who introduced Shakespeare to German audiences.

A most significant movement in the German theatre of the period was an expression of the spirit of the times, the *Zeitgeist* as the Germans call it. Germany, occupying an unspecified geographical area in the centre of Europe, has been the scene of constant political and religious aggression. Emperors and Popes have competed for the body and soul of the German people. A certain temperamental instability is therefore not perhaps surprising. So by the time of the eighteenth century it is understandable that the German people were some way behind the French and the English in finding much enlightenment (*Aufklärung*) in their society. In fact the term was first used by an influential philosopher named Emmanuel Kant in 1784. *Die Aufklärung* marked, he argued, the emergence of man from his self-imposed tutelage through daring to think for himself. The ideal state of man is to be reasonable, as the French had argued a hundred years previously, and this means that he must be natural. A natural man is a feeling man and this is as important as to be an intelligent man. And with a progressive weakening of the authority of the Bible, people began to think not that whatever God says, or is thought to have said, is right, but, in the words of Pope, whatever is is right.

Translated into human terms, all this means that there was a passionate concern for nature and natural things; for political freedom evoked by the despotic attitude of some of the princes. Criticism of politics led to a criticism of society. There developed, as in England but far more so, an idealization of the Middle Ages as a time of freedom, of romance, of sensationalism, and literature began to take over the décor of the Gothic novel of Horace Walpole and a writer known as 'Monk'

Lewis with their dungeons and subterranean passages, hermits, pilgrims, harpists, Minnesingers, gypsies, and bandits.

The result of all this was that before there was any 'enlightenment' in Germany, there was the opposite, a movement known as Storm and Stress (*Sturm und Drang*). It took its name from a play, *Sturm und Drang* (1776) which was concerned with the rivalry of two well-born Americans for the beautiful heroine. The author was Friedrich Maximilian Klinger (1752–1818), a handsome young man who wrote a number of plays, most of which were extravagant in both language and theme; but after the age of thirty he calmed down, joined the Russian army, rose to the rank of general, and married the daughter of the Russian Empress. Another member of the group was Johann Michael Reinhold Lenz (1751–92) whose potentiality as a playwright was limited by an unstable and neurotic nature. These and others, young men in their twenties, gathered round the charismatic character of the young Goethe. The movement was short-lived and confined to the 1770s. It produced no masterpieces but it was symptomatic of a kind of crisis through which German culture passed and which left its clear impression on the early works of the great writers, Goethe and Schiller.

Readers of German have the advantage of being able to read the Niebelungenlied *in the original. Another important and immensely readable German medieval poem, which has been translated into English, is Gottfried von Strassburg's version of* Tristan *which, in comparison with French versions of the story, has passages of the typically German mysticism to which we have referred.*

In case too much is made of a certain instability in the German national character, it must be remembered that this is the great age of German music. There is no artist whose work is more wholly stable than the great Johann Sebastian Bach (1685–1750). The exquisite Wolfgang Amadeus Mozart (1756–91) was in fact Austrian. Ludwig van Beethoven (1770–1827), less stable perhaps in character (as if this mattered) extended the emotional range of music prodigiously, and composed with an almost architectural sense of form.

76 | Goethe and Schiller

Johann Wolfgang Goethe (1749–1832) is one of the giants of European culture. Although as a young man he was involved in the Storm and Stress movement, he was of a very different calibre, both as man and artist, from the writers already mentioned. He received much of his education from a stern father and by the age of eight was practised in five European languages. At sixteen he went to study law in Leipzig where he came into contact with the leading artists of the day and the new movement in the theatre. He took part in amateur theatrical productions, translated French plays, and wrote original ones.

His interest in the theatre had been aroused when at the age of four his parents had given him a puppet theatre. In the course of the Seven Years War (1756–63) French troops had occupied Frankfurt (Main) and touring companies had given performances of French plays to entertain the officers, some of whom were billeted in his home. His passion for the theatre was a lasting one, and although in the course of a long and eventful life he became a public administrator, a distinguished scientist, and perhaps the finest lyric poet of the day, he wrote in all some fifty plays, sketches, and translations, although they have not all survived.

In his early twenties, which was passed between Strasbourg and Frankfurt, he fell in love repeatedly and wrote both poetry and plays. This was during the 1770s when he was the key figure in the *Sturm und Drang* movement. His many plays, sketches, scenarios, and opera libretti included the immensely influential *Goetz von Berlichingen*, a vast sprawling play about a heroic outlaw who defies authority for the sake of political freedom. He followed it with *Clavigo*, a rather melodramatic piece about marital infidelity; *Stella*, a 'drama for lovers' he called it, a striking play for its time about a young man who, unable to chose between two young ladies, sets up house with them both; and *Egmont*, an idealized picture of a Flemish hero who led a revolt against the Spanish domination of the Netherlands and goes to the scaffold dreaming of his country's liberation. (In 1810 Beethoven wrote a masterly overture and some incidental music for the play.) Goethe also wrote at this time the first draft of his eventual masterpiece, *Faust*.

In 1775 Karl August, the young Duke of Saxe-Weimar, who had been wildly excited by *Goetz*, invited Goethe to come and work for him. Goethe accepted and soon rose to the rank of Privy Councillor with a wide range of responsibilities which included the theatre. The Duke had already established the practice of inviting touring companies to play in Weimar, but as the theatre had been destroyed by fire in 1774 he had to be satisfied with amateur performances in whatever venue was suitable. Goethe threw himself into these activities with considerable energy as administrator, director, designer, and actor.

During his early years at Weimar he drafted two of his finest plays and completed them during a subsequent tour of Italy. These plays were *Iphigenia in Tauris*, a beautiful version of the story that had been handled by Euripides, and *Torquato Tasso*, a fictional study of the famous poet and his complex relationships with various personalities in the court of Ferrara.

His only other major work was the completion of the first part of *Faust* which was not published until 1808. The second part, which he composed late in life and which did not appear until after his death, is a strange and perplexing philosophical-allegorical vision. But his practical interest in the theatre continued throughout much of his life. In 1798 the theatre was rebuilt and Goethe began to establish his own style of playing and production as artistic director of a company which at one time included the fine actor August Iffland. His *Rules for Actors*, by no means acceptable today, show his anxiety to control the apparently rather exuberant style of German acting with an almost Gallic discipline.

His interest in the theatre was also cherished through close friendship with another great poet and playwright, Johann Christoph Friedrich Schiller (1759–1805). Schiller was a citizen of Stuttgart, in the Duchy of Württemberg, a small state which was ruled at the time by the somewhat despotically inclined Duke Karl Eugen. The young Friedrich Schiller suffered both from a tyrannical father, an army surgeon who ran his home with military discipline, and education at a military academy where the despotic principles of the Duke were imposed upon the young. Though Schiller wanted to read theology he was compelled to study medicine. His real love, however, was literature, and from the age of thirteen he began to sketch tragedies on biblical subjects. In 1777, when he was eighteen, he set to work on *The Robbers*. It took him four years to complete the play since he was obliged to arrange his papers so that they could be instantly covered by a medical textbook if a master entered the room without warning. He also hit upon the ruse of pretending to be ill, since he could work in sick-quarters uninterrupted, until the medical attendants began to question the constant ill health of an apparently robust young man.

In 1780 he finished both the play and his time in the Academy and was appointed physician to a regiment of Grenadiers. He gave his play to a publisher in Stuttgart who refused to handle it. Schiller decided to publish it himself. The printer was not only enthusiastic about the play but took a copy to the National Theatre in Mannheim and read it to the director, Baron Wolfgang von Dalberg, Electoral General Theatrical Superintendant. A production was arranged. But the Duke Karl Eugen heard what was afoot and refused Schiller permission to leave Stuttgart. Schiller escaped to Mannheim secretly and so was able to see for himself the tremendous effect of the play upon the audience. 'The theatre was like a madhouse', wrote someone who was present at that memorable first performance. 'There were rolling eyes, clenched fists, and hoarse outcries throughout the theatre. Strangers fell sobbing into each other's arms, women staggered to the door nearly fainting. It seemed as if dissolution into chaos was near!' The spirit of the time certainly seemed to lend a little hysteria to the German character.

Reading the play today it is difficult to understand how a piece that is little more than a farrago of romantic fustian can have made such an impact. Every emotion is pushed to its hysterical limit. The hero 'hangs in ecstasy on his beloved's lips', people foam at the mouth, passions are ungoverned, all authority is challenged. On its title-page the play bears as its dedication the words *In tyrannos* – 'Against tyrants'.

Karl Eugen did not wholly break off relationships with the young playwright, for a tyrant is always unwilling wholly to suppress someone who might bring credit to his regime. But Dalberg at Mannheim could spot a promising playwright when he met one and agreed to stage Schiller's next three plays. These were *Fiesco* (1782), a rather unsatisfactory piece about a Genoese conspiracy; the powerful *Kabale und Liebe* (*Love and Intrigue*, 1784), a play about the interplay of passion and intrigue in a small German court; and *Don Carlos* (1787). This tremendous play, which subsequently provided the libretto for a no less powerful opera by Giuseppe Verdi, involves two interrelated themes, the passion of the hero, Don Carlos, heir to the throne of Spain, for his stepmother, and the political problems facing Philip II in maintaining the military suppression of the Netherlands.

It was ten years before he completed another play. In the mean time Duke Karl August had invited him to Weimar while Goethe was in Italy and it was several years before the two poets became close friends. Schiller broke his dramatic silence with the *Wallenstein* trilogy (1798–9), the product of much reading and considerable creative agony. This great three-part political masterpiece established him as a major dramatist; with a secure position at Weimar and the support of Goethe, he applied himself to the composition of poetic drama. There followed *Maria Stuart* (1800), *Die Jungfrau von Orleans* (*The Maid of Orleans*, 1802), *Die Braut von Messina* (*The Bride of Messina*, 1804), an attempt to write a play in the manner of Greek tragedy, including a chorus, and *William Tell* (1804) in which he went some way to achieving an ideal that he and Goethe often discussed – the fusion between serious and popular drama in a fragmented society.

Opinions may vary as to the absolute value of the achievement of these two men. We do not really know whether their plays would live on the English stage since they have been so rarely produced. But in the many German theatres all the following plays have had more than two thousand performances since 1947 – and in this order of popularity – *Minna von Barnhelm* (Lessing), *Faust* (Goethe), *Maria Stuart* (Schiller),

Nathan der Weise (Lessing), *Die Raüber* (Schiller), *Don Carlos* (Schiller), *Wallenstein* (Schiller), *Iphigenie auf Tauris* (Goethe), *Wilhelm Tell* (Schiller). Goethe was less successful than Schiller as a playwright because in his maturity he gave less time to drama. He writes, morever, in a more constricted manner. He disliked disorder. He was bitterly critical of the French Revolution and even described Romanticism as a disease. Yet they both detested the tendency towards naturalism in the theatre. Schiller, on the other hand, was less concerned with conflicts in society than with conflicts in the soul of man, and in particular the relationship between reason and feeling (*Vernunft* and *Verstand*), realizing that since social behaviour is based on feeling, artistic creation requires the control of reason and intelligence. Goethe told his friend Eckermann late in life that Schiller was not always master of the philosophical ideas that interested him and these sometimes interfered with the dramatic development of his theme. Goethe believed that creativity was the result of a certain demonism which was related to the instincts and a poetic regard for nature, but this is more evident in his poems than his plays.

All the surviving plays of Goethe and Schiller are available in German; selected plays have been variously translated. Goetz von Berlichingen *has been translated by John Arden as* Ironhand. *Several comparisons will be found helpful, for instance Goethe's* Faust *with Marlowe's* Dr Faustus *shows how the ancient story was treated by a Renaissance and then a Romantic poet. Similarly the treatments of* Iphigenia *by Goethe, Euripides, and Racine crystalize the shifts in approach.*

77 | Later German Romanticism

When the Romantic theatre loses its reason there is usually little left but violent and unmotivated action, stock characters, and a crude theatricality. Even in the better plays of the period some of these elements persist but are sometimes acceptable when expressed in fine language. This is one of the impressive qualities of *The Robbers*, for example. But in the hands of the dramatic hack, the Romantic drama becomes a sensational melodrama, with all the defects of which Schiller was aware when he tried to give quality to material that is essentially popular. Such scruples, however, did not interest the many writers of popular melodrama who emerged in the early years of the nineteenth century to supply the professional theatres that were becoming established throughout Germany and were voracious for original plays. The chief exponent of melodrama in Germany was August Friedrich Ferdinand von Kotzebue (1761–1819), a man who had spent a short period of his life in Weimar, terminated by his inability to get on with Goethe. He wrote an immense number of plays of which upwards of forty were translated into other languages including English, and for a time ran a theatre in St. Petersburg. Even Richard Sheridan, desperate to fill the great spaces of Drury Lane, translated *Die Spanier in Peru oder Rolla's Tod* (*The Spanish in Peru or Rolla's Death*, 1796) as *Pizarro* (1799).

On quite a different level as dramatists were Heinrich von Kleist (1777–1811) and the Austrian, Franz Grillparzer (1791–1872). The latter was encouraged as a dramatist by the manager of the Burgtheater in Vienna, but discouraged by the censorship of the notorious Austrian chancellor, Prince Metternich, who played a big part in bringing Napoleon to justice. He was nevertheless a prolific dramatist. Between 1808 and 1838, when he gave up writing for the stage, he wrote a variety of plays. His earliest are in the *Sturm und Drang* tradition but over the years he wrote plays on the position of the poet in society, inspired by Goethe's *Tasso*, the nature of man, the Greek concept of fate, and human fallibility.

In Kleist there is a reversion to the hectic and morbid undertow that we tend to associate with German drama. Kleist was an unhappy and unstable personality, very much a man of his age, obsessed with the political insecurity of Europe as Napoleon careered victoriously around the continent. Although he wrote a number of comedies such as the very amusing and frequently staged *Der Zerbrochene Krug* (*The Broken Jug*, 1811) and some fascinating stories of which 'The Marquise of O' and 'Michael Kohlhass' are perhaps the most typical, it is in his tragedies that he expressed his tormented individuality. Of these the best known are *Penthesilea* (1808), a quite extraordinary play in which the related passions of love and aggression are most brutally considered, and the impressive *Prinz Friedrich von Homburg* (usually translated as *The Prince of Homburg*, 1810). Its failure led to his suicide.

A dramatist of even greater originality was Georg Büchner (1813–37). Yes, he died at the age of twenty-four. *Leonce and Lena* is an ambiguous fantasy, but it is in his two subsequent plays that he showed himself to be the outstanding dramatist of the age. *Danton's Death* (1835) is a remarkably shrewd political study of the French revolutionary leader. *Woyzeck* (1836), written in short staccato scenes, with a unique economy of means and an acute awareness of social realities, is a play that might have been written in the 1970s. One has only to compare Büchner's plays with those that were being written in contemporary France, Victor Hugo's *Ruy Blas*, for example, or England, where Browning's *Stafford* was being played, to realize how unique they are.

It was perhaps in music that German Romanticism expressed itself more freely, concepts of political radicalism are powerfully projected in Beethoven's great opera *Fidelio* (1805), while the founder of Romantic opera, with all its Gothic melodrama, is usually considered to have been Carl Maria von Weber (1786–1826) who died while on a visit to London to conduct *Oberon* at the invitation of John Philip Kemble.

Kleist's The Prince of Homburg *has been translated into English and is occasionally staged. Büchner's* Danton's Death *and* Woyzeck *(especially) are immensely popular and frequently revived. The play has been filmed and also made into a celebrated opera by Alban Berg.*

The period of Grillparzer, Kleist, and Büchner has not been adequately covered critically or historically, but for the late eighteenth century there is much interesting material in John Prudhoe's The Theatre of Goethe and Schiller *and W. H. Bruford's* Theatre, Drama and Audience in Goethe's Germany.

78 | Romantic Drama in France

British and German Romanticism was not based on rules. Goethe and many others discussed Romanticism in general and their own work in particular as is the way with committed people; William Wordsworth wrote a kind of manifesto in his Preface to *Lyrical Ballads* and Samuel Taylor Coleridge in *Biographia Literaria* writes fascinatingly about poetry in general and by implication the Romantic poets, but in no respect do either of them identify a movement.

It was otherwise in France. The French seemed to be unable to produce a work of art without a supporting body of theory, and as Romantic drama was based on a very different set of assumptions from neo-classical drama, they felt it necessary to define them. The novelist Stendhal wrote a curious little essay called *Racine et Shakespeare* in which he explains that Romanticism is concerned with giving pleasure, with contemporary events, that the action of a play should last several months and take place in a variety of situations. His model, of course, was Shakespeare, who was one of the inspirations of the Romantic movement in drama and whom he adored. He had little use for Schiller whom he found, not without a certain justification, a windbag (*rhéteur*).

The French Revolution did not have as great an effect on drama as might have been expected. In 1789 the Parisian crowds stormed the Bastille; in 1791 the revolutionaries imposed a reign of terror. In 1802 the young Napoleon Bonaparte made himself Consul for life and in 1804 promoted himself Emperor of the French (to Beethoven's disgust) and led his conquering armies all over Europe. The great battles of Austerlitz (1805), Jena (1806), and Wagram (1809) were splendid victories for the French nation but defeats for the ideals of the French Revolution which did little for the theatre but break the monopoly of the Comédie-Française.

Napoleon, however, reimposed theatrical censorship (in 1804) and in the course of his invasion of Russia in 1812, he found time to compose the Decrees of Moscow for the administration of the Comédie-Française in a manner that has required little subsequent modification.

Political instability is rarely good for the theatre which tends to be either too trivial to be taken seriously or too sensitive to uncertainty for comfort. The only significant dramatist of the period was Réné-Charles Guilbert de Pixérécourt (1773–1844), a counterpart of the German Kotzebue, the author of melodramas designed for audiences, as he himself claimed, who could not read. Many of them were translated into English.

On a more serious level the French were a divided people. They detested the British for their part in subduing their hero Bonaparte, while the theatre-going public adored Shakespeare. It was one of the achievements of Stendhal to help overcome this literary chauvinism. Then in 1827, when the political situation was more stable, John Philip Kemble led a company to Paris with a repertoire of Shakespearian tragedies. The effect was considerable. The great composer Hector Berlioz seduced the leading lady and made her his wife, a great poet, Alfred de Vigny, was inspired to translate *Othello*, and Victor Hugo was fired to write plays.

Victor Hugo (1802–85) was already a leading poet and a formidable political liberal. In 1827 he published his first play, *Cromwell*, having composed it for the actor Talma who died before the play was finished. It was not the play, however, that created the interest, for it is immensely long and virtually unactable, but the Preface which he appended to the published version. In this celebrated piece of pleading Hugo argues that art is concerned with what is truthful, but that true reality, and herein lies the sting, includes both the beautiful and the ugly, and this extends to the grotesque. He pursues this concept at considerable length, citing Shakespeare as its greatest exponent, followed closely by Dante and Milton, although it is in drama that the grotesque, together with its reverse, the sublime, is most finely expressed. The second part of the essay is taken up with a fierce attack on the rules, the creation, he says, of addle-pated pedants. One thing the stage must never be is commonplace, for it is the meeting-ground for everything of most significance in history, in life, in the world. The immensely colourful Romantic poet, Théophile Gautier, described this Preface as 'shining in their eyes like the tables of the law upon Mount Sinai'.

In spite of the failure of *Cromwell*, Hugo was encouraged to continue writing for the theatre by the success of a Romantic drama by Alexander Dumas whose remarkable piece of melodramatic historical fustian was staged at the Comédie-Française in 1829. Though still writing poetry, and in spite of having begun work on his great historical novel, *The Hunchback of Notre Dame*, he found time to write a five-act tragedy set in the days of Louis XIII. He called it *Marion de Lorme ou Un Duel sous Richelieu* (*A Duel at the Time of Richelieu*). But he was out of luck. It was banned by the censor for showing up a French king in a poor light. Hugo had a friendly conversation with the King himself, who freely discussed his lamented and lamentable ancestor, but refused to allow production of the play.

The King's sensitivity was not wholly due to pigheadedness. Political tension once again was running high. Little more than a year after the banning of *Marion de Lorme*, the tension between Charles X and Parliament became so extreme that the King abolished the liberty of the press and dissolved Parliament. Four days later he lost his throne. A second, though lesser, French Revolution had taken place.

Hugo, desperately short of money, with an attractive wife and two children to support, set to work on another play, *Hernani*. He wrote this masterpiece in twenty-six days. It was accepted for production by the Comédie-Française and immediately became a centre of controversy both inside and outside the theatre. First, there was trouble with the cast. Mademoiselle Mars, for example, the celebrated leading lady, objected to some of her lines. She disliked referring to the robber chieftain, Hernani, with whom she is supposed to be in love, as 'mon lion', preferring the conventional 'monseigneur'. This artistic controversy was a mirror of the political controversy that was being waged outside the theatre between the Republicans, who identified with the overt Romanticism of the play, and the Royalists who composed the Conservative opposition. On the first night in February, 1830, there was something of a battle. Four hundred supporters of Hugo took their seats in the theatre at midday. They were led by Théophile Gautier himself with Balzac, Vigny, Berlioz, and Dumas in support. There was uproar from the start. Every time a line offended traditional verse-forms, the traditionalists hissed and the romantics cheered. But the prodigious sweep of the play with its great *coups de théâtre* and the torrential splendour of its verse eventually won the day.

In the next ten years Hugo wrote six more plays but in 1851, with the failure of *Les Burgraves* and the coming to power of Louis Napoleon (with the establishment of the Second Empire), he gave up the stage, and at the same time was sent into exile in Jersey for eighteen years for his uncompromising liberal views.

After *Hernani* his most successful play was *Ruy Blas* (1838). It is another play which convinces through its own superb self-assurance. Its story, like that of *Hernani*, is a fatuous mixture of disguised identities, overheard conversations, unlikely coincidences, secret panels, and passionate vendettas. But the basic stupidity is swept aside by the magnificent poetry and the play's superb theatricality. Hugo creates his own glowing reality out of wholly unreal ingredients.

Running Hugo a close second as a Romanticist was Alexandre Dumas whose first and most successful play was *Henri III et sa cour* (1829) (*Henri III and his Court*). It depicts the events leading to the murder of a young noblemen by assassins employed by the Duc de Guise, a member of a family of great political power in the sixteenth century, whose unscrupulous methods in suppressing Protestantism won a prominent role in the plays of Marlowe and Chapman. The play is erratic in construction, crude in characterization and, being in prose, has nothing of the passionate sweep of Hugo's dramas. But Dumas learnt to be a reasonable craftsman and kept the theatre supplied with plays until the 1860s.

The final twist to Romanticism was given by Alfred de Musset (1810–57) who stands in relation to Hugo rather as Marivaux does to Racine. His plays are subtle, delicate, exquisitely contrived, and often with an irony that borders on the tragic. *Les Caprices de Marianne* (1833) and *On ne badine pas avec l'amour* (*There's no Joking with Love* (printed in 1834)) show a far greater degree of sensibility than is to be found in the poetic torrents of Hugo, the theatricalities of Dumas, or even in Musset's own tempestuous but morbid *Lorenzaccio* (1834).

*In the forty-nine plays produced at the Comédie-Française in the twenty-five years between 1954 and 1978, with more than one hundred performances, a clear indication of recent popularity, Molière appears seventeen times, Musset six, Marivaux four, Corneille twice (*Le Cid *and* Horace*), Victor Hugo once (*Ruy Blas*), and Racine once (*Andromaque*).*

79 Romantic Drama in England

Britain, at the turn of the nineteenth century, was a great deal more stable politically than France or Germany. Romanticism, therefore, had much less of a political flavour and is rather more difficult to identify. The poets, especially in their youth, were fascinated by what was going on in Europe and uneasy about the industrialization of their own country. It was not only for reasons of health that Lord Byron and Shelley went to live in Italy, and Wordsworth set up a permanent home in the Lake District.

Chronologically, the first of the great literary figures was Samuel Taylor Coleridge (1772–1823). As a young man at Cambridge he became friends with Robert Southey (1774–1843). They married sisters, planned to set up an ideal republic in the United States, and collaborated in writing a play to raise money for their venture. The play was called *The Fall of Robespierre* (1794). Though extremely undramatic, consisting of little but the judicial arraignment of the tyrant Robespierre, it avoids the false theatricality that mars so much of the drama of the period; but even its fine rhetoric sounds hollow beside the hard prosaic reality of Büchner's *Danton's Death.* Southey went on to become an indifferent poet. Four years later Coleridge wrote *Osorio* (1798) which was produced at Drury Lane in 1813 under the title *Remorse*; but it is a depressing return to the Romantic unrealities of disguises, rivalries, high virtue, low villainy, and unconvincing *coups de théâtre.*

Coleridge turned out to be not only a literary critic of the highest standing but a very great poet. At the time he was writing the non-sensical *Osorio* he was also composing some of the finest poems in the language, 'Christabel', 'The Ancient Mariner' and 'Kubla Khan'. He was by no means the only poet to switch off his critical faculties when writing for the theatre. One has the unfortunate impression that many writers were only interested in the theatre as a possible way of making money; and even then their lack of appreciation for dramatic crafts-manship is lamentable: they deserved to fail.

Another of Coleridge's friends was William Wordsworth (1770–1850). Wordsworth, who early in his life lived in Dorset, had been greatly influenced by the French Revolution and European Romanticism. He went so far as to write a play called *The Borderers*, somewhat on the lines of Schiller's *The Brothers*. It is about a group of voluntary outlaws who defend the weak against tyranny and injustice, but it does not ring with the authentic passion that seems to have invested Schiller, and he showed no more interest in the theatre. Coleridge, however, having visited Germany in the company of Wordsworth, translated the second and third parts of Schiller's great *Wallenstein* trilogy and was invited by Goethe to translate *Faust*. He did not accept the invitation and in 1816–17 wrote another worthless play, *Zapolya*.

In 1802 Wordsworth made a visit to Scotland and met the novelist, Sir Walter Scott (1771–1832) who by that time had translated Goethe's *Goetz von Berlichingen*. It was still many years before he began writing the succession of novels that made him influential throughout Europe. Between 1817, when he wrote *Devergoil*, and 1830, when he wrote the slightly better *Auchindrane*, he composed five plays on Scottish themes but they are of no great account and his brief references to his plays in his *Journal* show a most patronizing attitude towards the theatre.

Just as British writers were influenced by Goethe and Schiller, so European writers were influenced by Scott and Byron. George Gordon, Lord Byron (1788–1824) came nearest of all poets of the period, with the possible exception of Shelley, to writing successfully for the stage. He knew something about theatrical affairs since before he went into more or less voluntary exile in 1816 he had been a governor of Drury Lane. His first play, *Manfred* (1816–17), is an impressively original piece of work. It is really a dramatic poem or choral tragedy rather than a play, a kind of Faustian vision of man's impotence set in the typically Romantic décor of the Swiss Alps. One feels that a poet of great imaginative fertility, with a pen that could compose the most exquisite lyrics and the witty vernacular verse of 'Don Juan', need only to have taken the stage really seriously to have freed it from the galumphing tyranny of pseudo-Shakespearian blank verse.

But he went to Ravenna, in Italy, where there was no theatre to incite him although he seems to have found it necessary to go on writing plays. In *Marino Falieri, Doge of Venice* (1820) he reverts to the German model. The play is about a popular uprising to overthrow the Venetian patriarchs by whom the eponymous hero, the hero of the title, thinks he has been insulted. Good enough, but not good enough for a great poet. 1821, when he was living in Venice, was an extraordinary year. In May and June he wrote *Sardanapalus*, the first three acts in a fortnight, and dedicated it to Goethe. It is a lurid, colourful piece about the overthrow of a libidinous, self-indulgent, despotic Assyrian tyrant. Between 12 June and 9 July he wrote *The Two Foscari*, another play in the manner of *Marino Falieri*, about a Venetian Doge whose son is committed to torture and exile for crimes against the state. Between 16 July and 9

September he wrote *Cain*. This is a reversion to the style of *Manfred*, a kind of biblical mystery that owes something to *Paradise Lost*. He dedicated it rather surprisingly to Sir Walter Scott. Between 9 and 23 October he wrote *Heaven and Earth*, another mystery, this time on a theme from Genesis. It is decked out with visions of angels and archangels and a chorus of spirits and seems to owe something to Shelley, who the year before had completed *Prometheus Unbound*, and of whom he was seeing a good deal at the time. He then moved to Pisa and between 8 December and 20 January 1822, he wrote *Werner*, perhaps in a conventional sense the most actable of all his plays. In the summer of the same year he wrote *The Deformed Transformed*, a curious play about a club-footed hunchback who makes a Faustian compact with a Satanic figure to conjure up visions of beautiful men and heroic episodes. The play was no doubt related to his own club-foot.

Byron was the very incarnation of Romanticism. In England he was admired for his poetry, derided for his republican politics, and detested for his private life. In Europe he was regarded as the Champion of Liberty. As a man he was arrogant and self-centred. He was known to have dressed as a monk, to drink Burgundy from a human skull, to live in residences of wild and decayed splendour, and he traipsed round Italy with an entourage of servants, horses, birds in baskets, monkeys in cages, and enormous dogs. If he had been willing to focus on to the stage the twin aspects of his genius represented by 'Don Juan' and 'Childe Harold' or, on a lower level, *Werner* and *Cain*, the British theatre of the early nineteenth century might have been transformed.

This polarity which is so clearly marked in the poetry and plays of Byron was also to be found in Goethe. *Egmont* is written in something of the same vein as *Marino Falieri*. *Faust* is akin to *Manfred* and *Cain*. The same quality is to be found in Percy Bysshe Shelley (1792–1822) who combined, like Byron, a notorious and scandalous private life with a poetic power that made him the equal of Goethe. *Prometheus Unbound* is written in the style of *Faust* and *Manfred*, though in the form of a Greek tragedy, with direct reference to Aeschylus, and is more of a dramatic poem than a stage play, though no more so than *Manfred* and *Faust*. It is a superb statement of the power of the human mind to free itself from the self-created domination of the cruel Jupiter. It is a powerful restatement of Rousseau's stirring opening to *The Social Contract* – 'Man was born free but everywhere he is chains' – a statement that stirs the blood even if it does not stand up to critical scrutiny.

The other aspect of Shelley's dramatic ability is seen in *The Cenci* (1819), a Florentine tragedy that comes near to being a powerful, actable play. He wrote more for the stage but nothing comparable with these two masterpieces.

1819, however, was a phenomenal year for English literature. John Keats (1795–1821) was living not a wild and dissipated life in Italy but that of an invalid in Hampstead. In this year he composed 'The Eve of Saint Agnes', 'La Belle Dame Sans Merci' and the great odes during the composition of which he wrote a trivial historical tragedy *Otho the Great* and the fragments of *King Stephen*. It is suggested that he did so for money of which he was lamentably short, but also because he had been impressed by the acting of Edmund Kean whom he had seen playing at Drury Lane where he had been taken by his friend Charles Brown. Once again the theatre was lamentably undervalued by a poet who was far from lacking in critical intelligence.

Robert Browning (1812–89) had perhaps more potential than any to revive or recreate poetic drama. Between 1837, when he was twenty-five, and 1846 when he married Elizabeth Barrett and retired to Italy, he wrote eight plays. With one exception they are all in the heavy vein of historical or Romantic tragedy, without either the poetry or the theatricality to give them an even synthetic vitality. The exception is *Pippa Passes* (1841), a charming fantasy about the way in which the simple song of a girl from the silk mill is heard by various characters at a crisis in their life. This is the single occasion when Browning escapes the deadening effect of ponderous pentameters. Yet in those long dramatic monologues which he wrote later in life and which he published as *Men and Women* and *Dramatis Personae*, he finds a wholly new form of verse that might have been splendidly adapted to the stage.

His case is the more strange for in William Macready, Browning had an actor-manager who was tireless in developing new dramatists. But they do not appear to have made a successful relationship. Macready, who felt that *A Blot on the 'Scutcheon* (1843) needed a lot of rewriting, got little co-operation from Browning whom he describes in his *Diaries* as 'a very conceited man' and a few days later as 'a very disagreeable and offensively mannered person'. But then Macready himself was not always the epitome of tact.

There were other writers who tried to revive poetic drama but they showed little skill as poets or dramatists. The most prolific was James Sheridan Knowles (1784–1862) who wrote two plays in which Macready had some success, *Virginius* (1820) and *The Hunchback* (1832). Sir Thomas Talfourd (1795–1854) was a distinguished literary figure but had only one success on the stage and that was *Ion*, also staged by Macready. The most successful dramatist was Edward Lytton (or Lord Bulwer-Lytton, 1803–73), a prolific historical novelist and the author of one play in verse that was frequently revived in the nineteenth century, *Richelieu*, and two plays in prose which helped to initiate a new element in the theatre. These plays were *The Lady of Lyons* (1838), and even more important, *Money* (1840). All these plays were first staged by Macready and will be discussed later.

But there was yet another poet to flog the moribund tradition of poetic drama and that was Alfred, Lord Tennyson (1809–92) who when nearing seventy conceived a project for a series of verse dramas on 'the making of England'. He began with a sprawling chronicle play on *Queen Mary* (Tudor) and followed this with *Harold* (1876) in which there are some powerful scenes between the English King and Count William of Normandy (prior to the Norman Conquest). But the failure of both plays, in distinguished productions by Sir Henry Irving, as well as of subsequent shorter plays, *The Cup* and *The Promise of May*, discouraged him from his ambitious project. In 1884 he wrote the not very satisfactory *Becket* in which the conflict between the Archbishop and the King is interwoven with a rather tedious love story.

It was not until the present century that a new note was struck in poetic drama especially by W. B. Yeats and T. S. Eliot. Meanwhile the mainstream of British drama developed on wholly different lines.

Assiduous readers will taste for themselves some of the many plays that have been mentioned in this section. The biographical and critical literature on these poets is immense, but their own critical and prose works are usually readable and important. Coleridge's Biographia Literaria *is far less forbidding than the title suggests. Keats's letters give a penetrating picture of the act of poetic creation. Byron's voluminous correspondence is wonderfully vivid and discursive. But their rather stagnant plays should not deflect anyone from the splendour of their verse.*

80 Actors and Acting in the Eighteenth and Nineteenth Centuries

The old phenomenon is seen at work again: when play-writing is undistinguished, acting comes into its own. It is clear that, with the exception of Sheridan, it was the actors who brought what distinction there was to the stage between about 1720 and 1850. There is a problem, however, about recalling any stage performance or the work of any actor or actress who is dead. There are absolutely no means of judging the quality of their work except through what critics or members of the public may have written at the time. Even then it is a personal judgement. Critics are by no means impartial. They have their own personal standards of assessment; and history, along with the performers, is dependent on what they write. Some of them, fortunately, have written well.

Until dramatic cricitism became a regular feature of daily newspapers later in the century, we are grateful for occasional references to the theatre in the *Spectator*, as the following, by Joseph Addison, 18 April 1711. Having praised the splendour of the actress's dress in the production of a certain tragedy he complains about the necessity of having a boy in attendance to manage her train. 'The Princess is afraid lest she should incur the displeasure of the King her father, or lose the hero, her lover, whilst her attendant is concerned lest she should entangle her feet in her petticoat.'

During the eighteenth century, as heroic tragedy gave way to so-called bourgeois tragedy, and declamation was less the order of the day, so acting styles changed to accommodate the new style of writing. There was the irascible and rather unstable Irish actor, for example, Charles Macklin (*c.*1700–97), who acted a good deal for John Rich at Lincoln's Inn Fields, and was the first to play Shylock as a dignified and tragic figure, drawing from Pope the famous couplet, 'This is the Jew That Shakespeare drew'. But far away the most influential figure of the century, and one of the great theatrical personalities of all time, was David Garrick (1717–79).

Garrick made his début as an actor in 1741 and became manager of Drury Lane in 1747, remaining as such until 1776 when he handed over the theatre to Richard Sheridan. As an actor he introduced a new and more naturalistic style of playing than was general at the time. He was a versatile actor and extremely accomplished technically. As a manager he reformed and improved the general administration of the theatre, demanding and winning better and more attentive behaviour from audiences. He also did much to improve technical aspects of production, particularly in décor and lighting. He was also something of a dramatist himself, composed a number of comedies and after-pieces, by himself and in collaboration with other writers. Although he perpetuated the Restoration habit of adapting, and even rewriting Shakespeare to suit what he considered to be the taste of his audiences, he restored much of the original text, 600 lines of *Hamlet* and 300 of *King Lear*. When he died the great orator, Edmund Burke, said that 'He raised the character of

14. Actresses dressing in a barn
Drawn and engraved by William Hogarth, 1738. Even allowing for exaggeration on the part of the artist the picture suggests the chaotic conditions that travelling companies must have endured.

his profession to the rank of a liberal art, not only by his talents, but by the regularity and probity of his life and the elegance of his manners.'

It was at this time that attention was first given to the theory of acting.

The whole question of the extent to which acting was a matter of expressing natural emotion or shaping the performance in a rational manner became a matter of high dispute in France as a result of the rivalry between two leading actresses. A high sense of style and control marked the acting of Claire Léris de la Tude, who used the stage name of Madame Clairon (1723–1803). She was trained by the Italians but made her début at the Comédie-Française as Phèdre at the age of twenty-one. She then became the favourite actress of Voltaire and 'created' many of his heroines. In the latter part of her life she wrote her *Mémoires* in which she emphasizes the importance of a well-trained voice, constitutional strength, a body training through dancing, the study of drawing to acquire a sense of space, a feeling for all the varieties of language and speech, of geography and history, and above all the need for intense study of a character without which total identification is impossible.

Her great rival was Marie-Françoise Dumesnil (1713–1803), an actress whose style was founded on emotional power and what Voltaire called *le diable au corps* (the devil within her). Passion being her strength she had great success in the tragi-comedies (*pièces larmoyante*) of La Chaussée and Marmontel. She describes the emotional nature of her acting in her *Mémoires* which she wrote in retirement in answer to her rival. Clairon, she says, is all art. Her style of acting is highly finished. She arouses admiration. But real acting is more than this; it requires that deep inner feeling which alone gives an impression of absolute truth. What is necessary is the art which conceals art, the ability to move an audience deeply, not to admiration but to tears. It is 'd'avoir réçu du ciel l'influence secrète' (to have received from heaven a secret power). Clairon insisted on the fact that acting is an art: Dumesnil that it is all nature (which is a little different from being natural).

The debate was vigorously pursued by Denis Diderot who was never one to miss opportunity for an argument. Fascinated by the contrasting styles of Clairon and Dumesnil and by the technical facility of Garrick, whom he had met on a visit to London he wrote, between 1770 and 1778, his famous *Paradoxe sur le comédien*. In this fascinating work he discusses the question which is at the heart of all acting: to what extent does the actor feel subjectively the emotions he is expressing and how are they to be controlled? His conclusion is that to feel deeply is only part of an actor's gift: 'To encompass the whole range of a major role, to organise and to be equally in control of all the varied emotions of the part, to express variety in detail, harmony in the whole, and to perfect a style of speech which will sustain the highest flights of the poet, is the work of a cool head, profound judgement, painful study, long experience and an unusual tenacity of memory.' There speaks a critic of the eighteenth century.

This combination of a powerful emotional drive with strong control of expression (or technique) was clearly achieved by the great English tragic actress, Sarah Siddons (1755–1831). She combined a dignified, almost statuesque physical style with a rich voice and an ability to move an audience deeply. William Hazlitt said of her, 'The homage she has received is greater than that which is paid to Queens. The enthusiasm she excited had something idolatrous about it; she was regarded less with admiration than with wonder, as if a being of a superior order had dropped from another sphere to awe the world with the majesty of her appearance.' Her brother, John Philip Kemble (1787–1833), with a fine figure and Roman features, was a distinguished actor but without the genius of his sister. Leigh Hunt says of him 'that with the same solemn deliberation and the same loftiness of aspect, he has issued his commands, divided a word into syllables, and taken out his pocket handkerchief.'

Sarah Siddons and John Philip Kemble were really survivors, in their style of acting, of a former age; the great Romantic actor was Edmund Kean (1787–1833). Little is known for certain about the circumstances of his birth. Extraordinary stories are told about his childhood. He developed into an actor with a poor voice, no gift for comedy but an ability to express villainy and tragic passion of a remarkable kind. Hazlitt wrote that to see Kean acting was as if to read Shakespeare by flashes of lightning. He first appeared on the London stage in January 1814 as Shylock at Drury Lane. It was snowing heavily and there was a poor house. Hazlitt says that from his first appearance his performance was accompanied by frequent bursts of applause. He had brought a new spirit into the theatre. His performances were inspirational, in the manner of Dumesnil, rather than studied like those of Clairon. He was an unstable personality and frequently took to the bottle; but he was outstanding in his great roles – Othello, Iago, Barabas in Marlowe's *The Jew of Malta*, and Sir Giles Overreach in Massinger's *A New Way to Pay Old Debts*.

For the full deployment of his art an actor needs adequate theatres and good parts. We shall say something about the condition of the theatre at the time of Siddons, Kemble, and Kean in the following sections. But for a description of their performances we depend largely on dramatic critics. It is extremely fortunate that at the time of these three players and their contemporaries there lived and wrote two of the finest critics. William Hazlitt (1778–1830) wrote dramatic criticisms for various London newspapers between 1813 and 1818. He begins with Kean's début as Shylock and ends with Kemble's farewell performance as Coriolanus. The dramatic criticisms of Leigh Hunt cover a longer span, from 1805 until the 1830s. Although he was not capable of the sustained and detailed analyses of a performance in which Hazlitt excelled, he covered a wider range of subjects such as the architecture and décor of Drury Lane and Covent Garden, and is always readable.

Unfortunately the generally debased condition of the theatre and the romantic emphasis on feeling and what the French called *sensibilité* prevalent in the early nineteenth century put an end to theoretical discussion on the art of acting. The subject was not raised again until a change in the nature of plays compelled a similar change in the way they were to be played. This revolution in the theatre, which is associated with the name of Stanislavsky, will be the subject of later sections.

Hazlitt's dramatic criticisms are collected in A View of the English Stage. *He also wrote admirably and sympathetically about the stage in* On Actors and Acting. *He expressed his deep admiration for the Elizabethan and Jacobean dramatists in* The Characters of Shakespeare's Plays *and* The Literature of the Age of Elizabeth. *The best of Leigh Hunt's dramatic criticisms are to be found in his* Dramatic Essays. *Charles Lamb (1775–1834) was a literary rather than a dramatic critic and expressed his preference for reading Shakespeare's plays rather than seeing them on the stage. He wrote extensively on Shakespeare and the Elizabethans and makes occasional references to the theatre in his* Essays of Elia.

Sarah Siddons, John Philip Kemble, and Edmund Kean have all been the subject of biographies but readers should be warned that theatrical biography is very difficult to write, especially when there is a shortage of contemporary descriptions.

Amongst the great players of the nineteeth century, whom there is no opportunity to mention in the following pages, are the Italians, Tommaso Salvini, Adelaide Ristori, and Eleonora Duse.

81 | New Theatrical Forms

It is now necessary to go back a little. It will be remembered that competition between the two London theatres became fairly intense towards the end of the seventeenth century. John Rich at Lincoln's Inn Fields went one better than Drury Lane by providing a short Harlequinade at the end of the main play of the evening. This was called an 'after-piece'. The practice was copied by Drury Lane and became regular theatrical practice until well into the nineteenth century. The Harlequinade became an extremely popular form of entertainment and was enlarged into a full evening's performance as the pantomime. More will be said about this later.

The next event of considerable significance was the passing of the Licensing Act in 1737. This came about as a result of Henry Fielding's political satires. Sir Robert Walpole, the Prime Minister, felt affronted, and in the summer, shortly before the recess, he pushed through the Act which had considerable effect on the future development of the theatre. There were two particularly important clauses. The first was the establishment of the censorship of drama. A copy of every play to be performed in public was henceforth to be submitted, with an appropriate fee, to the Lord Chamberlain's office, who would give or refuse a licence or require alterations to be made. The proposal was strongly attacked in Parliament by Lord Chesterfield but without success. This clause was in fact only regularizing the old function of the Office of the Revels, but it was a singularly philistine Act, and the ludicrously inconsistent manner in which the censorship of plays has been carried out subsequently makes it all the more remarkable that the Act was not repealed until 1968.

The other clause in the Act was a reaffirmation of the necessity for theatres to be licenced. An actor who played in unlicenced premises was to be 'deemed a rogue and vagabond'. One can see how hard the iniquitous tradition was to die. The effect of this was to establish Covent Garden and Drury Lane as the two 'patent' theatres, with a limited licence granted to the Haymarket Theatre in 1766. This gave them the sole right of presenting what was known as 'straight' or 'legitimate' drama, in plain language, ordinary plays. Other theatres could exist – and in this lies the idiocy of the provision – but could only provide other forms of entertainment. The ingenuity of the managers was challenged. What forms of theatrical entertainment could be devised other than plays? The answer was music and dancing. And this is where the Harlequinade and pantomime came into their own, and is one of the reasons why from being short after-pieces they were blown up into a full evening's entertainment.

But in the process the whole nature of pantomime changed. Transvestism was common. The hero, known as the Principal Boy, was played by a young lady with shapely legs, a survival of the Restoration 'breeches' parts when plots often required women to disguise themselves as men.

Harlequin, developed into the strangest character of all, the Clown, another survival or recreation of the medieval Fool, who appears as a somewhat pathetic character in the plays of Shakespeare. But in the theatre of the early nineteenth century he was given enormous zest and authority through the genius of Joseph Grimaldi (1778–1837), who transformed the Italian Harlequin into the English Joey the Clown. Grimaldi was brought up, as they say in the theatre, in a skip (or hamper). He was immensely talented as an actor, singer, dancer, and acrobat. He was a rogue and fool of genius. London audiences, especially at Sadlers Wells where he most often performed, adored him.

Writing in 1831 Leigh Hunt, who took enormous delight in the high-spirited vitality of Harlequin, complains of contemporary pantomime being composed 'of tricks and transformations equally stinted and wanting in fancy, and a total departure from the old and genuine Harlequin plot, which consisted in the runaway vivacities of a couple of lovers full of youth and spirits (Harlequin and Columbine), the eternal hobbling after them of the decrepit Pantaloon, and the broad gluttony, selfishness and mischief of his servant the Clown'.

The change was due to the very popularity of the genre. Authors, in scraping round for subjects on which they could hang their spectacular effects and transformation scenes, their Principal Boys and Widow Twankys, collected an extraordinary jumble of subjects – Aladdin, Robinson Crusoe, Jack and the Beanstalk, Dick Whittington, Little Miss Muffet, Babes in the Wood, Cinderella, Puss in Boots, Sinbad the Sailor, and Mother Goose. In fact, as the nineteenth-century theatre pursued its erratic course, a whole jumble of theatrical forms developed both in association with and independent of the pantomime. There was the burlesque which was usually a parody of plays and operas in the main theatres. The most successful writer of the genre was H. J. Byron (1834–84) whose works had such titles as *Aladdin or the Wonderful Scamp* (1861). (The pun was the stock-in-trade of the burlesque.) The leading exponent of the extravaganza was James Robinson Planché (1796–1880), who was also a distinguished authority on heraldry and historical costume; while the burletta was the name given to any play that circumvented the Licensing Act by having at least five songs in each act. By this device a Shakespearian production, with musical additions, could be given in the minor theatres – *Macbeth*, for example, with a chorus of singing witches.

82 | Melodrama

The creation of melodrama (*melo-drama – music drama*) was another result of the Licensing Act. The possibility of successfully interposing songs into a dramatic text had been shown by the success of *The Beggar's Opera*. But what plays? It was clear enough that Shakespeare and the classics were not ideally suited to this kind of treatment. This is where the crude popular plays of the German Kotzebue and the French Pixérécourt came into their own. They had exciting stories with plenty of action and no irrelevancies such as subtle characterization. Music would not only help to legitimize the performance but even give additional colour to the action. Hero and villain would not only have their appropriate songs but heroic and villainous music to accompany their entrances and exits.

In the early nineteenth century melodrama moved rapidly away from Gothic castles with their haunting spectres, clanking chains, and exotic settings drawn from Romantic literature, and took its themes increasingly from contemporary life, exploiting the less attractive social conditions of the times – poverty, drunkenness, and gambling, material which at the same time a writer like Charles Dickens was handling with considerable literary skill. So we have Isaac Pocock's industrial melodrama, *The Miller and his Men* (1813), Douglas Jerrold's extremely popular naval melodrama, *Black-Ey'd Susan* (1829), and melodramas that exploited the horrors of the Crimean War.

A further comment on melodrama will be found in section 89.

The history of stage censorship has been wittily followed by Richard Findlater in Banned. *The history of pantomime has not on the whole been dealt with adequately. Victorian melodrama has now become a subject of academic study. Its history has been well described by Michael Booth in* English Melodrama.

Anthologies of selected melodramas are also available.

83 | Macready and the London Theatre of the Early Nineteenth Century

The difficulty of writing a history of the theatre that does not become too diffuse is that the theatre itself is a complex organization in which plays, styles of acting, theatre design, décor, and methods of production react upon each other. But the whole complex internal organization of the theatre must be seen against its social background. A theatrical performance is a social event in the sense that it involves the participation of members of its society as audience. So important decisions which managers have to make include the time of performance, for this must be adjusted to availability of transport, eating habits, and working hours. In the early eighteenth century the lack of street lighting or any policing of the streets made it injudicious for performances to close too late, while a six o'clock opening was a little early for those who had worked through the day and required a meal before their evening entertainment. So there developed a practice of attracting the late theatre-goer by reducing the price of seats after the third act of the main piece, a practice which gave additional importance to the after-piece. Changes in procedures by managers such as David Garrick and in particular John Philip Kemble, together with any attempt to increase the price of seats, met with strong resistance from the regular theatre-goers.

Managers who were also artists, such as particularly those we have mentioned, were faced with the double problem of staging plays which satisfied their artistic intentions, while attracting sufficiently large audiences to pay their way. One of the traditional ways of doing so is by building larger theatres and so getting bigger audiences. But a large auditorium imposes a certain style of playing on the actors. In 1794 Sheridan rebuilt Drury Lane with a capacity of 3,611. In 1809 the theatre burned down and was rebuilt and reopened in 1812 with a capacity of 2,226. In 1808 Covent Garden had been burnt down and rebuilt with a capacity of 2,190. These immense auditoria imposed on the actors a style of playing that was either declamatory, in the manner of John Philip Kemble, or highly emotional, like that of Edmund Kean. In either case it required a strong voice and broad gestures. Subtlety was not effective.

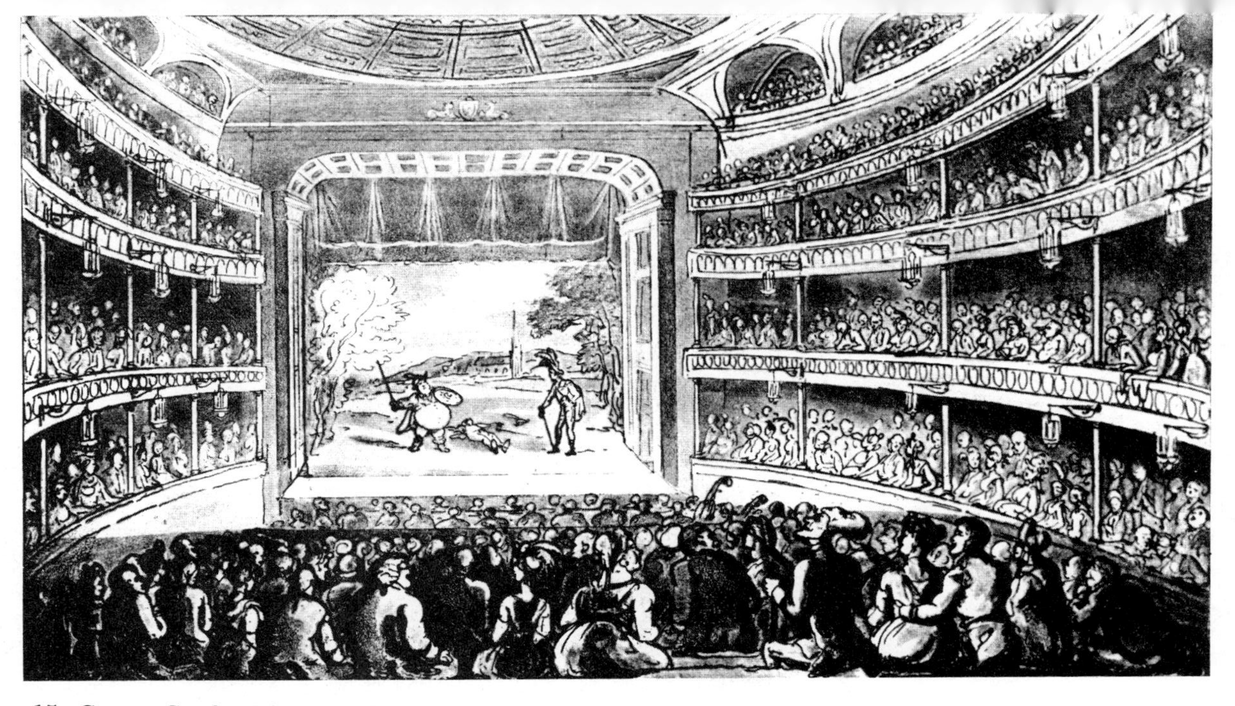

15. Covent Garden Theatre, c.1812
The picture by Thomas Rowlandson shows a scene from an extravaganza by C. I. M. Dibdin. It will be noted that there are five circles and a considerable orchestra.

But straight plays were not always sufficiently attractive to fill these vast theatres and even Sheridan had had to resort on occasion to equestrian displays and shows that were virtually circuses. In doing so he was trespassing into the area of the minor theatres, which did not have the right to reply by staging straight plays, although their smaller theatres would have been far more appropriate. It was as a result of such circumstances as this that Covent Garden became particularly associated with the staging of opera.

There was, however, another reason for the major theatres to have a large seating capacity. During the nineteenth century the population of London increased enormously. Between 1801 and 1841 it doubled from 1,115,000 to 2,235,000 and then doubled again to nearly five million by 1881. Thus there was an enormously increased potential public for the theatre. The managers of the major theatres responded, as we have seen, by increasing the capacity of their auditoria, often with unhappy consequences. But it was with the minor theatres that the most striking developments took place. As the size of Greater London grew along with its population, so speculators built theatres in all the developing suburbs. But they were still subject to the restrictions of the Licensing Act of 1737. This led to a proliferation of such 'bastard' theatrical forms as melodrama and pantomime, extravaganza and burlesque, equestrian shows and music halls. The situation was ridiculous.

At the same time there was another problem which had great effect on the internal running of theatres though less on the general public. To build a theatre required an increasing expenditure of capital. A man who invests capital in a building expects a return. The ownership and running of theatres therefore became a form of big business beyond the scope of the former actor-manager. So two kinds of managers developed, the so-called 'bricks-and-mortar' manager who owned the theatres and the producing managers, including the old actor-managers, who rented the theatre and staged the productions. It was, and often still is, an uncertain relationship as the rent charged by the theatre-owner can have a considerable effect on the artistic policy of the producing manager.

Among the first actor-managers to protest violently about the state of the theatre and to realize the necessity for reform was William Charles Macready (1793–1873). He was a remarkable man. As an actor he was limited by a rather heavy style and certain mannerisms but in his *Diaries*, which give a most vivid picture of the theatrical conditions of his time, he subjects his playing to constant self-analysis and criticism of the most remarkably honest nature. Related to his ability as an actor was his interest in what we should now call 'production' or 'direction'. He cared deeply about the ensemble, the way in which the play was mounted, adequate rehearsals, strict attendance by all members of the cast. But most important of all, perhaps, was the importance he attached to the whole status of the theatre and the theatrical profession. He was disgusted by prevailing conditions and frequently confessed to being ashamed of his profession. But he was a friend of most of the leading literary figures of the day, including Charles Dickens, and was responsible for staging some fifty new plays including works by Robert Browning, Sheridan Knowles, Thomas Talfourd, and Edward Bulwer-Lytton. This was a splendid achievement.

He is also notable for having restored Shakespeare's original texts to the stage. There was no lessening of Shakespeare's popularity. During the eighteenth century nearly a quarter of all productions at Drury Lane and Covent Garden had been of Shakespeare. But the texts were 'updated' to a greater or lesser extent to bring them into line with contemporary taste. This practice had been widely indulged by Restoration dramatists, who felt that they were only doing what Shakespeare himself would have done had he been alive. They wanted to make the morality of the plays more explicit and give the characters a clearer motivation for their actions. Davenant made a single play out of *Much Ado About Nothing* and *Measure for Measure* and called it *The Law Against Lovers*. Garrick wrote a death speech for Macbeth that ended,

> I cannot rise! I dare not ask for mercy –
> It is too late, Hell drags me down. I sink,
> I sink – Oh! my soul is lost for ever! (*Dies*)

Macbeth having previously said to his wife:

> Madam, I have observed since you came hither,
> You have been still disconsolate. Pray tell me,
> Are you in perfect health?

There are records of 123 adaptations of Shakespeare and there may have been many more. Some of them, such as Colley Cibber's *Richard III*, held the stage until the time of Macready.

The movement to re-establish the authenticity of Shakespeare's original texts was encouraged by a number of well-edited editions of Shakespeare that had been appearing with increasing regularity and scholarship from 1609 onwards. It was now known what Shakespeare wrote. But Macready had to struggle with a powerful theatrical tradition to ensure that what Shakespeare wrote was what was spoken on the stage.

Macready's illuminating Diaries *have been published in full but are difficult to obtain. An abbreviated version has been edited by J. C. Trewin.*

It is very difficult to get hold of copies of even the most popular of the old adaptations of Shakespeare; but they are well worth reading, not to jeer at, but to study changing literary and theatrical values.

84 | The Theatres Act of 1843

That the situation created by the 'patent' and the minor theatres was irrational, was in time accepted, and as a result of persistent lobbying by such Parliamentarians as Lord Lytton, the Theatres Act of 1843 was passed. The Act removed the anomaly of the patent and established the right of a theatre to choose its own repertory. Theatre buildings still required a licence, in London from the Lord Chamberlain, in the provinces from local Justices of the Peace. (The licensed theatre was usually called the Theatre Royal.) But the office of Examiner of Plays (censorship) was reaffirmed in spite of Bulwer-Lytton's protestations.

The passing of the Act did not recreate the brave new theatrical world which had been anticipated. This was not because the theatres did not know what to do with their newly-won freedom, but because the condition of the theatre, as it has been described, could not easily be changed. The theatre as a whole had not found an identity that enabled it to cater for, or win the support of London's rapidly growing population. Yet it was not simply a question of size of population: its characteristics were of great importance.

The Act made possible the establishment of some twenty-seven theatres in the Greater London area, but these only touched the fringe of the problem of providing entertainment for the huge working population. In this respect one of the most extraordinary developments was the Penny Gaff, a term of unknown origin. Penny Gaffs were real old theatrical glory-holes or 'blood tubs' as they were often called, improvised stages of the most uncomfortable kind where the crudest melodramas were staged, sometimes three or four times a night. In the mid-nineteenth century between eighty and a hundred are known to have existed in London and they were to be found in all the great industrial cities.

In what might be called the mainstream theatre there were a number of managers who, like Macready, brought some kind of distinction to the theatre. One of the most interesting was Lucia Elizabeth Bartolozzi (1797–1856) who, as a result of an early marriage, is usually known as Madame Vestris. Though gifted as a singer and dancer she made her greatest contribution to the stage as a manager. In 1830 she took over control of the Olympic, a theatre in the region of the Aldwych, where

16. Shakespeare's Henry V: the siege of Harfleur
One of Charles Kean's productions at the Princess's Theatre which he managed between 1851 and 1859 with a mixture of lavish theatricality and an obsession for antiquarian authenticity.

she made considerable improvements in the staging of plays, establishing box-sets with real ceilings for comedies, and paying detailed attention to costumes and properties. She advertised her productions without 'puffs' (exaggerated claims). Most of all she established rigorous artistic discipline within her company; and when for a short period she took over management of Covent Garden she applied her high artistic standards to the production of Shakespeare.

Another important manager was Ben Webster (1797–1882) who was lessee and manager of the Haymarket Theatre from 1837 until 1853. The Haymarket, it will be remembered, had enjoyed a limited patent to stage straight plays; but the success and distinction of Ben Webster's productions, in spite of the limitations imposed by the Act of 1737, constituted a serious rivalry to the two patent theatres, emphasized the anomaly of the situation, and helped to bring about the Theatres Act of 1843.

Then there was Samuel Phelps (1804–78) who had been a young actor in Macready's company. In 1843 he took over Sadler's Wells Theatre and by 1862 had staged imaginative productions of thirty-two of Shakespeare's plays. Shakespeare also provided a large part of the repertory of Charles Kean (1811–68), the son of Edmund Kean, during his tenancy of the Princess's Theatre between 1851 and 1859. He gave spectacular productions with considerable emphasis on historical accuracy in all the visual details of the performance.

But a living theatre is not created by revivals, however authentic, imaginative, or intelligent they may be. The theatre needed new dramatists of talent, and these were surprisingly long in coming.

85 | Music-hall

During the middle and latter part of the nineteenth century the music-hall became one of the most distinctive of all forms of theatrical entertainment. It owed its origins to two practices which were common in the eighteenth century. One was the Pleasure Garden. This had been established in Restoration times in the public parks.

Here there was food and drink, a variety of entertainments, games, and diversions. A number of such Pleasure Gardens existed, such as the celebrated Vauxhall Gardens in south London, and in Kilburn, Hampstead, and Belsize Park to the north.

As the Pleasure Garden provided a place of relaxation and entertainment for the middle classes, so the taverns did the same for the working population. Enterprising landlords began to attach music-rooms to their taverns where patrons could be entertained with popular songs while they drank. Since streets were dangerous at night, both taverns and their music-rooms became plentiful to prevent patrons having to walk too far at closing-time. The idea caught on and music-rooms became so popular that they were increasingly detached from the taverns and run independently. Publicans bought neighbouring premises and converted them into halls. With a swiftly growing population in the new suburbs, and with strict limitations on the building of new theatres, the music-halls increased rapidly in number, in popularity, and in the scope of the entertainment they provided. That is to say, they provided an opening for a new type of entertainer. Although in most cases singers provided the main entertainment they were joined by performers with a variety of skills – patter acts, ventriloquism, conjuring, juggling: the scop, the *jongleur*, the minstrel, the jester had become the music-hall artist.

In the early nineteenth-century the music-halls began to make common cause with the minor theatres, for this was a new form of entertainment that circumvented the Licensing Act of 1737. Some of the minor theatres turned themselves into music-halls.

But the Theatres Act of 1843 put no kind of a brake on the development of the music-hall. Many music-hall artists became stars of great individual distinction. They were quite different from actors in that they usually developed their own individual 'act' with their own costume and make-up, many of them maintaining this same stage 'character' throughout their lives. They 'worked a date' while actors 'played a town'.

In the second half of the nineteenth century, when there was a very considerable boom in theatre buildings, a very large number of theatres were built all over the country entirely devoted to Variety, as the music-hall industry had come to be called. A delightful feature of these Variety Theatres, or music-halls, was their architecture. Architects gave free rein to their fantasies, and built theatres in a variety of exotic styles, Moorish or Indian, or just richly decorated with cherubs and scrolls and cornucopia and plenty of crimson and gold. The celebrated Alhambra, which opened in 1854, has now been replaced by the featureless architecture of the Leicester Square cinema; but the

17. Canterbury Music Hall, Lambeth
Built and opened in 1849 by Charles Morton, it was known as 'the father of the halls'. With a seating capacity of 1500 it was successful for many years.

Coliseum, the Victoria Palace, the Palladium, the Hippodrome, now devoted to late-night cabaret, and the London Pavilion, of which only the façade now remains, were all originally music-halls. Some of the most delightful, however, were outside the West End. There was Collins Music Hall on Islington Green; the Metropolitan, Edgware Road; and the Granville, Walham Green, all in use until 1939.

The French form of the music-hall was Vaudeville. The derivation of this word is uncertain but it was first used in the seventeenth century to describe a political or satirical ballad. Subsequently, when the minor theatres of Paris, in the same position as those of London, were seeking for entertainment with which to circumvent the monopoly of the Comédie-Française, they strung these songs together rather in the manner of a ballad opera, and called them Vaudevilles. A partnership was established in due course between the Vaudeville and the Italian comic opera (*opera buffa*) which arrived in Paris in 1752. The result was the Opéra Comique, a theatrical form that became extremely popular in Paris of the nineteenth century through the stylish and amusing pieces of such composers as Jacques Offenbach (1819–80) and Johann Strauss II (1825–99).

The comic opera or operetta also became extremely popular in Britain. A theatre known as the Opera Comique was opened in the Strand in 1871 but was replaced ten years later by the Savoy Theatre which was built as a result of the outstanding success of the light operas of W. S. Gilbert and Arthur Sullivan. Light operas continued to be successful until the sentimental whimsicalities of Noël Coward and Ivor Novello, skilled entertainers but no great artists, were replaced in the post-war years by the far more vigorous American musicals such as *Oklahoma!*, *Kiss Me Kate*, and *Guys and Dolls*.

The history of the music-hall, like that of other forms of popular entertainment, tends to fall between the drily academic and the over chatty of which W. McQueen Pope's The Melody Lingers On *is an example. Harold Scott's* The Early Doors *is particularly good on the music-hall prior to 1843.*

86 | The Well-made Play

It is rather curious to find that in the course of the nineteenth century it was France, with an extremely unstable political history, which became the artistic centre of Europe. In 1815 her military power and the Empire of Napoleon Bonaparte were destroyed. There were revolutions in 1830 and 1848. In 1851 Louis Napoleon, a nephew of Bonaparte, seized power and established the Second Empire. In 1870 France was defeated by the Germans, who occupied Paris. The short-lived Paris Commune of 1871 was followed by the establishment of the Third Republic. (Louis Napoleon had gone into exile in Chislehurst, Kent.) In spite of these upheavals the French produced a succession of outstanding artists. The first exhibition of the Impressionist painters inaugurated one of the most splendid movements in the whole history of art; in many other respects the French had shown themselves to be a most cultured and civilized people.

This is partly because they have traditionally taken art seriously, even though they have been disposed to reduce it to a set of rules. While in some ways this is a very constrictive practice, obedience to rules necessitates a disciplined approach to a subject. Louis Napoleon, for example, made great efforts to ensure the beauty and splendour of Paris. The Goncourt brothers, in their *Journal*, tell us that under Louis Philippe (1830–48) the dominating spirit of Parisian bourgeois society was 'Enrichissez vous!' (Get rich quick!) while under Louis Napoleon the order of the day was 'Jouissez!' (Enjoy yourselves!). So even in the provision of entertainment there was professionalism, a serious approach to the provision of frivolous *divertissements*. There was of course a vigorous reaction against all this commercialization as well as against the academicism of much traditional art; the masterpieces of many of the finest artists and writers took the form of a protest at various features of a society which they increasingly detested.

Victor Hugo, in his Preface to *Ruy Blas* (1838) makes a very interesting analysis of audiences. The theatre-going public, he says, consists first of women, secondly of thinkers, and thirdly of the crowd. The latter want action, women want passion, thinkers are particularly interested in character; or, in other words and the same order, the theatre must provide sensation, emotion, and thought; or satisfaction for the eyes, the heart, the mind. So there is melodrama (action and sensation) for the crowd, tragedy (of passion) for women, the comedy of human life for the intelligentsia; though naturally, he adds, there is considerable overlapping.

Of melodrama something has already been said. The tradition that had been established by Pixérécourt continued throughout the century. Tragedy, as Hugo intended it, had no distinguished future, though at the end of the century Edmond Rostand (1868–1918) gave a final flourish to Romantic drama with a number of plays in verse of which the most popular was *Cyrano de Bergerac* (1897). What Hugo failed to recognize was the extent to which the interests of the middle-class theatre-goers conditioned what the playwrights produced. The first of a group of highly professional dramatists to write entirely for the mainstream theatre was Eugène Scribe (1791–1861). He was the author of more than three hundred plays, many on historical subjects but most of them depicting episodes from contemporary bourgeois society. None of them is a masterpiece of dramatic art; they tend to be trivial in theme, weak in literary quality, and poor in characterization; but they are so carefully constructed that they constitute a new theatrical genre, the well-made play (*la piéce bien faite*). They were elegantly staged in the boulevard theatres and played by actors and actresses who were developing commensurate standards of professionalism.

The tradition of the well-made play continued. A most notable exponent was Victorien Sardou (1831–1908). His early plays are comedies and farces modelled on the style of Scribe, but in the 1880s he wrote a number of heavy dramas that provided splendid roles for the great actress, Sarah Bernhardt, and in *Tosca* a colourful libretto for the composer Puccini.

Sardou's plays are rarely revived; their contrived theatricality and their complicated plots make them unfashionable. Even in their own day they were dismissed by Bernard Shaw, who was then a dramatic critic, along with the whole genre of the well-made play, as Sardoodledom. Yet the well-made play throws up some interesting problems. There is a certain satisfaction in seeing a play of this kind simply because it is well made. There is an initial situation, which is then developed in the second act, comes to a climax in the third or fourth, and is rounded off in the fifth. There are no loose ends. All satisfying aesthetically. But there are two snags. In order to achieve this orderliness of construction, the playwright is obliged to organize his plot in a manner that almost inevitably results in some kind of unnatural behaviour. Character is subservient to plot. Human beings tend not to behave in the theatrically consistent manner that is required by this kind of play. The second problem is related to the first. This logical sequence of events can be extremely unconvincing, unnatural, unlifelike. The technical problem is the same that faced the playwrights who tried to conform to the unities. Only a great master can write with absolute freedom in so constricted and disciplined a form.

A vivid picture of French society in the mid-nineteenth century can be had from three superb works, the Journals *of the painter Eugene Delacroix, the* Letters *of Gustave Flaubert and the* Journals *of Edmond and Jules de Goncourt. They have all been translated into English.*

Bernard Shaw's dramatic criticisms, which will have even greater relevance to a later section, have been collected in Our Theatre in the Nineties.

The structure of the well-made play has been analysed by another fine dramatic critic, William Archer in Playmaking.

Very few of the plays of Scribe and Sardou are available in English translation.

87 | Farce

The theory of the well-made play can be as well applied to comic as to serious themes. To do so adroitly was another achievement of the French.

If one removes character and emotion from tragedy one is left with narrative. If this narrative is 'action-packed', the chances are that one is left with melodrama. But if one removes character and emotion from a comic theme, one is left with farce. Melodrama and farce are therefore the two extremes of a dramatic action from which character and emotion have been removed to leave a vigorous sequence of actions and events. The naivety and crudity, though the entertaining theatricality, of what results can be seen in such famous English melodramas as *Maria Marten or the Murder in the Red Barn* (*c.*1840), *Lady Audley's Secret* (1863), and *Sweeney Todd, the Demon Barber of Fleet Street* (1862). Their theatrical appeal can be seen from the fact that they held the stage until the 1930s.

The French playwright, Eugène Labiche (1815–88), gave a kind of distinction to farce by applying to highly comical themes the rules for constructing a well-made play. Between 1837 and 1877 he wrote 173 plays of which among the most celebrated are *Le Chapeau de paille d'Italie* (*The Italian Straw Hat*, 1851) still often revived, and *Le Voyage de Monsieur Perrichon* (1860).

Next in the succession was Georges Feydeau (1862–1921). In his forty to fifty plays there is a much stronger sexual element than is to be found in Labiche. It is his heroines, whether the virtuous young lady of middle-class origins who dreams of adultery like the heroine of *La Puce à l'oreille* (*A Flea in her Ear*, 1862) or the cocottes of easy virtue who take a cynical attitude to marriage and establish the myth that every man has a mistress in the cupboard, that led to the frequently used term 'bedroom farce' (not to be confused with Alan Ayckbourn's play of the same name).

It is in the farces of the English dramatist, Sir Arthur Pinero (1855–1934) that one can see very clearly the basic pattern of the farce – the serious character who finds himself in a ludicrously inappropriate situation. Thus in *The Magistrate* (1885) the highly respectable protagonist finds himself in a night-club; *The Schoolmistress* (1886), headmistress of a seminary for young ladies, becomes a star of an operetta while her school goes to ruin; in *Dandy Dick* (1887) a bishop becomes involved in gambling on the horses and *The Cabinet Minister*, saddled with a spendthrift wife, is blackmailed by a socially ambitious moneylender.

During the present century the only writer of genuine farces has been Ben Travers (1886–1981); for farce, like the well-made play, has a basic artificiality which is not popular today. The form has been replaced by light comedies of which an outstanding example is Oscar Wilde's *The Importance of Being Earnest* (1895). Indeed, the situations of this exquisite play are farcical, but the elegance of the dialogue transforms it into high comedy.

Farce can only really flourish in a society which has strong class structure and widely accepted moral values. For farce in a way is anarchical. It is concerned with the overturning of values. If society accepts, as ours is inclined to do, that there is nothing improper in a magistrate visiting a perfectly well-run night-club, or a bishop having a flutter on the horses, the stuffing has gone out of farce. This provides yet another example of the manner in which theatrical forms are created by the society of their time.

The better-known farces of Labiche and Feydeau are available in translation. Dandy Dick *has been reprinted in recent years; it is regrettable that the other farces of Pinero have been out of print for so long. Ben Travers's so-called Aldwych farces were, of course, a feature of the London theatre in the 1920s and 1930s, owing much of their success to immaculate playing by a more or less permanent company.*

18. **Covent Garden Opera House**
The present building opened in May 1858, designed by Edward Barry. Frederick Gye, the owner and manager, also built a Floral Hall with materials left over from the Crystal Palace but it became used for promenade concerts and not a flower-market as had been intended.

88 London Theatre in the Late Nineteenth Century

It took twenty years for London managements to take advantage of the freedom allowed by the Theatres Act of 1843. In 1865 an actor-manager, Squire Bancroft (1841–1926), and his wife, Marie Wilton (1839–1921), took over management of a disused and rather disreputable theatre in Charlotte Street, a road that runs parallel to the Tottenham Court Road. They refurbished it, put in comfortable stall seats in blue velvet with lace antimacassars, for which they eventually charged 10/-, increased the salaries of their players and opened with the first of a number of plays they subsequently staged by a young playwright named Tom Robertson (1829–71). Tom Robertson's plays, of which the most successful were *David Garrick* (1864), *Society* (1865), and especially *Caste* (1867) are not masterpieces of dramatic art, but they are evidence of a new drama in the making. Robertson tackled contemporary themes in an unexaggerated fashion, using dialogue that rings true and staging his plays in box-sets with real doors, banishing for good the wing pieces with painted doors and windows. The Bancroft management took the first big step in creating a theatre that reflected the values of, and so was supported by the now powerful and influential middle classes. Squire Bancroft and Marie Wilton had a great success with their first venture in management. In 1880, therefore, they moved 'up-market' and took over management of the Haymarket Theatre. Here, with a kind of symbolic gesture, they had the proscenium arch rebuilt to form a large gold frame. Also, to the fury of their regular patrons, they abolished the pit and filled the parterre with stalls.

In some respects the most prestigious of all actor-managers was Sir Henry Irving (1838–1905), ruling the Lyceum Theatre in the Strand from 1871 until 1901. He was an actor of considerable power if limited scope; as a director he was responsible for a number of highly spectacular productions. Indeed, it was his lavish expenditure on staging that resulted in the final collapse of his management. But he was a figure of eminent respectability and the first man of the theatre to be knighted. (Thereafter most of the more distinguished actor-managers received a similar accolade.)

The period from about 1880 until the outbreak of the 1914–18 war was the heyday of the 'commercial' theatre. It has been recorded that between 1850 and 1950 there were over 900 theatres, music-halls, and theatrical venues in London. Over the whole country the number must have been prodigious. But in the mainstream commercial theatres the emphasis was on comfort and elegance. It was increasingly customary for evening dress to be worn by those occupying the stalls; in at least one theatre the front of the boxes were made of lattice-work so that the rest of the audience could appreciate the ladies' dresses; opening times were arranged so that patrons could dine before the show, programmes were better printed, bars were installed. And in the area of administration a large number of laws and by-laws were passed establishing standards of safety and hygiene on both sides of the curtain.

In all these developments the actor-managers played a significant part. There was Sir Herbert Beerbohm Tree (1853–1917), an eccentric character who built His (now Her) Majesty's Theatre in 1897 and carried on something of the Lyceum tradition of spectacular Shakespearian productions – Richard III on a real horse and *A Midsummer Night's Dream* with real rabbits. Sir George Alexander (1858–1918) managed the St. James's Theatre, now destroyed, with great distinction and authority between 1891 and 1917. Sir Johnston Forbes-Robertson was more successful as an actor than a manager but was responsible for some enterprising productions. Sir John Martin-Harvey (1863–1944), Sir John Hare (1844–1921), and Sir Charles Wyndham (1837–1919) who built both the Criterion and the theatre that now bears his name, all these and many more made their individual contribution to the theatre.

The theatre for which these men were responsible was on the whole extremely successful. Many of the actor-managers retired as wealthy men. They established theatre-going as a fashionable middle- and upper-class activity. But whether their work was artistically successful is open to question. There were many critics and men of the theatre at the time who said it was not. Among the most vociferous was the red-bearded Irishman, George Bernard Shaw, whose focus of attack was not standards of acting or production but the nature of the plays, many of which he considered to be lamentable examples of Sardoodledom. The validity of such criticisms depends on the point of view from which one regards the theatre. Shaw wanted it to be something other than it was. The middle classes, who largely supported the theatre, were well enough content.

The Bancrofts have left their own most readable memoirs. A detailed life of Henry Irving has been written by his son, Laurence Irving. Sir Charles Wyndham is subject of a biography by

19. Balham Hippodrome
This superb theatre was opened in 1899 as a music-hall to a design by W. G. R. Sprague who also designed, usually on more intimate lines, Wyndham's (1899), the Albery (1903), the Strand (1905), the Aldwych (1905), the Globe (1906), the Queen's (1907), the Ambassadors (1913), the St Martin's (1916), and several others now destroyed.

Wendy Trewin. Beerbohm Tree has received rather sensational treatment by his biographers. Short biographies of some of the others are to be found in Richard Findlater's The Player Kings, *Frances Donaldson's* The Actor-Managers, *and Hesketh Pearson's* The Last Actor-Managers.

89 | Playwrights (*c.*1880–1914)

The record of the actor-managers, together with London managers as a whole, in the production of new plays has been persistently good. The improved status of the theatre and the existence of managements ready to stage new plays stimulated that subtle kind of adrenalin in potential playwrights that encouraged them to turn their best talents to writing plays. One may or may not care for the plays of Arthur Pinero and Henry Arthur Jones, but like the plays of Sardou, they are serious examples of dramatic art and represent the strengths and weaknesses of a theatre that reflected, or projected a certain image of contemporary society.

Nevertheless the more serious plays of the period show that the tradition of the socially conscious melodrama died hard. The plays of Oscar Wilde (1854–1900), excepting of course the delightful *The Importance of Being Earnest*, are bogged down in the stuffy theatricalism of the social melodrama. *Lady Windermere's Fan* (1892), *A Woman of No Importance* (1893), and *An Ideal Husband* (1895) all deal in one way or another with that Aunt Sally of the Victorian society, the respectable woman with an unrespectable past. Nothing, in fact, demonstrates more clearly the brutal values of Victorian society than the manner in which he himself was destroyed by that very society whose values he is at pains to demonstrate in his plays.

It is the same with Sir Arthur Pinero (1855–1934). Having written four entertaining farces of considerable technical skill, he becomes preoccupied with marital problems created by the intransigent values of Victorian society. *The Profligate* (1889), *The Second Mrs Tanqueray* (1893), *The Notorious Mrs Ebbsmith* (1895), *The Gay Lord Quex* (1899), and *His House in Order* (1906) are serious, finely constructed plays, compulsively readable and theatrically fascinating. But they have the inherent weaknesses of the well-made play. The characters behave, not according to any natural instincts, or even on the basis of common sense, but according to the values and taboos of a patriarchal society which places women in a position of distinct social inferiority to men. A wife must be pretty, that is sexually attractive to her husband, but inflexible to the approaches of other men. She must run the house, while accepting that all major decisions are taken by her husband. A high premium is set upon virginity. The revelation of the slightest peccadillo in the early life of a married woman is social damnation. Bernard Shaw sums up the whole attitude of the dramatists in a comment he makes on *The Profligate*: 'Mr Pinero walked cautiously up to a social problem, touched it, and ran away.' A good example of Pinero's methods are to be seen in *The Benefit of the Doubt* (1895). The story turns upon an unhappily married young man who seeks innocent solace with a young married woman whose husband is often abroad. The jealous wife brings an action and the judge gives her 'the benefit of the doubt'. Thus we have the case of two young couples trying to establish a human but in no respect adulterous relationship with each other, wholly destroyed by an irrational moral order imposed by a tyrannical society. Pinero neither protests nor suggests that an element of common sense might not have been amiss, though perhaps he was twisting the screw to enhance the dramatic effectiveness of the play.

Henry Arthur Jones (1851–1929) is often coupled with Pinero as a fashionable dramatist, but his gift was for light comedy rather than serious drama, although *Mrs Dane's Defence* (1900) is an impressive example of the kind of subject that was exploited by Pinero. *The Case of Rebellious Susan* (1894), *Dolly Reforming Herself* (1908), and especially *The Liars* (1897) are delightful and well-written examples of their kind. He was perhaps a little less successful than Pinero because he was more divided in his aims. He tried to extend the frontiers of drama by writing plays such as *The Tempter* (1893) and *Michael and his Lost Angel* (1896). Their failure dispirited him. He valued the social importance of the theatre and argued vigorously that drama should play a significant part in national life. He wanted to relate drama more closely with literature. He went so far as to say in his older years that if he could live his life again he would devote it to literature. His long essay, *The Shadow of Irving*, is an example of the prose style of which he was master. But he lacked the artistic drive that would have enabled him to realize his ideals either in plays or argument.

The more naturalistic British dramatists, those that were influenced by and wrote in the aftermath of Ibsen, will be discussed in a later section. But up until the 1939–45 war the British mainstream theatre sustained a succession of playwrights of considerable professional ability even if one does not rate their work very high in creative power. By simply listing them there is no intention of belittling their immense contribution to the theatre; but in the proportions of this book one must either devote a paragraph to each of them or simply point out the pleasure to be had from reading and seeing the major plays of James Barrie, Noël Coward, Somerset Maugham, James Bridie, J. B. Priestley, and Emlyn Williams. The list could be made very much longer. But at a time when it is fashionable to disparage the so-called 'commercial' theatre, it is common justice to emphasize its record in the staging of new plays.

90 | Regional Theatre

The distribution of theatres in a country is dependent on a variety of demographic factors such as the distribution of the population and the geographical and political structure of the country. During the nineteenth and early twentieth centuries the theatre in England and France was centred on London and Paris because in the early seventeenth century, when the theatre first began to achieve economic independence and professional status for the actors and actresses, no other towns were large or rich enough to support more than sporadic theatrical enterprises. Even in the eighteenth century when the population of many regional towns was in excess of a hundred thousand, they continued to depend, as they had always done, on tours, most of which emanated from the capital. There was a far greater tendency for towns to support permanent theatrical companies in countries like Italy and Germany which for historical reasons had not achieved their national identity, or which in due course established a federal constitution. In these two countries, for example, there was no political unification and so no accepted seat of government until the 1870s. Prior to the unification of Germany, many of the theatres of the eighteenth-century dukes were taken over by municipal authorities in a manner that did not happen in England until the 1950s. So in England and France particularly, most of the venues outside London and Paris were touring theatres. The bigger theatres in the bigger towns took London companies – known until recently as number one tours – to play their most recent success. This was made possible by rapid improvements in railway travel. Indeed, the railway companies provided every kind of facility especially when the company included a star performer.

During the eighteenth century the size of provincial cities increased considerably. In many of them there was established a small professional company which would also go on tour, establishing a circuit in a certain area of the country. In Kent, for example, there was the Canterbury circuit which included Margate, Dover, Deal, Maidstone, Faversham, and Rochester; the Norwich circuit included Cambridge, Colchester, Bury St. Edmunds, King's Lynn, Ipswich, and Great Yarmouth.

All this can be followed clearly in the theatrical history of a flourishing commercial city like Bristol. There are records of small companies of professional actors visiting the town from early Tudor times. Throughout the seventeenth and well into the eighteenth century there was a struggle between those who wished to encourage the establishment of a permanent company in the town, as well as visits by touring companies, and the puritanical element on the town council which wanted to suppress all theatrical activities. Puritanical influence was so strong that although the exquisite Theatre Royal, still in use, was opened in 1766, it was seven years before the Justices issued the necessary licence for plays to be performed. Thereafter Bristol became a regular date for major tours and in 1912 the Hippodrome was built especially for that purpose.

In the early years of the present century there were regularly some hundred 'number one' tours and innumerable smaller tours on the road, but the establishment of permanent regional theatres was a slow process. Glasgow (1909), Liverpool (1911), and Birmingham were among the first, and by the 1930s there were as many as a hundred. They were known as repertory theatres – incorrectly, for a repertory theatre is one in which there is a repertory of plays ready for production, three or four of which may be given every week. Pre-war repertory theatres had much the same policy as present day regional theatres, producing one play at a time for a run of anything from a week to a month. The National and the Royal Shakespeare Companies, as administered in the 1980s, are proper repertory theatres.

The repertory theatre movement, however, was the first stage in a wholly new concept of theatre that became known as community theatre. The Irish national theatre was a clear forerunner, and Annie Horniman, undeterred by a certain failure in Dublin, offered her patronage to Manchester, where from 1907 she helped to establish the Gaiety Theatre as a regional repertory theatre and to encourage a school of regional play-writing. But the concept of national, regional, and community theatres will be developed in later sections of this book.

The development of the regional theatre in Britain has never been the subject of a major study but there are a number of short books on the history of the theatre in various cities. The local library should be a source of information on this interesting subject.

91 | Naturalism in the Theatre

Theatre in primitive society tends to be ritualistic. In content it is concerned with matters of life and death. In form it is poetic and wholly unrealistic because it is concerned with unrealistic matters. Under the pressures of what we are pleased to call civilized society, drama becomes increasingly less concerned with the survival of life than with the quality of life. As people's aspirations change, so drama becomes a projection of the different ways that people think and feel and what they think and feel about. Writers and actors and other artists are motivated by the wish to communicate something to their readers or their audience. Thus, under normal conditions, they are concerned with expressing themselves ever more clearly. Dramatists write increasingly in prose rather than verse and actors drop the declamatory style that was common at the beginning of the eighteenth century and adopt an increasingly naturalistic manner of speaking. By the middle of the nineteenth century most European dramatists were writing in prose, the actors wore realistic and appropriate costumes, whether historical or contemporary, and scenery was, as far as possible, a representation of real life.

But many writers felt that this trend towards naturalism could and should be taken much farther. With a good deal of justification they considered that a great deal of theatrical art was overlaid with a kind of false romanticism. Dickens, Balzac, and Flaubert were particularly concerned with depicting the society of their time and in the French theatre the younger Alexandre Dumas (1824–95) showed considerable interest in social problems. The heroine of his most famous play, *La Dame aux camélias* (*The Lady of the Camelias*, 1852), which he wrote to make money, is a lady of easy virtue whom he treats as a sympathetic character.

The new movement was announced by the French novelist, Emile Zola (1840–1902). His first play, *Thérèse Raquin* (1873), is a fairly crude melodrama: it is the Preface which is important. In this and his collected dramatic criticisms, which he published in 1881 under the title of *Naturalisme au théâtre* (*Naturalism in the Theatre*), he propounded his thesis. The theatre, he argued, must be brought into closer relationship with social reality and experimental science. Romantic tragedy with its secret doors, poisoned wine, and mislaid letters, and bourgeois realism with its false sentiments and unconvincing revelations, are both utterly dead. The new drama must throw aside all outworn conventions, theatrical language, and hackneyed situations and express a new reality. Naturalism must introduce a scientific analysis of the human being and reveal his spiritual and emotional reality. Fine words. But it was just about this time that doctors in Vienna were beginning to undertake that investigation of the human mind which introduced two important new words to European culture, psychiatry and psychoanalysis.

It is arguable, of course, that the novel provides a more satisfactory form for discussing the nature of human personality than drama, and many nineteenth-century novels had made profound comments both on human society and human nature. Drama was far behind. No plays had been written of the same class as the novels of Flaubert, Balzac, Dickens and many others. But naturalism in the theatre created problems. Since a stage play depends upon a certain amount of action, the result of dramatizing the novels of Zola was to turn them into crude melodrama. But other dramatists did better; and when eventually there was a theatre ready to stage their plays the naturalistic movement gathered momentum. The creation of such a theatre is an interesting story.

92 Le Théâtre Libre (The Free Theatre)

In the year 1887 André Antoine was a heavily-built, broad-shouldered, slightly stooping man of thirty-three with small blue eyes set rather far apart, stubborn jaw, and a rather high-pitched voice. He was inclined to be brusque in manner and ungainly in appearance. His employers, the Paris Gas Company, considered him to be a conscientious worker.

As a young man Antoine had had a passion for literature and went without meals to buy books. In the 1880s this was supplanted by a passion for the theatre and he went without meals to buy theatre tickets. He became an enthusiastic amateur actor and joined a group called the *Cercle gaulois* run by a retired army officer known as Père Krauss. This elderly gentleman had acquired a hall at the end of a narrow gloomy passage in Montmartre called L'Elysée des Beaux Arts in which he built a small stage. But Antoine was critical of Père Krauss's choice of play and suggested they produce something more interesting. One thing led to another and in due course Antoine and his colleagues had collected four new one-act plays, one of which was a dramatization of a story by Zola. This scared Père Krauss and members of the circle, for Zola was known to be a provocative figure, and Antoine was forbidden use of the hall for rehearsals although he could hire it for performances. Antoine had to raise the necessary hundred francs himself. The performance was a success. Zola's name may have frightened the Circle but it drew the critics. Antoine could continue with periodic performances.

He called his theatre Le Théâtre Libre, the Free Theatre; but freedom from what? Basically from what he considered to be the limitations of the boulevard theatre. He never had any intention of creating a theatre for the staging of naturalistic plays, but since these were the most fresh and original plays then being written, and since there was no satisfactory place for them in the boulevard theatres, they tended to dominate his repertory. Moreover he was strongly supported by two of the leading naturalistic novelists of the day, Edmond de Goncourt and Alphonse Daudet. Plays such as *Die Weber* (*The Weavers*,

1892) by the German dramatist Gerhart Hauptmann (1862–1946) and Ibsen's *Ghosts* created a sensation. Antoine himself describes how in playing Oswald in *Ghosts* he experienced a kind of loss of personality, so fully did the role grip him, and George Moore, the Irish novelist, who saw the performance, describes how he became involved in the performance in a way he had never previously experienced in the theatre.

Antoine kept the venture going until 1894, gradually creating a fully professional organization. During these seven years he introduced Paris audiences to the work of Ibsen, Hauptmann, Strindberg, Bjornson, Becque, Brieux, and many other French and European writers. The naturalistic plays he staged had been either rejected by or not even submitted to the boulevard theatres, not because they were naturalistic but because they dealt with subjects that were socially taboo, such as venereal disease, class war, sexual relationships, but handled in as honest and naturalistic a manner as possible without the artificialities imposed by the well-made play. Yet it was not just the subjects that disturbed people: it was that they were treated realistically. For many the truth is only palatable when it is sentimentalized.

Soon after the creation of the Théâtre Libre, similar ventures were started in other European cities to stage the new drama of which Henrik Ibsen was the leading figure. In 1880 Otto Brahm (1856–1912), a dramatic critic, founded Die Freie Bühne in Berlin, developed it on similar lines, and injected renewed vitality into the German theatre. In 1891 a Dutch critic who had become a naturalized Englishman, J. T. Grein, founded the Independent Theatre in London especially to stage *Ghosts* and went on to give the first productions of the earliest plays of Bernard Shaw, who was one of the most vigorous supporters of the whole movement, and particularly of Ibsen.

It is disappointing that Antoine's most interesting Mémoires du Théâtre Libre *has not been translated into English. There is no comparable history. Translations exist, however, of the better-known plays of most of the dramatists mentioned in this section.*

93 | Ibsen

Henrik Ibsen (1828–1906) began life as a chemist's assistant in the small town of Grimstad on Oslo fiord. Although he was a lonely and reticent boy he took to writing plays before he was twenty. While still a young man he secured a job as dramatic author attached to the theatre in Bergen which was dedicated to the creation of a Norwegian national drama to help displace the Danish influence which was dominating Norwegian culture. During his five and a half years at Bergen he was involved in staging 145 plays, an experience which brought him into close contact with European Romanticism as well as the neatly constructed plays of Eugène Scribe. Both these influences can be seen in his later work.

While at Bergen he devoted himself seriously to the task of becoming a dramatist, continuing to write plays when in 1857 he became artistic director of a theatre in Christiana, now rechristened Oslo, where he stayed until 1864. None of his plays, most of which were on historical subjects, had any great success. He was disgusted with his country's attitude towards the growing power of Germany, and having been granted a small state pension he left Norway and settled in Rome. Except for a couple of brief visits it was twenty-seven years before he returned.

Between 1864 and 1867 he completed two of his most impressive works, *Brand* and *Peer Gynt*, the first occasionally, the second frequently revived. *Peer Gynt* is in many respects unique in European dramatic literature for its poetic vigour, its huge canvas, and its curious mixture of fantasy, satire, and tragic realism.

The immense and virtually unstageable *Kejser og Galilaeer* (*Emperor and Galilean*, 1869–73) was his thirteenth play and he was half-way through his life. His next twelve plays, which he wrote between 1873 and 1899, are of a wholly different kind and constitute one of the greatest achievements in the whole history of dramatic writing. This change in spirit was partly the result of the German defeat of France in 1870–1, which Ibsen saw as the final destruction of eighteenth-century ideals of liberty, equality, and fraternity. What was needed, he wrote, was a revolution in the spirit of man.

These twelve plays are all set in contemporary Norway. They are written in prose and in some respects they can be seen as naturalistic dramas. Plays such as *Et Dukkehiem* (*A Doll's House*, 1878–9), a powerful study of the ignominious manner in which wives are treated by husbands, *Gengangere* (*Ghosts*, 1881), a deeply disturbing play about inherited venereal disease, and *En Folkefiende* (*An Enemy of the People*, 1882), about a public official in conflict with a corrupt society, are powerful social tracts; but in his following plays, from *Vildanden* (*The Wild Duck*, 1883–4) to the last extraordinary *Naar vi Dode Vaagner* (*When We Dead Awaken*, 1897–9), he faced a new dramatic problem.

It was this: in changing the subject of his plays from the false values of the world in which many people live to the struggle of men and women with their own false values, the corrupting reflection of a corrupt society, he had to find theatrical means of expressing these far more abstract concepts. He had discovered the limitations of naturalism. He solved the problem by developing a style of symbolism which enabled him to use concrete objects and ideas to represent abstract ones. Thus in *The Wild Duck* there is a little attic which represents the remote and unreal world of some of the characters; in *Fruen fra Havet* (*The Lady from the Sea*, 1888) references to the eternal movement of the ocean represent the restless longings of an unsatisfied woman; and in *Rosmerholm* (1886), the mill-race at the bottom of the garden represents the violent passions of the protagonists. This is a subject, however, on which critics of Ibsen have a great deal to say.

Though disgusted with the spiritual poverty of middle-class society, Ibsen was in no respect a socialist. He had no belief in the efficacious virtues of politics or religion. Yet he was in no way a pessimist. Men and women, he believed, bring destruction on themselves by refusing to face the realities of the world they live in. His protagonists tend to be people of enormous energy. The hero of *The Master Builder* destroys himself by climbing to the pinnacle of one of his own buildings. John Gabriel Borkman is a great industrialist destroyed only by his own false illusions. *When We Dead Awaken* ends with the artist and his former model climbing a mountain to their death rather than descending to safety and everlasting mediocrity. The play is taken to be symbolic of Ibsen's own life.

Contemporary audiences tended to react with horror and disgust at plays which seemed to challenge the very structure of social life. Bernard Shaw has collected the abusive epithets with which critics described *Ghosts* at its first production in London. Society has now assimilated these extraordinary plays and disgust has turned to admiration. Ibsen is now subjected to a good deal of criticism for his sometimes faltering technique, and for the excessive theatricality that mars some of his earlier plays. But he stands among the masters.

Ibsen's plays generally received early publication in editions amounting to 10,000 copies, and were fairly widely translated; but it was only in Germany and the Scandinavian countries that they were immediately produced. In England they were given single performances as a result of the efforts of individual critics such as William Archer and Bernard Shaw and actresses such as Janet Achurch.

Far from being the demonic and destructive figure that bourgeois society considered him to be, Ibsen was a very monument of respectability. For twenty-seven years he lived in voluntary exile, not so much a lonely as a totally independent figure. As he grew older and more famous, his coat-tails became longer, his side-whiskers bushier, his habitual expression more taciturn. He abhorred literary parties and artistic cliques. He was personally unattractive, short in stature, and accustomed to walk with little short steps. He conducted his life with scrupulous regularity down to the last detail of his dressing. But he enjoyed the minor pleasures of life and was devoted to his wife and child, a boy who grew up to marry the daughter of another Norwegian dramatist of some distinction, Bjornstjerne Bjornson (1832–1910), who had given Ibsen much encouragement in his years of struggle.

Bjornson in fact treated some of the same subjects as Ibsen. His plays are intelligent, not without interest, but thin in texture. A comparison of the plays of the two dramatists shows very clearly what one means by the imaginative depth and the intellectual concentration of Ibsen's masterpieces.

All Ibsen's plays have been translated into English. Many critical studies have been written and there is a superb biography by Michael Meyer. Readers might be particularly interested in Bernard Shaw's The Quintessence of Ibsenism, *which records the critical epithets that were levelled at* Ghosts.

Some of Bjornson's better-known plays are available in English.

94 | Strindberg

August Strindberg (1849–1912) is one of the few great Swedish playwrights. He is a dramatist of the greatest interest, for he wrote plays in many of the styles that were current at the time; but while a knowledge of Ibsen's life is unnecessary for an understanding of his plays, Strindberg wrote in so subjective a manner that it is necessary to know something about what kind of a man he was.

Strindberg was the son of ill-matched parents who had eight children and went bankrupt. As a child he was intensely sensitive and prone to tears. He loathed school and adored his mother, who died when he was thirteen, and resented his father's marriage to his housekeeper. He grew up to be neurotic and unstable and found it difficult to apply himself to a steady job. It was through his first wife, an actress called Siri van Essen, whom he married in 1877, that he took up the serious writing of plays. He began with historical subjects, a children's play, *Lycko-Pers Resa* (*Lucky Peter's Travels*, or *The Wanderings of Lucky Per* 1882) and *Herr Bengt's Wife*, a kind of riposte to *A Doll's House*, for he did not care for Ibsen's so-called emancipated women. Then the marriage took a turn for the worse and restlessly seeking a solution in travel, the couple moved to Paris and then Switzerland. Two of his most original and gripping plays, *Fadren* (*The Father*, 1887) and *Froken Julie* (*Miss Julie*, 1888), stem from his disastrous sexual relationships. In Paris he had become familiar with the work of Zola and Antoine and became excited with the naturalistic style of writing. He explains his intentions in a fascinating Preface to *Miss Julie*.

> I have avoided the logically symmetrical construction of French dialogue and let people's brains work irregularly, as they do in actual life, where no topic of conversation is drained to the dregs, but one brain receives from another a cog to engage with. Consequently my dialogue too wanders about, providing itself in the earlier scenes with material which is afterwards worked up, repeated, developed and enriched, like the theme of a musical composition.

The Father and *Miss Julie* were produced by Antoine at the Théâtre Libre. Strindberg, envisaging the creation of a theatre entirely devoted to the production of his own work, wrote a group of short but intense plays which included *Fordringsagare* (*Creditors*), a psychological masterpiece which he considered to be among his best works. But the project collapsed along with his marriage. In 1891 he divorced Siri and returned to Sweden. In 1893 he wrote another group of fine short plays still of a realistic nature. But his emotional condition deteriorated. He made a second marriage which lasted for less than a year and then returned to Paris where *The Father* was being staged for the second time. Between 1894 and 1896 were the years he afterwards referred to as his Inferno. He took up physics and chemistry; lived as a recluse; charred his fingers making chemical experiments; delved into the occult and black magic; was at various times in prison, in hospital. The loyalty of his friends, the philosophy of Swedenborg, and the promises of religion helped to restore him to something approaching normality and he returned to Sweden.

His next group of plays included some historical dramas, which are rarely played outside Sweden, and two more plays on sexual relationships. *Dodsdansen* (*The Dance of Death*, 1901) is perhaps his masterpiece. Some critics say that this play established Strindberg as a supreme misogynist, but this is to take a very superficial view of his work. Strindberg depicts with supreme honesty and considerable penetration the nature of marriage which locks couples into a close and inescapable relationship, as stifling as imprisonment. Far from hating women, Strindberg cares for them so much that weaknesses in relationships between man and woman are a kind of torment to him.

The next group of plays is coupled with his third marriage to another actress, Harriet Bosse. These plays are broadly symbolic plays, not in the manner of Ibsen, but in a style that was popular in Paris in the 1890s and which will be described in a later section. They are compounded of a variety of personal, religious, and mystical experiences, and although they are difficult to understand, they are wonderfully visionary. *Svanehvit* (*Swanwhite*, 1902) is an exquisite piece of writing.

It was at this time that he heard that the German producer, Max Reinhardt, had opened a chamber theatre (*Kammerspiel*) in Berlin and lamented once again the absence of a similar theatre in Stockholm where his own plays could be produced. A young actor-producer named Augustus Falk came forward with a practical scheme and in 1907 opened a Strindberg Theatre in Stockholm. Unfortunately it was as unsuccessful as other seasons of his plays had been, and this is hardly surprising when one considers the plays he wrote to be performed there. *Brande Tomtem* (*After the Fire*) shows us the burnt-out ruins of a house, the former residents poking about among the charred remains which evoke memories, fears, anxieties that have remained suppressed until this moment. *The Ghost Sonata* is about a group of barely-related people from whom Strindberg has stripped the conventional masks of their identity leaving them like so many boney skeletons. These chamber plays are masterpieces of their kind but Strindberg's intensely personal imagery makes them very difficult to come to terms with.

This great writer, in short, poses in the most acute way the basic problem of the playwright – how to find a theatrical form, a vocabulary of images and symbols with which he can present his innermost thoughts and feelings in terms of actors and actresses moving on a stage. A novelist or a poet has far greater freedom in this respect. A dramatist is severely limited by the conventions of the theatre; a dramatist of this period particularly so, since writers like those with whom we are now dealing were interested in the spiritual life of their characters, not their actions. Or, one could say, their actions in so far as they are a reflection and a projection of their inner life.

Strindberg has not on the whole been well treated by biographers. The most accessible biography is by Elizabeth Sprigge. Most of his plays are available in translation.

95 | Chekhov and the Russian Theatre

In the Russian theatre of the nineteenth century there was much going on of considerable interest; but natural development was held back in two ways. One was the domination of Russian by French and German culture. Educated Russians had acquired such a feeling of inferiority that many of them spoke French and German in preference to their own language. The other hindrance was the censorship. Tsar Nicholas I (Tsar 1825–55) with a well-organized secret police, kept a strict control on the freedom of the theatre. His son, Nicholas II (Tsar 1894–1917) learnt nothing. His repressive methods were directly responsible for the Russian Revolution of 1917.

Nevertheless there was a surge of nationalism brought about by the unsuccessful Napoleonic invasion of 1812, and it was first expressed in literature by such writers as Alexander Pushkin and Mikhail Lermontov. The first Russian plays to achieve a European reputation were *Gore ot Ooma* (usually roughly translated as *Woe from Wit*, 1833) by Alexander Griboedov and two comedies of Nicolai Gogol (1809–52). Gogol was a rather unbalanced and unhappy man and so sensitive to criticisms of his work that he spent twelve years of his life travelling round Europe. His exquisite comedies, *Revizor* (*The Government Inspector*, 1842) and *Zhenitba* (*Marriage*, 1847) had too sharp a satirical quality for success in their own day, but the former has become a classic, frequently staged throughout Europe.

The most prolific dramatist of the time was Alexander Ostrovsky (1823–86). He was the author of some fifty plays and a number of translations of European classics. As early as 1868 a Scottish critic was asking why his plays were not better known in English; to which the answer is probably the insularity of the English and the intensely Russian quality of Ostrovsky. Nevertheless, many of them are extremely amusing, full of richly rounded characters, and far fresher than anything else being written in Europe at the time.

The playwrights were encouraged by the existence of some fine actors. Among the most oustanding were Vasily Andreyevich Karatygin (1802–53) and Pavel Stepanovich Mochalov (1800–48).The former was what can be called a classical actor. He studied his roles carefully, took considerable trouble with what he wore, yet opposed a more realistic style of acting that was adopted by his near contemporaries. Mochalov, on the other hand, was a romantic, emotional actor who left things to the inspiration of the moment. He excelled in *Hamlet* and the exuberant heroes of Schiller. In their contrasted styles the two can be compared to the French actresses, Mesdames Clairon and Dumesnil. Perhaps the greatest of them, though the eldest, was Mikhail Semenovich Shchepkin (1788–1863) who is thought to have synthesized the two styles. After considerable experience in various parts of Russia he came to Moscow in 1822, played the lead in Gogol's plays and established the school of acting on which the Moscow Art Theatre was ultimately based.

The middle of the nineteenth century was also a particularly rich period for the Russian novel. There was Ivan Turgenev (1818–83) who spent many years of his life abroad, due largely to the critical reception of his novels. Among his plays, *Myesyats v Derevne* (*A Month in the Country*, 1850) is a haunting play about the rivalry of a married woman and her ward for the love of her son's tutor. Then there was Feodor Dostoevsky (1821–81), the author of such tremendous novels as *The Brothers Karamazov* and *Crime and Punishment*, but he wrote no plays. Leo Tolstoy wrote three major plays in the latter part of his life, after he had completed his great novels, *Voina i Mir* (*War and Peace*, 1864–9) and *Anna Karenina* (1873–6). These plays are *Vlat' T'my* (*The Power of Darkness*, 1886), which gives a curiously brutal picture of life among the Russian peasants; *Plody Prosveshcheniya* (*The Fruits of Enlightenment*, 1890), a play that is not often performed outside Russia, and *Zhivoi Trup* (*The Living Corpse*, 1900), about a man who tries to step aside from and avoid the responsibilities of society and personal relationships. Each projects one of the obsessions of this extraordinary man.

The period, nevertheless, was a far from easy one for writers. On the one hand there was a powerful movement of both nationalism and political radicalism and on the other a repressive censorship, but for which the theatre might well have played a more significant part; for it is an interesting comment on the potential effectiveness of the stage that in many times and places the drama has been subject to far greater censorship than any other form of literature or art. Thus there is no difficulty in understanding why it was that political conditions discouraged Tolstoy from writing more for the theatre. This is yet another example of how, in the eyes of the bureaucrat, the theatre, with its power of affecting an audience with possibly subversive emotions and ideas, is more to be feared, and so more in need of censorship, than literature.

The vitality of the Russian literary tradition is evident again in the work of Anton Chekhov (1860–1904) who had written some six hundred stories by the time he was twenty-eight before he had any success as a playwright. Of most of his earliest plays only the titles remain. Then from about 1885 he began writing a succession of one-act farces, or vaudevilles as he called them. 'It is easier to write a great play, about Sokrates', he said, 'than a simple comedy about peasant life'. His first major play was *Ivanov* on which he worked between 1887 and 1889. But then his troubles with the theatre began. For his particular form of naturalism was wholly new to the theatre and actors and producers did not know how to handle it. Chekhov does not simply make stories out of contemporary society but seems to analyse the frustrations of people who compose that society. He does not create types, with the result that actors did not know whether they were playing a heroic, a comic, or a tragic character, nor audiences whether to laugh or cry. The failure of *Ivanov* was repeated with *Leshy* (*The Wood Demon*, 1889–90) which he wrote the following year. Such failures were to be expected. Chekhov's style was wholly different both from the well-made play with its tightly-knit story, the social naturalism of Zola and his kind such as Henri Becque, and even Ibsen whose plays he disliked intensely; and although there are elements suggestive of Chekhov in *A Month in the Country* and *The Storm*, his style is altogether more elusive and his characters more complex than anything that had preceded him.

None of Chekhov's complex characters is more unsure of himself than Chekhov was about himself at this stage of his career. He went through a period of self-appraisal, of his stories, his plays, his private life, his political commitment, a subject on which he was challenged by Tolstoy, who had now become an eccentric propagandist for all kinds of unusual opinions. He was an enthusiastic do-gooder, yet he hated having to commit himself to any kind of a programme; he like pretty women, yet he lived by the strongest puritanical convictions. He loved to fill his house with guests and play practical jokes, and wrote half-a-dozen hilarious farces; yet his stories and plays are filled with melancholy, frustrated men and women.

In 1895, turning to the theatre again, he wrote *Chayka (The Seagull)*. He read it to his friends who made nothing of it. He sent it to a young friend of his, Vladimir Nemirovich-Danchenko, who replied with a long and sympathetic criticism. So encouraged he sent the play to his publisher, Alexei Suvorin, who offered the play to the Imperial Alexandrinsky Theatre in St. Petersburg (now Leningrad). Unhappily the play was accepted for production. It was under-rehearsed and wholly misunderstood by cast and public. The first performance began with titters and ended with jeers. The critics said the play was not merely bad but idiotic. Chekhov vowed he would never write another.

Two years went by and he received a letter from Nemirovich-Danchenko telling him that he and his friend Konstantin Stanislavsky had founded a people's theatre and asking permission to include *The Seagull* in the repertory of their first season. Chekhov agreed only after considerable persuasion.

The first season of the Moscow Art Theatre, as the venture came to be called, opened shakily. Plays by Tolstoy, Shakespeare, Hauptmann, and Andrev had nothing like the success that was needed to keep the venture going. The future of the whole enterprise depended on *The Seagull.* But the first performance turned out to be one of the great events in theatrical history. At the end of the first act the applause broke out with what Nemirovich-Danchenko afterwards described as a 'deafening crash' and the success was maintained until the end. A seagull was immediately adopted as the emblem of the theatre.

But Chekhov's relationship with the Moscow Art Theatre remained uncertain. The direction of the company was in the hands of Stanislavsky, whom Danchenko has described as a 'wealthy Muscovite knowing nothing of the frustrated provincial world of which Chekhov wrote' and who, Chekhov was convinced, did not understand his plays at all. Stanislavsky made them too gloomy, too theatrical, too fussily naturalistic. Accordingly he sent his next play, *Dyadya Vanya* (*Uncle Vanya*, 1899), a reworking of *The Wood Demon*, to the Maly Theatre and to the Moscow Art Theatre only when the Maly asked for extensive revisions. Even then it was only a modest success.

He then set about writing the most complex of his plays, *Tri Sestri* (*Three Sisters*, 1901). 'I am writing a play with four heroines', he wrote to a friend in a typically ironic vein. He attended rehearsals, had a furious row with Stanislavsky, and left Moscow. The masterpiece was staged in 1901, again with only moderate success. But his relationship with the Moscow Art Theatre was preserved by a fortunate accident. In May, 1901, he married Olga Knipper, one of the most loyal members of the company. She ensured that her husband's last play, *Vishnyovii Sad* (*The Cherry Orchard*) should be staged by no one else, and Chekhov was to be present at rehearsals to ensure that the play was acted as a comedy and not a bourgeois tragedy.

Chekhov's plays did not shock the Russian or European public like those of some of his contemporaries; but they certainly puzzled them, and Stanislavsky and his company were by no means alone in not knowing how to stage them. His plays are in the naturalistic tradition. They depict ordinary people who speak ordinary language. But his characters are far from ordinary. In a sense no one is really ordinary. It is only the image that people present to the world that is ordinary. Chekhov's characters are rich, complex, and fully rounded. They are conceived with great sympathy. And although he uses only very moderately the symbolic devices of Ibsen or the Symbolists he manages to create profound reverberations between them. The delicate balance between tragedy and comedy, between tears and laughter, is a part of this subtle, reverberating world. In this respect Chekhov's plays are the final outcome of the Romantic movement which recognized that human emotions are rarely polarized but compounded of a variety of often contradictory feelings all at the same moment.

In the Soviet Union Chekhov is not held in such high esteem as his immediate successor, Alexei Maximovich Pyeshkov, always known by his pen-name of Maxim Gorky (1868–1936). This may be the result of a political rather than a literary judgement, for Gorky was a good supporter of the regime, a champion of the underdog, and a dramatist, in his early plays, of class war.

It was Chekhov who introduced Gorky to the Moscow Art Theatre and persuaded him to write a play for them. Gorky's first play was *Meshcane* (*Small People*, 1902) and it was soon followed by his masterpiece, *Na dne* (*The Lower Depths*), an intensely naturalistic play about a crowd of down-and-outs living in a kind of slum workhouse. Stanislavsky explains how the social unrest that finally erupted in the Revolution of 1905 was already apparent and the censor made frequent use of his blue pencil. Although Gorky went on to write one or two plays in the manner of Chekhov such as *Dachniki* (*Summerfolk*, 1905) he was in almost constant trouble with the authorities and spent much of his life in Italy, until after the revolution. But the Soviet authorities are not slow to immortalize their supporters. The Moscow Art Theatre is now resident in the Gorky Theatre, and Nizhni-Novgorod, the town where Gorky was born, has now been given the name of this most distinguished author.

The British Theatre is slowly becoming aware of the quality of Ostrovsky's plays through productions of The Storm *and* The Forest *by the Royal Shakespeare Company; and some of his plays have been (on the whole rather poorly) translated into English.*

The life of Tolstoy is as extraordinary as any of his works, and in a biography such as Henri Troyat's quite as readable.

There are a number of biographies of Chekhov; but anyone wishing to understand this remarkable man should also read some of his short stories, the best of which are available in various collections, and his Letters *which are both readable and revealing.*

Gorky has been quite inadequately dealt with in terms of both biography and translation; but Enemies *staged by the Royal Shakespeare Company, gives a moving picture of a contest between management and workers.*

The Russian theatre as a whole has also been poorly dealt with in English but there are valuable comments on the Russian theatre in general and Chekhov in particular in those two fine books, Stanislavsky's My Life in Art *and Nemirovich-Danchenko's* My Life in the Russian Theatre.

Inconsistencies in the spelling of Russian proper names is due to problems of transliteration.

96 | Shaw, Barker, and Galsworthy

These were the three dramatists who carried the tradition of social realism into the mainstream of the British theatre. Bernard Shaw (1856–1950) was an Irishman who came to London in 1876, lived off his mother, and wrote some unsuccessful novels until the critic and first translator of Ibsen, William Archer, suggested he turned his attention to the theatre. Shaw was as great an admirer as Archer of the Norwegian dramatist and in 1891 wrote *The Quintessence of Ibsenism*, a fascinating introduction to the plays; but there is nothing of Ibsen in his work. For one thing he was much more of a propagandist; his intellectual passions were far wider; he was as deeply interested in political as in social problems. The other difference lay in his prodigious sense of humour. He had a remarkable facility for turning the most commonplace situations upside down and by this means extracting a maximum of ridicule. So although he is an immensely commonsensical writer he is in no way a naturalistic one. His prose, which often drowns the action, has a highly wrought rhythmical structure, and his finest plays, *Man and Superman* (1903) (Superman is woman), which includes the great Juan in Hell scene, *Heartbreak House* (written between 1913 and 1919), *Saint Joan* (1923), considered by many to be his masterpiece, and the extraordinary *Back to Methuselah* (1920–2) show an imaginative range that few other dramatists have equalled.

Bernard Shaw was established as an important dramatist by the

Barker-Vedrenne management of the Court Theatre (now Royal) between 1904 and 1907, when 701 performances were given of eleven of his plays. John Vedrenne was the business side of the partnership, but Harley Granville Barker (1877–1946), though a less charismatic figure than Shaw, was an outstanding man of the theatre, supremely gifted in many respects, and somewhat like his contemporary, Jacques Copeau, in being even greater for what he stood for, the dignity, stature, and importance of the theatre in a nation's culture, than for anything he actually achieved. Barker was an actor of talent, an outstanding director, a brilliant Shakespearian scholar, and the author of some masterly plays. He was also a persistent advocate for a national theatre.

It is arguable that these plays are models of what can be achieved in the naturalistic convention; for they are firmly constructed without the artificial compression of the well-made play, and written in dialogue which combines literary expressiveness with the flexibility, hesitations, and innuendoes of ordinary speech; while their subject-matter is of great social relevance. *The Marrying of Anne Leete* (1902) is about a bourgeois young lady who marries her gardener; *The Voysey Inheritance* (1905) concerns a respectable solicitor who is discovered by his son to have gambled away his clients' money; *Waste* (1907) is about a young politician whose career is destroyed by the pregnancy of his mistress, and *The Madras House* (1910) is about irregularities in a family business.

To find a way of handling social themes in prose dialogue that was reflective of ordinary speech was one of the great concerns of John Galsworthy (1867–1933), and he again shows the strengths and limitations of the convention. Galsworthy is a most interesting character, for although he was a respectable member of the upper classes and an exceedingly successful novelist – *The Forsyte Saga* is comparable with Thomas Mann's *Buddenbrooks* as a picture of middle-class decay – he wrote a number of plays which show an intense awareness of social injustice. Such was his first success, *The Silver Box* (1906), which depicts the wholly different values that pertain to the rich and the poor; *Strife* (1909) is about an industrial strike; *Justice* (1910) includes a horrifying picture of solitary confinement; while *The Skin Game* (1920) and *Loyalties* (1922) deal with class and racial prejudice.

Yet Galsworthy's plays, for all their intelligence and relevance, are far less interesting than Ibsen's. And the reason seems to be that they are intensely prosaic. They wholly lack penetration, further layers of meaning, symbolic relationships to which poetry gives rise; and by poetry one does not mean verse. The prose plays of Ibsen and Chekhov are intensely poetic.

Bernard Shaw, who was anxious that his plays should be read as well as staged, appended to the published version of each a Preface in which he discusses not only the play but the whole background to the subject the play is about. These collected Prefaces are immensely entertaining. The dramatic criticisms he wrote as critic of the Saturday Review *between 1895 and 1898, published under the title* Our Theatre in the Nineties, *are masterpieces of their kind and give a vivid picture of the theatre of the period. There are many critical and biographical books on Bernard Shaw.*

97 | Wagner

The cultural map of Europe in the second half of the nineteenth century became increasingly confused. In general terms this was the result of the industrial revolution. The population of most countries had increased enormously with the gap between the land- and property-owning class and the industrial worker becoming increasingly marked. Karl Marx sat in the British Museum and analyzed the whole process in an immensely influential but rather unreadable book called *Das Kapital* (*Capital*, published 1867), having been obliged to leave Germany for having written the *Communist Manifesto* (1848).

It is understandable, therefore, that in this overpopulated, politically unstable, materially-oriented Europe there should be many social tensions, many differing points of view, many cliques, movements, and what are now called sub-cultures. The artists whose names crop up most frequently in a book of this kind tend to be those who crystallize one of these movements or attitudes. In this way their work has an importance other than the intrinsic value of the work itself. Works of this kind are Victor Hugo's *Hernani*, Gustave Flaubert's *Madame Bovary*, Emile Zola's *Thérèse Raquin*, J.-K. Huysmans *A Rebours* (a novel whose importance will be described in the next section), the Impressionist painters and the operas of Richard Wagner.

Richard Wagner (1813–83) was the most original composer of the mid-nineteenth century. This is not to say that he was a better composer than, for example, Giuseppe Verdi, but that his operas and his attitude towards opera were of an outstandingly individual kind. People need time to become accustomed to originality and his early operas were not successful. These were *Rienzi* (1840), *Der Fliegender Holländer* (*The Flying Dutchman*, 1843), *Tannhäuser* (1845), and *Lohengrin* (1847). Wagner as a young man was politically inclined towards the left and sided with the liberal intellectuals in opposition to the reactionary policies of the German dukes who were terrified of the aftermath of French revolutionary ideas. He took an active part in the revolutions of 1830 and 1848, and in the latter got his fingers burnt. With a warrant issued for his arrest he fled to Paris and then to Switzerland and remained in exile from Germany for nearly ten years. With plenty of opportunity for contemplation he produced an immense amount of theoretical writing in which he worked out his artistic objectives. The two most relevant of his books are *Opera and Drama* and *The Art Work of the Future*.

The substance of Wagner's theories is the fusion of music and drama and this is what he achieved in his subsequent masterpieces, the great tetralogy, *Die Niebelungenring* (*The Ring of the Niebelungs*, completed 1876), *Tristan und Isolde* (1865), and *Parsifal* (1882). He worked out his theories like this. Music is the highest expression of feeling, but since it is an abstract expression it must be made intelligible through poetry, which will ensure that the action embodies the original feeling. But to ensure that this action is expressed in the most concentrated emotional form, the verbal poetry must be expressed in melody. Thus the word-poet expresses the action which is clarified in the words, and the tone-poet, who may well be the same person, provides this action with concentrated emotion by means of melody, while distinguishing different kinds of emotion through the use of harmony. Thus the words provide intelligibility and the orchestra the emotion. At the same time the most physical of all gestures is dance-gesture, and this bears the same relationship to orchestral melody as word-verse bears to vocal melody. Thus the complete realization of the composer's aim is achieved by means of the most lucid expression of word-verse melody through the perfected language of the orchestra, with all its possible variations in harmony and instrumentation, in alliance with gesture.

For subject-matter, or story, Wagner turned to myth which he considered to be an ordering of human experience of a kind that was deeper and more lasting than scenes from history, literature, or everyday life.

Although in his early operas he was beginning to put his theories into practice, it was in his later works that he realized them even more intensely. For the great tetralogy of *The Ring of the Niebelungs*, composed of *Das Rheingold*, *Die Walkyrie*, *Siegfried*, and *Gotterdämmerung* (*The Twilight of the Gods*) he turned to an ancient myth that was common to Nordic and Teutonic culture and which enabled him to depict heroes 'ruled by unbridled elemental passions which have stirred men's hearts since time immemorial'. In *Tristan and Isolde* he took up the most ancient of sexual myths, expressing erotic passion with unsurpassed intensity.

These operas sent shock-waves round Europe. They were in direct opposition to the theories and the work of Wagner's young contemporary, Emile Zola and the naturalistic writers. But they were a source of enormous encouragement to all those who were aware of the limitations of naturalism to express anything but the most superficial aspects of life.

Outwardly Wagner's operas revert to the twilit medieval world of knights and castles, giants and dwarfs, and buried treasure. But one of the virtues of a myth is that one can read into it almost anything one wants to find. And so it was, particularly with *The Ring*. Bernard Shaw's remarkable interpretation is to be found in *The Perfect Wagnerite*. Subsequent productions in opera houses throughout the world have shown the enormous variety of ideas thrown up by these prodigious pieces. One may not care for them, but they are not to be dismissed.

98 | The Symbolists

Even before Wagner was dead French artists begun to meditate on the possible harmony of poetry, music, and dance. It became a preoccupation of the poet Stephan Mallarmé (1842–98) who enjoyed considerable authority in Parisian artistic circles. He envisaged a union of poetry (the intellectual element), music (the emotional), and gesture (the physical). And the art which seemed to unify the arts was dance. That dance excluded poetry did not seem to worry him: it was the unspecific nature of dance that was particularly attractive. A French poet writing in 1889 dreamt of 'white terraces and steps leading to gardens bathed in light, with distant blue perspectives, waves of sound, and men and women beautifully draped, moving and speaking a vague but sonorous verse'.

The movement came to be called Symbolist because the symbol was seen as a means of embodying concepts, feelings, apprehensions too abstract to be expressed in the usual artistic forms. The great artist Gustave Courbet had said that 'an abstract object does not belong to the domain of painting'. The Symbolists believed the opposite, that it was the domain of art to clothe ideas in sensuous form, to form a relationship between the material and the spiritual world. Huysman's novel, *A Rebours*, is a paean of sensuality in which the bored and decadent hero encrusts the shell of a tortoise with jewels to deaden the brilliant tones of the carpet.

This begins to explain the fascination for the Symbolists of dance. The dancer for them was the embodiment of feeling. Mallarmé in his poetry used words with great precision to create imprecise sensations. But the dancer could do this without the use of words. The idol of the Symbolists was the American dancer, Loie Fuller, who, making use of the flexibility of electric light, filled the stage with diaphanous scarves, swirling around in parabolas of coloured light.

The initiator of the movement was the American writer, Edgar Allan Poe (1809–49) who wrote in the Preface to *Eureka*, a strange, visionary, part-scientific, part-visionary essay, that the realities of the world seemed to him like visions, while the material of dreams was the very substance of his existence. Elsewhere he added that an artist has nothing to do with imitating real life: art is the reproduction of what the senses perceive in nature. This is echoed by something that Wagner wrote in 1864: 'The highest work of art should take the place of real life; it should dissolve the reality in an illusion as a result of which it is reality itself which seems illusory'; and the English critic, Arthur Symons, himself a Symbolist poet, explained that 'art is the symbol by which the soul of things can be made manifest'.

The attempt to create a Symbolist theatre was the work of Paul Fort (1872–1960). He was a curious and precocious young man who called himself 'the Prince of Poets' and envisaged a theatre where the spectator would 'abandon himself completely to the will of the poet and see charming and terrible visions in a world which only the poet can penetrate'. In 1890, while he was still only eighteen and still at school, he collected some young actors from the Conservatoire, some Symbolist painters from the Boulevard St. Michel, where artists then congregated, and subscriptions from wealthy patrons and created the Théâtre d'Art. Over the next three years he staged a succession of one-night productions in a variety of venues with a varied repertory that included existing plays, such as Marlowe's *Dr Faustus*, and new plays by, for example, the young Belgian Symbolist poet, Maurice Maeterlink (1862–1949). These plays were *Les Aveugles* (*The Blind*) and *L'Intruse* (*Interior*), and very strange, remote, and static plays they are. He staged dramatic readings from Plato's dialogues and a play with a second act that takes place in the human brain; texts from the Hindu scriptures and the Bible, and poems by leading poets such as Rimbaud's *Le Bateau ivre*. He integrated words, music, and lighting even more closely than Wagner had done and one occasion introduced perfumes (or smells). His final production included a play rather typically called *Les Noces de Satan* (*The Marriage of Satan*), and a rather feeble dramatization of a passage from the *Iliad*. It was a disastrous failure. A consistently hostile press attacked him even more fiercely and a Russian princess, on whom he had depended for funds, withdrew her support.

He handed over his theatre to a young man with far less quixotic and whimsical tastes. Aurélien Lugné-Poe (1869–1940) had been a member of Antoine's Théâtre Libre before being called away on military service. He was a friend of many of the leading poets and painters of the day – Verlaine, Vuillard, Bonnard, Roussell, and Gauguin. He went some way to reconciling the works of the Symbolists with the naturalists – he staged their one major play, Maeterlink's *Pelléas and Melisande* (1892). But he was not well supported by the public and was criticized for doing too many foreign plays, especially Ibsen's. He closed his theatre, the Théâtre de l'Oeuvre, in 1899 but, like Antoine, continued as an independent director, with the first production of many new and foreign plays to his credit.

Apart from Maeterlink, the Symbolists produced no significant dramatists. This is perhaps because the theatre is altogether too substantial a form of art for the private and subjective fantasies which the Symbolists expressed in their paintings and their poetry. But the movement had a very considerable impact on the theatre and this will be described in the following sections. And they did a great deal to free the theatre from the rather coarse theatricality of which Ibsen himself was by no means free. It was Maeterlink who summed up this aspect of their work in a famous essay, *The Tragic in Everyday Life*. Here is an often-quoted passage:

> There is a tragic element in the life of every day that is far more real, far more penetrating, far more akin to the true self that is in us than the tragedy that lies in great adventure . . . Its province is rather to reveal to us how truly wonderful is the mere act of living, and to throw light upon the existence of the soul . . . to hush the discourse of reason and sentiment . . . Is it beyond the mark to say that the true tragic element of life only begins at the moment when so-called adventures, sorrows, and dangers have disappeared? . . . Must we indeed roar like the Atrides, before the Eternal God will reveal Himself in our life? and is He never by our side at times when the air is calm, and the lamp burns on, unflickering?

Materlink's essay is to be found in a collection of essays called The Treasure of the Humble.

Since the Symbolist theatre was largely French there are few English works on the subject. The interest of the Symbolists in dance has been fully discussed by David Daiches in The

Romantic Image. *The whole subject of Romantic and Symbolist art has been very fully dealt with by Mario Praz in* The Romantic Agony.

There are, of course, many books of reproductions of Symbolist painters.

Those that can read French should turn to the poets that have been mentioned in this section.

A useful anthology of English prose and poetry, in which the French influence is clearly marked, is Writing of the 'Nineties *edited by Derek Stanford in the Everyman Library.*

99 | Yeats and the Irish Theatre

Although the Symbolist movement produced only one playwright, Maurice Maeterlink, its influence is evident in the work of a number of others, notably August Strindberg and W. B. Yeats (1865–1939).

Yeats's achievement, however, was not to have written Symbolist plays, but poetic plays, plays in poetry, and a poetry that uniquely avoided the reverberations of the outworn Shakespearian-Romantic tradition. In the 1890s Yeats had many English poets for friends but was introduced to French Symbolism by Arthur Symons, one of the leading supporters of the movement with whom for a short time he lived. But Yeats's central problem at this time of his life was to reconcile his three abiding interests, poetry, philosophy, and Irish nationalism. Drama was not another interest but a way of expressing these three profound concerns. He therefore lived to the full both a private and a public life and this polarity is evident in many of his essays. While on the one hand he recognized the responsibility of the poet to write about things that matter, he was strongly opposed to the kind of externality that marked the work of naturalistic writers.

Early in his career Yeats turned to the theatre, not so much because he had a passion for the stage, but because he thought that plays would be more effective than lectures to further the cause of Irish nationalism, a movement which in the 1890s had been gathering considerable momentum. He was given a great deal of help by a remarkable lady, Lady Isabella Augusta Gregory (1852–1932), whom he met in 1898. On the death of her husband she too had begun to devote herself to Irish literature and history by making collections of old Irish folk tales and Celtic legends. Yeats therefore satisfied his poetic sensibilities by writing plays, not on contemporary political or social themes, but on the myths and legends which Lady Gregory drew to his attention.

In the late 1890s there was virtually no Irish drama. The Dublin theatre was usually occupied with English touring companies playing recent London successes. Yeats had to create his own theatre.

He began in 1899 by founding the Irish Literary Theatre which gave a performance in the Ancient Concert Rooms of his own play *The Countess Cathleen* and *Heather Field* by Edward Martyn, another Irish nationalist. Further performances of Irish plays, usually including at least one by Yeats, were given in 1900 and again in 1901.

One of Yeats's greatest problems was finding the right kind of actors, and how to stage his own plays which were deceptively simple: plays ostensibly about Irish peasants were at heart profound moralities. There were no precedents for this kind of drama. Then in 1902 he met Willie and Frank Fay, two brothers who had been working with a small group of amateur actors. Together they created a new organization, the Irish National Drama Company, which began operations by staging A.E.'s (pen name for George Russell) *Deirdre* and Yeats's *Kathleen ni Houlihan*.

In May 1903, when the company paid a short visit to London, A. B. Walkley, writing in the *Times Literary Supplement*, described the acting like this:

> As a rule they (the actors) stand stock-still. The speaker of the moment is the only one who is allowed a little gesture . . . The listeners do not distract one's attention by fussy stage business; they stay just where they are and listen. When they do move it is without premeditation, at haphazard, even with a little natural clumsiness.

The stillness of the actors was the result Yeats's insistence that the greatest possible emphasis should be given to the speaking of the text. There was nothing naïve about Irish actors. Indeed, the Abbey players were soon to achieve an international reputation.

Yeats got an idea how his plays should be staged when he visited a production of Purcell's opera, *Dido and Aeneas*, at the Hampstead Conservatoire of Music, Swiss Cottage, in 1901. The production was by Edward Gordon Craig. Yeats said subsequently that the production had the only good scenery he had ever seen. The two men became friends but their various activities kept them apart and it was not until 1909 that they met again and Craig was able to help Yeats to solve some of the technical problems that were bothering him. Basically the problem was the same as had exercised the Symbolists. This was how to isolate the actor so that his voice and movements had particular significance while at the same time providing a background that was expressive in itself, yet did not distract the attention of the audience from the players. Craig's solution was in the use of movable screens. He built a little model theatre for his friend and Yeats has described how thereafter he made constant use of it while composing his plays. Ninette de Valois says that in fact he had far more help from Edmund Dulac, who designed most of his productions.

Another good friend came to the help of the Irish National Theatre in the person of Miss Annie Horniman (1860–1937), a tea heiress, who in 1904 gave Yeats money for the acquisition of the Abbey Theatre which became the permanent home of the company.

The movement then went from strength to strength. Yeats was a remarkable character – from 1922 a senator, involved in building the Republic of Ireland; the guiding spirit of the Abbey Theatre throughout most of his working life; and a poet of international reputation, who never allowed the enormous demands of his many responsibilities to interfere with his spiritual development. It was often a rough ride, for while the Irish nationalists considered that the Abbey was not sufficiently political, there were others who felt that the Irish theatre would become narrowly parochial if it ignored the European theatre at large.

The existence of a lively theatre and a fine company of players produced further dramatists. Among the first and most gifted was John Millington Synge (1871–1909). Yeats had met him in Paris and persuaded him to return to Ireland. He wrote six plays before his early death and these included the tragic *Riders to the Sea* (1904) and one of the great comedies of the English language, *The Playboy of the Western World* (1907). Lady Gregory was another, the author of a number of short comedies based on the lives of the peasants whom she knew well from her home in south-west Ireland (where Yeats often stayed and wrote some of his finest poetry). And there was Lennox Robinson (1886–1958) whose comedies *The White-headed Boy* (1916) and *The Far-off Hills* (1928) should be far better known than they are. Robinson was for many years Yeats's loyal assistant in running the Abbey.

Then there came that giant among dramatists, Sean O'Casey (1880–1964) with his savagely humorous plays of Dublin life at the time of the troubles – *The Shadow of a Gunman* (1923), *Juno and the Paycock* (1924), and *The Plough and the Stars* (1926). In 1928, when the Abbey turned down *The Silver Tassie*, O'Casey went into voluntary exile in England where he exasperated admirers of his early plays by experimenting in a variety of styles and techniques. He was a brave man and saw no purpose in repeating himself. It is difficult to guess how his later plays will survive, although there can be little question of the grandeur of *Cock-a-doodle Dandy* (1949). But all his plays are rich in that marvellous language for which so many Irish writers have a special gift.

Yeats, whose *alter ego* wanted to be a man of action, continued to develop as a poet and a poetic dramatist. In the latter respect he was greatly helped at one time by his secretary, a young American poet called Ezra Pound who introduced him to the Japanese Noh drama, a formal ritualistic and highly poetic form of theatre that was concerned with confrontations between mortals, gods, and strange spirits. The Noh stage was very simple and the actors, whose movements were of a dance-like quality, wore masks. Yeats was fascinated and wrote *At the Hawk's Well* (1916), the first of his four *Plays for Dancers*. It was staged in a drawing-room in Dublin for reasons that Yeats explained himself.

> I want to create for myself an unpopular theatre and an audience like a secret society where admission is by favour and never too many . . . I desire a mysterious art . . . doing its work by suggestion, not by direct statement, a complexity of rhythm, colour, gesture . . .

Yeats was helped to stage his play in the style of the Noh by a Japanese dancer named Michio Ito who then had to return to New York. Yeats found no one to replace him until the Scottish poet, Gordon Bottomley, introduced him to Ninette de Valois, herself Irish, who had been working on the choreography for the *Oresteia* at the Festival Theatre, Cambridge (see section 101). Yeats tried to persuade her to form a small ballet company attached to the Abbey; but she had other ambitions. She helped him to stage his *Plays for Dancers* and then returned to England.

In 1938, shortly before his own death, he wrote the last of his *Plays for Dancers*, *The Death of Cuchulain*. This play, like much of his earlier work, is of more interest to specialists than to the general theatre-going public. But this does not lessen its importance. For he was far and away the most important dramatist the European theatre has produced in showing the possibilities as well as the limitations of poetic drama. For Yeats's plays are not Romantic dramas written in blank verse: they are the uncompromising work of a poet whose conceptions, verse-form, and methods of staging are seen as a single creative process.

Of the success of Yeats's other great achievement, the creation of an Irish national theatre, the proof lies in the continued lively existence of the Abbey Theatre.

Yeats's principal writings on the theatre are to be found in The Irish Dramatic Movement *which is published in a collection of essays entitled* Explorations.

There are a number of histories of the Irish national theatre, the most recent being by that distinguished theatre director, Hugh Hunt.

A definitive biography of Sean O'Casey has yet to be written. He is far more informative on the subject of his plays in his published collection of Letters *than in his four-volume autobiography. His* Letters *include his bitter controversy with Yeats over* The Silver Tassie.

100 The Development of Theatre Dance

Dance meanwhile had become something more than exotic performances by Loie Fuller to excite the Symbolists. Classical ballet had been established by Louis XIV as a new and independent form of dance. But the dancing masters at the Académie Royale de Musique had perpetuated the neo-classical symmetrical arrangements of Beaujoyeux and developed a very precise vocabulary of steps, turns, gestures, attitudes, which are still the basis of the classical technique.

Two teachers and choreographers were responsible for bringing classical ballet into the theatre and developing it as a theatre art. One was Louis Dupré (1697–1774), who as a young man danced in John Weaver's *The Loves of Mars and Venus* (Weaver, it will be remembered, had made a study of French dancing); the other was his pupil, Jean Georges Noverre (1727–1810), who was both a dancer and a choreographer. In the latter capacity he staged ballets in a number of French and European cities. Garrick invited him to Drury Lane in 1755 when war with France was imminent; but the audience, believing him to be French when in fact he was Swiss, broke up the theatre. Noverre was clearly an innovator and as such a thorn in the flesh of the ballet 'establishment'. For he insisted that dancers must not put precision of technique in place of genuine feeling: 'Renounce cabriolets, entrechats and over-complicated steps, renounce that slavish routine which keeps your art in its infancy', he wrote, 'let your *corps de ballet* dance while at the same time expressing an emotion. . . To be successful in theatrical representations, the heart must be touched, the soul moved, the imagination inflamed'. Noverre was clearly something of a romantic.

Classical ballet was able to make a very close relationship with Romanticism since the subject-matter of ballet was that world of myth and fancy which was the stock-in-trade of many Romantic artists. Théophile Gautier, the most Romantic of French poets, wrote the ballet *Giselle* for the Italian dancer, Carlotta Grisi (1819–99). Giselle, the country girl who kills herself when her lover deceives her and rises from the grave to dance with other spirits (Wilis) in the moonlit forest, was, and still is, the very archetype of this classical-romantic school. Ballet responded in a curious manner by establishing the virtual domination of the ballerina. This is not to say that there was no place for male dancers, but that in most nineteenth-century ballets a woman, a ballerina, is the central character. The great dancers of the period were women, not men: Marie Taglioni, who first got dancers on their 'points'; her great rival Fanny Elssler, a Viennese; and the Italians Carlotta Grisi and Fanny Cerito.

During most of the century the French preserved the tradition of classical ballet, while the Italians, in their slightly ostentatious way, staged immense spectacular ballets somewhat in the manner of a Verdi opera. But with the appointment of Marius Petipa (1822–1910) as *maître de ballet* at the Marynsky theatre, St. Petersburg, the initiative passed to the Russians. Petipa created fifty-four ballets including the two masterpieces for which Tchaikovsky wrote the music, *Sleeping Beauty* (1890) and *Swan Lake* (1895), and established new standards of dancing and choreography.

Petipa's work was advanced still further by the remarkable character, Serge Diaghilev (1872–1929). He was in fact neither dancer nor choreographer but an impresario. In his early years he was involved with painters and in 1906 staged an exhibition of Russian art in Paris. The next year he added concerts of Russian music, and in 1908, ballet. The Russians indeed had something to boast about. A choreographer of great originality and genius, Michel Fokine (1880–1942), had developed a company of outstanding dancers of both sexes – Anna Pavlova, Tamara Karsavina, Vaslav Nijinksy, and many others. Diaghilev's particular contribution was to establish, what so many others had tried to do without much success, the integration of music and décor with dance. He commissioned scores from the leading composers of the time, however avant-garde they may have been. There were furious demonstrations at the first performances of Stravinsky's great ballet, *Le Sacre du Printemps* (1912). He employed leading painters to provide décor. Such Russian artists as Alexandre Benois, one of Diaghilev's closest collaborators, and even more so, Leon Bakst, used colour more daringly than anyone had done before; and in due course Pablo Picasso designed some fine sets. At the same time he encouraged his choreographers to enlarge the scope and vocabulary of dancing without actually destroying the classical style. The theatrical vitality of Diaghilev's ballets was so tremendous that the company's regular visits to London throughout the 1920s were attended by all the leading directors, producers, and theatre people of the time.

The pressure for ballet dancers to escape the rigid domination of the classical technique came from a remarkable American dancer called Isadora Duncan (1891–1927). After an unsuccessful début in Chicago in 1899 she came to Europe where she remained throughout the rest of her somewhat stormy career. Isadora Duncan believed in a natural style of dancing. She danced in a simple tunic, with bare arms and legs and bare feet. Having a powerful and sensual personality she created extremes of admiration and distaste in no way allayed by her irregular private life.

The influence of Isadora Duncan was immense. She demonstrated a natural and expressive form of dance that did not require immense technique. The possibilities were immediately apparent to educationists, theatre directors, and the world at large. Dance could now be made accessible to many people who had no capacity for or interest in the classical ballet, yet wanted a form of dance far more expressive than the foxtrot or *Selinger's Round*.

An example of such a person was Margaret Morris who did much to establish a free and natural form of dance. She was inspired by Isadora Duncan's brother, Raymond, whom she met while he was in London lecturing on Greek dance, was helped by the author, John Galsworthy, to found a dancing school in Chelsea, married a man who lived in Paris and greatly admired the Diaghilev ballet, and collaborated with the composer, Rutland Boughton.

Rutland Boughton was a kind of Christian Communist who held similar views on music for the people that Margaret Morris held on dancing. He was engaged on an enormous operatic cycle on Wagnerian lines on the legend of King Arthur. In 1913 the two of them staged a scene from this great work which featured 'moving scenery' (at a summer school at Bournemouth). A male chorus constituted the walls of Tintagel Castle singing 'dark and strong Tintagel Castle stands', while twenty female students in flowing blue and green dresses advanced and retreated with tossing arms telling in verse of 'the splash and surge of the sea on the rocks of Tintagel'.

While it is easy to laugh at this kind of thing it represented a tremendous new departure in theatrical art. Music, poetry, dance were being used in new relationships to enlarge the expressive possibilities of theatre beyond anything that had been conceived before. A kind of manifesto on these lines was written by the highly eccentric Terence

Gray who talked about 'the new and potent medium of light, colour and mass, that is of expressive and changing scenic design revealed by means of the atmosphere it creates and reveals and intensifies the emotions (the actor) is expressing on the stage. At such moments, in fact, the character should dance.'

In 1926 Terence Gray took over management of the Festival Theatre, Cambridge, which over the next few years he made the most remarkable experimental theatre in the country. It was a wonderfully stimulating venue for undergraduates interested in the theatre. He opened his first season with the *Oresteia*. To choreograph the choruses he employed the services of his niece, Ninette de Valois, who had been a member of the Diaghilev company and who was then considering the possibility of creating the impossible – a British national ballet (which she eventually achieved at Sadler's Wells Theatre under the management of the even more remarkable Lilian Baylis). Another of Terence Gray's early productions was Yeats's *On Baille's Strand*.

An interesting survivor of the Diaghilev ballet was Rupert Doone who in 1931 joined the company of the Festival Theatre. Unable to continue his career as a dancer he was instrumental in forming the Group Theatre, an ensemble that was based on very similar principles to those of the French Compagnie des Quinze and the American Group Theatre. Some of these principles have yet to be described but relevant to the present section was his intensive training of the actor in a wide range of physical and vocal skills, and his encouragement of W. H. Auden as a poetic dramatist. Auden wrote *The Dance of Death* and *The Dog Beneath the Skin*, which were staged at the Westminster Theatre in 1935 and 1936. At the same time discussions took place between W. B. Yeats, T. S. Eliot, and W. H. Auden, the three most distinguished poets writing in English, on the establishment of a theatre for poets; but the concept was perhaps too visionary to be realizable, especially by three men so different in age, background, and attitude. But Yeats's *Plays for Dancers*, Eliot's *Sweeney Agonistes*, and Auden's *The Dance of Death*, both the latter produced by the Group Theatre, were all extraordinary and wholly different examples of a new poetic drama. But the outcome was deeply disappointing. Yeats died in 1939 and no one followed up his ideas. Auden wrote two or three more plays, but the powerful and original poetic element was increasingly lost; and although Eliot went on to write some fine plays in verse, such as *Murder in the Cathedral* (1935), *The Family Reunion* (1939), and *The Cocktail Party* (1949) among others, all with some arcane reference to or basis in Greek tragedy, neither he nor any other poet who wrote plays in verse, and one must include Christopher Fry, pursued the particular kind of integration that had once been so promising.

There are plenty of books on the romantic ballet, many of them replete with romantically photographed ballerinas. Ivor Guest's The Dancer's Heritage *is clear and compact. Richard Buckle's* Diaghilev *is most informative about this remarkable man. Isadora Duncan wrote her own autobiography and is the subject of, or discussed in, many books. The early productions at the Festival Theatre, Cambridge, are described by Norman Marshall in* The Other Theatre. *Ninette de Valois's* Step by Step *describes the creation of the Royal Ballet. British culture in the 1930s has been dealt with in a number of books but the radical theatre movement of the period inadequately. There are biographies of W. H. Auden by Charles Osborne and Humphrey Carpenter.*

101 | The Emergence of the Director

The changes that took place in the European theatre in the last decades of the nineteenth century were immense. The development of the railways gave a new impetus to touring; but the traditional procedure had been for the 'star' performer to go on tour in one of his celebrated roles and for the characters to be filled in by the local stock company, as it was called. But these stock companies were becoming increasingly ill-equipped to cope with the new drama which audiences were interested in seeing; moreover they themselves were being displaced by a far better quality of actor who was thrusting his/her way into the profession. They were well-educated men and women responding to the new middle-class interest in the theatre and increasingly able to cope with the demands of the new drama.

The result of these, and similar pressures, was the emergence of a new specialist in the theatre, the producer. He is now known as the director, to bring the theatre into line with the film industry. The present-day producer is the man with the money; he rents the theatre, chooses the play, and hires the team, including the director, who is responsible for the actual staging of the play.

Until the end of the century there was no distinctive role for the producer/director, but a gradual improvement in standards of presentation by the actor-managers led to particular interest in this aspect of their work. Macready, Phelps, Charles Kean, Henry Irving, and others were clearly able, even brilliant directors in matters of presentation but were less interested in the new drama and how it was to be performed.

Commercial considerations also led to the creation of the director, since some of the managers who were prepared to invest money in a production knew nothing about the workings of the theatre and had to employ someone to stage the play. This someone was the producer/director.

A further reason lay in a problem that has been touched on continually in the last few sections. Plays were being written which the actor-managers did not know how to stage. Chekhov is an outstanding example. Thus there emerged a new specialist in the theatre, the producer, in the shape of men like André Antoine, Paul Fort, Aurélien Lugné-Poe, and Konstantin Stanislavsky who may or may not have been actors but made their mark as producers.

The first autocratic, independent, free-standing producer is generally taken to have been, of all unlikely people, the prince of a small German duchy, George II, Duke of Saxe-Meiningen. He took his hitherto unknown company to Berlin in 1874 and astonished his audiences with disciplined integrated acting, historically accurate sets and costumes, and a rare concentration upon the meaning of the text. Antoine said that the ensemble was marvellous but that his lighting was poor and his scenery inadequately painted, while Stanislavsky was horrified by the dictatorial methods used at rehearsals by Ludwig Chronegk, the Duke's stage-director.

No director made a greater contribution to the art of the theatre than Konstantin Stanislavsky (1865–1938). In his fascinating autobiography, *My Life in Art*, he describes how he made a close study of the methods employed by various actors and actresses and how this led him to collaborate with Vladimir Nemirovich-Danchenko in forming the Moscow Art Theatre where they would develop a company of real theatrical artists, playing with truthfulness and sincerity in contrast to the false theatricality that was still prevalent. Stanislavsky spent the rest of his working life not merely as principal producer of the Moscow Art Theatre but in working out with astonishing persistency an approach to the art of acting that would encapsulate his principles. In this respect Stanislavsky exercised the most important formative influence on the theatre of the twentieth century.

Stanislavsky is always associated with an attempt to probe, to analyse, and to master the psychology of the art of acting. Of a very different temperament was Vsevolod Meyerhold (1874–1938), originally an actor with the Moscow Art Theatre, but who, on becoming an independent director in 1902 conducted a remarkable variety of theatrical experiments. He tried to synthesize the work of author, actor, designer, and composer. He became obsessed with the need for the actor to be able to reveal, through movement and gesture, the inner life of the character. He disliked intensely the cultivated naturalism of the Meiningen company and the Moscow Art Theatre. This style of acting he considered to be too subjective, too introverted. He tried to create a style of acting that was nearer to dance, having been influenced by Isadora Duncan. He often placed his actors on a bare stage with a simple background and worked towards a kind of stylization that would reveal, or be expressive of the inner life of the character the actor was playing. He had a great deal in common with the Symbolists. After the Russian Revolution he ran foul of the authorities by carrying his experiments to unacceptable extremes, having invented a form of movement he called 'bio-mechanics'.

The work of the director is closely related to that of the architect who has designed the stage-space in which the actor works and the relationship of that space with the disposition of the audience. This was a subject in which the young German director George Fuchs was particularly interested. It is also related to the work of the stage designer. In the case of Adolphe Appia and Gordon Craig it is very difficult to make distinction between their work as designers and directors for they conceived productions in visual terms.

Adolphe Appia (1862–1928) was a Swiss. He lived largely as a hermit, immured in a castle on the shores of Lake Geneva. Though trained in medicine he adored music and was horrified at the staging of Wagner's operas in Bayreuth. His practical productions were few: Byron's *Manfred* with music by Schumann in Paris (1912); Gluck's opera *Orfeo* at the Dalcroze Institute, Hellerau (1913); *Tristan and Isolde* under Arturo Toscanini at La Scala, Milan (1923), and Wagner's *Rheingold* and *Walkyrie* at the Basel Stadttheater (Town theatre, 1924). But these productions together with his two books, *Mise en scène du drame Wagnerien* (*Production of Wagnerian Opera*, 1895) and *Musik und Inscenierung* (*Music and Staging*, 1899) were enormously influential.

Appia's achievement consisted partly in applying the use of electricity to the staging of opera. He envisaged abstract but architectural stage-settings composed of varying levels, slopes, planes, and three-dimensional spatial form and on this open stage and architectural setting light would play with varying degrees of concentration and so throw the actor, singer, or dancer into isolation. It was a realization of the problems which had faced the symbolists.

It should be mentioned here, perhaps, that the first theatre to be lit wholly with electricity was the Savoy built in 1881 for the Gilbert and Sullivan operas. Although electricity was far easier to control than gas, safer and more flexible, it was generally thought to give a far inferior quality of light.

Appia's ideas were reinforced and even extended by Edward Gordon

Craig (1872–1966), a man whose influence on the European theatre was immense. He was the son of Ellen Terry, who for many years was Henry Irving's leading lady at the Lyceum, and joined the company as an actor. In 1897 he broke away and developed his true vocation of theatrical visionary. He saw the stage as a painter sees his canvas, a three-dimensional area on which he could create his visions in which the actors were only part of the whole immense design. Great cloud-capped towers reared above immense architectural forms creating on many levels a chiaroscuro of light and shade in the middle of which great crowds of actors moved beneath fluttering banners.

But there was another side of his art which he expressed in his production of *Dido and Aeneas* in 1900 and again in 1901. He threw the singers into relief against beautifully painted drapes. Yeats wrote of his purple backcloth that it made the lovers appear to be 'wandering on the edge of eternity', which was doubtless Craig's intention. This simplicity also emerged in the arrangement of screens which he designed for a production of *Hamlet* at the Moscow Art Theatre, and which were so great a source of inspiration to Yeats.

At the heart of all this there were two fundamental traditions: one focused on the truthfulness and creativity of the actor; the other on the playing-space, the stage. Since the aim of the Symbolists, of Appia and Craig, had been to rid the stage of representational scenery and create an environment in which the actor could develop his creativity to the full, there were directors who saw the possibility of synthesizing the two traditions. One of these was Jacques Copeau (1878–1949). Among his earliest achievements was the founding, in collaboration with his friend the novelist, André Gide, of the publishing house, La Nouvelle Revue Française. His work in the theatre began in 1913 when he opened the Théâtre du Vieux Colombier, in the Latin quarter of Paris on the south bank, with a refreshingly simple programme. 'Pour l'oeuvre nouvelle qu'on nous laisse un tréteau nu', he wrote (for new work let's have a bare stage). On this bare stage only poetic texts would be mounted (which does not necessarily mean plays in verse). These plays would be realized by actors trained to pay absolute respect to the text and at the same time able to use their bodies with the utmost physical expressiveness. This was a kind of combination of Stanislavsky and Meyerhold with a certain implied contempt for the former; but Copeau's nephew, Michel St. Denis, has described their delight at the exquisite truthfulness of the Russian players whom they first saw when the Moscow Art Theatre visited Paris in 1926.

After the war Copeau formed a company of young actors and actresses which he called Les Copiaux, and established a school in Burgundy for intensive training. When Copeau retired from active involvement with the company, his work was carried on by Michel St. Denis who in 1931 formed the Compagnie des Quinze, a company whose frequent visits to London were a source of constant inspiration to many British actors and directors. With the demise of the Quinze in 1934 St. Denis settled in London and through his teaching at the London Theatre Studio, and then the Old Vic Theatre School, he established new methods of training actors.

Copeau's inspiration was evident in the work of a group of superb French actors and directors. There was Charles Dullin (1885–1949) who developed his interest in classical training with his company at the Théâtre de l'Atelier, and Louis Jouvet (1887–1951) whose ravishing sense of style made his productions of Molière and Jean Giraudoux at the Théâtre de l'Athénée unforgettable occasions. And then there was, there is, Jean-Louis Barrault (b.1910) who developed his outstanding gifts as director and actor into a concept of total theatre. By this he did not envisage the *gesamtkunstwerk* of Wagner, the synthesis of all the arts, but the total expressiveness of the actor through his voice and body. Nevertheless his productions of Paul Claudel's *Christoph Colomb*, which included the use of film and an orchestral score by Darius Milhaud, and his own version of Rabelais's *Gargantua*, were supreme examples of a full deployment of the total resources of the theatre.

The most distinctive development in Germany will be described in the next section. The most important director in the early years of the century was Max Reinhardt who worked in a great variety of styles. The two most important British directors were William Poel and Harley Granville Barker. William Poel's achievement was to free the production of Shakespeare's plays from the clutter of spectacular scenery which had been exploited by Henry Irving and Beerbohm Tree and to show the value of reproducing as nearly as possible the conditions under which his plays were first staged, a large bare playing-space, with a minimum of scenery, continuity by action between one scene and the next, and a cast of actors and actresses with expressive voices and a sensibility for poetic diction.

Harley Granville Barker (1877–1946) was a many-sided man of the theatre who in addition to his achievements as dramatist and manager did much to advance the art of theatrical production, particularly in the staging of Shakespeare. In a short season at the Savoy Theatre, 1912–14, he staged *A Midsummer Night's Dream*, *Twelfth Night* and *The Winter's Tale*, extending the work of William Poel with emphasis on simple and imaginative staging and speed in delivering the verse. In his important theoretical writings he argued the case for a national theatre with remarkable understanding, and for the educational importance of drama in a civilized community.

In recent years, with a poverty of new writing for the theatre it is not the actors who, as has happened in the past, have come into their own, but the directors. Their authority and power has become immense. Since by the very nature of their position in the theatre they cannot be prime creators, this development has not always been in the best interests of the theatre. The work of a director is to help the actor to reveal the intentions of the playwright. Far too many directors have used a play as a vehicle through which to project their own theatrical images. Although they have led the theatre in many interesting directions they have failed the theatre in their responsibility to encourage new playwrights, and they have failed to give the actors the help and support they need in mastering the great classic roles.

An illuminating history of the director is to be found in Norman Marshall's The Producer and the Play *and Edward Braun's* The Director and the Stage. *There are two excellent books on Meyerhold,* Meyerhold on Theatre, *a collection of his own writing, edited by Edward Braun, and Edward Braun's biography,* Meyerhold. *A useful summary of the theories of Appia, as well as of other luminaries mentioned in this section, is to be found in Eric Bentley's* Theories of the Modern Stage. *The work of Copeau has not been adequately dealt with in English. In French there are plenty of books by and on Copeau, Jouvet, and Dullin. Barrault's theory of total theatre, as well as much other material of great interest, is to be found in his two books,* Reflections on the Theatre *and* The Theatre of Jean-Louis Barrault. *His autobiography,* Memories for Tomorrow *is informative but a little whimsical. The latest biography of Granville Barker is by Eric Salmon. Barker's own important works include* The Exemplary Theatre *(1922) and* A National Theatre *(1930). Gordon Craig's* On the Art of the Theatre *is one of the great classics of theatrical literature.*

102 | A Note on Theatre Architecture

The variety of theatre practice that has emerged over the last hundred years has presented theatre architects with considerable problems. (One includes of course the even more important person who has the responsibility of briefing the architect, that is of telling him broadly what kind of a theatre he must design.) To build a theatre requires a great deal of capital. Logically, therefore, it should be built substantially

20. Shakespeare Memorial Theatre, Stratford-upon-Avon, 1879
The first permanent memorial theatre, designed by Messrs Dodgshun and Unsworth of Westminster and opened in 1879 through the initiative of C. E. Flower. The style of architecture was known as 'modern Gothic'.

to last. But a solid structure is far too inflexible to adapt to the variety of arrangements that contemporary directors require.

One of the solutions to this problem was prevalent in the 1960s when there was a considerable amount of theatre building in Britain. This was to build small flexible theatres in which the seating could be rearranged, without too much trouble, to give different kinds of playing-spaces and different actor-audience relationships. But this is only practicable with relatively small theatres.

The alternative solution is the one adopted by the architect of the National Theatre and by many other theatres in Britain and throughout

Europe, which is to provide a variety of auditoria and stages. The Olivier Theatre has an immense open stage rather on the lines of the Elizabethan; the Lyttleton has an uncompromising proscenium arch; the Cottesloe is a studio in which the most flexible and varied arrangements are possible. Fine, but extremely expensive.

There is no completely satisfactory solution. Large-scale opera and ballet require a theatre with provision for a large orchestra. It is interesting to note that the theatre in the Barbican, the London base of the Royal Shakespeare Company, has a large open stage on the lines of the Olivier. But some of the most interesting and original work in the contemporary theatre, in opera and ballet as well as drama, is being done by medium-sized and small companies which require smaller theatres.

the social side of the theatre, companies that have a permanent base are often insistent that their theatre should be situated not 'up-town' but in a suburban or working-class area. In such circumstances the 'theatre'

21. Shakespeare Memorial Theatre, Stratford-upon-Avon, 1932
The Victorian theatre was burnt down in 1926 and replaced by the present theatre, designed by Elizabeth Scott and opened on 23 April 1932 through the initiative of Sir Archibald Flower. It is now the base of the Royal Shakespeare Company.

22. The British National Theatre, London
Designed by Denys Lasdun and opened in 1977. The photograph has been taken from the north bank of the Thames which flows between the parapet and the theatre. It is interesting to compare the linear, practical, undecorated design with the confident opulence of a Victorian suburban theatre such as the Balham Hippodrome.

is usually a converted hall in an arts or community centre. This is why there is much talk now about 'venues' rather than theatres.

Thus over the whole field of theatrical activity there is a constant interaction between all the different people involved: the playwrights envisage a certain kind of production of their play, the actors want a certain kind of relationship with their audience, the directors want a certain kind of stage, dancers want plenty of space, musicians want certain acoustics, the managers want theatres big enough to make money, and each of these interests impinges upon the others. None is self-exclusive: actors are interested in play-writing, directors are interested in dance, designers are interested in theatre architecture. But it is from this jostling of often conflicting interests that a lively theatre emerges.

103 | The Soviet Theatre

The Russian Revolution of 1917 was one of the most significant political events in the whole history of man. It resulted in one-sixth of the earth's surface coming under the control of a regime that set itself up in direct opposition to the political and economic system of the Western world. There were many people who at the time, and in the following years, believed that the Revolution inaugurated a new phase in the history of man, in which the Romantic ideals of liberty, equality, fraternity would be finally realized. These expectations, however, were not, on the whole, fulfilled.

There was a period, nevertheless, during the early years of the Soviet rule when all the cultural aspirations of the new regime seemed to be expressed in the theatre. There was nothing particularly outstanding about early Soviet literature, music, or art; but during the 1920s and early 1930s the Soviet theatre was the astonishment of Europe. This was largely the achievement of the first Commissar of Education, Anatoly Lunacharsky who, with the backing of Lenin, first of all assured the survival of all that was best in the theatre of the past, including the Bolshoi Ballet and the Moscow Art Theatre. The importance of this decision is that it established in a most definitive way that a new culture should be built upon such traditions of the old as are worth preserving.

But it was the creation of the new Soviet theatre that astonished the world. First of all in extent: new theatres were built in all the Republics of the Union and theatrical activity of all kinds, both amateur and professional, was encouraged.

It was a director's theatre. One of the few criticisms raised by those who took a deep interest in Soviet artistic achievement was of the paucity of new writers. This may have been due to some kind of intellectual imposition by the authorities, but it was not enough to dampen the vigour of the directors. Space prevents any kind of analysis of the various directions taken by the Soviet theatre: a few examples must serve.

We have seen something of how Stanislavsky tried to exploit the actor's subconscious powers in the cause of creating theatrical truth, and how a contrary method was adopted by his one-time pupil, Vsevolod Meyerhold. It was Meyerhold, in fact, who after many years of experimenting with a variety of theatrical forms, became one of the most influential figures in the newly-created Soviet theatre. A critic describes how the actors in Meyerhold's theatre 'did not "experience" feelings and thoughts of the characters they portrayed . . . they did not identify with their roles or attempt to present an illusion of life . . . They presented the character they were playing by means of a highly conventionalized technique'. But his dictatorial and highly formalized methods and egocentric manner were not popular with the authorities and in due course he was tragically 'removed from the scene'.

His enthusiasm and his experimental zeal were infectious. Most of the Soviet directors had some kind of grounding with Stanislavsky but found a new creative energy in the opportunities provided by the Revolution. Stanislavsky's methods, they seem to have felt, were fine so far as they went, but required excessive introspection; they did not provide a technique that would allow them to express all the vitality of the new society. Meyerhold had gone perhaps too far but he had established a kind of theatrical authenticity that was different from the psychological truth demanded by Stanislavsky. Some sort of synthesis was clearly required. Although Eugene Vakhtangov (1883–1922) was potentially the most interesting of the new wave of Soviet directors – he died before he could fully realize his promise – it was Alexei Popov who introduced a style known as socialist realism. (Popov had been trained at the Moscow Art Theatre, had directed at the Vakhtangov Theatre, and then become director of the Theatre of the Revolution which had been created by Meyerhold.) In the event, however, socialist realism, instead of providing a model that subsequent directors could follow, became a dead end. The Soviet theatre lost its abounding vitality and originality and it remained for Bertolt Brecht to achieve a living synthesis between psychological truthfulness and social reality.

In the late 1920s and early 1930s the Soviet Tourist Agency organized frequent tours of the Soviet theatres. Their astonishing productions are vividly described in a number of books. Among the most memorable are Norris Houghton's Moscow Rehearsals, *particularly good on methods of production. The same author followed this with* Return Engagement *written twenty years later. The comparison is fascinating. Joseph Macleod's* Actors across the Volga *contains valuable chapters on the pre-Revolutionary Russian theatre and his* The New Soviet Theatre *describes the theatre in the various Republics. P. A. Markov's* The Soviet Theatre *describes the more important elements. But there are many other books on the subject.*

Stanislavsky's books, which through no fault of the English publisher, have been produced piecemeal, are badly in need of translation from the properly edited eight-volume edition available in the Soviet Union. The first to be based directly on Russian sources is J.-N. Benedetti's Stanislavski: an introduction.

104 | Expressionism and the German Political Theatre

The influence of the Soviet theatre on the rest of Europe has been less than its high quality might have warranted. Even in its most vigorous days Soviet theatrical productions were rarely exported, and in recent years Western Europe has seen little of the Soviet theatre apart from the Bolshoi Ballet and occasionally its opera. Even in the 1920s, when Communism was a potent element in German politics, the influence of the Soviet theatre was minimal and Germans developed their own brand of political theatre, Communist in direction but not based on any theory of socialist realism.

The modern history of Germany dates from her victory over France in the war of 1870–1, which made possible the creation of a united country. The 1914–18 war was a culmination of this period of Prussian imperialism. Defeat is always hard to accept, but it was particularly so for the Germans whose political unification had been achieved so recently and whose political structure was not sufficiently adaptable to come to terms with the unstable aftermath of the war. The near political chaos of Germany in the 1920s was barely held in control by an administration which based itself in Weimar to avoid the Prussianism associated with Berlin.

The 1914–18 war was a horrifying experience for all who had been involved in it. For those already critical of society it was confirmation of their disgust. What the Communists had achieved in Russia, socialists saw the possibility of achieving elsewhere. The promise (or threat) of a Communist-led revolution hung over Europe throughout the 1920s, particularly where there was economic and political instability.

The post-war malaise, outstandingly evident in defeated Germany but shared by many other countries, was the culmination of many decades of unrest. It took an artistic form that was known as Expressionism, a movement that involved the direct expression of emotion. Every aspect of art was to be used for its expressive possibilities. It may therefore be seen as the final outcome of Romanticism. It was not an artistic movement with a clearly defined programme and historians have found it difficult to define. In some ways it was a kind of generalized protest against man's increasing enslavement of man, resulting from the industrial revolution, and the maiming of the human spirit by a world that put increasing emphasis on material production. Technological developments increasingly concealed, it was claimed, disastrous psychic disorder in the soul of man. In more simple terms, it was a cry of anger against the bestiality of the war and widespread industrialization.

The most eminent personality in the creation of an Expressionist theatre was Erwin Piscator (1893–1968). He had a fairly conventional upbringing but was persuaded by the events of 1918 to adopt the cause of socialism. In 1920 he opened his Proletarisches Theater. This consisted of groups of amateur working-class actors meeting in halls in industrial districts without proper stage, costumes, or lighting, playing short pieces of political satire and propaganda that came to be known as agit-prop. 'We look on the theatre', he wrote at this time, 'as a means of disseminating a specific political idea'. But just how to do this he soon found to be a complex business. In realizing and so rejecting the limitations of naturalism he found himself experimenting with a variety of theatrical forms, not for the sake of experiment, but because he was trying to use the theatre in a new and revolutionary manner. He wanted to present on the stage the troubled political situation, the great themes of war and socialism and unemployment; but there were no models to help him. When in 1924 he was appointed director of the Volksbühne, the most prestigious theatre in Berlin, and in 1927–8 of the Theater am Nollendorfplatz, he developed a number of striking technical innovations – mobile platforms, belts, and a considerable use of film. In 1928 his work foundered through sheer financial bankruptcy. It is difficult to say whether his work had failed artistically because the very word is inappropriate. He was trying to create a political theatre and not an art theatre. In the sense that the theatre is an art, he was trying to create a political art. Some people dispute the possibility of this. But it must be remembered that art is the servant of man; it is for man to use as a means of projecting his view of society. Piscator and others who worked in and for a political theatre are often criticized by people who disapprove of their aims before sneering at their achievements.

In any case Piscator's contribution to the theatre was immense. His original methods of production were widely influential. But he had little success in encouraging new playwrights. From the whole output of German Expressionist drama only two writers stand out in any significant way: Georg Kaiser (1879–1945) who is likely to be remembered for his play *Von Morgen bis zum Mitternacht (From Morn till Midnight*, 1916), rather than for his more ambitious but usually rather confused plays, and Ernst Toller (1893–1939) whose *Masse-Mensch* (*Masses and Man*, 1921) is usually considered to be the prototype of Expressionist drama.

The political background of this important period is well described in Peter Gay's Weimar Culture *and the work of Piscator in C. D. Innes's* Irwin Piscator's Political Theatre.

The spirit of German Expressionism is particularly evident in the work of such Expressionist painters as Max Bechmann and George Grosz. Though wholly irrelevant to the theme of this book, one of the most interesting manifestations of German culture of this period was the work of the artists who were associated with the Bauhaus, a movement intended to create a synthesis between design and industrial techniques. Its leading spirit was the architect, Walter Gropius, who designed a fascinating project for a total theatre which, unhappily, never materialized.

105 | Brecht

The most significant theatrical survivor of German Expressionism and the Weimar Republic was Bertolt Brecht (1898–1956), a curiously ambiguous figure whose theories and plays have dominated the post-war European theatre. He was born of a fairly well-to-do family and went to university in Münich. He had a short but bitter experience of the war as a hospital orderly and was demobilized during the economic chaos. He worked for a time as literary adviser to the Münich Kammerspiel Theater but soon left for Berlin, where he worked for both Reinhardt and Piscator. He soon showed himself to be a poet and playwright with an extremely individual, ironic, and caustic style. In addition to a considerable amount of poetry, he wrote some forty plays, radio plays, and adaptations in a variety of forms.

Not only was Brecht not an Expressionist writer but he was strongly opposed to the emotionalism of the movement. He did not wholly approve of Piscator's practice of turning the theatre into a public meeting and loading the stage with machinery. His aim was to create a theatre for a scientific age. (The phrase is one he often uses.) This required a clear analysis of social realities. Since society is in a state of constant change, he felt that this could not be done by using the form of theatre he associated with Aristotle and Ibsen, which he considered to be too static. Nor did he care for Bernard Shaw's practice of turning plays into debates, although Shaw was a writer he much admired. He therefore placed emphasis on narrative, took Shakespeare as his model, and created a form of theatre he called 'epic', a term which had also been used by Piscator. This explains why he wrote his plays in many short scenes, often broke up the action with songs, and sometimes suggested that the moral of the scene be written on a placard clearly visible to the audience. All this was to avoid the deep emotional involvement of audience and actors which he considered to be a kind of hypnotism and put the critical faculties to sleep.

His tactics are clear in all his early plays from *Baal* (1918) to *Die Dreigroschen Oper* (*The Threepenny Opera*, 1928). This last is a sharp and witty satire on capitalist society which, with its haunting astringent music by Kurt Weill, was an immense success and established his position as a major dramatist.

With the depression of 1929, and the political instability of Germany that led to seizure of power by Hitler and the National Socialists, he felt the need for greater political awareness and wrote a number of short plays which he called *Lehrstücke* (learning pieces). *Die Massnahme* (*The Expedient*, 1930) is the most interesting example.

When the Nazis came to power Brecht went into exile and settled for a time in various Scandinavian countries. His next group of plays were sharply anti-Nazi – *Die Mutter* (*The Mother*, 1930–1) after a story by Gorky, *Die Rundkopfe und die Spitzkopfe* (*Round Heads and Pointed Heads*, 1931–4), and *Furcht und Elend des Dritten Reiches (Fear and Misery of the Third Reich*, 1935–8). With the outbreak of war Brecht obtained a visa to settle, surprisingly, in the United States, a country he had frequently attacked for its apparently total commitment to the evils of capitalism. It was here that he wrote his finest works – *Galileo* (1937–9), *Mutter Courage und Ihre Kinder* (*Mother Courage and her Children*, 1938–9), *Der Gute Mensch von Sezuan* (*The Good Person of Szechwan*, 1938–42), and *Das Kaukasische Kreidekreis* (*The Caucasian Chalk Circle*, 1943–5).

On his return to Europe after the war he settled in East Berlin and became director of the Berliner Ensemble, a company that specialized in his own plays and with which he was able to develop his theories.

Brecht was clear about and generous towards the contribution that Stanislavsky had made to the theatre, although he strongly opposed what he considered to be a static Aristotelian approach to the theatre with too much psychological introspection. But in the United States he found a widespread perversion of Stanislavsky's teaching known as The Method. He therefore developed a theory that had long interested him: it requires that an actor should not become wholly immersed in his feelings, but play his role and demonstrate its characteristics to the audience in a more objective fashion. Of all Brecht's theories this is not only the most difficult to understand but certainly the most difficult for an actor to put into effect.

This *Verfremdung*, or Alienation Effect, as he called it, was all part of his determination to keep players and audience critically alive. He never wanted the audience to become so absorbed in the performance as to forget that it was in a theatre. He therefore advocated the practice of using bright lights and of having all stage lanterns visible to the audience, a practice now often used for convenience and not for the reasons that Brecht intended.

Brecht is full of contradictions. His plays are emotionally cool and often intellectually demanding. But he at least hoped that they would never be dull. 'The theatre of the scientific age', he wrote, 'is in a position to make dialectics into a source of enjoyment'. The unexpectedness of logically progressive or zigzag development, the joke of contradiction . . . all these are ways of heightening our capacity for enjoying life'. He was far too much a man of the theatre to risk boring his audiences; and he was a great joker himself, full of a teasing and ironical wit.

Another important element in his plays is his passion for music. Many of his plays include songs and *The Threepenny Opera* and *Augstieg und Fall der Stadt Mahagonny* (*Rise and Fall of the Town of Mahagonny*, 1927–9) are virtually light operas. He enjoyed the collaboration of some of the best composers of the day – Kurt Weill, Hans Eisler, Paul Dessau, Paul Hindemith, and others. He considered that these songs helped the Alienation Effect by breaking up the continuitiy of the action and helping to prevent any chance of the audience becoming hypnotized by the performance.

Brecht always collaborated with artists of distinction. His composers have been mentioned. For décor he worked frequently with his school-friend, Caspar Neher, and for actors he chose the best that were available. It is in no way surprising that this rare mixture of high professional competence, a powerful imagination, a conceptual originality, and a mind of the greatest ingenuity have made him so powerful an influence in the theatre of his times.

There is an enormous amount of critical literature on Brecht. But before becoming involved in what other people have said that Brecht said, or what he meant by what he said, it is helpful to read what Brecht himself said. His theories are expounded in numerous essays, newspaper articles, and interviews. His most substantial piece of critical writing is his Kleines Organon für das Theater *(*Short Organum on the Theatre, *1948).*

An invaluable selection from all his notes and theoretical writings is to be found in John Willett's Brecht on Theatre.

106 Experimental and Alternative Theatre

The political and socially-conscious theatre of Soviet Russia, and Germany under the Weimar Republic, had its influence on other countries, though to a very minor extent on the mainstream theatre. In

Britain and France the creation of a political theatre in Piscator's sense, a theatre with a strong working-class support, giving plays with an explicit social message, was largely the work of amateurs. This amateur socialist theatre movement was fostered by the Soviet Union during the late 1920s through festivals held in Moscow and in various countries by their Communist Parties.

By the 1930s the workers' theatre movement had gathered its own momentum. In Britain the two most significant companies were Unity Theatre, which had developed on the basis of previous groups such as the Rebel Players and Theatre Union, the creation of Joan Littlewood. Between 1936 and 1939 Unity had considerable success with a programme of such uninhibitedly socialist plays as Clifford Odets's *Waiting for Lefty* (1935) and Herbert Hodge's *Where's that Bomb?*, a Living Newspaper on a London Bus Strike – the American influence was strong in a number of respects – and the first production of Sean O'Casey's *The Star Turns Red.* Joan Littlewood's greatest years came after the war. (The Living Newspaper has now been superseded by the documentary.)

In other countries other theatrical movements signalled the emergence of a theatre that stood well apart in aims, methods, and material from the mainstream theatre. In France, for example, the Dadaists and the Surrealists made attempts to give theatrical expression to their anarchistic and fantastic visions. In Italy the emphasis of the Futurists was increasingly on performance. It is interesting to find that the inspiration and driving force behind many of these theatrical movements were the painters who turned to the theatre, or theatrical forms of expression, as an active way of forcing their ideas and experiments upon the public. But in most countries the pattern of work was roughly the same. Such a wide range of experimental theatre was carried out that it is difficult to imagine that anyone can ever find anything new or original again. It is difficult even to describe these experiments since the relationship between the different arts was so close that it becomes impossible to identify where the contribution of one art ends and another begins. Lines of demarcation were unknown. And then there was a curious love-hate relationship between these various artistic movements and Communism. For many artists the Russian Revolution suggested the possibility of a brave new society until they came up against the unanswerable question, whether one changed society through art or art through society. It was only when Soviet society itself became caught up in the problems of establishing its own independent identity that a certain momentum went out of the experimental theatre movement.

The 1939–45 war changed the situation profoundly. The war ended with far less hysteria and chauvinism than had attended the end of the 1914–18 war, and a far greater determination to reconstruct a more just society. In Britain these ideals were incorporated into a great deal of the legislation that was passed in the late 1940s, while Germany achieved prodigies in reconstructing her ruined cities. One of the unspoken assumptions of this reconstruction was that central government must take responsibility for certain aspects of a country's culture and art. This led in many European countries to a considerable amount of building and rebuilding of theatres. In the Federal Republic of Germany (West Germany) theatres were sometimes built before homes for the people, suggesting the importance that the public authorities attached to providing for the spiritual and cultural life of the people.

In Britain a new theatrical movement emerged during the 1950s, closely associated with the Royal Court Theatre which was directed by George Devine. It was identifiable not through the use of any new theatrical form, but in an increased awareness of society and a more intensive kind of naturalism. This did not result in the stages being cluttered with an increasing amount of naturalistic scenery and properties but in a sharp analysis of social trends and human relationships. The drama of the 1950s and 1960s was dominated by the plays of John Osborne, Arnold Wesker, John Arden, and other writers, most of them associated with George Devine at the Royal Court Theatre. John Osborne's *Look Back in Anger*, Arnold Wesker's *Roots*, and John Arden's *The Workhouse Donkey* can be taken as typical of the movement.

One of the strangest phenomena of the period was a form of drama that came to be known as the Theatre of the Absurd. Yet 'absurd' is a wholly inadequate description for the plays, among others, of Samuel Beckett, Arthur Adamov, Eugene Ionesco, Jean Genet and Harold Pinter which depict a world in which, in the words of Martin Esslin, 'the unshakeable basic assumptions of former ages have been swept away' and a sense of metaphysical anguish at the absurdity of the human condition predominates. Many of the plays of these dramatists are at the same time amusing and deeply moving.

A shot in the arm came from a visit by the young Polish director, Jerzy Grotowski, and his company together with the publication of his book, *Towards a Poor Theatre*. Both events turned attention once again to the importance of the actor's role in the theatre and the value of intensive training. But there was more to it than this. Grotowski was part of a growing interest in non-verbal forms of theatre. This was partly the result of increasing discontent with the domination of literary values and a loss of confidence in the spoken word as a form of artistic expression. But more positively it was the result of the experiments conducted in the 1920s and 1930s in a great variety of intrinsically theatrical forms. One of the great visionaries was a tortured Frenchman called Antonin Artaud who advocated what he called a Theatre of Cruelty. His ideas were important to Grotowski and even more to Peter Brook whose theatrical experiments, though hardly deserving the term cruel, have revealed new concepts of theatrical art, sometimes of a non-linguistic nature.

Then in the 1960s there was something of an invasion from the United States. American companies visited Britain and toured Europe with plays and productions that combined social and political awareness with highly original and unconventional methods of presentation. Some Americans settled in this country and established important theatres and theatre groups. All this was associated with the curious student unrest that manifested itself throughout Europe in 1968. (There is perhaps a tenuous connection between this movement and the final removal of the censorship from the British theatre which took place in the same year.)

These events seemed to provide a stimulus for the emergence, the creation, the coming together of a large number of groups which were now identifiable as a movement. In Britain they found a rallying point in the Edinburgh International Festival where they constituted what was described as a 'Fringe' to the main events. Similar groups started up throughout Europe and although they commonly refer to themselves as 'free' theatres, they are best described as 'alternative', for the term describes precisely what the movement is, an alternative to the mainstream theatre in venue, in management, in content, and in styles of performance.

The range of work that is covered by the alternative theatre is immense. On the one hand there are companies which are interested in exploring new theatrical forms, the theatre of gesture, for example, or various aspects of what has been called performance theatre, which usually involves some kind of mixed-media presentation. At the other extreme there are the overtly political groups, highly critical of bourgeois society, and using the stage quite deliberately to effect social change. Perhaps the most common element in the whole movement is the determination to create a new audience for the theatre, or to play to audiences who do not visit the mainstream theatre. There is plenty of scope for this. In most European countries the regular theatre-going public constitutes about five per cent of the total population, and is almost wholly middle- and upper-middle-class in composition. Thus there is a huge audience waiting to be tapped, to be given an alternative to films and television. But the success of alternative theatre groups in reaching this public is open to question. Any company, of whatever artistic or political persuasion, that becomes known for the vitality or originality of its work, is visited by the regular middle-class theatre-goer who has come to be rather contemptuously dismissed as the 'radical chic'.

It is probably in the field of play-writing that the alternative theatre has had its greatest success, especially in Britain. Small companies have offered a stage and a production to playwrights as a form of apprenticeship. Those with talent have had little difficulty in progressing to the mainstream theatre which is as anxious for good original work as it has ever been. The success of the alternative theatre in this respect has been largely the result of a close collaboration between players and playwrights. The creative potential of the actor, which was released by Stanislavsky, has now begun to narrow the distinction between acting and writing. Some playwrights are deeply disturbed by the development and consider that the actors are trying to displace them. But taking a broader view, this is undoubtedly another example of the situation we have noticed constantly throughout the history of the theatre, that when the pen of the playwright falters, the actor tends to take over. There are many pens at work today but the quality of the penmanship leaves plenty of scope for improvement.

The alternative theatre movement looks longingly back at periods in the history of theatre where there seems to have been a closer link between society and its theatre, a genuine community theatre. If this ever was the case, it was the result of a wholly different set of social and cultural circumstances. The movement can take courage from the fact that this is the first time in the history of the theatre that the profession itself has made vigorous attempts to reach a bigger public. In one sense, it is a matter of survival: the challenge of television is a most serious one. But the need for missionary zeal has had the beneficial result of compelling all theatre workers to consider the basic nature of theatrical art; there is no point in trying to do what film and television do better. But a cultural revolution is not achieved overnight, and theatre workers are faced once again by the dilemma that faced the progressives in the early 1920s: can they change society through the theatre or does new work in the theatre depend upon a change in society? Only time will tell.

Roselee Goldberg's Performance *gives a detailed and very well-illustrated account of theatrical experiments between 1909 and about 1978. The story of the British Fringe during the 1970s will be found in Katherine Itzin's* Stages in the Revolution *and Sandy Craig's* Dreams and Deconstructions. *Artaud's* Theatre of Cruelty *and Grotowski's* Towards a Poor Theatre *are available in English. Peter Brook's* The Empty Stage *is an important discussion on basic attitudes towards the theatre.*

Playwrights of the Royal Court and other groupings are fully discussed by John Russell Taylor in Anger and After.

107 The European Theatre in the 1980s

The traditional theatre, to which the developments described in the last chapter provide a recent alternative, has never played more than a limited role in the cultural life of Western Europe, though from time to time it has been an important role, encapsulating more surely than any other art the spirit of the times. But with its possible collapse after the 1939–45 war, the governments of Europe took steps, each in its own way, to ensure survival. The reasons for possible collapse were entirely economic. In the Federal Republic of Germany many theatres had been destroyed, but there was a tradition of public responsibility. Italy, faced with the total destruction of the Fascist regime, had to rebuild a democratic state in which art and culture should clearly play an important part. In France there had been a modest tradition of state intervention in the arts and this was energetically revived by the Ministry of Fine Arts (as it then was) which began by establishing five regional subsidized theatres. (The number has now grown to nineteen.) In Britain a wartime initiative, the Council for the Encouragement of Music and the Arts, was converted into the Arts Council of Great Britain which, beginning with a subsidy of £235,000 in 1945, will receive a Treasury grant for 1982–3 of over £86 million. And similar developments took place elsewhere.

The question remains whether the traditional unsubsidized theatre would have survived without government support. The answer is that it has survived, to a certain extent and at a certain price. The traditional mainstream theatre has always survived on its ability to attract an audience simply by what it has to offer. The success of a theatre has depended on the ability of a manager to judge public taste. When he has failed he has shrugged his shoulders and tried again. This procedure, common throughout industry, of measuring the success of one's product against the willingness of the public to buy it has become known as the 'market-test'.

But theatre artists have felt increasingly that whatever the validity of the test in a free capitalist society, it was not good enough for the theatre, or any art, for that matter. For one thing, the cost of producing a play in the 1980s has become so high that a manager is compelled to play safe and aim for the lowest common factor in public appreciation. This prevents the production of many fine plays which are expensive to stage and not likely to enjoy the long run which will ensure a substantial return on outlay.

Related to this is the argument that a responsible theatre constitutes a public service and should cater, as television does, for a wide variety of tastes by offering a great variety of plays, classics, foreign plays, new plays, and experimental plays, whether they are cheap or expensive to mount. Some plays, for example, can be adequately rehearsed in a few weeks while others may require several months, especially if the director wishes to create a new style of presentation.

The concept of theatre as a public service has led many countries to establish some kind of system for subsidizing the theatre from public funds. Whether or not we accept this practice, the fact is that otherwise there would be very little theatre in any European country, and that in Britain there would be no National Theatre, no Royal Shakespeare Theatre, and very few regional theatres. Most countries in Western Europe give about 1 per cent or less of their total 'income' to subsidizing the arts and of this the theatre receives a small proportion. This does not seem to be a high price to pay to preserve so crucial a part of our culture.

The subject of this section has been fully covered by John Allen in Theatre in Europe.

A number of books have been written on the Arts Council of Great Britain. The book that treats the subject most fully is The State and the Arts, *edited by John Pick. The history of state involvement in the arts has been admirably dealt with by Janet Minihan in* The Nationalization of Culture.

108 | Conclusion

In 1981 the National Theatre in London included in its repertory a production of *The Oresteia* of Aeschylus. Many people who saw the performance left the theatre feeling that they had been through an experience more real than the world in which they were living.

Clytemnestra had murdered her husband and in revenge had been murdered by her son who was then put on trial. Nothing more. But the sordid story seemed to be more real and far more significant than anything in the world outside the theatre.

The explanation must lie in the intensity of the experience. There was nothing outwardly real or natural about the performance: the actors wore masks and spoke an artificial kind of English; and yet the result was more real than reality. And this is what the theatre at its most serious has always tried to do, to present a moment of real life with as much intensity and concentration as author, composer, and performer can achieve.

The value of a history of the theatre is therefore to enable one to consider the many different ways in which playwrights, directors, and players have set about creating this artificial sense of reality. It is sometimes called a theatrical convention. This simply means that we accept the whole game of actors and actresses dressing up and pretending to be other people as something to take seriously. A more far-reaching way of looking at it is to see a theatrical performance as a great symbolic act in which the actors and actresses and the accepted conventions of the performance are a representation of imaginative ideas or abstract concepts.

The most pervasive of these conventional elements of symbolic forms is probably the custom of making characters speak in verse. This is because poetry itself is the most intense form of literature; and this intensity is expressed by the poet not only in his choice of words but in the form in which he couches them; and this poetic form, which often includes a powerful metrical element, is of a physical nature and therefore extremely actable.

It will have been apparent to anyone reading this book straight through that most plays were written in poetry until comparatively recent times, until, in fact, the so-called naturalistic revolution in the theatre gave greater importance to fact than fantasy, and so more value to prose than poetry. This was a reversal of an ancient tradition, for many critics from the Greeks to the Elizabethans considered that fiction, which enabled the writer to create his own reality, was a higher form of art than history, which requires the writer to stick to the facts so far as he understands them.

But playwrights had to choose the nature of their poetry very carefully. T. S. Eliot says that 'What we have to do is to bring poetry into the world in which the audience lives and to which it returns when it leaves the theatre; not to transport the audience into some imaginary world totally unlike its own . . .' This puts the problem very clearly. The poet/playwright has to use conventions and symbols and language which the audience understands and accepts. More than this: the very material he writes about must be of the kind that makes sense to the audience even if it is the intention of the playwright to disturb or shock them. All this explains why we are able to accept a kind of theatrical or poetic reality in plays that are written in a far from naturalistic manner.

But in practice it isn't as easy as that. The Victorians read poetry. Tennyson's poems sold in tens of thousands of copies. A playwright could write in verse reasonably confident that the public would accept the poetic convention he was using. In the late twentieth century people no longer read poetry. T. S. Eliot (1888–1965) wrote his plays in a kind of verse that was as resonant as he could manage of the rhythms of ordinary speech. In fact he began his work as a playwright with *Sweeney Agonistes* which is written in what one might call a jazz idiom, a style in which regrettably he did not persist. Christopher Fry had a brief period of success in the 1950s with plays that astonished audiences with the brilliance of their word-play; but without a more significant content this is not a quality that is likely to ensure the endurance of his plays.

Another poet who made a courageous attempt to write poetic drama was W. H. Auden (1907–73); but having written the immensely original *The Dance of Death*, staged by the Group Theatre in 1934, and the only slightly less interesting *The Dog Beneath the Skin* a year or so later and *The Ascent of F6*, he sheered rapidly away from the theatre, yet not before, together with T. S. Eliot, he had shown the way in which a variety of metres and verse-forms could be used dramatically and in so doing had freed the British drama from the debased jog-trot pentameter.

On the other hand we have a great creative artist like the Frenchman, Paul Claudel (1868–1955) who wrote a number of powerful plays in a kind of poetic prose. Critics have grumbled that he saddled himself with the worst of both worlds, prose that was too dense for clarity, and poetry that was too leaden to dance. Nevertheless plays such as *Partage de midi* (1906) and *Le Livre de Christoph Colomb* (*The Book of Christopher Columbus*, 1927), both of which were superbly staged by Jean-Louis Barrault, have that density of texture, and particularly in the case of the latter, a theatrical inventiveness that make them two of the greatest plays of the century.

Federico Garcia Lorca (1898–1936), the Spanish poet, was able to discover a folk tradition in the Spanish people that he was able to exploit in a number of fine plays, poetic fantasies like *La Zapatera Prodigioso* (*The Shoemaker's Extraordinary Wife*, 1930), and savage tragedies such as *Bodas de Sangre* (*Blood Wedding*, 1933) and *La Casa de Bernarda Alba* (*The House of Bernard Alba*, 1936). But as this is not a folk world any more than it is a poetic world, this was not a form that other playwrights could develop.

It has been constantly noted in this book that playwrights reflect in their material and their style something of the culture of the age in which they live. This is virtually what T. S. Eliot was saying when he proposed that poetry in the theatre must be of the world in which the audience is living. But Emile Zola, who was no poet, and Bertolt Brecht who was a fine poet, both claimed that we are living in a scientific age. Playwrights have responded in different ways. Brecht related science to sociology and wrote about man as a social animal. A playwright such as the Italian, Luigi Pirandello (1867–1936) picked up the theme of the nature of human identity and exploited it in a number of brilliant plays. This is a reflection of the century's profound interest in that most dubious of sciences, the analysis of the human psyche. Sigmund Freud and his fellow psychologists and psychoanalysts revealed a source of material that offers limitless opportunities for exploitation by all kinds of writers. In plays like *Sei Personaggi in Cerca d'Autore* (*Six Characters in Search of an Author*, 1921) and *Enrico Quarto* (*Henry IV*, 1922), Pirandello found a way of creating magnificent plays out of the contemporary preoccupation with the identity of a human being.

Somewhat the same theme is handled by the most curious French playwright, Jean Genet (b.1910). In *Les Bonnes* (*The Maids*, 1947) there is a most subtle reversal of roles, while in *Le Balcon* (*The Balcony*, 1956), which is set in a brothel, the inmates play out their fantasies and assume a variety of roles in very much the same way, so the author implies, as many people do in ordinary life.

These are examples of playwrights who have managed to create a theatrical convention enabling them to handle themes which earlier playwrights could not have considered for a moment even if they had been interested which, on the whole, is most unlikely. But perhaps the most remarkable playwright of the century is the Irishman, Samuel Beckett (b.1906), who has lived for most of his working life in Paris. For he more than any other writer has found a way of exploiting the century's growing disenchantment in the power of speech and language for purposes of human communication. And in creating a convention by means of which he can dramatize what he sees as the hopelessness of the human situation, he has found at the same time a way of writing with an intensity of experience which is usually associated with poetic dramatists. Plays such as *Waiting for Godot* (1952), *Endgame* (1958), and *Happy Days* (1961) are remarkable examples of plays in which language is reduced to a minimum but where the most commonplace word assumes, from its context, tremendous suggestiveness. It is a remarkable achievement.

At the beginning of this book we quoted Jean-Louis Barrault's remark that the theatre is the 'conscience of mankind'. Many years ago Bernard Shaw wrote words to the effect that the theatre is 'a temple in the ascent of man' and a good deal more in a similar vein. There are some to whom such statements may seem a bit steep. But Barrault and Shaw were great men of the theatre, and their statements do not so much describe the theatre as it usually is, but what on rare occasions it has proved to be. Those occasions include Aeschylus's *Oresteia*, Shakespeare's *King Lear*, Racine's *Phèdre*, Chekhov's *The Cherry Orchard* – every reader will add his own titles to the list. But what is the chance of there being new playwrights to join this illustrious group? The chances are good if certain conditions are fulfilled.

A community, whether it be town, conurbation, county, or country, must take the theatre seriously. By that I mean that the community clearly must expect the theatre to present a responsible projection of contemporary thoughts and feelings. It does not matter whether this projection is cast in a comic, a tragic, or any other kind of vein as long as it epitomizes a moment of human consciousness or social responsibility. That is all there is to it. All else follows. It is a matter in the first instance of community responsibility, since no artist will take his creation into a community which he feels will not be interested. But the reverse is even stronger. No community that does not believe in the importance of art will itself create an artist of stature. The one gives birth to and then accepts responsibility for the other. But the artist likewise has responsiblities. He must use whatever language he is using to the full, whether that language be words, sounds, the human body, paint, or clay or stone. And he must use that language intelligibly so that the community as a whole, and not just a few who have had a special training in appreciation, can understand it.

Then if it is so simple to be a great artist, the reader may ask, why are there not more of them? And the answer is quite simply this: that although the conditions are undemanding, they are rarely fulfilled. If society as a whole is interested in the theatre only as a low-brow form of entertainment, so be it. But do not let anyone raise their eyebrows in surprise. If society is interested in the theatre as a temple in the ascent of man, dramatists, choreographers, and composers of genius will soon emerge. While 95 per cent of the present population of Europe does not mind whether the theatre exists or not, there is not much to be hoped for. When the figures are reversed there will be a theatre to wonder at.

Selected Bibliography

Allen, John, *Theatre in Europe*, John Offord, 1981
Ansorge, Peter, *Disrupting the Spectacle*, Pitman, 1975
Axton, Richard, *European Drama of the Early Middle Ages*, Hutchinson, 1974

Baker, Michael, *The Rise of the Victorian Actor*, Croom Helm, 1978
Baldry, H. C., *The Greek Tragic Theatre*, Chatto and Windus, 1974
Barrault, Jean-Louis, *Reflections on the Theatre*, Rockliff, 1951
——, *The Theatre of Jean-Louis Barrault*, Barrie and Rockliff, 1959
Beare, W., *The Roman Stage*, Methuen, 1968
Beauman, Sally, *The Royal Shakespeare Company*, Oxford, 1982
Bentley, Eric (ed.), *The Theory of the Modern Stage*, Pelican, 1968
Bevington, Donald, *From Mankind to Marlowe: Growth and Structure in the Popular Drama of Tudor England*, Harvard, 1962
Bieber, Margarete, *The History of the Greek and Roman Theatre*, Princeton, 1939
Booth, Michael, *English Melodrama*, Herbert Jenkins, 1965
Bradbrook, M. C., *The Rise of the Common Player*, Chatto and Windus, 1962
Braun, Edward, *The Director and the Stage*, Methuen, 1982
Brereton, Geoffrey, *French Tragic Drama of the 16th and 17th Centuries*, Methuen, 1973
Brook, Peter, *The Empty Space*, MacGibbon and Kee, 1968
Brown, Ivor, *How Shakespeare Spent the Day*, The Bodley Head, 1963
Bruford, W. H., *Theatre Drama and Audience in Goethe's Germany*, Routledge and Kegan Paul, 1950
Browne, E. Martin, *The Making of T. S. Eliot's Plays*, Cambridge, 1969
Buckle, Richard, *Diaghilev*, Weidenfeld and Nicholson, 1979

Chambers, Sir E. K., *The Medieval Stage* (2 vols), Oxford, 1903
——, *The Elizabethan Stage* (4 vols), Oxford, 1923
Cibber, Colley, *An Apology for his Life*, Everyman
Clark, Barrett, H., *European Theories of Drama*, Crown, New York, 1947
Clemen, Wolfgang, *English Tragedy before Shakespeare*, Methuen, 1955
Cole, Toby, and Chinoy, Helen, *Actors on Acting*, Crown, New York, 1949
——, *Directors on Directing*, Bobs-Merrill, Indianapolis, 1963
Cook, Anne Jennalie, *The Privileged Playgoers of Shakespeare's London*, Princeton, 1981
Craik, T. (ed.), *Revels History of Drama in English* (8 vols), Methuen
Cornford, F. M., *The Origin of Attic Comedy*, Cambridge, 1914
Craig, E. Gordon, *On the Art of the Theatre*, Heinemann, 1911
Craig, Hardin, *English Religious Drama of the Middle Ages*, Oxford, 1955

Duchartre, Pierre Louis, *The Italian Comedy*, Harrap, 1929
Donaldson, Frances, *The Actor-Managers*, Weidenfeld and Nicholson, 1970
Duckworth, G. E., *The Nature of Roman Comedy*, Princeton, 1952

Elsom, J. and Tomalin, Nicholas, *The History of the National Theatre*, Cape, 1978
——, *Post-war British Theatre*, Routledge and Kegan Paul, 1981
Esslin, M., *The Theatre of the Absurd*, Heinemann, 1962

Findlater, Richard, *Banned! A Review of Theatre Censorship in Britain*, MacGibbon and Kee, 1967
——, *Lilian Baylis*, Allen Lane, 1975
Frank, Grace, *The Medieval French Drama*, Oxford, 1954

Garten, H. F., *Modern German Drama*, Methuen, 1964
Glasstone, Victor, *Victorian and Edwardian Theatres*, Thames and Hudson, 1975
Goldberg, Rose Lee, *Performance*, Thames and Hudson, 1979
Goldman, Albert and Springhorn, Evert, *Wagner on Music and Drama*, Gollancz, 1970
Gozzi, Carlo, *Useless Memoirs*, Oxford, 1962
Green, F. C. (ed.), *Diderot's Writings on the Theatre*, Cambridge, 1936
Grotowski, Jerzy, *Towards a Poor Theatre*, Methuen, 1968
Guest, Ivor, *The Dancer's Heritage: a History of Classical Ballet*, A. and C. Black, 1960

Harrison, G. B., *Shakespeare at Work 1592–1603*, Routledge, 1933
——, *Elizabethan Plays and Players*, Michigan, 1956
Harrison, Jane, *Ancient Art and Ritual*, Thornton Butterworth, 1913
Hodges, C. Walter, *The Globe Restored*, W. Norton and Co, New York, 1973
Houghton, Norris, *Moscow Rehearsals*, Allen and Unwin, 1938
——, *Return Engagement*, Putnam, 1962

Itzin, Katherine, *Stages in the Revolution*, Eyre Methuen, 1980
Innes, C. D., *Erwin Piscator's Political Theatre: the Development of Modern German Drama*, Cambridge, 1972

Jeffery, Brian, *French Renaissance Comedy* (1552–1630), Oxford, 1969

Kahrl, Stanley, J., *Traditions of Medieval English Drama*, Hutchinson, 1974
Kitto, H. D. F., *Greek Tragedy*, Methuen, 1950
——, *The Greeks*, Penguin, 1951
——, *Form and Meaning in Drama*, Methuen, 1964
Knights, L. C., *Drama and Society in the Age of Jonson*, Chatto and Windus, 1937
Komisarjevsky, Theodore, *The Theatre*, The Bodley Head, 1935

Leacroft, Richard, *The Development of the English Playhouse*, Eyre Methuen, 1973
Lough, John, *Seventeenth-Century French Drama*, Oxford, 1979

Mackintosh, Iain and Sell, Michael, *Curtains!!! or A New Life for Old Theatres*, John Offord, 1982
Macleod, Joseph, *The New Soviet Theatre*, Allen and Unwin, 1943
Mander, Raymond and Mitchenson, Joe, *The Theatres of London*, Rupert Hart-Davis, 1961
Marshall, Norman, *The Producer and the Play*, Macdonald, 1957
——, *The Other Theatre*, John Lehmann, 1947
Mongrédien, Georges, *Daily Life in the French Theatre at the Time of Molière*, Allen and Unwin, 1969
Moore, Robert Etheridge, *Henry Purcell and the Restoration Theatre*, Heinemann, 1961
Murray, Gilbert, *The Rise of the Greek Epic*, Oxford, 1907
——, *Five Stages of Greek Religion*, Oxford, 1935
——, *Aeschylus*, Oxford, 1904

Nagler, A. M., *A Source Book in Theatrical History*, Constable, 1952
Nemirovich-Danchenko, Vladimir, *My Life in the Russian Theatre*, Geoffrey Bles, 1937
Nicoll, Allardyce, *The Garrick Stage*, Manchester, 1980

Orgel, Stephen and Strong, Roy, *Inigo Jones: the Theatre of the Stuart Court*, Sotheby Parke-Bernet, 1973

Pearson, Hesketh, *The Actor-Managers*, Methuen, 1950
Pickard, Cambridge, Sir Arthur, *Dithyramb Tragedy and Comedy*, Oxford, 1927
——, *The Dramatic Festivals of Athens*, Oxford, 1968
——, *The Theatre of Dionysus in Athens*, Oxford, 1946
Prudhoe, John, *The Theatre of Goethe and Schiller*, Blackwell, 1973

Raynor, Henry, *A Social History of Music*, Barrie and Jenkins, 1972
Reese, M. M., *Shakespeare: His World and his Work*, Edward Arnold, 1980
Roose-Evans, J., *Experimental Theatre*, Studio Vista, 1970
——, *London Theatre from the Globe to the National*, Phaidon, 1977
Rowell, George, *The Victoria Theatre* 1792–1914, Cambridge, 1978
Rosenfeld, Sybil, *A Short History of Scene Design in Great Britain*, Blackwell, 1973

Salmon, Eric, *Granville Barker: A Secret Life*, Heinemann Educational Books, 1983
Sandbach, F. H., *The Comic Theatre of Greece and Rome*, Chatto and Windus, 1977
Schoenbaum, S., *William Shakespeare*, Oxford, 1978
Scott, Harold, *The Early Doors*, Nicholson and Watson, 1946
Shaw, Bernard, *Major Critical Essays: The Perfect Wagnerite*, Constable, 1922
——, *The Quintessence of Ibsenism*, Constable, 1932
——, *Our Theatre in the Nineties*, Constable, 1932
——, *Prefaces*, Constable, 1934
Shergold, N. D., *A History of the Spanish Stage*, Oxford, 1967
Southern, Richard, *The Staging of Plays before Shakespeare*, Faber, 1973
——, *The Seven Ages of the Theatre*, Faber, 1962
Speaight, Robert, *William Poel and the Elizabethan Revival*, Heinemann, 1954
Stanislavsky, *My Life in Art*, Geoffrey Bles, 1924
Steiner, George, *The Death of Tragedy*, Faber, 1963
Strong, Roy, *Splendour at Court; Renaissance Spectacle and Illusion*, Weidenfeld and Nicholson, 1973

Taplin, Oliver, *Greek Tragedy in Action*, Methuen, 1978
Taylor, John Russell, *Anger and After*, Methuen, 1962
Thomson, George, *Aeschylus and Athens*, Lawrence and Wishart, 1941
Trewin, J. C. (ed.), *The Journal of William Charles Macready*, Longmans, 1967
Tydeman, William, *The Theatre in the Middle Ages*, Cambridge, 1978

Valois, Ninette de, *Step by Step*, W. H. Allen, 1977

Walton, J. Michael, *Greek Tragedy Practice*, Greenwood Press, 1980
Wardle, Irving, *The Theatres of George Devine*, Eyre Methuen, 1978
Wickham, Glynne, *Early English Stages 1300–1600* (4 vols), Routledge and Kegan Paul, 1959–81
——, *The Medieval Theatre*, Weidenfeld and Nicholson, 1974
Willett, J., *The Theatre of Bertolt Brecht*, Methuen, 1960
——, *The New Sobriety: Art and Politics in the Weimar Period 1917–33*, Thames and Hudson, 1978
Williams, Raymond, *Drama from Ibsen to Brecht*, Chatto and Windus, 1968
Wilson, J. Dover, *The Essential Shakespeare*, Cambridge, 1932

Index

Plays are assigned to their authors. They are given in whatever language seems to make them most readily identifiable. Titles in the original language are given in the text.